CRACKING THE
JAVA CODING
INTERVIEW

200 Tips & Non-Technical Interview Questions & Answers.
2000+ Java Questions & Answers.

-Harry.

(*IT Manager* & *Anonymous Hacktivist @ Anonymous International*)

Author Note:

Every possible effort has been made to ensure that the information contained in this book is accurate, and the publisher or the Author can't accept responsibility for any errors or omissions, however caused.

All liability for loss, disappointment, negligence or other damage caused by the reliance of the Technical Programming or other information contained in this book, of in the event of bankruptcy or liquidation or cessation of trade of any company, individual; or firm mentioned, is hereby excluded.

All other marks are property of their respective owners. The examples of companies, organizations, products, domain names, email addresses, logos, people, places, and events depicted herein are fictitious. No association with any real company, organization, product, domain name, email address, logo, person, place, or event is intended or should be inferred.

The author and publisher have taken care in the preparation of this book, but make no expressed or implied warranty of any kind and assume no responsibility for errors or omissions. No liability is assumed for incidental or consequential damages in connection with or arising out of the use of the information or programs contained herein.

This book expresses the author views and opinions. The information contained in this book is provided without any express, statutory, or implied warranties. Neither the authors, and Publisher, nor its resellers, or distributors will be held liable for any damages caused or alleged to be caused either directly or indirectly by this book.

Dedication

"This book is dedicated to all those who make the daily sacrifices,
Especially those who've made sacrifice, to ensure our freedom & security."

You told me that everything will be okay in the end,
You also told me that, if it's not okay, it's not the end.

"I'll search for you through 1000 worlds & 10000 lifetimes until I find you"

About Author:

Harry, is an **Anonymous *Hacktivist,*** World Famous computer Programmer and Bestselling Java Author and **scientifically Hacking professional** has a unique experience in the field of computers Programming, **Hacking and Cyber Security.**

*H*e has helped many Countries Governments and many multinational Software companies of around the globe to secure their networks and securities. He has authored several books on Various Computers Programming Languages and computer security & Hacking. **He is basically known for his international bestselling Programming book "Core Java Professional."**

*H*e is technically graduate software engineer and Master. He is the leading authority on C Programming and C++ Programming as well as on Core Java and Data Structure and Algorithms. His acclaimed C and C++ ,C# & Java books. He has over 5 years of experience as a software methodologist. His teaching and research interests are in the areas of artificial intelligence, programming languages.

*H*e is living two lives. One life, He is a Computer program writer for a respectable software company. The other life is lived in computers, where he go by the hacker alias 'Harry" and are guilty of virtually every computer crime. Currently he is working as offline IT manager @ world famous community *Anonymous international Community.* *-Team Anonymous.*

Author side :

You may have noticed something missing here: no impressive of credentials. I haven't been a professor at a Prestigious University for a quarter-century; neither am I a top executive at a Silicon Valley giant. In some ways, I'm a student of Technology, just like you are.

And my experience over the years has shown me that many of the people who know the most about how technology works also have rather limited success in explaining what they know in a way that will allow me to understand it. My interests, and I believe my skills, lie not in being an expert, but an educator, in presenting complex information in a form that is sensible, digestible and fun to read my books.

"What is real? How do you define *real*? If you're talking about what you can feel, what you can smell, what you can taste and see, then real is simply, electrical signals interpreted by your brain."

"... I am just now beginning to discover the difficulty of expressing one's ideas on paper. As long as it consists solely of description it is pretty easy; but where reasoning comes into play, to make a proper connection, a clearness & a moderate fluency, is to me, as I have said, a difficulty of which I had no idea ..."

– Harry.

∞ Inside Topics at a Glance ∞

Preface

∞ Essential Java Interview Skills--Made Easy! ∞

Please Hold On !

I know many people do not read the preface, But if you really want to crack the coding interview, Then I would strongly recommend that you go through the preface also every single page lines as well. The reason for this, is that this preface has something different to offer.

The main objective of this interview book is not to give you just magical interview question & tricks, I have followed a pattern of improving the question solution with deep Questions-Answers explanations with different interview complexities for each interview problem, you will find multiple solutions for complex interview questions. I mentioned approx 2000+ Java Technical Questions and 200+ Non- Technical Questions for before the technical round. *This book is world's Biggest Java Interview book you ever read.*

What Special –

In this book I covered and explained several topics of latest Java 8 Features in detail for Developers & Freshers, Topics Like– Lambdas. *Java 8 Functional interface, Stream and Time API.*

As a job seeker if you read the complete book with good understanding & seriously, i am 101% sure you will challenge any Interview & Interviewers (Specially Java) in this world. and this is the objective of this book. This book contains more than Two Thousands Technical Java Questions and 200 Non-Technical Questions like before

*T*his book is very much useful for I.T professionals and the students of Engineering Degree and Masters during their Campus Interview and academic preparations. If you read as a student preparing for Interview for Computer Science or Information Technology, the content of this book covers all the required topics in full details. While writing the book, an intense care has been taken to help students who are preparing for these kinds of technical interview rounds.

Hello! Now I want to share something important with you. For those of you new to IT/Technical or any other job interviews, the process can seem overwhelming Interviewers throw questions at you, expect you to whip up brilliant algorithms or Program Codes on the spot, and then ask you to write beautiful code on a whiteboard luckily, everyone else is in the same boat, and you're already working hard to prepare Good job! So, throw the ball back in the interviewer's court.

✓ *As you get ready for your interviews, consider these suggestions:*

Always Write your Code on Paper:

Most interviewers won't give you a computer and will instead expect you to write code on a whiteboard or on paper To simulate this environment, try answering problems by writing code on paper first, and then typing them into a computer as-is Whiteboard / paper coding is a special skill, which can be mastered with constant practice. I mean suppose your thoughts are interviewer and your mind is compiler. Simple!

First Know Your Resume:

First at all, I want to share something important thing with you that you don't know. I am talking about differences! Yes, the Difference between,

A CV (Curriculum Vitae) & Resume. Curriculum Vitae is a document prepared by the fresher's or students searching a job. It provides the academic details of the student, another hand a resume is prepared by the experienced professionals, which emphasizes job history and on-the-job skills and experience.

While technical skills are extremely important, that's no reason to neglect your own resume make sure to prepare yourself to give a quick summary of any project or job you were involved with.

And Don't Memorize Solutions:

While this book offers a representative sample of interview questions, there are still thousands of interview questions out there Memorizing solutions is not a great use of your time Rather, use this book to explore approaches to problems, to learn new concepts, and to practice your skills.

So, Talk Out Loud:

Interviewers want to understand how you think and approach problems, so talk out loud while you're solving problems let the interviewer see how you're tackling the problem, and they just might guide you as well.

Finally remember -- interviews are hard!

In my years of interviewing at IBM, I saw some interviewers ask "easy" questions while others ask harder questions but you know what? Getting the easy questions doesn't make it any easier to get the offer Receiving an offer is not about solving questions flawlessly (very few candidates do!),

But rather, it is about answering questions better than other candidates. I'm excited for you and for the skills you are going to develop Thorough preparation will give you a wide range of technical and communication skills It will be well-worth it no matter where the effort takes you!

For Entry level jobs, the IT industry requires students and young professionals with good programming, especially the world most demanded Java language and problem solving skills. For jobs that require programming skills most of the IT companies look for candidates with good C, C++ (lesser extent) and very specially Java Programming Skills.

Finally the key point-

Is that java programming skills are essential for getting almost any software related job now a days in IT companies (Particularly in Apple, IBM, HP, HCL, MICROSOFT,INFOSYS, ACCENTURE, FACEBOOK GOOGLE, YAHOO, & other).

Many programming-

Books are already available in market, but most of books are tutorials or text books on different programming languages.

It is very difficult to crack an IT interview by just reading any of these books or by writing a few programming that can easily creates a *doubt like you are a most devil dare programmer on this earth.*

Every IT Interview focus on problem solving skills from a programming perspective and hence, the questions asked are considerably different from those covered in textbooks because textbooks only covers pedagogical questions and solutions that are meant to teaching you how to write a simple program.

Target Audience:

This book is designed specifically for students and programmers & Software Professionals attending Campus or offline interview for software companies with the objective of helping those clear written tests and interviews.

The Campus placement in IT Companies typically consists of written tests and interviews. In written test with objective Questions of C & C++ and Java. They want to check if a student or professional knows the fundamentals of programming concepts and has basic programming and problem solving skills.

As a software professional or student-

By reading this book you can easily crack both written tests and interview. In this book I used every aspect of Java programming with more than Two thousand Questions & Answers including ten high definition pictures for interview dress up - Dress Appropriately & Body language and FAQ'S etc.

Another hand-

For experienced software programmers are quite different from the written test/interviews conducted for freshers. Except a very few ones, good IT companies do not conduct written tests for programmers with prior work experience.

The interviews are designed to assess a candidate's practical experience in programming and his/her ability to solve the problems faced in day-to-day programming & projects. The programming logic questions and puzzles are also much more complex than those that students are asked, finally a programmer can benefit from this book while preparing for such job interviews. This book is really a great book for java interview and other section focused on several interview related preparation.

"A Stone is broken By the last Stroke Of Hammer. This doesn't mean that the 1st Stroke is useless. Success is the result Of Continuous effort..!!! So, Stand up, be bold, be strong. Take the whole responsibility on your own shoulders, and know that you are the creator of your own destiny."

Chapter - 1
Interview Myths

One important reason people fail at interviews is because of several misconceptions, or myths, about what really happens during the course of an interview. All of us know that the purpose of interviews is for an interviewer to hire someone who will perform well in a particular job, but beyond that few people fully grasp how interviews really work and what makes one candidate stand out more than another.

This lack of understanding represents a major obstacle to maximising performance when sitting before an interviewer and trying to give your best answers.

Interviews are no different to other endeavors in life: the better you understand how they work (or don't work), the higher the probability of tackling them successfully. An understanding of the underlying dynamics inherent in most interviews is an important start to improving your interview performance.

Myth no. 1: The best person for the job gets it-

Sometimes this is true—especially in a situation where everyone knows everyone else, such as when a company is recruiting internally. However, this is often not the case. In order for the best person for the job to win it, a number of very important things need to be in place (and even then, there's no guarantee).

These include:

+ The interviewer knows what questions to ask and how to search for the truthfulness in answers. These two things may sound simple enough, but I can assure you that a large proportion of people conducting interviews have received no training, lack interview experience and often do not even go to the trouble of preparing for the interview.

+ The interviewer is not taken in by the charm, good looks, great humour or any other aspect of the interviewee. This can be a difficult obstacle, even for experienced interviewers.

+ The interviewee has learned how to clearly articulate their skills, key achievements and how they can add value to the organisation.

+ There is no personality clash between interviewer and interviewee.

+ Neither party is having a bad day.

Some employers usually the ones who have been badly burnt by hiring the wrong people in the past—go to great lengths to set up professional hiring procedures designed to minimise hiring mistakes. Whilst some of these procedures are effective in improving candidate selection, they do not guarantee that the best person for the job will actually win it.

In the final analysis, choosing someone for a job involves at least one human being making a decision about another, and no matter what we do to eliminate subjectivity, as human beings it is impossible to put aside our predispositions, predilections and personal preferences—no matter how much we may try to.

In an ideal world, the best person for the job would always win it; however, the reality is that it is often the person who performs best at the interview who wins the prize. The important lessons here are:

+ Don't automatically pull out of applying for a job if you know someone better suited for the job is also applying for it. If you go to the trouble of preparing properly for the interview, there's a good chance that you may be seen as the preferred candidate especially if the other person takes the interview for granted and fails to prepare.

+ If you happen to know that you're the best person for the job, avoid taking the interview for granted. Behave as though you're competing against formidable rivals. Take the time to prepare properly. Just because you've got a lot of experience does not mean you know how to convey this message at an interview.

Myth no. 2:

Interviews are like school exams- The more you say, the better you'll do -

*Y*es, interviews are a bit like exams in so far as that you're asked a number of questions to which you need to respond intelligently, but there the similarities end. Unlike exams, where lots of accurate detail is important, interviews are more about interacting and rapport building whilst simultaneously articulating smart answers. And a smart answer is often not the most detailed. In fact, long and overly detailed answers can drive interviewers to distraction, despite their technical accuracy. Knowing when to stop talking is a skill all successful interviewees have.

*A*lso unlike many exams, there are often no right or wrong answers in interviews. We're all different and come to interviews from different backgrounds and business sitations. What is important at an interview is to justify your actions and talk about your achievements in a confident manner.

Myth no. 3: Interviewers know what they're doing-

*S*ome interviewers are very good at what they do, especially full time professionals (provided they're not suffering from interview fatigue). However, many managers and owners of small businesses often flounder because interviewing is not something they do on a regular basis.

Some sure signs of a bad interviewer are:

- They do most of the talking.
- They sound as though they've made up their mind about you in the first five minutes.
- They seem to pluck their questions randomly out of the ether.
- Their phone keeps ringing and they answer it.
- They sound like very sharp and less-than-honest salespeople when it comes to selling the job.

Some sure signs of a good interviewer are:

- They have their questions carefully prepared in advance.
- They want to know what you've done and how you've done it, including specific examples.
- They let you do most of the talking.
- They may want to interview you more than once.
- They will try to make you feel at ease.
- They are genuinely interested in your accomplishments, skills and the type of person you are.

*I*nexperienced interviewers generally don't ask the right questions and can easily be swayed by factors that have little to do with your ability to perform in the job. So if you are being interviewed by an inexperienced interviewer, don't wait to be asked a good question one that will allow you to talk about all your wonderful skills and qualities.

*R*ather, take the initiative in as unobtrusive a way as possible and talk about the things you feel the interviewer might really want to know. Unfortunately, this may not always be possible especially if you're being interviewed by a forceful personality who loves the sound of their own voice.

*I*f ever you find yourself in such a situation, don't panic. Remind yourself that interviews are just as much about rapport-building as they are about answering questions. So nod your head, smile and make all the right noises talkative interviewers love people who agree with them.

Myth no. 4: Never say 'I don't know' -

*I*nterviews are about making a positive impression by answering questions intelligently and building rapport with the interviewer. To this end, many interviewees feel that they have to provide the perfect answer to every question put to them, irrespective of whether or not they actually know the answer.

*C*learly, a great interview is one in which you can answer all the questions (and you should be able to do so if you take the time to prepare correctly); however, if you don't know the answer to something, it is better to admit to it rather than pretend to know and start waffling.

*M*ost interviewers can pick waffling a mile away and they don't like it for a couple of very important reasons: first, it is likely to make you sound dishonest; and second, it will make you sound considerably less than intelligent. You may as well not attend the interview if you give the impression that you're neither honest nor bright.

*T*rying to answer a question that you have little idea about could undermine an otherwise great interview. This does not mean that you cannot attempt answers that you are unsure of. There's nothing wrong with having a go, as long as you make your uncertainty clear to the interviewer at the outset. Here's what an answer may sound like:

I have to be honest and say that this is not an area I'm familiar with, though I am very interested in it. If you like, I'm happy to have a go at trying to address the issue, as long as you're not expecting the perfect answer.

Or:

I'd love to answer that question, but I need to be honest upfront and say that this is not an area that I'm overly familiar with, though I'm very interested in increasing my knowledge about it.

Myth no. 5: Good-looking people get the job -

I suppose if the job was for a drop-dead gorgeous femme fatale type in a movie, then good looks would certainly help, but for most other jobs the way you look is not as big a deal as many people make out.

*A*s we've already discussed, there will always be an inexperienced employer who will hire on the basis of superficial factors, but most employers are smarter than that.

*T*he claim that good-looking people get the job over plain-looking people makes one seriously flawed assumption that employers make a habit of putting someone's good looks before the interests of their livelihood. All my experience has taught me the contrary. Most businesses find themselves in highly competitive environments and employers are only too keenly aware that a poor hiring decision can prove very costly.

*T*his is not to say that appearance and a bright personality are not important factors at an interview. It is very important that you dress appropriately and try your best to demonstrate all your friendly qualities. Good looks are certainly overrated in interviews, but an appropriate appearance and a friendly personality are not.

Myth no. 6:

If you answer the questions better than the others, you'll get the job -

Being able to articulate good answers in an interview is very important, and failure to do so will almost certainly mean you don't get the job. However, interviews—as we've already seen—are much more than just giving good answers.

They're also about convincing the interviewer that you will be a nice person to work with. To put it another way, it doesn't matter how good your answers are technically, if the interviewer doesn't like you there's not much chance you'll get the job (unless your talents are unique, extremely difficult to find or the interviewer is desperate).

So avoid thinking about interviews just in terms of answering questions correctly. Interviews are also about establishing rapport and trust, and whilst there is no fail-safe method in doing this, there are things you can do (and things you should not do) that will go a long way towards improving your skills in this all-important area of interviewing.

Myth no. 7:

You should try to give the perfect answer -

I've heard too many people stumble over their words, repeat themselves and talk in circles because they're trying to articulate the perfect answer—or what they think constitutes the perfect answer.

Some people are so obsessed with delivering the perfect answer that they don't stop until they produce what in their opinion is a word perfect response. Because we can never be entirely sure of what the interviewer wants to hear, some of us will keep on talking in the hope that we'll cover all bases. The problem with this approach is that we end up talking too much, leading to the interviewer losing concentration which, of course, is the last thing you need at an interview.

The reality is that in most cases there is no such thing as the perfect answer. The lesson here is: it makes a lot of sense to settle for a good answer that gets to the point rather than meander all over the place searching for the elusive perfect answer.

Myth no. 8:

You must ask questions to demonstrate your interest and intelligence -

Many interviewees are under the mistaken belief that they must ask questions at the end of the interview. There seems to be a common belief amongst many interviewees that this makes them sound more intelligent as well as more interested in the job.

This is not true. Asking questions simply for the sake of doing so won't improve your chances of getting a job. It could even make you sound a little dull especially if you ask questions about matters that were already covered during the course of the interview.

Only ask a question if you have a genuine query. Acceptable questions include those relating directly to the job you're applying for, as well as working conditions and company policies on such things as on pay, leave, and so on. Interviewers never mind answering questions about such matters, but they do mind answering questions they perceive to be irrelevant.

If you have no questions to ask, simply say something like: 'Thank you, but I have no questions. You've been very thorough during the course of the interview and have covered all the important matters regarding the job.' There's nothing wrong with including a compliment to the interviewer about their thoroughness and professionalism—provided it doesn't go over the top or sound like grovelling.

Two further points need to be made about asking questions. First, avoid asking too many questions. On the whole, interviewers do not enjoy role reversals. Second, never ask potentially embarrassing questions. These can include:

+ A question relating to a negative incident;
+ something that's not supposed to be in the public domain;
+ A difficult question that may stump the interviewer.

The rule of thumb is: if you think a question may cause embarrassment, err on the side of caution and avoid it.

Myth no. 9: Relax and just be yourself -

Whilst it is important to be relaxed and show your better side, it is also very important to understand that interviews are not social engagements. Most interviews are highly formalised events in which otherwise innocuous behaviours are deemed unacceptable.

In short, being your usual self could spell disaster (as contradictory as that may sound). For example, if being yourself means leaning back on your chair, dressing somewhat shabbily and making jokes, you might find yourself attending an inordinate number of interviews.

Whilst interviewers like people to be relaxed, they also have definite expectations about what behaviours are appropriate for an interview and you violate these expectations at your peril!

Myth no. 10: Interviewers are looking for flaws

The danger with this myth is that it can easily lead to interviewees adopting a defensive, perhaps even distrustful, attitude during the interview.

If you believe that the interviewer is assiduously searching for your flaws, it will more than likely undermine your attempts to establish that all-important rapport and trust.

It may also prevent you from opening up and giving really good answers. Rest assured that most interviewers do not prepare their interview questions with a view to uncovering your flaws. Questions are mostly prepared with a view to giving the interviewer an overall or holistic insight into what you have to offer the company. A good interviewer will indeed uncover areas in which you are not strong, but that is a far cry from thinking that the interviewer is hell bent on uncovering only your flaws.

It is very important to treat every question as an opportunity to excel rather than being unnecessarily guarded. It is only by answering the questions that you can demonstrate how good you are. To treat questions as objects of suspicion makes no sense at all.

Understanding the myths surrounding interviews gives you a great start for success. Remember, interviews are no different to other endeavors in life: the better you understand their underlying nature the higher the probability you'll tackle them successfully. An insight into common interview myths will arm you with the information you need to prevent you from falling into those disheartening traps.

Just as importantly, a clearer picture of the true nature of interviews better informs the rest of your preparation and will contribute to your confidence and performance.

Summary of key points

- The best person for the job does not necessarily win it—often it's the person who gives the best interview.

- Interviews are more than just giving technically correct answers. They're also very much about building rapport.

- Not all interviewers know what they're doing; your job is to know how to handle the good and bad interviewer.

- It's better to be honest and admit ignorance than try to pretend you know an answer and come across as disingenuous and less than bright.

- Good looking people win jobs—maybe in Hollywood movies, but on the whole, employers are keen to hire talent over superficial factors.

- Striving to give the perfect answer can get you into trouble. It's betterto give a good answer that's to the point rather than searching forperfection; besides, often there's no such thing as the perfect answer.

- Do not ask questions for the sake of it. Only ask a question if you have a genuine query that has not been covered.

- Interviews are formal occasions requiring relatively formal behaviours. Interviewers will expect this and may react negatively if they don't see it.

- Interviewers do not spend all their time looking for your flaws. They're more interested in getting an overall picture of who you are. Avoid answering questions defensively. It's much better to see every question as an opportunity to highlight your best points.

"Just know, when you truly want success, you'll never give up on it. No matter how bad the situation may get." – Harry.

Chapter - 2

Convincing them
you're right for the job

Doing well at interviews is not nearly as difficult as many people think. With correct preparation and a little practice, most people who dread interviews can learn to excel. The important thing to note is that performing well at interviews is a learned process. Highly effective interviewees are not born with interview skills; rather, they teach themselves what to say, how to say it and how to behave during an interview.

Common interview mistakes -

All of us have made mistakes during interviews, and most of us have walked out of interviews thinking of all the great things we forgot to mention and all the things we shouldn't have said. But the most important thing about mistakes is learning from them and not repeating them. Here are some common interview mistakes:

+ Failing to express oneself clearly. Often, because of anxiety and wanting to say things perfectly, we try too hard and turn what should be simple sentences into convoluted nonsense. Simple language is always the most effective. Avoid trying to sound knowledgeable by using jargon or complex sentences.

+ Not being aware of one's body language. Many interviewees succeed in alienating the interviewer because they pay little or no attention to their body language. Body language is an extremely powerful communicator, and failing to use it effectively will almost certainly put you at a significant disadvantage. Eye con tact, sitting position and facial expressions are all very important aspects of interviewing, and need to be thought through before the interview.

+ Failing to control those nerves. Sometimes people allow their nerves to get so out of control that they fail to establish rapport and even forget their answers.

Feeling anxious before and during an interview is common. In fact, a touch of nerves can be a good thing. But there is no need to be the victim of debilitating nerves. As you read through this book, you'll gradually learn how to lessen your anxiety.

+ Failing to give appropriate examples. Failing to give examples, or giving inappropriate examples, will spell disaster. Before the interview, it is important to think of relevant examples of what you've achieved and how you went about realising those achievements.

Saying that you achieved something without being able to back it up with specific examples will only get you a rejection letter. Your examples need to be easy to understand, follow a logical sequence and be relevant to the needs of the employer. None of this happens without preparation.

+ Trying too hard to please the interviewer. Whilst building rapport and trust during the interview is critical, few interviewers appreciate interviewees going overboard with their behaviour. Obsequious behaviours are generally seen as a form of deceit and carry little weight—in fact, they can undermine your efforts to create trust.

There's nothing wrong with you

You've probably committed at least some of the mistakes listed above. It's very important to realise that making such mistakes is common. In other words, there's nothing wrong with you. In the vast majority of cases, performing poorly at an interview happens because of the very nature of interviews—it's the interview process that is the culprit.

So an awareness of the basic nature of interviews is the first step in a step-by-step process by which you can significantly improve your performance. A great place to start is to ask: 'What does it take to convince the interviewer that you're the best person for the job?' The answer to this question can best be summarised in four parts:

+ *correct preparation;*

+ *knowing the things that are important to interviewers;*

+ *practising your answers;*

+ *perseverance.*

Correct preparation -

How well you perform at an interview will largely depend on how well you have prepared for it. Failure to correctly prepare almost certainly means you will not perform at your best. In some cases, it will mean performing quite badly, which may contribute to the erosion of your confidence.

Even if you're lucky enough to be the favoured candidate, and are almost certain to win the position by just turning up, you should still take the time to prepare because the better you perform, the greater the likelihood that you will negotiate a better salary and often the difference in money can be substantial.

We've all heard people boast that they've never prepared for an interview in their lives and have done all right. Whilst this boast may not be an idle one, closer inspection will usually reveal that these people were:

+ *Lucky—that is, in the right place at the right time;*

+ *Well connected;*

+ *Working in a favourable labour market where there was a huge*

+ *Demand for employees coupled with low supply;*

+ *Applying for jobs well within their comfort zone—that is, not*

+ *Stretching themselves to improve their position; or*

+ *Applying for jobs internally and competing mainly against external candidates.*

The case for preparation -

The argument for interview preparation becomes compelling when you give some thought to the basic nature of interviews.

Not only are you expected to sell yourself in a competitive environment, but you're also expected to compress large and often complex pieces of information into neat and highly articulate answers that avoid any negative connotations and contain the information the interviewer wants to hear.

It's no wonder people's stress levels increase. But it doesn't end there. There are three additional reasons that make the case for interview preparation even more compelling:

- Interviews are rare events, thus making them unfamiliar and awkward.

- Many people find it very difficult to sell themselves at interviews because they've been conditioned by family and society not to blow their own trumpet. Making simple statements such as 'I am very good at selling xyz' can be quite an obstacle to overcome.

- In most interviews, coming second isn't good enough. It's not just a matter of performing well; it's also a matter of beating everyone else. It is unimaginable that you would fail to prepare for an event that is infrequent, competitive and requires behaviours not normally used. Yet that is exactly what people do when they walk into an interview without preparation.

What is incorrect preparation?

Incorrect preparation is any preparation that will not optimise your performance at an interview. Rote-learning generic answers that someone else has prepared has limited value.

At best, they can give you an insight into what may constitute a good answer; at worst, they simply lead you astray. It is important to understand that, in the vast majority of cases, there's no such thing as a single answer to a question. What may constitute a great answer for one employer may be viewed as quite ordinary by another.

One of the worst things you can do is learn other people's responses off by heart and repeat them at an interview. Repeating other people's so-called great answers can make you sound disingenuous and make you look a bit ridiculous when asked a probing follow up question. It makes a lot more sense to prepare your own answers.

Advantages of preparation -

Taking the time to correctly prepare for an interview will:

- Improve your confidence levels;

- Assist you in answering questions succinctly, as opposed to taking forever to make a simple point;

- Help you know what to say and how to say it;

- Assist you in handling difficult questions;

- Help you avoid saying things that willmake a negative impression;

- Improve your rapport-building skills.

Knowing the things that are important to interviewers -

One of the keys to knowing what to prepare lies in understanding the needs of the interviewer. Once you know the things that are important to interviewers, interview preparation suddenly becomes a lot clearer and a lot more manageable.

The vast majority of interviewers—whether or not they realize it—want to hear three things from you. In fact, nearly all good interview questions boil down to these three key generic questions:

+ Can you do the job? In other words, do you have the skills, knowledge, experience or potential to perform well in the job? Most interviewers will spend the majority of the interview probing you on this question. They'll want to know what you've done, how you did it and what the outcomes were. In the event you have not performed a particular duty, they will try to ascertain your potential to do the job.

+ Are you the sort of person they can work with? Another way of stating this question is: Will you fit into the existing culture of the organisation? Or, in the case of small organisations: Will you get on with the boss? Whilst interviewers generally spend a lot less time on this question, it is nevertheless a vitally important one that's because no one wants to work with someone they don't like, even if they can do the job.

+ How motivated are you? In other words, what energy levels and drive do you bring to the position? You may not even be asked a question about your motivation levels, but you fail to address it at your peril. As we all know, highly motivated employees are keenly sought after by employers—with good reason.

There are two significant benefits in knowing that interviewers are keenly interested in these three generic questions, and that the vast majority of questions they can ask fall under one or more of these categories. First, it guides you in the preparation of your answers (a large part of this book is based on answering these three key questions). Rather than spending lots of time wading through randomly selected questions in the hope that you will have prepared the right answers, an understanding of the significance of the three key generic questions provides a direction and platform for your preparation. In short, you are able to plan your preparation around the following issues:

+ Your skills, knowledge and experience—can you do the job?

+ Your personal attributes—are you the sort of person they can workwith?

+ Your motivation levels.

Second, it provides a useful way to deal with questions at the actual interview. By sorting interview questions into one or more of the three generic question categories, your answers will gain added structure and a clearer direction simply because you know what the underlying purpose of the questions is.

By learning how to recognize the real intent of a question, you minimise your chances of giving the wrong answer and/or waffling.

Practice -

The third aspect of convincing an interviewer that you're the best person for the job is practice. Unfortunately, there are no shortcuts to developing great interview skills.

Once you've prepared your answers, you need to sit down and practise them as much as you can. The more you practise, the better you'll be. As the old saying goes, 'success is one part talent and nine parts perseverance'. How you practise is up to you. Do it in front of the mirror, sitting on your couch, pacing your room or while driving your car but avoid

practising in front of your boss!

Practising your answers aloud It is important to practise your answers aloud, rather than just mentally rehearsing them. That's because the human brain distinguishes between talking and thinking and you need to stimulate the talking part of your brain. Thinking your answers at an interview will get you nowhere, unless the interviewer is a mind reader.

Get some feedback -

Ideally, you should do your practising at real interviews. The more interviews you attend, the better—even if you have to attend inter- views for jobs that you're not really interested in. After the interview—assuming you're not the winning candidate—ring back the interviewer and ask for feedback on your performance.

Some interviewers are happy to provide this feedback; however, many prefer not to because they find it threatening and a waste of their time. These people will either avoid you altogether or provide you with such watered-down feedback that it will be virtually useless.

In some instances you may not be able to resolve this problem; however, you can increase your chances of getting honest feedback by making interviewers feel as comfortable as possible.

You can do this by a) assuring them that you only want five minutes of their time; and b) telling them that the only reason you're seeking feedback is to improve future interview performance.

Mock interviews -

If you cannot get yourself to as many interviews as you would like, it's a good idea to set up mock interviews with someone you can work with. The more closely you can simulate a real-life situation, more benefit you will derive.

An effective way to conduct mock interviews is to get into role and stay in it for the entire interview. No distractions, no small talk and especially no starting again. If possible, avoid providing the questions to your helpers let them come up with their own.

If your helpers are not in a position to do this, give them lots of questions and ask them to choose the ones they want. The important thing for you is to get yourself used to answering unexpected questions.

Furthermore, if you feel your helper can provide you with honest feedback on your performance, do not shy away from asking. You never know what you may learn. Often it's the small things that make a big difference. But be on your guard for overly positive feedback. Chances are that your helper will be a friend, and friends are well known for avoiding negatives.

Perseverance -

The worst thing you can do when setting out to improve your interview performance is give up because it all seems too hard. Quitters invariably get nowhere. They certainly don't land great jobs and build great careers. On the other hand, people who persevere very often gain valuable insights simply because they have the stamina to stick it out.

The people we admire most are often those who face seemingly insurmountable obstacles yet instead of quitting, quietly resolve to overcome them. On the other side of the coin, the people we generally least respect are those who are forever starting things without finishing them.

They tend to be the same people who make grandiose claims but end up delivering little or nothing. One common characteristic that chronic quitters tend to have is low self-esteem they don't really believe in themselves. And if you don't believe in yourself, others usually don't believe in you either—not a great place to be when you're trying to convince interviewers to believe in your abilities.

These are the people who are often heard saying things such as: 'That's too hard', 'I can't learn that', 'What will others think', etc. They also tend to be the people who are always complaining about things but never seem to take any action to correct them because there's always an excuse.You don't have to be a chronic quitter or burdened with low self-esteem to give up on working on your interview skills there could be any number of other reasons.

However, if you're reading this book there's a good chance that improving your interview skills is an important priority in your life, and therefore should not be let go easily. If you feel you might be one of those people who is standing on the precipice of quitting, here is a little exercise that can assist you to take a step or two back from the edge.

Suggested activity: Neurolinguistic programming -

Based on neurolinguistic programming (NLP), this exercise is designed to influence how you feel. People often quit because they associate negative feelings with what they're doing. People who persevere have the power to feel good about their actions no matter how tedious or unconstructive these actions may seem to others.

If you can make yourself feel good about the process of improving your interview skills, then there's a good chance that quitting will be the last thing on your mind. Next time you feel like quitting, you might like to find a quiet spot and take the following steps:

- Close your eyes and imagine yourself performing extremely well in an interview. Take your time to view this picture in as much detail as you can. Picture the faces of the enthusiastic interviewers, noticing how attentive they are and how impressed they are with your responses. Immerse yourself in the experience. Pay attention to the details, including sounds, smells, colours, temperature, and so on. Above all, capture the feeling of being successful. Do not hold yourself back. The better you make yourself feel, the more powerful the exercise will be.

- Keep on repeating this exercise until you capture that feeling of excitement. You may be able to generate greater excitement by picturing yourself in your new job. Imagine how good it is going to feel winning a great job. Imagine getting that all important phone call informing you of your success. Picture yourself in the position doing all those things you've dreamt of doing. The key to this exercise is to generate the great feeling that goes with succeeding at an interview. Your only limitation is your imagination.

- Once you've captured that feeling, the next step is to recreate it when you need it—in other words, when you feel like quitting. An effective way of recreating the feeling of excitement is by installing what NLP refers to as an anchor. An anchor is a stimulus that triggers the desired feelings when you want them. An anchor can be something you do, say or imagine. Action anchors usually work best. For example, you might cross your fingers or jump up in the air or pull your ears. It doesn't matter what it is, as long as you can do it easily when you want to and trigger the desired feelings. Every time you're afflicted with the scourge of quitting, use your anchor and let your ability to influence your feelings do the rest.

Summary of key points

- Because of their nature, interviews are inherently challenging. Making mistakes at an interview is something that everyone does. The good news is that we can overcome our errors by correct preparation, practice and perseverance.

- Beware of faulty preparation. Avoid rote learning of other people's answers. Always prepare your own.

- Knowing what employers want to hear at an interview constitutes a great start for preparing your own answers and simplifies interview preparation. What most employers want to hear can be represented by three key questions:

- ✓ Can you do the job?

- ✓ Are you the sort of person they can work with?

- ✓ How motivated are you?

- Get in as much practice as you can and always ask for honest feedback.

- Perseverance is everything.

- Banish all thoughts of quitting by teaching yourself to associate strong feelings of excitement with improving your interview skills.

"I don't regret the things I've done, I regret the things I didn't do when I had the chance." – Harry.

"Challenges are what make life interesting and overcoming them is what makes life meaningful." – Harry.

"In order to succeed, your desire for success should be greater than your fear of failure." – Harry.

JAVA
United Hills.

Effective
Core Java

The Complete Core Reference.

TENTH EDITION 2014.

Harry- H.Chaudhary.

Chapter - 3

Can you do the job?

*B*efore an employer decides to give someone a job, they need to be convinced that the person can either do the job properly or learn it quickly. It comes as no surprise to learn therefore that 'Can you do the job?' questions are the most common. They're also the ones people spend most time preparing for.

'Can you do the job?' questions are those that directly or indirectly seek to ascertain your ability to perform the duties inherent in a job. They include questions that seek to clarify your:

- *Skills;*
- *Knowledge;*
- *Experience;*
- *Key achievements;*
- *Potential performance.*

Examples of 'Can you do the job?' questions include:

Can you give us an example of a time you had to communicate something that was complex and controversial? How did you go about it?

- Tell us about one of your key achievements?
- An irate client rings and gives you a blast over the phone. How do you handle it?
- What do you think you can bring to this position?

- Can you give us an example of a project that you had to plan and organise? What steps did you take?
- How would you describe yourself?
- (At first glance this may not strike you as a 'Can you do the job?' question, but effective interviewees always look for ways to highlight their skills.)
- What would you say makes an effective manager of people?
- Why should we employ you?
- What do you regard as your greatest strength?
- The most important duty in your job will be to look after the x, y and z. Tell us how you intend going about it.

Three types of 'Can you do the job?' questions –

Unless you're being interviewed for a job that's almost identical to one you've already had, it is likely that you will be asked three types of 'Can you do the job?' questions. These are:

- Questions about duties that you have performed before.
- Questions about duties that you have not performed but whose skills you have mastered.
- Questions about duties that are entirely new to you.

Finding out as much about the job as possible -

The first thing you need to do is take a very close look at the duties and requirements of the job you're applying for. It is these duties and requirements that will form the basis of your answers. There are several ways of collecting this sort of information:

- Scrutinising the job advertisement;
- Accessing a duty statement—if there is one;
- Contacting the employer or recruitment agent to clarify the main responsibilities of the job.

In an ideal world, you would have access to a detailed job advertisement, an up-to-date duty statement and an employer happy to discuss the main responsibilities of the job. Unfortunately, all too often the reality is that job ads are thinly worded, duty statements are non-existent and employers do not have time to return your calls.

However, it is critical that you find out as much about the job as possible before sitting down and thinking about your answers. The best source of information is either the employer or the recruitment agent.

Job ads and duty statements are useful (sometimes they're all that you will have); however, duty statements can often be out of date and job ads can lack sufficient information.

Talking to the right people can provide you with insights that often cannot be picked up from the written word. You might find out, for example, that the position you're applying for was made vacant because the previous incumbent had poor interpersonal communication skills and became aggressive when anyone expressed a differing opinion.

In such a case, it is likely that the employer will be looking for a replacement with excellent interpersonal communication and team player skills. You'd have a far better chance of winning the job if you had accessed this information before the interview and taken the time to prepare your answers.

Talking to an employer to find out more -

If you're able to talk to the employer, be sure you've got your questions prepared. The last thing you want to do is waste their time by stumbling through poorly thought-out questions.

If the employer does not return your call, do not throw in the towel. Often the person who answers the phone can be an invaluable source of information—especially in small to medium sized enterprises.

There's a good chance that they know a great deal about the position, or they might know someone else who does and is willing to talk to you. Here are some useful rules when talking to an employer before the interview:

Avoid small talk and get straight to the point. Small talk will be seen as sucking up—which, of course, it is!

+ Avoid asking too many questions—just ask the important ones, unless the employer has made it obvious that they've got lots of time on their hands and is willing to talk to you.

+ Never ask frivolous questions—those that can be answered from the advertisement or that a good applicant would be expected to know the answers to.

- Where necessary, provide a succinct reason why you're asking the question—the employer may not understand the significance of the question and could draw the wrong conclusions.
- Thank them for their time and tell them you're looking forward to the interview.

A quick word about duty statements -

Duty statements are simply a summary of the main duties of a job. Whilst they're a great source of information, they can be out of date. So, if you've been sent one, make the effort to find out whether the information on it is still valid.

Checking on a duty statement can represent a great opportunity to contact the employer and ask a few questions. Unfortunately, duty statements are usually the preserve of large organisations. Smaller companies generally lack the resources to write them.

Gleaning information from a job advertisement -

When you scrutinise the job advertisement, make a list of all the duties/requirements associated with the position. The idea is to try to read between the lines as much as possible. The more duties and requirements you come up with, the more thorough your preparation will be, which will lessen the chances of being caught unprepared at the interview.

The four steps to interview success-

The four steps to interview success are designed to capture all the relevant information you need to construct interview answers within a simple-to-manage framework. This method features four columns, with the headings shown below in Table 3.1.

Table 3.1 The four steps to interview success –

Step 1	***Step 2***	***Step 3***	***Step 4***
Duties/requirements of the position I'm applying for.	What I've already done that relates directly to the duties listed in step 1, including overcoming obstacles.	Current or past context.	Outcomes—organisational and personal.

By filling out each of the columns in the table, you are effectively collecting all the information you'll need to answer a broad range of questions. Most importantly, it's your relevant information, not information gathered from other people's answers you've read elsewhere.

Once you've captured the required information, your next step is to put it together in response to a range of likely interview questions and then practise your answers.

Behavioural questions -

One of the key advantages of the four steps method is that it lends itself to addressing a popular questioning technique commonly referred to as behavioural questioning.

You can recognise one of these questions every time an interviewer asks you for specific examples to back up a claim you have made, including the steps you took and the obstacles you encountered.

Behavioural questions are designed to uncover the actions (behaviours) behind an outcome or a duty, and cannot be successfully answered without preparing the third column.

If you're a graduate or a new entrant to the workforce, there's still a good chance that you will be asked behavioural questions; however, they will be limited in scope. Instead of asking for employment-related experience, interviewers will ask for study- or life-related incidences.

For example, the interviewer may want to know how well you function in a team, so may ask you about the last time you had to complete an assignment with a group of students. The same principle applies to communication skills, planning and organising, conflict resolution, your ability to cope with change, and so on.

Using the four steps -

Once you've come up with as much information as you can about the job, you need to start thinking about preparing your answers regarding duties you've performed before. All you need to do is recount your past actions and achievements and link them to the new job.

But be careful not to take these interviews for granted. It is all too easy to fall into the trap of not preparing because you think that the questions will be easy.

However, just because you've performed the same duties does not mean you will be able to articulate the details of what you did and how you did it. There's a big difference between doing something and actually having to talk about it in a succinct and coherent fashion.

Your first step is to select all the duties/requirements of the new job that you have performed before and recount your past actions and achievements in a way that will make the creation of effective answers easy.

Use Table 3.1 to capture all the information you will need, including what you did, how you did it, the context in which you did it and the outcomes. A more detailed explanation of each of the steps, including what to include and not include in each column, follows.

Step1: Duties or requirements -

List the duties and requirements of the job you're applying for in the first column.

Step 2: What you did and how you did it -

The second column (step 2) contains the core of your answers, including the obstacles you overcame to satisfy the duties or requirements listed in step 1. When filling out this column, avoid writing broad-ranging or general answers, though this may not always be possible.

The idea is to break up the duty or requirement listed in step 1 into its primary tasks or components. It helps if you ask yourself the following question: In order to complete the duty or requirement in step 1, what individual actions did I take, including any actions I took to overcome obstacles? Then list these in a logical sequence.

Avoid rushing through this step, especially if it has been a while since you've performed a particular duty. A good idea is to write all the things you can think of and then reduce the list down to the key points. Include specific examples.

Be careful not to over-elaborate when filling out the second column. Doing so can inadvertently lead to answers containing far too much detail. Given that many interviewees feel they have to show off their hard-earned knowledge, it is easy to go overboard in step 2.

But, in the vast majority of cases, you are not required to cover every contingency when answering a question. Try to avoid talking for longer than you should, thus boring the interviewer. Most interviewers are able to draw sensible inferences from the main points in your answer.

If they want more information, they'll ask for it. If you do have lots of great information that you absolutely feel cannot be left out, then go ahead and list them in the second column, but be selective about what you use at the interview.

Only choose the most relevant points. You can leave your other points for other questions or, if there are no follow-up questions, pat yourself on the back for being thorough in your preparation.

Not providing exhaustive answers at an interview makes a lot of sense when you factor in the importance of rapport-building during the course of an interview.

Remember: building rapport with the interviewer is the most important thing you can do at an interview and talking too much works against that all-important goal.

How long should my answers be?

Some answers can be as short as one word; others may run into many sentences. It all depends on the question and the circumstances. Here are some helpful guidelines on keeping your answers within acceptable parameters.

Let's make some reasonable assumptions. Say your interview will run for 40 minutes. Take away five minutes for settling and the exchange of pleasantries. That leaves you about 35 minutes. (It never hurts to ask how long the interview will run, but ask before the interview, not at the actual interview, lest you give the impression that you're in a hurry to be somewhere else.)

Now, let's say the job contains ten main duties and requirements and that the interviewer has prepared two questions per primary duty/requirement.

That means you have to answer, at a minimum, twenty questions within 35 minutes, which means you'll have a little under two minutes per question. This does not mean that you set your timer at one minute and fifty seconds for every question—it simply means that it is reasonable to assume the interviewers have left a little less than two minutes to get through their primary questions.

However, it is also reasonable to assume that the interviewer may want to spend more time on particular questions. If you've done your homework, there's a good chance that you'll know beforehand which questions the interviewers will wish to spend a little extra time on.

If not, it's up to you to be as alert as possible during the interview. Look out for any clues (such as body language and tone of voice) that may indicate the interviewer is placing extra importance on particular questions. The point is that it's OK to spend a little extra time on these sorts of questions.

Avoid subjective or liberal interpretations of questions. Listen very carefully to the question, and answer it. This sounds obvious, but people do have a bad habit of assuming that the interviewer is wanting to hear a whole lot of other things.

Just stick to the question. If interviewers have other questions, there's a good chance they'll ask them.

Step 3: Context -

Once you've listed what you did and how you did it under step 2, it is important to give some thought to the context or situation in which you did it. Without context, your answers will sound empty or only half-completed.

In fact, as we shall see a little later, it is often a good idea to begin your answers by giving the interviewer an insight into the context in which you performed the duties.

For example, it's better to start an answer by saying, 'I planned and organised my work in a fast-paced entrepreneurial environment where clients wanted everything in a big hurry', rather than saying, 'I planned and organised my work by ensuring that my work schedule took upcoming events into account'.

Whilst there's nothing wrong with the latter, the former is a better beginning because it sets the scene and gives the interviewer a better insight into the environment in which you worked.

By talking about context, you're giving the interviewer a better appreciation of the work you did, as well as its relevance to the job you're applying for. Without a clearly articulated context, your answers will consist of little more than a bunch of tasks you completed.

And there's a good chance interviewers will adopt one of those indifferent expressions indicating that, no matter what you say thereafter, they have decided you're not getting the job.

Please note that you only need to establish context once for each job you did. Repeating context for the same job is nonsensical and is likely to make the interviewer think that you bumped your head against something hard on your way to the interview!

Step 4: Outcomes -

This step involves writing down the key outcomes or results of your actions. One of the things I've noticed over the years is that many people find it difficult to articulate the good things that have resulted from their work.

When I ask them why, I soon discover it's because many of them don't think in terms of outcomes. Unfortunately, their thinking is primarily confined to what they did, and sometimes how they did it.

However, outcomes or achievements are arguably the most important aspect of your work. There's little point in doing all the right things if you don't achieve any positive outcomes.

From an interviewer's point of view, outcomes are critical. When thinking about outcomes, it is useful to separate them into organisation and personal categories.

Organisational outcomes -

Organisational outcomes include any improvements accrued by the organisation as a result of your work. Sometimes these are easy to quantify, especially if you've been involved in making, selling, installing or changing something. When thinking about organizational outcomes, many people confine themselves to the evident outcomes— or the things they actually did.

Examples of evident outcomes include such things as implementing a new filing system, changing report templates or building a new database for keeping track of customer contacts. Needless to say, it is important to mention these outcomes at an interview.

However, the shortfall with evident outcomes is that they fail to articulate their primary benefits to the organisation. Saying you implemented a new filing system is great, but your answer would be much better if you also articulated the benefit of this new filing system to the employer.

Finishing your answer with an outcome or outcomes -

As much as possible, try to conclude with a positive outcome. Summarising the above points, here's what a question and a full answer might sound like:

Question: *Tell us about the way you dealt with working in a fast- paced entrepreneurial environment.*

Whilst working for this company, an important client needed changes made to one of the orders she had placed and she needed these changes completed within a very short space of time. Given that a number of our clients worked in unpredictable environments, these requests were not uncommon. Our job was to ensure that we could meet them, otherwise we'd effectively be out of a job.

This establishes the context step 3. Amongst other things, this opening tells the interviewer about the significance of your work. The way I dealt with working in such a demanding environ- ment was to ensure that my planning took into account the fact that matters could change at any minute. For example, I made it very clear to my clients and colleagues that, due to the nature of my work, I might be changing appointments or sending someone else instead of myself.

I also avoided making long-term commitments. Coping in such a hectic environment also meant that I had to make some fundamental changes in the way I thought about work.

I had to quickly jettison the idea of working predictable hours and performing foreseeable tasks. I also had to come to terms with the idea that work can often be unpredictable requiring a great deal of flexibility. Now I could never see myself going back to a settled working environment.

I also had to be prepared to learn new things quickly as the need arose. For this job, I had to learn the basics of PowerPoint and Access in a few days and apply them on the job. Retraining becomes a way of life, as does learning to work well with others.

This reflects step 2: what you did and how you did it. The answer clearly and succinctly states what actions were taken (planning), and gives specific examples of how they were taken (e.g changing appointments).

The outcomes of my work were very motivating for me. Not only did we consistently meet the client's requests, but we had an excellent record in terms of our customer service levels as measured by our twice yearly customer service survey.

This is an illustration of step 4: outcomes. In this case, two organisational outcomes have been stated: 'consistently met client's requests' and 'excellent customer service'. And there is one personal outcome—'high levels of motivation'. This answer is a thorough one, and you would probably not use all of it in response to a single question.

However, thorough preparation is a wise precaution. Youmay choose to use only a part of this answer in response to a team player question and keep the rest in reserve for another team player question or a question requiring similar skills. Feel free to 'cut and paste' your answers as the need arises.

The elements of a good interview response contained in this answer include the following:

+ It provided specific examples.

+ It mentioned learning the basics of PowerPoint and Access.

+ It stated what you did and how you did it—for example, changing appointments; avoiding making long-term commitments; learning new things quickly as the need arose; retraining; and letting go of the idea that work is predictable and inflexible.

+ It stated outcomes and mentioned being motivated by outcomes, including consistently meeting clients' requests and an excellent record in terms of customer service levels.

+ It avoided meandering all over the place. One of the strengths of the four steps is that we can answer a range of questions relating to the duty or requirement under step 1.

Below are responses to some other questions relating to working in an entrepreneurial environment.

Question:

Which part of working in an entrepreneurial environment did you find most challenging?

Given the short time frames and levels of work required, the most challenging aspect for me at least in the beginning— was meeting the client's tight deadlines. (step 3).

I met this challenge by improving the way I planned for contingencies, by training myself in several software packages including PowerPoint and Access, and by putting into place measures that improved the communication amongst key stakeholders. (step 2). The outcomes were very positive. Not only did I begin to meet the client's deadlines, but I also put into place communication procedures that improved organizational efficiency. (step 4).

Question:

What did you enjoy most about working in an entrepreneurial environment?

The part I enjoyed most was meeting the tight deadlines set by the clients. I always felt a deep sense of satisfaction every time we successfully overcame a difficult challenge (step 4). A lot of planning and well-organised work needed to be completed before the deadlines were successfully met. (steps 2 and 3).

For example, we needed to ensure that all members of the team were continually communicating with one another and that everyone had the required training. I enjoyed working in a fast-paced and challenging environment which stretched me on a daily basis.

Question:

How do you manage the pressures of working in a fast- paced entrepreneurial environment?

I manage it quite well. In fact, I'd go so far as to say that I enjoy working in such an environment. The strategies that work for me consist of ensuring that I've got all the right skills to do the job, including good communications skills and the ability to work well with others. Just as important as skills, however, is the right state of mind. I enjoy working at a fast pace and in a challenging environment where change is the only constant. I could not imagine myself working in a slow-paced and predictable environment.

Remember, the four steps simply provide a means by which you can capture lots of relevant data in a simple way. There's no reason why you cannot alter some aspects of the model to suit your own needs. It is designed to be flexible. Here are two important examples of how the four steps can be used differently.

First, you do not have to fill each column. For example, if you have no personal outcomes worth mentioning, don't invent them for the sake of filling out that section. The same goes for the obstacles under step 2.

In some cases, people encounter very minor obstacles when performing certain duties—so minor, in fact, that they're really not worth mentioning. Always leave out trivia. The idea is to fill each of the columns only with information that was important to the job and that you think will be relevant to the interviewer.

Second, you can alter the headings under the four steps to suit the question you're addressing. For example, for questions that relate to qualities or issues that are not skills related and/or do not readily lend themselves to step-by-step procedures, the heading of the second column can be adjusted to simply read 'Examples'. Such qualities would include loyalty, honesty, integrity, work-related values or beliefs, and hobbies.

Because values-related characteristics such as the above are qualities which do not require skills or technical knowledge, and which do not lend themselves to a sequence of actions, this column would simply list examples of when you behaved loyally or honestly (rather than how you did something). Here are

some examples of questions where step 2 may be adjusted:

- Tell us about some of your interests outside of work.

- We're loyal to our employees and would like to think they are loyal to us. Can you give us an example of you behaving in a loyal manner?

- Do you prefer a quiet workplace or one in which there is some noise?

- Do you enjoy following rules?

- Do you prefer following established step-by-step procedures or making it up as you go?

Suggested activity: Using the four steps

- Select a duty or a job requirement that you're familiar with and, using the four steps to interview success, capture all the relevant information you can think of (see Table 3.1).

- When you've entered all your information, pose yourself two questions using the behavioural questioning technique referred to in this chapter.

- Practise your answers aloud until you've reached a satisfactory level of fluency.

Summary of key points

- 'Can you do the job?' questions are generally the most common questions asked at interviews. They are concerned with ascertaining your skills, knowledge and experience.

- 'Can you do the job?' questions can be split into three categories: questions about duties that you have performed before;

- Questions about duties that you have not performed but whose skills you have mastered;

- Questions about duties that are entirely new to you.

- Your first important step to preparing your interview answers is to find out as much about the job as possible.

- The four steps to interview success provide a simple-to-use framework with which you can capture all the relevant information you need to construct interview answers. As well as capturing what you did and how you did it, it also compels you to think about context and outcomes. It is ideally suited for answering behavioural questions and can be used in a flexible way.

Beware of long-winded answers.

The most effective way of putting together the information you capture using the four steps is to pose to yourself hypothetical interview questions and then answer them out loud until you become fluent.

A good interview answer will generally contain the following points:
– a context;
– specific examples;
– what you did and how you did it;
– outcomes;
– it will get directly to the point.

"When you say "It's hard", it actually means "I'm not strong enough to fight for it". Stop saying its hard. Think positive!" – Harry.

The
C
Programming Language.

Printf(" Authored By Harry. H. Chaudhary.");

Golden Beginner's To Experts Edition.

Chapter - 4

Your potential to tackle New Tasks

At times, you'll be asked questions that have nothing to do with your past duties and achievements. To make matters worse, the skills inherent in these duties will be substantially different to the skills you already have, thus making these the most challenging of all interview questions.

Typically, you are asked these type of questions when you are starting off in your career, changing careers or going for a promotion that entails brand new duties such as managing a team of people.

Clearly, when you have not performed the duties before, making a direct link to past duties or skills becomes problematic. However, there's no reason for despair. There are plenty of interviewees who successfully tackle these sorts of questions on a regular basis. As you have already learned, the key to success is correct preparation.

Break down the duties -

The first step involves taking each of the new duties and breaking them down into the individual skills and knowledge they comprise. The individual pieces of information you come up with will constitute the core of your answers. In terms of our four steps, this information will go under step 2.

Breaking down a duty that you've never performed before can sometimes be a tricky exercise, particularly if you've had no experience in doing it. But don't give up after a couple of tries it becomes easy. Here are some guidelines that you should find useful. Begin by asking yourself the question, 'In order to perform a particular duty or requirement, what steps would I need to take?' Conduct a brainstorming session. Do not overlook any - detail, no matter how trivial you may think it is.

Write down everything and anything that comes into your head. You can throw out the unimportant stuff later. What may strike you as being trivial and not worth mentioning often turns out to be an important skill. A good example of this is listening skills.

Most people don't even think about mentioning this skill, yet good listening skills are critical to effective interpersonal skills—including being a team player, problem-solving and conflict resolution. It's also a very hard skill to master, especially when you're hearing something that you don't agree with.

If you're having problems coming up with ideas, don't worry. Contact a friend, a work colleague, a former manager or anyone you think may be able to shed some light on the matter. You'll soon find that two or three heads are better than one.Whatever you do, don't give up. You will do it—it's just a matter of getting the hang of it.

If your friends can't help, don't panic. It's time to consult a book or an expert in the field. If, for example, you're applying for a manager's position and you've never managed people before, it makes sense to talk to someone who knows what's involved. As much as possible try to list the component skills in a logical, sequential order.

Before you finalise your list, you must scrutinise your answers. Because you've never performed these duties before, it stands to reason that some of your answers may be somewhat naïve or just plain wrong. Scrutinise the quality of your answers by talking to someone who knows and/or by asking yourself the all-important question, 'Can I credibly support my answer if questioned in more detail by the interviewer?'

In most circumstances, there are no absolutely right or wrong answers to how duties are performed. Questions requiring highly technical answers which need to be very specific are, of course, the exception. As unique individuals working in varied environments, we face differing challenges which affect the way we do things.

So the way I work in an entrepreneurial environment, or plan and organise my work, may be different to someone else's method—but it is no less valid or effective. In terms of interviews, the important thing is to provide a succinct and logical answer that can withstand scrutiny if the interviewer decides to delve deeper into your answer.And good interviewers always dig deeper.

You need to have faith in what you think is the right way to perform a duty, but be sure you have thought your answer through. Ask yourself, 'Why would I take a particular course of action?' By all means consult experts and listen carefully to what they say, but at the end of the day it has to be your answer.

Let's look at a common example of a new duty: managing people in the workplace. Managing staff, as anyone who has been thrust into that - position knows, requires a range of new skills some of which can be quite challenging. Given the importance most organisations place on effective people management, how you respond to this type of question could easily make or break your interview. Here are a few examples of managing staff questions:

+ How would you go about leading a team of highly trained professionals?

+ As a manager of people, how would you go about motivating them and maximising their performance?

+ Describe your ideal manager. Duties inherent inmanaging people in the workplacemight include:

+ Delegating work appropriately, taking into account the abilities of staff and multi-skilling considerations;

+ Giving timely and objective feedback;

+ Consulting on matters that affect staff;

+ Acknowledging and recognising their efforts;

+ Treating everyone equally.

Using the four steps, you would include these duties—or others you might regard as important—under step 2 (see Table opposite).

Create a relevant context -

Given that you've never performed this duty, it stands to reason that you cannot provide a real-life context as you would for the duties you had actually performed.

However, this should not prevent you from making up a context—one that will be the same or similar to the job you're applying for. Doing this compels you to go a step further by placing your step 2 answers in a 'real life' situation.

By doing this, you'll be in a better position to make your answers sound more convincing.

In an interview, you are likely to be asked a contextualized question—that is, one which asks how you would perform a duty within a certain situation or context. So, instead of being asked 'How would you go about managing staff?' (no context), it is likely you'll have to answer a question more like 'How would you go about managing a team of highly motivated professionals in a fast-paced environment?'

If you do happen to be asked a question without a context (inexperienced interviewers have been known to ask decontextualised questions), being able to put it into a context that is relevant to the job you're applying for is likely to impress the interviewer.

Without context, your answers will sound only half-completed. Place your imaginary context under step 3 in the four steps to interview success table (see Table opposite). Expected outcomes Given that you've never performed this duty before, it's nonsensical to talk about real outcomes. However, it is a good idea to think in terms of expected outcomes—that is, what is likely to happen if you manage people effectively.

The advantages of thinking about expected outcomes are twofold. **First,** because outcomes are similar to goals, it will demonstrate to the interviewer that you're thinking in terms of goals or final results rather than just process. Remember, it is achieving goals that matters most to employers.

Second, many interviewers are fond of asking annoying questions like, 'And what do you see the results of your peoplemanagement approach being?' and, 'What can a good manager of people achieve with his/her staff?' Filling out the step 4 column with your expected outcomes will help you to formulate effective answers to such questions (see Table below).

Be aware that some companies prefer not to use the term 'managing' people. Instead they favour the term 'leading' people. If you're preparing answers to a set of managing/leading people questions, make sure you acquaint yourself with the company's management language. Sometimes, just using the right word can make a big difference.

Step 1	Step 2	Step 3	Step 4
Duties/ requirements of position	What would I do to ensure the duties listed under step 1 are performed properly, including overcoming obstacles • Delegating work appropriately, taking into account abilities of staff and multi-skilling considerations • Giving timely and objective feedback • Consulting on matters that affect staff • Acknowledging and Recognizing their efforts	Imaginary context	Expected outcomes organisational and personal Organisational • Maintain or improvemotivation of staff, which will contribute to improved individual and team performance, including possible improvement in rates of absenteeism and turnover Personal • Demonstrated an ability to quickly learn about the products I was selling
Managing people in the workplace		Managing a sma team of highly motivated professionals in fast-paced environment	

Putting it all together –

Let's take a look at a likely question and a possible response.

Question: *How would you go about leading a team of highly trained professionals?*

I would certainly take into account the fact that I am dealing with professionals—that is, highly trained people who should know what they're doing (step 3). In delegating work, I would take into account their abilities, preferences and current workloads. I would make sure that work was distributed evenly, taking organisational needs into account (step 2).

I'm a great believer in giving people feedback. Without feedback staff often are unaware of important matters relating to their performance. I would ensure that my feedback was timely and objective—that is, based on facts rather than conjecture (step 2).

I also believe in consulting with staff in matters relating to their work. Not only do staff feel more valued when they're consulted, but often management can be made aware of important matters that they previously were not aware of (step 2).

Acknowledging and recognising individual and team effort is, I think, also very important—especially when it comes to giving staff a feeling of - being appreciated. I know that when my manager acknowledged something special that I did, I always felt good about it (step 2).

I strongly believe that effective people management is vital to the success of any team. Good managers are able to motivate and bring out the best in their people. This in turn contributes significantly to the performance of the team. It would be my objective to maximise the performance of my team by implementing the techniques already mentioned (step 4).

The strengths of the above answer are as follows:

+ Acknowledging the professional context of the team to be managed;

+ Articulating the points in a clear and sequential order;

+ Giving reasons why certain actions would be taken;

+ Finishing off with an expected outcome.

Suggested activity: Your potential to tackle new tasks -

To help you prepare your answers to at least one duty which is substantially different to anything you've done before, follow the guidelines described above that is:

+ Break the duty down into its individual components.

+ Use the four steps and put those individual components under step 2.

+ Use an imaginary context that is likely to come up in an interview.

+ Include expected outcomes.

Summary of key points

+ Questions about duties which are substantially different to anything you've done before are generally the most challenging in an interview.

+ There is often no one single answer (nor one right answer) about how duties are performed. We all come from different work backgrounds and bring with us different ways of doing things.

+ The names of steps 2, 3 and 4 will change slightly, reflecting the different challenges posed by these sorts of questions. In particular, the context (imaginary context) and outcomes (expected outcomes) headings change to take into account the fact that you've never performed these duties before.

Chapter - 5
Employers Love
Motivated Employees.

*E*xperienced employers know that highly motivated employees are invaluable. Motivated employees tend to learn things quickly, complete their duties enthusiastically, care about the business and often go beyond the call of duty. Contrast this with an unmotivated employee. Even highly talented people who lack motivation can border on the ineffectual. As one successful employer said to me:

"Give me motivation over talent any day. Motivated people develop talent by their drive and enthusiasm. They ask questions, volunteer for jobs and overcome any shortcoming they may have. They're worth twice as much as talented people who lack motivation. An unmotivated talented person is an oxymoron."

Communicating your motivation levels -

At interviews, the motivation levels of the candidate tend to be inferred by the interviewers. In other words, the interviewer picks up on signals given by the interviewee. These signals can be broken down into three groups:

- *What is said;*
- *How it is said;*
- *Body language.*

This chapter will focus on the first two groups what is said and how it is said. Last Chapter will discuss body language. Suffice to say that convincing employers you're highly motivated rests on more than just the words that come out of your mouth. Your body language and the way you say things are both critical.

Despite the critical importance of motivation in the workplace, motivation questions are not as common as they should be. One reason for this is that there are many inexperienced interviewers out there who are not sure how to construct a motivation question.

Questions such as, 'How motivated are you?'

sound embarrassingly amateurish and tend to attract answers such as, 'I am very motivated. If you give me this job I'll work very hard.'

+ *When direct motivation questions are asked, they usually begin with the words 'why' and 'what'. Here are some classic examples:*

+ *Why do you want to work here?*

+ *Why do you want to do this job?*

+ *What interests you about this job?*

+ *What are the things you like about working in this sort of environment?*

+ *What do you love about this work?*

+ *What are the sorts of things you enjoy doing at work?*

A useful way to prepare for all of the above questions is to ask yourself 'What are the things that I like about this job?' Or, to put it another way, 'Why do I like this sort of work?' When thinking about what you like about a particular job, you need to look at the duties of the job very carefully.

Your next step is to make a list of all the things that attract you to the job, being as specific as possible. You need to be specific, otherwise your answers may sound hollow.

A broad-ranging statement such as 'I love retail', for example, is not nearly as convincing as 'I love interacting with people on a daily basis' or 'I love the thrill of making a sale and watching a happy customer leave the store'. That's because the last two statements not only tell the interviewer that you love retail, but also explain why. Here are some examples of motivation statements that excite employers (but make sure you've got the specific examples to back up your statement):

+ *I love working with people.*

+ *I very much enjoy challenges of the sort you mention.*

+ *I really like working with numbers.*

+ *Interacting with people is what gets me out of bed in the mornings.*

+ *I really enjoy working on my own.*

+ *I love learning new things.*

+ *I love Programming.*

+ *Solving complex problems is what I love doing most.*

+ *I get a deep sense of satisfaction when I make a customer happy.*

+ *I'm very keen on solving technical issues.*

+ *I love working on computers.*

+ *I really go for working in this sort of environment.*

+ *I can't get enough of this kind of work.*

Don't hide your enthusiasm -

You will have noticed that all of the above statements have one very important quality in common: they're all enthusiastically expressed. Avoid timid or uncertain language because you will sound unconvincing. Put yourself in the shoes of an employer and compare the following two answers about customer service. Which of the two would you rather hear at an interview?

Answer 1: On the whole I like dealing with customers even though they can be really irritating and do ask stupid questions. But I do realise that without customers I'd be out of a job so I make a big effort to satisfy them.

Answer 2: I love dealing with customers. I really enjoy the interaction with people, including answering all their questions—no matter how trivial they may seem. I get a deep sense of satisfaction when I can solve problems for customers or help them out in some way.

Clearly, the second answer is the better one. It starts off with a very enthusiastic statement and reinforces this with several more affirmations. It is full of positive energy and gives the clear impression that the person is highly motivated in terms of providing high standards of customer service.

Notice also that this answer makes a value statement—that is, 'I get a deep sense of satisfaction'. By doing so, it gives us an insight into the beliefs or values of the speaker and hence partly addresses the 'Are you the sort of person we can work with? question.

On the other hand, the first answer sounds as though the person provides good customer service because they're forced to. We all know that customers sometimes ask stupid questions, but interviews aren't the place to articulate such views.

The information you've gathered using the four steps can also be used to address motivation questions. The information under step 2 can be a rich source of specific information when addressing the motivation question.

Let's say, for example, that you're applying for a job in which you have to lead a team of people and you're asked one of the classic motivation questions. Here's what the exchange might sound like:

Question: *What interests you about this job?*

There are many things that really interest me about this job. One of them is the opportunity to lead a team of hard-working people. I love bringing out the best in people and watching them get the most out of their work. I am able to do this by applying sound principles of team leadership.

For example, when delegating work, I take into account people's abilities as well as workload. I give timely and consistent feedback designed to improve people's performance. I consult with people, acknowledge good work and treat everyone equally. Getting respect from your team is a highly motivating experience.

The bold section of the above answer is taken directly from the second column of Table By stating specifically what you do to successfully lead a team of people, you're giving credibility to your claim about enjoying 'bringing out the best in people'.

The exciting thing about this answer is that it works on several levels:

 + *It answers the question directly.*

 + *It tells the interviewer that you're probably a great team leader.*

 + *It tells the interviewer that bringing out the best in people is something that motivates you a great deal.*

 + *It does all of the above without waffling.*

A word of warning about motivators -

When compiling your answers about the things that you like about the job, there are some things that you need to be careful with. These include:

 + *Money;*

 + *Proximity to where you live;*

 + *Convenient hours;*

 + *Friends working there.*

All of these can be important motivators for many people—and can, of course, be mentioned during the course of the interview. However, they should not be mentioned as primary motivators because none of them has anything to do with you performing well in the job.

Primary motivators should be linked to the nature of the work itself, and should demonstrate an ability to perform well in key areas of the job. It is much more effective to say that you love working with people rather than that you love the money or your travelling time will be halved!

Suggested activity: Motivation -

Make a list of all the things that attract you to your chosen job. If you're having problems coming up with answers, take a close look at the main duties and ask yourself, 'What is it about these duties that I like?' Remember to avoid broad statements. Be as specific as you can. Once you've compiled your list, answer the following questions. Keep on practising your answers until you're happy with your fluency.

Question 1: Why have you applied for this job?

Question 2: What are the sorts of things that motivate you?

Summary of key points

+ Convincing interviewers that you're highly motivated requires more than saying the right things. Body language and how you say things are just as important.

+ When preparing your answers to motivation questions, one of the helpful questions you can ask yourself is 'Why do I like this kind of work?' Your specific responses to this question will constitute the core of your motivation answers.

+ Express yourself with enthusiasm. Interviewers expect to see keenness in motivated candidates.

+ Step 2 of the four steps is often a good source of information for motivation questions.

+ Avoid mentioning motivators such as money and travel time—they do not contribute to your ability to perform well in the job.

"Don't worry about failures, worry about the chances you miss when you don't even try." – Harry.

"The pain you feel today is the strength you feel tomorrow. For every challenge encountered there is opportunity for growth."

– Harry.

JAVA
United Hills.

Effective
Core Java

The Complete Core Reference.

TENTH EDITION 2014.

Harry- H.Chaudhary.

Chapter - 6
The 'Big Five' Questions.

There are five very common generic questions which crop up in virtually every interview. They relate to:

- *Being a good team player;*
- *Planning and organising your work effectively;*
- *Good interpersonal communication;*
- *Coping with change in the workplace;*
- *Providing effective customer service (including internal customers).*

Using the four steps, this chapter poses the questions about these issues and suggests possible responses.

The importance of the 'big five' questions -

The skills listed above are vital to most jobs. It is hard to think of a job in which all five do not come into play at one stage or another, and impossible to think of a job in which at least one of them is not relevant. For this reason, the 'big five' actually constitute hundreds of interview questions.

Once you've learned how to answer the 'big five' questions, you will be able to respond to many other questions because there is a great deal of overlap amongst them. For example, if you can answer the basic question, 'What makes you a good team player?' you should also be able to respond to a range of similar team player questions, including:

- *How do you like working in a team?*
- *Do you consider yourself a good team player?*
- *Describe your ideal team.*
- *What does it take to be an effective team player?*

However, be aware that, while learning how to respond to one generic question allows you to answer many similar questions, this does not mean you will be able to answer every conceivable question asked. It's up to you to be diligent and look for questions within the genre that may be slightly different or unexpected.

Given the common nature of the above skills, they will be treated as if they have been performed before.

Answering a 'team player' question -

Most people work in teams. Even people who appear to work on their own often have to interact with others in the organisation, thus creating one or more loosely formed teams. Some teams need to work closely together, others less so; some teams work together all the time, whereas others meet only periodically. The important point is that employers rely heavily on the smooth functioning of their teams and are keen to hire effective team players. Here are some examples of team player questions:

- *What makes you a good team player?*

- *How do you find working in a team?*

- *Do you prefer working alone or in a team? Why?*

- *What do you dislike about working in a team?*

- *What would you do if one of your colleagues was not pulling their weight?*

- *Describe your ideal team.*

- *Can you give us examples of what you've done to ensure that your role in a team was a positive one?*

- *How would you handle a team member who was loud and aggressive at team meetings and dominated proceedings by intimidating others?*

Now let's use the four steps to prepare the information needed to respond to 'team player' questions: Here's a sample interview question and a possible response.

Question: Are you a good team player? Can you give us examples of you demonstrating team player capabilities?

*Y*es, I consider myself to be an effective team player. In my previous job I was part of a team of four people who were responsible for paying the salaries, including overtime and bonuses, of approximately 2000 employees When I first started work in the team, there were communication problems between several team members. As well as affecting our performance, these problems were straining relations between certain members of the team. After several weeks, I thought that if we introduced more regular meetings and a rotating chair, communications might improve.

When I made this suggestion, the team members agreed to it and, to make a long story short, the new meeting format turned out to be a success. Both communications and performance improved I also demonstrated my team player capabilities by making a point of acknowledging my colleagues' opinions and contributions, as well as helping team members when they were having problems.

I think when you're willing to help others, they'll help you when you need it in return and that can only be good for the team. I also made a point of sharing all information I thought my colleagues needed to know. I would mention even seemingly unimportant information such as individuals griping about their pay and minor mishaps with the software because often it can be the little things that cause big problems down the line.

According to my colleagues, my presence in the team led to improved communications amongst team members, as well as with our clients, which contributed significantly to our overall performance. In particular, our error rate was halved within two months.

Remember that, unless the interviewer has specifically told you that the company is placing a great deal of emphasis on hiring someone with effective team player skills, chances are that you would not use every aspect of the above answer in response to a single question.

You may decide to use parts of it and keep the rest in reserve for a follow-up question or a question seeking information about similar skills. It is wise to over-prepare and even wiser to know when to stop. The same principle applies to the rest of the 'big five' questions.

Answering a planning and organising question –

It is difficult to think of a job in which is no planning and organizing are involved. If we accept that technology has largely taken over many of the repetitive tasks performed by people in the past, most jobs these days involve some sort of planning and organising. Planning and organising questions are therefore likely to be high on the agenda of many interviewers. Here are some typical planning and organising questions.

- *Tell us how you go about planning and organising your work schedule.*

- *Can you give us an example of when you had to plan and organise an important event or work-related activity? What steps did you take?*

- *Do you consider yourself a good planner and organiser? Why?*

- *What do you do when your manager asks you to complete a task but you've already got a very full agenda?*

- *How do you prioritise your work?*

- *Describe your approach to planning and organising your work.*

Now let's look at a sample interview question and response.

Question: Can you give us an example of when you had to plan and organise an important event or work related activity? What steps did you take?

When I was working in the administration support unit for Michael Angelo Enterprises, I was responsible for planning a broad range of activities ranging from the timely ordering of paint supplies to security, building maintenance and assisting departments and managers with basic infrastructure needs Juggling all these activities simultaneously meant I had to plan my work in great detail as well as be very well organised.

There was one time when we had to install new security systems and new computer graphics software, as well as answering the multiple requests made by our clients. In order to deal with all of this, I needed to diarise my work on a daily, weekly and monthly basis and ensure that I continually kept up to date with what everyone else was doing.

I made sure I attended as many meetings as I could and kept my ear to the ground. Given the multiple tasks I had to complete, I found it important to prioritise my work according to the needs of the organisation, as opposed to the needs of a few individuals. Getting the new security systems in place had to come before some of the requests made by managers.

And, finally, it was important to learn how to say 'no' to some requests. In my view, a good planner knows how much is enough. Taking on more work than one can handle only leads to poor-quality service or even failure to do the work.

As well as learning a great deal about what it takes to maintain an organisation in terms of infrastructure support, one of the great outcomes of my actions was that my clients rated my service as 'very high' for three years running, which gave me a great deal of satisfaction.

*A*nswering an interpersonal communication question Interpersonal communication skills are not just about clear communications. They are also about the way we interact with others. People with effective interpersonal communication skills are much more likely to get on with others in the workplace (and thus get ahead) because they demonstrate a range of behaviours that bring out the best in the people they interact with.

*T*hey are good listeners, avoid inflammatory language (including body language), acknowledge others' contributions, consult before making decisions, and so on. People with effective interpersonal communication skills are highly prized by employers because they bring harmony to the workplace. *T*hey usually make people feel better about themselves and their contributions—which, of course, is important to employers in terms of maintaining a happy and productive workforce.

Here are some typical interpersonal communication skills questions:

+ *Do you enjoy working with people?*

+ *How would you describe your relations with others in the work place?*

+ *Describe yourself. (Whilst this question does not confine itself to interpersonal communication skills, it does provide an excellent opportunity for you to briefly mention them.)*

+ *Tell us about a time when you had a disagreement with some one at work. What were the circumstances and how did you deal with it?*

+ *Can you give us an example of when you had to communicate a complex and sensitive issue? How did you go about it?*

+ *Describe the colleague with whom you enjoyed working most.*

+ *How do you deal with an angry person at work?*

+ *Would you prefer to be seen as a well-liked person or an effective person?*

A clear overlap exists between interpersonal communication skills and team player skills. Many of the points can therefore be used interchangeably. Here's an example of a possible interview question and response.

Question: Can you give us an example of when you had to communicate a complex and sensitive issue? How did you go about it?

*W*hen I was working for Magellan, I was on the team that was responsible for introducing a new performance appraisal system for all of the crew on our ship. Working on this project, I was often required to communicate complex and sensitive information to individuals and groups. I'd like to emphasise that performance appraisals were an extremely sensitive issue because people's pay was being attached to the results.

I was successful in communicating the relevant information because I adhered to a number of sound interpersonal communication principles—principles that I have successfully implemented in the past. For example, I made a point of taking people's sensitivities into account and addressing them early on in our conversations.

I avoided any form of jargon, and often assumed that my audience had very little prior knowledge about the issues at - hand. I used positive, non threatening body language—especially when I was confronted by the sceptics who belittled the program despite their lack of knowledge about it. I also acknowledged other people's opinions and never made disparaging comments about suggestions, no matter how outlandish they were.

*F*urthermore, I always made the effort to consult with key stakeholders before finalising decisions. The very fact that you make the effort to consult and explain the parameters within which you have to work often minimises levels of dissatisfaction, even though people may not entirely agree with you.

*A*s a result of my efforts, opposition to the program was virtually non-existent. The crew demonstrated a constructive attitude and gave it their best. As a result, we were able to successfully implement the program within our timeframe and budget.

Coping with change in the workplace-

Unlike the workplace of yesteryear, when people could be performing the same set of duties for many years, today's work environment is characterised by constant change.

In fact, it can be argued that the only constant is change. All this, of course, means a flexible employee is a highly valued one. Change can take the form of any number of things, including:

- *New machinery;*
- *New procedures or guidelines;*
- *New legislation;*
- *New management structures;*
- *Company takeovers;*
- *Downsizing;*
- *New software;*
- *The effects of new competition.*

Organisations that are unable to adapt quickly to changing circumstances often lose market share and can easily go out of business. Therefore, how you respond to 'coping with change' questions is very important. Here are a few examples of the form they may take:

- *Tell us about a time you had to learn new things about your job. How did you cope?*
- *Do you enjoy changing duties?*
- *How do you cope with constant change in the workplace?*
- *Do you regard yourself as a flexible sort of person?*
- *How do you think you would react if you suddenly had to abandon a project you were working on and start a new one?*
- *What are your views on learning in the workplace?*

Now let's look at a sample question and a possible response.

Question: *Tell us about a time you had to learn new things about your job. How did you cope?*

When I working for Northern Legions building Hadrian's Wall, senior management decided to invest heavily in new technology which was designed to improve quality and save us a great deal of time. This new technology involved an array of new equipment, software and work procedures, and represented a sea change in how I performed my duties.

Initially, all of us were slightly daunted at the grand scale of the changes; however, I soon realised that the changes were inevitable if our company was to remain competitive.

I also quickly came to the realisation that, if I was to remain a valued member of the company, I would need to quickly learn how to work under the new regime. This realization ensured that I embraced the changes enthusiastically. Whereas some of my colleagues saw it as a burden, I saw it as the way of the future which is how I've come to view change generally.

As well as attending all the required training sessions, I attended extra ones as well. I studied hard, asked questions and gained as much experience as I could. I soon became the acknowledged expert in certain areas, and people started coming to me for advice.

As a result of our efforts, the new technology was successfully implemented. My team was working with the new technology within the timelines and budget allocated to us. And I learned a whole new way of doing things.

Summary of key points-

*T*he importance of the big five questions is that they are based on skills required for most, if not all, jobs. This makes it highly likely that you will be required to answer a number of questions relating to these. As well as the universality of these skills, they are also critically important to most employers (good interpersonal communication skills, for example, are seen as central to establishing harmonious work relationships and effective performance).

Chapter - 7
Building Rapport and Trust

Managing perceptions and preconceived views-

Interviews are largely about managing the perceptions of the interviewer. Studies show that people look for things that they believe (perceive) will be there, and conversely ignore or pay less attention to those things that don't fit into their preconceived views.

If interviewers think that you are an outstanding prospect, there's a good chance that they'll be looking for, and registering, all the things that will support their preconceived notion.

In other words, if two interviewees perform roughly the same at an interview, the interviewee with the better reputation prior to the interview will most likely be rated higher.

So, as much as possible, make the best impression you can beforeor at the very start of the interview. You can do this by:

+ *Ensuring that your resume is the best that it can be;*

+ *Sending a positive and very brief pre-interview letter thanking the interviewer for the opportunity to be interviewed and stating how much you're looking forward to meeting them;*

+ *Contacting the company to make sensible pre-interview inquiries Contacting the company before the interview demonstrates appropriate interest and a professional level of preparation.*

First impressions-

In addition, it is important to note that the first few minutes (some say seconds) of an interview are also very important in swaying the interviewer's mind. As the old adage goes, first impressions tend to be lasting impressions. Briefly (we'll cover these in more detail later on), the things to look for include:

- *Dress;*
- *Handshake;*
- *Eye contact;*
- *Facial expressions;*
- *Tone of voice.*

Last impressions-

People tend to recall more of what happens at the beginning and the end of an event than they do of what occurs in the middle. This does not mean you concentrate on the beginning and end of your interview and neglect the middle, however.

It is a reminder to be careful about what you do and say towards the end. Some interviewees fall into the trap of over-relaxing (usually as a result of over compensating for their initial tension) and straying into inappropriate behaviours such as becoming overly familiar and adopting an 'I'm at a barbecue' style of body language. So make sure you maintain appropriate interview behaviours right to the very end.

Communication is more than just words-

One of the most important lessons you can learn about improving your rapport and trust ability is that there's much more to communication than the words that come out of your mouth.

Communications experts constantly remind us that about 10 percent of communication is represented by what we say, 30 per cent by how we say things and 60 per cent by our body language! So if, in your preparation for an interview you've been spending all your time concentrating on the content of your answers, you have effectively been spending 100 per cent of your efforts on 10 per cent of overall communication. This may go a long way towards explaining why so many people who give technically brilliant answers don't get the job.

Admittedly many interviewees understand intuitively that successful interpersonal communication (face-to-face communication) relies on much more than just the words used. However, for reasons too varied and complex to discuss here, there are many people whose interpersonal communication skills are not as well honed and/or who are unable to demonstrate their otherwise effective communication skills during an interview—probably because of heightened anxiety.

Once you understand that successful communication relies on a whole range of factors other than words, an entirely new world of communication begins to emerge. The focus of your interview preparations should shift from strict word preparation to include a whole range of non-verbals including such things as appearance, the way you sit and even when you nod your head. Sometimes a friendly smile and an acknowledging nod can be worth a lot more than the best verbal answers.

Acknowledging the power source-

In most interviews, there is an important yet unspoken dynamic lurking just beneath the surface. This dynamic is as old as the first time humans eyeballed each other and opened their mouths to grunt. Naturally, I'm talking about power.

More specifically, I'm talking about acknowledging the fact that, in the vast majority of cases, the interviewer has the real power. (The exception to this is when you are lucky enough to possess a unique set of skills and/or knowledge that the employer is desperate to have.) If you are serious about maximising your rapport, it's important to demonstrate to the interviewer that you understand they have all the power when it comes to giving you the job.

As an interviewee, you too have power—primarily through the fact that you control what the interviewer will hear. However, this does not eliminate the reality that the power to hire (or not) lies exclusively with the interviewer.

Interviewees who acknowledge the interviewer's power stand a better chance of being liked (and therefore winning the job) because, to put it bluntly, most human beings have a weakness for feeling important and having their egos stroked. Intuitively, many of us understand this dynamic but not everyone proactively demonstrates it during the interview. An interviewer may not even be aware of this dynamic (you can usually pick the ones who enjoy their power), but this doesn't mean it's not there.

Avoid groveling –

*A*cknowledging the power dynamics inherent in most interviews does not mean grovelling. As already mentioned, throwing yourself at the feet of the interviewer or laughing yourself hoarse at a lame joke will more than likely be seen as a form of deceit.

*T*he lesson here is a simple one: be aware of the underlying power dynamics present at most interviews and avoid behaviours (such as arguing a point or openly disagreeing with the interviewer) that will more than likely put the interviewer off.

Body language issues-

Sitting -

*T*he way you sit communicates a great deal about a whole range of issues, including how important you think the interview is, how nervous (or confident) you are, and your understanding of the underlying power relations. Some people's sitting position exudes over-familiarity and even arrogance, whereas others communicate a serious lack of self-belief.

*T*he golden rules in sitting are: avoid anything that will distract the interviewer from concentrating upon the content of your answers; and avoid making the interviewer feel uncomfortable. Interviewers generally do not feel comfortable if you sit in an aggressive way (leaning forward too much) or in an overly passive way (leaning back and crossing your legs at the thighs). In short, good sitting goes unnoticed by the interviewer.

Here are some tips on what you should avoid:

- *Leaning back. Gives the impression that you're not taking the interview seriously.*

- *Crossing your legs at the thighs. Too familiar, especially at the beginning of an interview.*

- *Sitting with your legs wide apart. Far too familiar for an interview situation, and can be both distracting and uncomfortable for the interviewer.*

- *Leaning forward too much. May make some interviewers feel uncomfortable, especially if you're physically big and talk loudly.*

- *Slouching. Gives the impression that you're not taking the interview seriously and will likely slouch in your duties.*

Tips on good sitting practice include:

- *Straight and upright body. This is a neutral sitting position that interviewers expect to see.*

- *Male legs. Males can keep their upper legs facing straight forward and adopt what is commonly referred to as the starters position that is, the dominant foot flat on the ground with the other foot having only the front part touching the ground.*

- *Female legs. Females can cross their legs at the ankles and position the legs slightly to one side.*

Facial expressions and eye contact-

Facial expressions are extremely powerful communicators. If you're sitting correctly, the interviewer should spend most of the interview looking at your face and eyes.

The two golden rules of sitting also apply here: do not do anything that will distract interviewers or make them feel uncomfortable. Anything that is overdone will almost certainly give the interviewer pause for concern, whether it be too much smiling, nodding or eye contact.

During the course of an interview, it is very important to control your facial expressions, especially if you feel the interview is not progressing to your satisfaction or you're hearing something you don't like—otherwise you may be communicating unwanted information to the interviewer.

Failure to control your facial expressions will undermine your credibility by sending conflicting signals to the interviewer.

For example, say the interviewer suddenly tells you that the job will include a new and important duty that was not mentioned in the job ad and your immediate gut feeling reaction is,

'*Oh* no I didn't prepare for this new duty, and what the hell are they doing changing the job at this late stage and I know nothing about this new bloody duty!' But you say (or try to say), 'New duty, that's fine. I'm used to taking on new duties. I'm a fast learner and enjoy the challenge.'

In this situation there's a good chance that the terror registered on your face will undermine your words and leave the interviewer unconvinced despite a reasonable answer.

Controlling one's expressions is harder to do than many people realise. Often our faces work independently of our wishes. And usually they communicate our deepest (darkest) feelings, which it may not be in our best interests to reveal. But with a bit of knowledge and practice we can go a long way towards controlling what our faces say.

Becoming aware of the communicative power of facial expressions represents a good start to controlling unwanted communication. Next time you feel that your face may be communicating something that you don't want it to, stop and force yourself to change it. You'll probably find it a little awkward at first, but with a bit of perseverance you should be able to control it at will. With enough practice, it will become second nature.

Smiling -

If you were standing outside a room seconds away from being invited in for an interview and I happened to be passing by and you grabbed me with a desperate look in your eye asking me for one piece of advice, I would say, 'Don't forget to smile'. Smiling is a highly effective communicator and sends all the right signals to the interviewer, especially for building rapport.

A smile can often achieve what the best of answers cannot— softening the interviewer. Very importantly, when you smile at people it usually makes them feel better, which tends to draw out their better nature exactly what you want to be doing at an interview. It also signals to the interviewer that you have well-developed social skills, are a nice person and do not suffer from anti-social tendencies.

Here are some tips about smiling:

Be genuine. Avoid grinning or putting on a forced smile. There's nothing worse than someone trying to smile but only succeeding in demonstrating the art of teeth clenching.

Don't overdo it. Overdoing it may run you the risk of appearing disingenuous.

Avoid mimicking the grim-faced interviewer-

It is not uncommon to mimic others' facial expressions (and body language), even though we often don't realise we're doing it.

If you encounter the grim-faced interviewer, try not to fall into the trap of being grim-faced yourself. This is not as easy as it may sound because human beings, being what we are, usually require positive feedback in order to continue behaving in certain ways.

In other words, if you smile and the other person refuses to smile back, there's a good chance you will stop smiling. So: do not allow a dour interviewer to put you off. Stick to your guns and produce your warmest smiles, no matter what!

Nodding your head-

Nodding of the head represents another extremely powerful communicator. When you nod your head at something, people say you are telling them that you agree with them, and you do so without interrupting, which is an ideal rapport-building technique when the interviewer decides to expound on a topic. But be careful: as in smiling, the danger with nodding your head is overdoing it.

Eye contact -

The key to successful eye contact is avoiding extremes. Overdoing it can put people off, as can making hardly any eye contact at all. Staring will almost certainly raise a big question mark about your social skills. Even worse, it may frighten the interviewer.

Not making enough eye contact will more than likely signal that you lack confidence and perhaps suffer from low self-esteem issues. Bear in mind that interviews are largely about imparting impressions. You may in reality be a confident and outgoing person who enjoys a great social life, but if you fail to make enough eye contact with the interviewer, you will probably fail to communicate that reality.

Like so many of the non-verbal communicators, appropriate levels of eye contact during an interview differ between cultures. It is important that you ascertain the cultural norm before walking into an interview.

Hands and arms-

The big mistake with arms is to fold them across your chest. Doing so is tantamount to placing a barrier between you and the interviewer. Other transgressions include sitting on your hands or pretending you don't have any. There's nothing wrong with using your hands to emphasise a point it shows you're human. However, avoid overdoing it.

Handshake-

A good handshake is a firm one. If you are a young male, avoid the primal urge to crush the hand bones of the interviewer. Remind yourself that the purpose of handshaking is to establish rapport, not to demonstrate how - strong you are. Avoid also the limp handshake, the long handshake (remember to let go) and the three finger handshake.If you suffer badly from sweaty palms, bring a handkerchief, but if your sweat glands are running riot it would be a good idea to warn the interviewer first before drenching their palm.

Dress and appearance -

Some people persist in thinking that their appearance has very little to do with their ability to perform in a job, and so give little consideration to how they dress for an interview.

Whilst the logic in this thinking may be unassailable, it is a dangerous thing to do because it fails to take into account that interviews are largely about managing perceptions. Interviewers have certain expectations about dress codes. Failing to meet those expectations is dangerous.

The rule of the thumb for dress and appearance is to err on the side of caution. On the whole, interviewers tend to be cautious and conservative when hiring someone.

The last thing an employer wants to do is to hire the wrong person. Reliability, loyalty, consistency, trustworthiness and dependability are qualities that all employers seek in employees, no matter what type of job it is. Your task at the interview is to signal to the interviewer that you have all those qualities, and dressing appropriately represents a good start.

Here are some tips:

*Always make a point of wearing clean clothes and shoes.

*Jeans (or anything else) with holes in them may make a posi- tive impression on the dance floor, but are unlikely to inspire an interviewer.

*Avoid excessive jewellery and makeup.

*A designer stubble may make you look manly and represent the latest word from the fashion gurus; however, it's likely to make the interviewer think that you didn't think the job was important enough for you to bother shaving.

*Avoid extreme hairstyles.

*Avoid displaying too much skin.

There is a sensible school of thought that advocates dressing according to the nature of the job you're applying for. So, if you're applying for an accountant's position, you wear a business suit, whereas if you're applying for a labourer's position on a building site, a business suit is inappropriate.

All this is true; however, the above tips on dress and appearance remain important.

Interview behaviours -

Body language and personal appearance represent one side of the equation to building rapport and trust during an interview. The other, equally important side, is how you behave and express yourself during an interview.

Never argue -

One of the worst things you can do at an interview is argue with the interviewer. Even a very polite argument should never be considered. Arguing will more than likely convince the interviewer that you are argumentative by nature, which is not a trait that excites employers.

This is a point some interviewees forget—especially when they're convinced they're in the right or the interviewer says something that is evidently wrong.

Also, some interviewers (usually inexperienced ones) tend to downplay some of the things interviewees say and add their own information or even make corrections (or what they believe to be corrections).

Encountering this type of interviewer can be a very frustrating experience. It is at times such as these that your smile can turn into a grimace and the rest of your body can look like it is ready to launch into battle.

However, the effective interviewee will maintain discipline and continue to smile, nod happily and utter little gems like, 'Yes, that's right,' and 'I couldn't agree more'.

You may be thinking, 'I would never want to work for an interviewer who is so disagreeable, so why should I be so agreeable?'

Whilst this is not an unreasonable thought, there are good reasonsto ignore it:

+ *The interviewer may not be the employer or your direct supervisor.*

+ *Bad interviewers do not necessarily make bad employers.*

+ *The interviewer may be inexperienced, nervous or having a bad day.*

Always do your very best at an interview, no matter how objectionable you may find the interviewer. The whole idea of attending an interview is to be offered a job. It's up to you on whether you accept the offer or not later on.

Avoid negatives –

There is no point in attending an interview if you're going to sit there and highlightmany of your flaws and defects. Here are some examples of negative statements that send interviewers ducking for cover:

- 'I would have been able to finish the project had I not been clashing with my teammates.' (You may have been working with the teammates from hell, but the interviewer is likely to ques- tion your team player abilities.)

- 'I love working in software Company, but sometimes customer inquiries or my Boss drive me batty.'

- 'I generally enjoy managing people except when they start complaining about their work. I don't like whingers.' (Most people complain about work from time to time the job of a good manager is to listen and help, not think of staff as whingers.)

- 'I don't like things changing all the time. Just when you learn one thing you need to unlearn it and learn something different. There's too much instability in some workplaces.' (Unless you're applying for a rare job where things always remain the same, this answer given today's rapid rate of change could easily enter the hall of fame for bad answers.)

- 'I don't like pressure.' (Avoid this one unless you're applying for a fantasy job you've created in your head.)

- 'I don't like being told what to do.' (You should be giving serious consideration to starting your own business.)

- 'I suffer from high levels of stress, so I need a stress-free job.' (Another fantasy job.)

- 'I don't like working overtime.' (A lot of people don't like working overtime but it's not the sort of thing to say at an interview. Unless pressing commitments don't allow you to, most jobs require people to stay back sometimes.)

- 'I get annoyed when people don't understand what I'm talking about.' (Perhaps you've got a communication problem.)

- 'I don't know why, but people seem to be frightened of me.' (Perhaps you've got a problem relating to people.)

- 'I'm a slow learner.' (Ouch!)

Negative statements frighten interviewers a great deal remember, they're a conservative bunch. Being critical about your past performances is tantamount to giving interviewers a reason for not hiring you. Also, negative statements because they scare interviewers tend to invite follow-up questions, which is the very last thing you want happening at an interview.

The whole idea is to say things that will invite positive questions that is, questions that allow you to talk about all your strengths and wonderful

achievements. Some people think that pointing out negatives is a way of demonstrating their honesty to the interviewer. Unfortunately for them, the interviewer will only be thinking of ways of terminating the interview.

Other than things that will have a direct bearing upon the job (such as a problem back in a job which requires heavy lifting), it is no one's business what your foibles may be. What you may perceive as a weakness about yourself may not be regarded as one by others. At the end of the day, interviews are about making the best impression possible.

Overcoming shortcomings -

Not talking about negatives is different to talking about overcoming shortcomings. For many high achievers, work is largely about overcoming shortcomings in their skills and knowledge in order to achieve their aims. Rather than being frightened by new things, they embrace them as learning challenges and look forward to overcoming them.

Often the difference between a highly effective employee and one who is struggling has little to do with talent and much to do with this attitude towards learning.

Employers like nothing more than hearing about how you overcame a skills or knowledge deficit in order to complete a project. Overcoming deficiencies demonstrates to the interviewer that you are the sort of person who is able to learn on the job and, as a result, get the job completed. Here's what an 'overcoming a skills/knowledge deficit' answer may sound like:

After receiving the assignment, we soon realised that some of us on the team did not have the required knowledge to maximise our contribution. My deficit was in understanding how to use several complicated software applications that were crucial to the quality control side of the assignment.

My challenge was to learn how to use these applications within a very short space of time and reliably apply this knowledge. Because we were working under a very tight timeline and the rest of the team were relying on me, there was very little margin for error.

Fortunately, I was able to apply my newfound knowledge, as did the other members of the team, and we successfully completed the assignment.

This answer not only tells the employer that you can learn complicated information whilst working on an assignment, but that you can also do it under pressure and deliver the required results.

Dealing with the weakness question: *What not to do*

The 'What are your weaknesses?' question is not an ideal one for interviewers to be asking. Some of the problems inherent in this question include:

+ *Many interviewees do not recognise they have a weakness in the first place.*
+ *Others perceive they have a weakness but in fact do not have one at all.*
+ *Some interviewees mistakenly see this question as an opportunity to demonstrate how honest they are and say much more than they should.*
+ *Many interviewees are extremely reluctant to be forthcoming about their weaknesses in an interview.*

Despite these problems, many interviewers persist in asking about your weaknesses. Your job is to learn the best way to handle such questions. At the very least, you should be minimising the potential damage and at best you should be turning the question around and demonstrating to the interviewer that you're the sort of person who can not only overcome weaknesses, but by doing so achieve your goals.

One of the worst things you can do in response to answering this question is to say you don't have any weaknesses. This would signal to the interviewer that you had lost some of your grip on reality and/or that you had a monstrous ego, neither of which would do you any favours. Here are some other things to avoid:

- Do not offer more than one weakness and do not set off on a monumental discourse about your failings and their possible origins. Stick to one weakness unless pressed for a second.

- Avoid talking about personality/character type weaknesses such as impatience, quickness to anger or intolerance of mistakes.

- Generally speaking, these types of weakness frighten employers more than skills deficiencies. Where the latter can normally be rectified with a bit of training, personality/character type weak- nesses may be less easy to remedy and more difficult to deal with.

- Avoid clichés such as: 'I work too hard. I don't know when to stop. I don't know how to say no to work requests.' The problem with these answers is twofold: first, a lot of other people use them, which means you're failing to stand out from the pack; and second, all of the above answers may signal to the astute interviewer that you have a serious problem with managing your workload.

- Do not mention things that are really going to hurt you. Mis- takes you have made in the dim past should remain in the past.

- Don't go digging them up—especially if you've learnt the error of your ways and have moved on.

Hopefully, you will not be applying for jobs for which you are unsuited in the first place. If, for example, you have a great fear of heights and part of the job involves working in high locations, then you shouldn't be wasting anybody's time by applying.

However, if the same job also requires skills that you have in abundance, feel free to ring first and tell them about your situation. The employer may value those other skills and be willing to at least talk to you.

Warning: If you have committed a legal offence that may be relevant to the job you're applying for, you should investigate what your legal obligations are in terms of disclosure before attending the interview. Avoid going on hearsay. Disclosure laws are sometimes changed and may differ from state to state.

Dealing with the weakness question: What to say -

An effective way of dealing with the weakness question is to locate the weakness (preferably a skills deficiency) at some time in the past and then describe the steps you took to overcome it (similar to overcoming shortcomings, see above). The idea is that you show the interviewer that you are able to overcome your weaknesses. It's also good to try to finish your answer on a positive note. Here's what an exchange may sound like.

Question: Tell us about your weaknesses.

When I was working for Chaos several years ago, one of my weaknesses was in the area of making presentations to clients and internal staff. Not that my presentations were disasters far from it—but they lacked the polish of other more experienced presenters.

So I approached a presenter whose style I admired and asked her if she could give me some tips on how I could improve my skills. Fortunately, she was very happy to help me, including sitting in one of my presentations and giving me feedback about my weaknesses. I took her feedback on board and made several changes, which led to my presentations improving significantly.

If the interviewer is not happy with this type of answer because it fails to talk about a current weakness, simply provide a skills-based weakness that is not going to undermine your chances of winning the job—in other words, a weakness that is not very relevant to the job.

Handling objections -

Employer objections usually take the form of 'I like you but . . .'statements. For example, 'I like you, but my main concern is that most of your experience lies in retail which is not relevant to our needs.' You will encounter objections most often when going for promotions or jobs in different vocations or industries. Whilst there is no one correct way to deal with objections there is a three-step method that you may find useful:

1. *Agree with the objection: 'Yes that's correct. Most of my experience does lie in retail.' Agreeing tends to soften the inter- viewer. Disagreeing will probably make you sound unreasonable, if not desperate.*

2. *State why you think the objection does not represent a problem: 'I'd like to point out that in retail most of the work I've been doing is directly relevant to this job. Even though the industry is not the same the skills are. For example, the skills required in delivering high levels of customer service and resolving customer complaints are the same as those you require.'*

3. *Affirm that the difference is not a problem and finish on a pos- itive note: 'In fact I see bringing in a fresh perspective to your business as an advantage. I believe I can introduce new ideas that will drive your business forward.'*

Avoid uncertainty -

One of the golden rules in interviews is to avoid doubt or hesitancy as much as possible. Saying you can accomplish something with hesitancy in your voice or using tentative language is almost the same as saying that you cannot really do it. Steer away from expressions such as:

- *I think I could . . .*
- *I'm not sure about that but perhaps . . .*
- *Perhaps I would . . .*
- *Maybe I could . . .*
- *I feel that I would be able to . . .*

Confidence is one of the keys to establishing rapport in an interview. Interviewers love hearing confident answers because it helps them to overcome their doubt about the interviewee's abilities. Even if you're asked a question about a duty you've never performed before, it is better to say you've never performed it but feel confident about accomplishing it because of all the skills and knowledge you bring to the job, rather than admitting to never having performed the duty and expressing a string of uncertainties.

Remember, how you say things is more important than what you say. Compare the following answers from two candidates, both of whom are responding to the question 'How do you think you would cope with managing a team of professionals?'

Candidate one: I'm not entirely sure whether I could manage a team of professionals. I've never done it before so it would be a whole new experience for me, but I think with a bit of application I could manage it. Certainly I'd like to have a go. It's an area that I'm very interested in.

Candidate two: I'm confident that I could do a good job. I'm comfortable with working with high achievers, I have good interpersonal communication skills and managing people is an area I have a lot of interest in. Even though I've never managed a team before, I feel ready to meet this new challenge in my career.

Essentially, both of the above candidates are saying the same thing. Both are admitting to having no experience in managing a team of professionals, yet both are interested in taking on this new responsibility. The beginning of the first candidate's answer would probably cost them the job, however. I doubt many interviewers would be seriously listening to anything after that first fatal sentence.

There is an attempt to recover in the last two sentences but it's too late by then. On the other hand, the second candidate inspires confidence right from the start. There is a complete absence of uncertainty in this answer, even though the candidate admits to having no experience in managing professionals.

Many interviewees struggle with using highly positive language when talking about duties they've never performed before. This is not unusual, given that in non-interview contextsmost people use tentative language when talking about things they've never tried before. Your aim should be to leave all tentativeness outside the interview door. If you're not going to be confident about doing a good job, how do you expect the interviewer to be confident about you?

Positive statements -

An effective way of getting yourself accustomed to using positive language is to practise using positive statements before the interview. Make a list of positive statements relevant to your situation and start saying them aloud. You may feel a little awkward in the beginning, but repetition will soon take care of that. Keep on practising until you feel very comfortable. Here are some beginnings to help you get started:

- *I can definitely do/finish/write/analyse . . .*
- *I am confident about . . .*
- *I feel very comfortable at the prospect of . . .*
- *I am very secure in the knowledge that . . .*
- *I feel at ease about doing all those things you mentioned . . .*
- *I am positive about taking on . . .*

Third-person statements.

Instead of using first-person statements ('I' statements) all the time, such as 'I did so and so . . .' and 'I am a very good at . . .', it is often better to use third-person statements. The advantage of these types of statements is that they allow you to quote what others have said about your achievements, rather than what you think. Here are some examples:

- ❖ My boss frequently commented on how quickly I was able to get through my work. (as opposed to 'I was often able to complete my work very quickly')
- ❖ My colleagues, very generously, voted me the most valuable team player.
- ❖ Clients often gave me positive feedback about my customer service skills.
- ❖ The team I worked in consistently gave me top marks for my personal communication skills and willingness to help others.

Credit others.

Despite what some people may think, in the vast majority of cases getting something done within the workplace requires the assistance and cooperation of others. Acknowledging the valuable input of others when it comes to your accomplishments is a great way of achieving interview humility. Here's what an answer might sound like: Successfully completing the project on time and within budget meant a great deal to my employer. Had I not delivered the goods, there was the possibility of people beingmade redundant.

However, I would like to stress that the only reason I was successful was because of the valuable help I received from my colleagues.Without their unstinting support I would have failed. Without acknowledging the input of colleagues, this answer runs the risk of sounding somewhat arrogant, but the crediting of others ensures that the speaker comes across as humble without reducing the magnitude of the accomplishment.

+ Avoid repeating your key achievements. In a normal social context, we don't like people going on about their achievements adnauseum one mention is generally enough. The same applies in interviews. Whilst it is essential that you learn how to talk up your key achievements, you should only state achievements once. If you repeat them, you risk giving the impression that you either don't have many to talk about or that you're showing off.

+ Avoid 'big noting' yourself. This may sound a little strange coming from an interview skills book, but it is crucial if you are to avoid portraying yourself as too big for your boots. 'Big noting' your- self means actually saying that you are good or great, or any other descriptor you care to choose—for example, 'I am a fantastic communicator'. It should be left up to the interviewer to infer this by listening to you talk about the sorts of things you've done in this area. In other words, instead of describing yourself,

Say what you did and how you did it and let those actions speak for themselves. Here are some examples:

Avoid: I was a great manager of people.

Do say: By applying sound principles of people management, I was able to lead my team effectively.

Avoid: I've got great customer service skills.

Do say: My manager often commended me on my customerservice skills, in particular my understanding of our products and my ability to link this knowledge to the needs of our customers.

Avoid: I am hard-working.

Do say: In my previous job I always made sure the work was done properly before I went home. If that meant staying back, then that's what I did.

Avoid criticising the boss. We all know that there are mediocre to poor managers out there, and undoubtedly many interviewers have had the - misfortune to work for them.

Despite this, another of the golden rules is: never criticise your bosses. The reason for this is simple: the interviewer does not have the benefit of listening to both sides of the story and therefore is not in a position to know who was really at fault. In other words, when you criticise your boss, you are effectively creating doubts about yourself in the mind of the interviewer. To criticise more than one boss is virtual interview suicide.

If you're in a situation where the poor performance of your boss prevented you from accomplishing key achievements and you're faced with a persistent interviewer who insists on getting to know the ins and outs of what happened, instead of blurting out something critical about your boss, like 'We didn't achieve our targets because our team leader couldn't tie his shoe laces', you could try something like this:

Unfortunately we came up short of reaching our targets. One of the reasons for this was because certain members of our team lacked the necessary experience to overcome some of the obstacles we encountered. Had we had the right experience,

I'm sure we would have succeeded.

Avoid saying anything that may remotely sound like the following:

I had an awful boss.

My boss was a real Nazi.

I couldn't stand my boss and he couldn't stand me.

I wouldn't feed my ex-boss.

My boss suffered from an extremely low IQ.

Nobody liked my boss because he looked like a monkey.

Recruit your voice-

Interviewees who know how to use their voices properly enjoy an advantage over those who do not. Your voice is the vehicle by which you deliver your sentences, and you neglect it at your peril.

A good interview voice is clear and emphasises important points without too much of a fuss. It is confident and in control, but never overbearing. It rises to the occasion subtly and imperceptibly fades when it has to but always keeps your attention. It is pleasant to listen to.

Here's what not to do:

- Avoid a flat monotone—in fact, avoid any sort of monotone.
- Avoid shouting or raising your voice too high—you'll more than likely frighten the interviewers or have themshouting back at you.
- Avoid an overly soft or shy voice. You don't want the interviewer straining to hear you.
- Avoid extreme changes such as very loud to very soft or very emotional to very measured.

If you've been told, or you suspect, you have a flat or uninspiring voice, practising is the key to changing it. Enlist the help of a good friend or vocal coach.

Telephone interviews –

More and more companies are starting to realise that, because much of their work is done over the telephone, it makes sense to interview candidates using this medium. If you're wanting a job in Software sales, customer enquiries etc, it would be a good idea to prepare yourself for a telephone interview.

Some companies are generous enough to informyou exactly when they will ring you, but many do not. The number one complaint I hear about telephone interviews is that the call invariably comes at a time when people are not ready for it.

One minute they're engrossed in a personal conversation, the next they're talking to an interviewer who insists on asking them a range of ugly questions. Given that you cannot put your life on hold for that one telephone call, it makes a lot of sense to prepare a summary of your answers and leave it next to your telephone so that when the call does come, you'll have the main points of your answers right at your fingertips, and can read them out if you have to.

This simple strategy is notmeant to be a substitute for proper preparation, but it can help you to focus very quickly. It's all in what you say and how you say it In terms of content, the answers for a telephone interview should not be any different to the answers you would provide in a normal interview.

The fact that a telephone interview does not provide you with the opportunities to 'distract' the interviewer with your dazzling smile and wonderful body language means that there is even more emphasis on what you say. The idea that you do not have to prepare as much because you will not be sitting face to face with the interviewer is a dangerous one.

The big difference with telephone interviews lies in the voice. Whilst voice is important in all interviews, it naturally assumes far more importance in a telephone interview. In fact, one could say that voice is the body language of telephone interviews. Here are some more things to avoid when being interviewed over the telephone:

- Long pauses;
- Too many 'umms' and 'ahs';
- Coughing or sneezing directly over the mouthpiece;
- Background noises including television, music, screaming kids, etc.;
- Long sighs.

Negotiating a salary -

Often interviews contain a discussion about salary expectations. If handled correctly, this can go a long way towards helping you maximise your earnings. Here's what to do.

Give a good interview-

It is crucial to understand that salary negotiation starts the second you walk into the interview room, not when the discussion turns to money. In other words, one of the most important things you need to do to maximise what the employer is willing to pay you is to really stand out during the entire course of the interview. Clearly, employers are much more predisposed to giving away more of their money if they think they will be getting value.

Do your research -

Trying to negotiate your salary without having done basic research is a bit like trying to hit a target blindfolded. Your research should focus on two areas. First, find out what themarket is paying for people such as yourself. You will need to take into account all your qualifications, experience and key achievements. Importantly, you will also need to take into account the industry you will be working in because some industries pay more than others for people of comparable experience and abilities. The same goes with location.

Salary survey firms, good recruitment consultants and relevant professional organisations can usually provide you with reliable salary information. Be sure all your sources are credible and that you use more than one. Your case will quickly collapse (asmight your credibility) if your sources are found wanting—and they will be if you're facing an experienced negotiator who knows themarket.

Never go on hearsay and never quote what your friends claim they earn. Your second area of research should focus on the company itself. You may not be able to get all the information you want, but this should not stop you from trying (just don't make a nuisance of yourself). Things to investigate include:

Remuneration policies.

Sometimes, especially with smaller companies, there is a noticeable absence of such policies. However, if they do exist and you're able to access them, you may be able to use this information to your benefit. For example, if you know that the company reviews performance and salaries every six months, you might be able to negotiate a deferment of a higher salary until you've had six months in which to prove yourself on the job rather than accept a lower amount for an indefinite period.

Levels of pay.

This can be tricky because information regarding people's pay is often shrouded in mystery. But if you are able to get an insight you will at least know what you're up against. Knowing, for example, that the company is inclined to pay its employees above market value can be a very useful piece of information when negotiating salary.

How well the company is travelling. Companies which are doing well are generally more inclined to pay more than companies which are struggling financially. The last thing you want to be doing is selling yourself short for a company that is riding high.

How desperate they are to fill the position. Some jobs are harder to fill than others, whilst other jobs are crucial to the success of the company. If your research indicates that the position you're applying for happens to fall in either of these categories, then it is reasonable to assume that you have greater leverage in your negotiating.

Avoid mentioning money up front -

An important principle in negotiating salary is leaving the discussions right to the end. The idea is to make as good an impression as humanly possible before talk about money arises. This is no different from any salesperson trying to sell a product.

Price is only mentioned after all the great features and benefits of the product are discussed. To talk about price before highlighting features and benefits doesn't make for a good sales approach, nor does it make for good salary negotiations.

First talk about your skills and knowledge and how they can benefit the business before quoting your price. If you happen to come across an interviewer who wants to talk about money up front, try (politely) to convince them otherwise.

You can try saying something like: 'I'd prefer to leave discussion about salary until the end of our talk. I'd really like you to get a better understanding of what I have to offer the company and for me to learn more about the job before money is discussed.'

If that doesn't work and the interviewer is adamant, then you're left with no choice but avoid quoting a specific amount. Instead, quote a range (see below). Doing so will leave you with room with which to manoeuvre later on.

The first principle of quoting employers a range of money that you're willing to consider is realism. Quoting unrealistically high amounts will more than likely damage your credibility and can undo much of the good work you put have in. The following guidelines are designed to help you work out a range.

Establish your bottom line -

Give serious thought to determining what your bottom line is—that is, the absolute minimum amount you're willing to work for. Three factors you should take into consideration include:

- Your cost of living, taking into account expected rises;

- What the market will bear given your levels of experience. Do not go below the bottom point of the market range. If the market range is between $45 000 and $65 000, your bottom line should not go under $45 000. On the other hand, if circumstances are favourable enough, you can exceed the top point;

- How much you want the job. People are often willing to settle for less because of a variety of important personal reasons such as more suitable hours, minimal travelling time or because the job represents the first step to a career change.

Work out a range-

Once you've worked out your bottom line, it is important that you stick to it. Accepting a lesser amount will more than likely lead to disappointment later on. Your minimum amount will represent the absolute bottom point of your salary range.

How wide you wish to make the range should be contingent upon all the factors discussed above, but mainly on what the market is paying and your levels of experience.

Here's one possible approach. Let's say you've decided that your absolute minimum amount is $50 000. You have lots of experience and you know both that the company really likes you and that they have been experiencing difficulties filling the position.

You also know that the top end of the market in your industry is $60 000. In such a favourable situation, it would not be unreasonable to quote a salary range starting above your minimum and going above the top end of the market's top end—say, $55 000 to $65 000. If, on the other hand, you know that there is tough competition for the job and your experience is not outstanding, then quoting $50 000 to $58 000 would make more sense.

Another, less conservative, approach to establishing a salary range in the above favourable scenario would be to have the range but quote a higher minimum—say, $60 000 to $65 000. The advantage of this second approach is that it increases the chances of getting the employer to automatically pay your quoted minimum and it fully recognises your powerful bargaining position.

A less than flush employer (but one that you're keen on working for) may be frightened off by your expectations, but you should be able to overcome this by agreeing to drop your quoted minimum.

*T*here are no hard and fast rules about establishing either a minimum amount of money you're willing to work for or a salary range. The above guidelines are simply illustrations of possible approaches. *T*he most important thing is to do your research first and then avoid quoting employers unrealistic amounts.

How to respond when you've been sacked from a previous job -

On the whole, employers do not enjoy sacking people. Firing someone is fraught with difficulty and often causes a great deal of angst for both parties. Unfortunately, however, there are employees whose actions give employers no choice but to exercise the ultimate sanction.

However, there are also instances in which employees are sacked through no fault of their own. These unfair dismissals can come about from a variety of reasons, including grossly incompetent management, very poor job design (some jobs—especially new ones—have not been thought through and often set people up for failure), poor recruitment practices or lack of training.

The issue here is how someone who has been unfairly dismissed responds to the barrage of questions at their next interview. In particular, how do they respond to the ubiquitous question, 'Why did you leave your previous employer?' when we can reasonably assume that telling an interviewer that you were sacked (albeit unfairly) may border on interview suicide? As already mentioned, interviewers tend to be a cautious bunch (generally with good reason) and have only your word to go by when you try to explain how hard done by you were.

Unfortunately, some recruiters (especially in an over-supplied labour market) will demonstrate considerable reluctance to hire someone who was sacked from their last job, even if that person was blameless. Much of their reluctance stems from a fear that the formerly sacked person won't work out in the new job. In such a scenario, the recruiter may end up looking incompetent.

The cold, hard reality is that people who have been sacked from their last job generally start the interview race some distance behind the rest of the field. However, all is not doom and gloom—it just means they have to try that much harder. There are several things such interviewees can do to increase their chances of success.

Describe what happened in detail -

One option is to draw a very clear picture of the circumstances that led to your dismissal. One of the keys here is not to use pejorative terms. Avoid descending into abusive language or insulting your former employer, hard though it may be. Just stick to the facts and present your case dispassionately, using measured language. Four things you could include to bolster your case are:

- *Similar experiences with other employees. This is a powerful argument. If others were treated in a similar way to you, then that is compelling evidence condemning the employer.*

- *Broken promises. Employers who dismiss employees unfairly usu- ally make lots of promises which they break.*

- *Examples of poor management practices. These could include any number of things, including: no training where training was essential; significant changes without any warning; zero consul- tation or feedback; abusive behaviours; or major changes to your job duties without any warning or consultation.*

- *What you did to save the situation. This would include attempts you made to improve matters, including suggestions you made or any actions you took. Here's what a good answer to the dreaded 'Why did you leave your former employer?' question may sound like:*

> *Unfortunately we parted ways because of a string of negative incidences. My former employer was under some pressure and had great difficulty in coping. He often took out his frustration on his staff, including using abusive language and making all sorts of threats.*

> *As a result of this, many of his staff were terrified of him and were actively looking for other work. In fact, staff turnover was very high. He was also in the habit of making important commitments but very rarely keeping them.*

> *One example of this was a promise he made that we would receive training on new machinery. This training would have improved our productivity levels significantly* and made everyone's life much less complicated, yet the training never arrived. When I approached him about the matter, he told me to mind my own business. When I tried to explain to him that my concern was for the welfare of the business he got very angry and dismissed me on the spot.

Compare the above answer to the following:

I left because I got fired, which was the best thing that could have happened to me. My former boss was terrible. As well as having no idea on how to run a business, he had no people skills whatsoever. He was a bully and an idiot and could not cope with pressure. No one could stand him and those who weren't jumping ship were looking for other work.

I got fired because I told him we needed training on new machinery training he promised we would receive and which would have improved our productivity levels significantly.

Last I heard he was going broke, which surprises me not at all. Even though both of the above answers say essentially the same things, on one level they are complete opposites.

The first answer is dispassionate, avoids using abusive language and makes a compelling case before raising the dismissal. By the time the first speaker gets to the dismissal, there's a good chance that he has recruited the sympathy of the interviewer.

Whereas the second answer, apart from being abusive and emotional (which would worry any interviewer), begins perilously because it mentions the sacking in its opening sentence. Mentioning the dismissal in your first sentence simply does not give you the opportunity to soften the interviewer.

Avoid mentioning the sacking -

The second option involves keeping your mouth shout. Given the stigma attached to sacked employees, it makes little sense to mention the sacking and inevitably frighten the interviewer, especially where your employment period was for a short period of time or performed in the distant past.

At the risk of offending those who enjoy occupying the moral high ground, it is my view that there are times when certain things need not be revealed to interviewers. At the end of the day, all employers are entitled to know only whether you can do the job, whether you will fit into the culture of their organization and what your motivation levels are like.

Group interviews -

An increasingly popular form of interviewing is the group interview, in which a collection of interviewees come together and are given a set of tasks to work through as a group (though some tasks may require that you act by yourself, such as giving a presentation).

Examples of group tasks can include any exercise that requires problem-solving, coming up with creative solutions, planning and organising, defining and setting goals or resolving conflict. Whilst the group is working through these tasks, the situation is monitored carefully by an assessor, or a group of assessors, whose job it is to observe how you interact with the group and what your contributions are.

Based on your observable behaviours—that is, what you say, how you say it, what you do and how you interact with the others in your group— the assessors will draw conclusions about your suitability. In a way, the group interview is the ultimate behavioural interview.

The key to group interviews is to ensure that you demonstrate the required behaviours and avoid undesirable behaviours. Desirable and undesirable behaviours at group interviews Be sure you contribute.

Your contribution should be designed to facilitate the smooth functioning of the group and the completion of the tasks. Avoid any behaviours that might undermine these two primary objectives. Undermining behaviours can include anything that can reasonably be seen as aggressive or overly dominating behaviour, such as:

+ *Intimidating others;*
+ *Insisting on your own way;*
+ *Not listening to or dismissing other people's contributions;*
+ *Hogging the limelight.*

Equally as bad are overly passive behaviours. Sitting there and not contributing, or contributing very little, will do you no favours.

It is important that you have the confidence to make a contribution. Don't sit there thinking, 'Oh my God—what if they all laugh at my suggestion?' It is far better to make a less than spectacular contribution than to sit there in silence.

Listen to and acknowledge what other people say. If someone makes a good suggestion, acknowledging it will win you brownie points. But avoid acknowledging for the sake of doing so. And, what- ever you do, do not pay homage to every single suggestion.

Where possible, help others but do it properly. Avoid embarrassing group members or taking over their task. Don't lose sight of the purpose of the task. If you see the group straying from task, try to bring them back on course by reminding them of the objectives.

Try to work out what behaviours the task has been designed to elicit. For example, if you think the task has been designed to draw out behaviours relating to solving problems within a group, then your job is to demonstrate those behaviours. These might include:

- *Getting everyone to agree on what the actual problem is (problem definition);*
- *Initiating a discussion on possible causes of the problem;*
- *Finalising the most probable cause/s;*
- *Suggesting a brainstorming session on possible solutions;*
- *Getting agreement on best solutions;*
- *Drawing up a plan of action designed to implement solutions;*
- *Remembering to avoid dominating procedures.*

Hopefully I've convinced you of the importance of establishing rapport and trust and that winning a job depends on more than just answering questions correctly. While all of us are different and bring different communication styles to interviews, the experts agree that some behaviours are more effective than others in terms of building rapport and trust. It is important to familiarise yourself with these behaviours so you can maximise your effectiveness.

You may find some of the techniques described above a little difficult to master in the beginning. That's not because they are inherently difficult—in fact, most of them are straightforward. The challenge will be in unlearning current behaviours, but with a little perseverance you will be amazed at how quickly you can begin changing; it really is worth the effort to keep at it until you've mastered all the techniques.

Suggested Activities-

To help you achieve mastery of these techniques, here are some suggested activities to help you along the way.

1. As mentioned above, begin modelling the behaviours of people whose interpersonal skills you admire.

2. You can practice many of the techniques in most social situations. Next time you're having a conversation with someone give some thought to your body language.

Does it lend itself to improving communication, rapport and trust? And what can you do to improve it? After a while you'll find that this kind of self-awareness becomes second nature.

Summary of key points

Building rapport and trust requires three things: answering questions intelligently and honestly; ensuring all your non-verbal communication (body language and personal appearance) does not give cause for apprehension in the interviewer; and conforming to acceptable interview behaviours, such as never arguing.

Be aware of first and last impressions—people tend to better remember what happens at the beginning and end of any interaction, including interviews. Smiling, using appropriate facial expressions and nodding your head at the right time all give a positive impression.

For telephone interviews, recruit your voice; it replaces your body language when talking on the phone.

Remember the key do's and don't's: give credit where it's due and avoid criticising others, including previous bosses; use positive statements but avoid big-noting yourself; mention any shortcomings or hurdles you've overcome but avoid embellishments.

When negotiating your salary, do your research first—don't undersell yourself, but be realistic in what you ask for. Avoid discussing money before you've highlighted what you can bring to the company.

In panel interviews, make sure you familiarise yourself with everyone's name. In group interviews, be pro-active in demonstrating behaviours the interviewers are looking for.

"The only thing that stands between you and your dream is the will to try and the belief that it is actually possible."

"Self confidence is the most attractive quality a person can have. how can anyone see how awesome you are if you can't see it yourself?"

"The biggest failure you can have in life is making the mistake of, never trying at all."

Mastering
Algorithms with C
Perfect Beginner's Guide 2014.

Brain Washer

Harry H. Chaudhary.

Chapter - 8

10 Effective Answers
To Common Questions

*B*y now, as well as recognising the basic ingredients of a good interview response, you should also be able to put together your own effective answers. You should know how to:

find out as much about the job as possible before finalising your answers;

⚓ *Use the four steps to bring together the major parts of your answers, including what you did, how you did it, the context in which you did it and the outcomes;*

⚓ *Put all your information together so you can articulate clear and coherent answers which do not meander all over the place;*

⚓ *Answer a broad range of questions, including those concerning duties that you have performed before, duties that you have not performed but whose skills you have mastered and duties that you have not performed and don't yet have the skills for;*

⚓ *Use your body language and other interpersonal communication skills to establish and maintain rapport.*

There's no simple formula for a good answer -

It is important to reiterate at this juncture that, even despite useful guidelines on how to answer questions, there is no single blueprint or structure for an answer that is applicable to all interview questions.

Sometimes it may be appropriate to give a three-part answer which includes the context, what you did and how you did it, and an outcome. At other times it may be more appropriate to talk about your ability to do the job, your cultural fit and motivation levels.

Often, it may be more appropriate to mix and match from the above. At the end of the day, it is up to you to recognise a suitable structure or approach for each question. And one approach may be just as good as the next remember, there's no perfect answer. Practice will give you the ability to provide the best possible response.

This chapter presents some good and not so good answers to common interview questions, as well as brief explanations of why they work. By learning to recognise a less effective answer, you should be in a better position to avoid it.

Question: *Why did you choose this job?*

Good answer -

Ever since I can remember, I've been interested in this line of work. What attracts me to it is the opportunities it gives me to interact with people, solve problems and work autonomously.

I love the fact that one day I could be out on the road helping clients with their problems whereas the next day I can be in my office working with a team of people trying to solve a complex technical problem. I very much enjoy working in a service industry such as ours where I can satisfy clients.

Not so good answer -

Actually I stumbled into it quite by accident. I always wanted to be an actor, but getting work was next to impossible. I suppose the reason I'm still in this line of work is because I've picked up all the skills and knowledge and know my way around the traps. I've been doing it for a while now and I suppose you could say I'm an old hand and know how to deliver the goods.

Comments -

The first answer responds to the question promptly and then proceeds to highlight the main duties of the job—interacting with people, problem-solving, etc.—as the reasons why the candidate chose the job. Just as importantly, we get a strong sense of the candidate's high motivation levels and the desire to give good service. It also implies that the candidate enjoys working in a team and can do the job, thus addressing the three things employers want to hear.

In the second answer we have to wait until the third sentence before the question is addressed—far too late. Despite the candidate's experience, we get a strong sense of indifference towards the job.

We're left with the impression that it's just a job, whereas the first answer is brimming with enthusiasm.

Question: What factors do you think determine a person's progress in an organisation?

Good answer -

In my view, there are three things that determine a person's progress in an organisation. These are, first, an ability to do the job well, including a willingness to learn new things and adapt to changing circumstances; second, to be able to fit in with the culture of the organisation (i.e. be able to get on with colleagues); and third, to have high levels of drive and motivation.

Certainly these are the three things that I insist upon for myself in the workplace. If at any time I feel I'm not at my very best in all three areas, I stop and ask myself what I can do to improve matters. I don't think anyone can truly be happy in their work if all three areas are not being satisfied. So far they've held me in good stead.

Not so good answer -

Keeping on the boss's good side is probably the number one thing I can think of. It doesn't matter how good you are if you don't get on with your boss, I think your days are numbered. Of course, it also helps to be good at your job, but being able to play the game that is, navigating through the minefield of organisational politics is I think more important. I realise this may sound somewhat cynical, but all of us know that to get to senior management one needs to know how to play the game.

Comments -

A question such as this should immediately be recognised as an opportunity to highlight your strengths. The first answer talks directly about the three things all employers want to hear—ability to do the job, cultural fit and motivation and then goes a step further and states that all three are qualities that the candidate offers. The second answer is far too cynical and fails to emphasise the candidate's strengths. There is little doubt that an ability to 'play the game' can have a bearing on a person's progress, but to throw all your eggs into that basket is a fatal mistake.

Question: *Why would you like to work for our organisation?*

Good answer -

Yours is the sort of company in which I could maximise my contribution. All my research has revealed that you are not only market leaders in service standards and product innovation but that you also have a great work culture.

Everyone I've spoken to has talked about the high levels of support, training and recognition employees receive. You offer great career prospects, interesting work and family-friendly policies. Above all, I've always been very keen to work for a company that offers challenging and cutting-edge work.

Not so good answer -

I know your organisation really looks after its people— everybody I talked to wants to work here. You pay well and look after your employees. You're a large company, which means that my prospects for career enhancement would be increased and hopefully I wouldn't be doing the same kind of work all the time. I like the idea of getting rotated and learning new things.

Comments -

The tone of the first answer is set in the opening sentence, where the candidate talks about wanting to contribute which is the sort of thing that excites employers. The answer recognises all the good things about the company, but very importantly links these plusses to contribution on the part of the candidate.

In other words, it's not just about what the candidate can get from the company but also what the candidate wants to give back. The overriding problem with the second answer is that it's all about what the candidate can get out of the company. No overt link is made between what the company offers and how these factors can increase the candidate's contribution.

Question: *What do you want to be doing in your career five years from now?*

Good answer -

I'd like to be doing what I'm doing now—that is, enjoying my work, working hard and contributing to the best of my abilities. Of course, I'd expect that in five years time my added experience would hold me in good stead for greater responsibilities, which is something I look forward to taking on when-

the time comes. The most important thing, however, is to be happy, productive and a valued member of the team.

Not so good answer -

Basically, I'm ambitious and hard-working, so I expect to further my career considerably. My aim is to work hard and get as far as I can. I think I'd be looking at some sort of management position with greater responsibilities and of course greater rewards.

Comments -

There's nothing crushingly wrong with the second answer; in fact, it makes several good points—namely, it gets right to the point and promotes the candidate's hard work and ambition to get ahead. The reason it is not as good as the first answer lies in its limited approach: the candidate's primary goal is one of promotion only.

The sub-text is that if there's no opportunity for promotion, the candidate might leave. On the other hand, the first answer acknowledges the importance of hard work and promotion but very wisely goes on to say that getting promoted is not the only thing that matters. The first answer is less egocentric and more aware of the importance of making a contribution to the company.

Question: *Describe your ideal job.*

Good answer -

This job that I'm applying for contains many, if not all, of the ingredients of my ideal job. It contains a lot of variety, is intellectually challenging, will allow me to work on my own as well as in a team environment (the best of both worlds),

And will also allow me to offer creative solutions to clients. I've always thrived in challenging and results-driven environments and this job offers me all of that.

Not so good answer -

My ideal job would be one in which I'd work hard but I wouldn't be too stressed out all the time.

It would have lots of variety and a good amount of challenges with plenty of opportunities for advancement. It would include great people to work with as well as a good boss.

Comments -

One of the reasons the first answer is so effective is that it links the candidate's ideal job to the actual job in question. Telling an interviewer that the job you're applying for is one you consider ideal makes a lot of sense. Note that all the main ingredients of the job variety, challenge, working solo as well as in a team environment, and providing creative solutions to clients.

Once again, the second answer is not a fatally flawed one. Its major mistake is mentioning stress. The instant you mention stress, the interviewer's alarm bells will start ringing. They'll want to know how much stress is too much and what things stress you out not what you want to be talking about in an interview.

Question: What motivates you?

Good answer -

There are lots of things that motivate me in the workplace, but three of my biggest motivators would have to be problem solving especially highly technical problems that require specialised knowledge; learning new things and keeping up to date with all the changes in my field; and working in a cooperative team environment where we're throwing ideas off each other and coming up with creative solutions. I love the camaraderie that goes with that.

Not so good answer -

Probably my biggest motivator is having a fun job, one I really look forward to and excel in. There's nothing worse than turning up to a job you don't enjoy day in day out. Also, I love having great work hours. I don't mind staying back occasionally and lending a hand, but I wouldn't want to be doing that all the time. I also love working in the city because it's easy to get to from where I live and it gives me easy access to great shops and restaurants.

Comments -

The first answer would only be an effective one if the duties mentioned in it solving highly technical problems, keeping up to date with the latest innovations and enjoying working creatively in a team were all part of the job description . . . the point is that an excellent strategy for answering the motivation question is to go to the main duties of the job and talk about those. The second answer begins well but fails to mention what constitutes a fun job. Thereafter it is a fatally flawed answer. Working hours and location of work may very well be motivating factors, but they should never be mentioned because they fail to demonstrate how you will add value to the job.

Question: *What qualities do you think are important to be successful in this field?*

Good answer -

The qualities necessary to be successful in this field would include the skills and knowledge to actually do the job properly.

I'm not just talking about all the technical skills, such as knowing how to operate the various software programs and a comprehensive knowledge of the relevant legislation and how to apply that legislation,

But also an ability to get on with people, possess great communication skills and know how to plan and organise your work whilst working under considerable pressure.

I also think high levels of motivation and drive are very important. These are all qualities that I possess and can bring to this position from day one.

Not so good answer -

The qualities necessary to be successful in this field would include a detailed understanding of all the various software programs required to complete operations. Not only does one require knowledge of how to operate the software but also how to fix things when they go wrong and something is always going wrong.

The same can be said for the complex legal technicalities. As you well know, in our industry the devil is in the detail and a superficial understanding of the legislation can lead to a lot of trouble. As well as having a thorough understanding of all the programming requirements of this job, I also have a comprehensive knowledge of the legal subtleties.

Comments -

This type of question invites you to go directly to the main duties of the job you're applying for and use those as your answer (it is the same strategy that's used in answering the motivation question).

The first answer does just that. It is superior to the second response because it covers more bases. As well as talking about the technical skills, it also talks about getting on with people, planning and organising, and good communication (the generic competencies).

The second answer is not a bad one, but it falls into the common trap of only focusing on the technical side of the job.

Question: *Tell us about a time you handled a difficult situation with a coworker.*

Good answer -

Last year one of our colleagues was displaying a lot of aggressive behaviours, including dominating team meetings, belittling other people's ideas and not cooperating.

I approached the rest of my colleagues about him and soon realised everyone was feeling the same as I was. We decided not to take the matter to our manager until we had the opportunity to talk to him first. So we decided that at our next meeting we would raise these issues with him. I was chosen to initiate the discussion.

At the meeting I avoided personalising the problem and I avoided using inflammatory language. I also adopted an upbeat and optimistic tone. The results were better than we anticipated. He thanked me for the delicate manner in which I raised the issues and also thanked us all for talking to him first before taking it further. After our meeting, his behaviours changed markedly for the better.

Not so good answer -

There was one time when one of my colleagues was not pulling his weight, nor was he being at all cooperative with other members of our team. The manager failed to pick it up because some members of the team covered for his mistakes and he would always go out of his way to be extremely friendly when the manager was around. So one day when he was being uncooperative I pulled him aside and let him know what I thought about him. Ever since that day his behaviour towards me changed. He went out of his way to be friendly towards me and he made sure all the work that I needed was done properly. Unfortunately, his behaviour towards the other members of our team did not alter at all. The lesson I learned was that you have to stick up for yourself because no one else will.

Comments-

The first answer demonstrates an ability to consult with colleagues, the capacity to solve a problem on your own rather than immediately escalating it to management, and an ability to communicate highly sensitive information in an appropriate manner. It also demonstrates a great outcome for everyone involved. The second answer is too narrow in its focus. It solved the problem only for that individual but fails to address the broader issue of team harmony and cooperation.

Question: *Tell us about a time you had to meet a very tight deadline.*

Good answer -

When I was working for the Interplanetary Commission, I was required to meet multiple tight deadlines. I was able to consistently meet all my deadlines by adhering to sound planning and organising principles.

These included planning my work well ahead so there were no surprises, ensuring that everyone in my team was well trained and well aware of their responsibilities, always having various contingency plans for when things went wrong, and never accepting more work than we could handle.

The effectiveness of these practices was highlighted by the fact that my team never missed a deadline and was seen as the standard-bearer for performance within the organisation.

Not so good answer -

The way I meet tight deadlines is by making sure that I stay back and put in the hard yards. When something unexpected arises or we are experiencing a particularly busy period, I'm not one to shirk my responsibilities. If it means staying back to complete the work on time, I'll do it. In my view there's no substitute for hard work.

Question: *What sort of manager would you like to work for?*

Good answer -

I'd like to work for a manager who knows how to do his or her job properly as well as knowing how to lead staff. It's important that managers know how to do their job well, otherwise they can lose credibility amongst their staff and a manager without credibility will soon lose the respect that is needed to be an effective leader.

My ideal manager would understand and practise sound leadership principles such as consulting with staff, acknowledging people's hard work, providing regular feedback and not intimidating or bullying people. My view is that a good manager is a firm but fair one and knows how to gain the commitment of staff.

Not so good answer -

I think it's important for a manager to have good people skills. The best manager I worked for was able to get on with her staff in the workplace as well as outside. She was a good friend to all and everyone knew they could turn to her in time of need. She never turned anyone away and always tried her best to look after us. More people turned up to her farewell dinner than to the general manager's.

Comments -

The second answer is too narrow. Good managers need to be more than just liked by their staff. They also need to be good at their jobs and firm with staff when and if the need arises. It's possible that well liked managers may be operating inefficiently in order not to lose popularity amongst staff.

The first answer is a more complete one. Not only does it acknowledge the importance of getting on with people, but it also acknowledges the importance of being firm when the need arises as well as having good work skills.

Question: *Have you performed the best work you are capable of?*

Good answer -

Yes I have, and I'd like to think that I do it on an ongoing basis, not just on so-called important occasions. Performing the best work you are capable of, in my view, requires high levels of motivation and a willingness to work hard and learn from your mistakes.

These are qualities that I bring to the workplace every day, and I believe the proof of this can be seen in the quality of my work and the praise I have received from former employers. My work on the Odysseus Project, where I exceeded all my targets and played an important role in bringing home the goods, is an example of my daily work rate and contribution.

Not so good answer -

Yes I've managed to perform at my best on several occasions. I tend to be at my best when the pressure is on. If I know there's a lot at stake I roll the sleeves up and really give it all that I've got. If that requires working late and on weekends then so be it, as long the job gets done. I love a challenge and enjoy delivering the goods under pressure.

Comments -

The strength of the first answer is its argument that performing at one's best is something the candidate does all the time rather than an occasional approach reserved for special circumstances. It also lists the qualities required for someone to perform at their best and then goes on to give a specific example.

The second answer is commendable for the candidate's willingness to roll the sleeves up when there's a lot at stake; however, an employer would like that sort of dedication all the time.

Question: How do you deal with criticism?

Good answer -

I view positive criticism as being the same as constructive feedback—something which is designed to improve my performance, which is important to me. If I'm criticised about an aspect of my work I try my best to locate the source of the problem and do my best to rectify it. Viewed in that light, criticism can be a great learning tool. On the other hand, I do not take kindly to criticism that is not constructive, where the main objective is to hurt or undermine the other person.In such cases I'm inclined to approach my critic in an open manner so we can work things out. I don't think there's a place for negative criticism in the workplace it just under- mines morale.

Not so good answer -

I don't like people criticising my work. No one's perfect and I never go around criticising other people's work. Let he who is without fault cast the first stone. Of course, I expect my team leader to criticise my performance if I make a mistake, but I think it's important that the criticism be delivered in the proper manner, with no belittling or bullying. I've seen too many people get crucified over minor mistakes which undermines their commitment to the organisation.

Comments -

The first answer's strong suit lies in its ability to distinguish between constructive and negative criticism and its statement of how the candidate would respond to each of those. The second answer's weakness lies in the candidate's reluctance to be criticised by colleagues. Even though the part about belittling and bullying is good, one comes away thinking that the candidate may be a little too sensitive to criticism.

The above answers have been written to give you an insight into what an effective interview might sound like and the reasons employers prefer to hear some answers rather than others. Performing well at interviews is not as difficult as many people think. The key to success lies with correct preparation and practice. Knowing what to prepare and how to prepare, then giving yourself the opportunity to apply your newly acquired skills, is a tried and tested formula for success.

Remember, great interviewees are not born with effective interview skills they develop their skills by following this formula. Completing this book means your awareness of the realities of the interview process has increased significantly. It's also highly likely that your interview skills have already inproved. It is important to note, however, that the more you think about your answers and the more you practice them the better you will become. Great interview skills are not developed overnight; they improve with time and correct application.

Nine key points to remember from this book

1. Don't waste your time looking for quick fixes they don't exist. They could even make matters worse. Great interview performances come from proper preparation and practice.

2. Avoid memorising other people's answers.

3. Remember that interviews are about more than just giving good answers; they're also about building rapport and trust.

And building rapport and trust is contingent upon more than simply words body language and attitude are very important.

4. All interviewers want to know three things:

 + *Whether you can do the job;*
 + *How motivated or driven you are; and*
 + *Whether you'll fit into the existing workplace culture.*

5. Using the four steps gives you a simple-to-follow system by which you can organise and bring together large amounts of disparate information about your work achievements, to help you form clear and articulate answers.

6. The vast majority of jobs have skills or duties that overlap. These include:

 + Being a good team player;
 + Planning and organising your work effectively;
 + Good interpersonal communication skills;
 + Ability to cope with change in the workplace; and
 + Ability to provide effective customer service (including to internal clients).
 + Awareness of these allows you to anticipate the nature of some of the questions you may be asked.

7. Do not fall into despondency if you have a bad interview. Everyone has them, even good interviewees. The key is to learn from it and get yourself ready for the next one.

8. Often, interviewers are not experienced and can ask questions that are not well considered. Your job is to know how to handle both the novice as well as the experienced interviewer.

9. Believe in yourself. Now that you know what to do there's no reason not to.

-Good luck Champs.

The Apple Interview

Much like the company itself, Apple's interview process has minimal beaucracy. The interviewers will be looking for excellent technical skills, but a passion for the position and company is also very important while it's not a prerequisite to be a Mac user, you should at least be familiar with the system.

The interview process typically begins with a recruiter phone screen to get a basic sense of your skills, followed up by a series of technical phone screens with team members.

Once you're invited on campus, you'll typically be greeted by the recruiter who provides an overview of the process you will then have 6-8 interviews with members of the team for which you're interviewing, as well as key people with whom your team works.

You can expect a mix of 1-on-1 and 2-on-1 interviews Be ready to code on a whiteboard and make sure all of your thoughts are clearly communicated Lunch is with your potential future manager and appears more casual, but is still an interview Each interviewer is usually focused on a different area and is discouraged from sharing feedback unless there's something they want subsequent interviewers to drill into.

Towards the end of the day, your interviewers will compare notes and if everyone still feels you're a viable candidate, you'll interview with the director and then VP of the organization you're applying to While this decision is rather informal, it's a very good sign if you make it This decision also happens behind the scenes and if you don't pass, you'll simply be escorted out of the building without ever having been the wiser (until now).

If you made it to the director and VP interviews, all of your interviewers will gather in a conference room to give an official thumbs up or thumbs down The VP typically won't be present, but can still veto the hire if they weren't impressed Your recruiter will usually follow up a few days later, but feel free to ping your recruiter for updates.

Well, when I applied through a recruiter and the process took 2 months - interviewed at Apple.

Interview Details Met Apple recruiter through *Hacktivist*. I've been applying online for ages without hearing anything back, so I guess Apple recruiters prefer candidates they've met in person.

I had two phone screens next month. The first one was technical and pretty easy. The second was behavioral. I actually was really surprised, I had expected Apple's screening process to be a lot more difficult. I was asked to interview on-site next month.

The on-site interview was way more challenging than the phone screens. I was still in college, so I knew a lot of things, but none in depth. The questions asked were directly related to the team's work, unlike most other companies -- where NCG's are usually asked questions based on what they've learned in school. I guess Apple's teams look for people they specifically need for a position even for college grads.

I was able to hold my own for most of the first technical interview, but I started losing confidence and getting very nervous. By the third interview, I was a mess. It took me 5 minutes to actually understand what the interviewer was asking of me. The last two interviewers asked me about my experience and projects I had undertaken in college and at my internships. They were pretty impressed, but I knew it was too late by then. Sure enough, I was escorted out right after.

I guess I was caught off guard by how much more difficult the on-site interview was than the phone interviews, and by how specific the questions were to the team.

Interview Question – Create a synchronization primitive for the operating system/kernel from scratch. I created a spinlock with test-and-set. Next, create a primitive that doesn't waste CPU cycles. (Essentially, how would you create a mutex inside the kernel?)

Given an array with N - 2 elements (two missing) from 1 to N, find the two missing elements in linear time and constant memory usage & Core design concepts.

I did fairly well in technical interview, I believe I wasn't well prepared for it, specially behavior interview . Questions were related to Design patterns, data structures, algorithms (BST related multiple problems, queues, linked lists etc). There were follow up question, how would you improve time/space complexity. And several questions from core Java. I got *$30,000 USD/A offer*.But I declined and showed my second finger up to them.

Interview Question – how would you design evernote app, find circular loop in linked list, and other simple questions related to java.

"Life has two rules: #1 Never quit #2 Always remember rule # 1." – Harry.

The Google Interview

There are many scary stories floating around about Google interviews, but it's mostly just that: stories The interview is not terribly different from Microsoft's or Amazon's However, because Google HR can be a little disorganized, we recommend being proactive in communication.

A Google engineer performs the first phone screen, so expect tough technical questions On your on-site interview, you'll interview with four to six people, one of whom will be a lunch interviewer. Interviewer feedback is kept confidential from the other interviewers, so you can be assured that you enter each interview with blank slate your lunch interviewer doesn't submit feedback, so this is a great opportunity to ask honest questions.

Written feedback is submitted to a hiring committee of engineers to make a hire/no-hire recommendation Feedback is typically broken down into four categories (Analytical Ability, Coding, Experience and Communication) and you are given a score from 1 0 to 4 0 overall.

The hiring committee understands that you can't be expected to excel in every interview, but if multiple people raise the same red flag (arrogance, poor coding skills, etc), that can disqualify you A hiring committee typically wants to see one interviewer who is an "enthusiastic endorser " In other words, a packet with scores of 3 6, 3 1, 3 1 and 2 6 is better than all 3 1s Your phone screen is usually not a strong factor in the final decision.

The Google hiring process can be slow if you don't hear back within one week, politely ask your recruiter for an update a lack of response says nothing about your performance.

Tip: Definitely Prepare:

> As a web-based company, Google cares about how to design a scalable system. So, make sure you prepare for questions from "System Design and Memory Limits" Additionally; many Google interviewers will ask questions involving Bit Manipulation, so please brush up on these questions.

Tip: What's Different?

> Your interviewers do not make the hiring decision. Rather, they enter feedback which is passed to a hiring committee. The hiring committee recommends a decision which can be—though rarely is—rejected by Google executives.

The Microsoft Interview

Microsoft wants smart people Geeks People who are passionate about technology You probably won't be tested on the ins and outs of C++ APIs, but you will be expected to write code on the board.

In a typical interview, you'll show up at Microsoft at some time in the morning and fill out initial paper work You'll have a short interview with a recruiter where he or she will give you a sample question Your recruiter is usually there to prep you, and not to grill you on technical questions Be nice to your recruiter Your recruiter can be your biggest advocate, even pushing to re-interview you if you stumbled on your first interview They can fight for you to be hired - or not!

During the day, you'll do four or five interviews, often with two different teams Unlike many companies, where you meet your interviewers in a conference room, you'll meet with your Microsoft interviewers in their office This is a great time to look around and get a feel for the team culture.

Depending on the team, interviewers may or may not share their feedback on you with the rest of the interview loop.

When you complete your interviews with a team, you might speak with a hiring manager If so, that's a great sign! It likely means that you passed the interviews with a particular team It's now down to the hiring manager's decision. You might get a decision that day, or it might be a week after one week of no word from HR, send them a friendly email asking for a status update.

Tip: Definitely Prepare:

"Why do you want to work for Microsoft?"

In this question, Microsoft wants to see that you're passionate about technology. A great answer might be, "I've been using Microsoft software as long as I can remember, and I'm really impressed at how Microsoft manages to create a product that is universally excellent.

For example, I've been using Visual Studio recently to learn game programming, and its APIs are excellent." Note how this shows a passion for technology!

What's Unique?

You'll only reach the hiring manager if you've done well, but if you do, that's a great sign!

The Yahoo Interview

Resume Selection & Screening:

While Yahoo tends to only recruit at the top 10 - 20 schools, other candidates can still get interviewed through Yahoo's job board (or - better yet - if they can get an internal referral) If you're one of the lucky ones selected, your interview process will start off with a phone screen Your phone screen will be with a senior employee (tech lead, manager, etc)

On-Site Interview:

You will typically interview with 6 - 7 people on the same team for 45 minutes each, Each interviewer will have an area of focus For example, one interviewer might focus on databases, while another interviewer might focus on your understanding of computer architecture Interviews will often be composed as follows:

Minutes:

5 minutes: General conversation Tell me about yourself, your projects, etc.
20 minutes: Coding question For example, implement merge sort.
20 minutes: System design For example, design a large distributed cache These questions will often focus on an area from your past experience or on something your interviewer is currently working on.

Decision:

At the end of the day, you will likely meet with a Program Manager or someone else for a general conversation (product demos, concerns about the company, your competing offers, etc) Meanwhile, your interviewers will discuss your performance and attempt to come to a decision The hiring manager has the ultimate say and will weigh the positive feedback against the negative. If you have done well, you will often get a decision that day, but this is not always the case There can be many reasons that you might not be told for several days - for example, the team may feel it needs to interview several other people.

Definitely Prepare:

Yahoo, almost as a rule, asks questions about system design, so make sure you prepare for that. They want to know that you can not only write code, but that you can design software. Don't worry if you don't have a background in this - you can still reason your way through it!

What's Unique? Your phone interview will likely be performed by someone with more influence, such as a hiring manager. Yahoo is also unusual in that it often gives a decision (if you're hired) on the same day. Your interviewers will discuss your performance while you meet with a final interviewer.

The Facebook Interview

Interview Details –

I personally interviewed by Facebook. The process started out with a pre-screening test which was coding based. There was one question to be done in 60 minutes.

The question was fairly simple for me and I completed it quickly. Then, I was called for the onsite interviews a week later. The interview was supposed to last for 45 minutes. Now, in my interview, I was first (She, she was so beautiful- Melody) asked about the best experience I have had in my last two years. I said, you are beautiful, I met you before 5 min ago, this is my best experience I have had. She smiled and she forwarded me to next.

Then, the interviewer quickly moved on to the coding questions. There were two questions for which I had to explain my solution and then code it on the whit board. I was able to both the questions, but I guess the interviewer have liked the way I had explained my approach as FB team called me for the next interview but I showed my second finger Up !.

The interviewer was not very vocal and did not really participate in the discussion where you explain the approach. That is why it becomes difficult to detect if the interviewer is understanding your words or not. Anyways, it was a some experience.

Interview Details:

There were a total of 1/2/3 interview rounds depending on the performance on previous interviews. The Facebook recruiter and other staff were very pleasant.

My Interview Rounds:

Round 1: Given an undirected graph and a node, modify the graph into a directed graph such that, any path leads to one particular node.

Round 2: Given a matrix of size mXn, and a list of cells, find the number of paths from the top left cell to the bottom right cell.

Round 3: Solve a linear equation in one variable, where the possible operands are +,- and * along with brackets. For e.g. $(2x + 5 - (3x-2)=x + 5)$ So, as I know they are very serious about Coding (c & c++ and java & web based programming & math's) and communication skills,

INTERVIEW FAQ'S - I

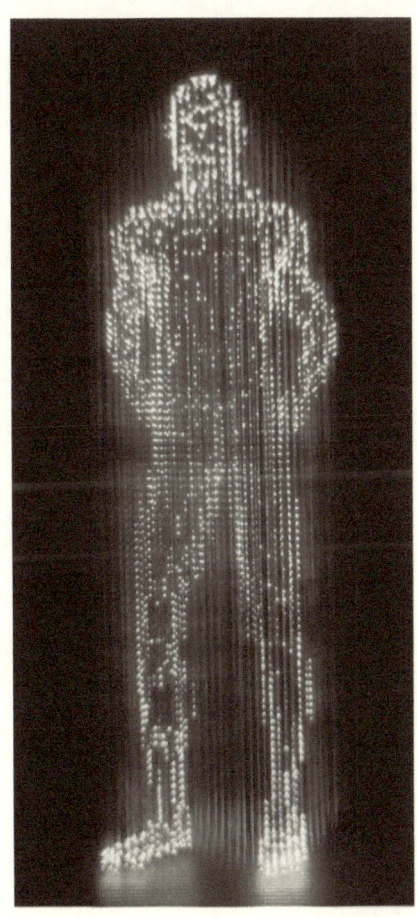

1. What skills do IT Companies look for in prospective candidates?

Answer: IT companies look out for various technical skills and soft skills in candidates, In soft skills, communication skills are very important other soft skills includes presentation skills, Team work, writing skills, leadership etc and In technical skills, companies expect the candidates to have good expertise in their area of graduation. For example C & C++, Operating system & networking and Core java –DSA-DBMS etc.

2. When should I start preparing for placement?

Answer: For soft skills, it is better to start preparing one year before the placement start.

3. How should I prepare for written tests?

Answer: following should be taken care of:

- Programming Aptitude in (C-C++, Data structure, Algorithms, Java)
- Reasoning section.
- Verbal skills (Synonyms, Grammar, Compositions, etc)

Read Following books on Amazon.com & Google Books || Google Play- I'am listing some great books for students with beginners to experts. Serious Note : **Purchase only Paperback formats (Amazon.Com) or Digital PDF formats (Google Books or LuLu.com). Don't Buy Kindle Format.**

1. **Accelerated C** : Practical Programming in Very Easy Steps by 2000+ C Examples. ISBN- 9781500521950

2. **Your Brain On C++** : Learn C++ Very Fast & Very Easy. ISBN- 9781500349578

3. **Thinking In C#** Programming : Professional Beginner's Guide 2014. ISBN- 9781500192693

4. **Mastering Algorithms with C** : Perfect Beginner's Guide 2014. ISBN- 9781500137137

5. **Effective Core Java** : The Complete Core Reference : TENTH EDITION 2014. ISBN- 9781499642582

4. *How many interviews do I have to clear to get a job?*

Answer: It is usually a minimum of three interviews: A telephonic interview before calling them for face to face interview. And second are a technical interview and an HR Interview. In some big MNC'S there will be multiple technical interviews. Unless the hiring company is satisfied with your technical skills & communication skills.

5. *Tell me about yourself.*

Answer: This is first question that interviewers ask at the beginning of the interview to know more about you, they also use this question to get an idea of how you look at yourself and your achievements. So, briefly explain your professional background, the projects you've done, significant contributions you've made in your previous jobs, and conclude with a note about your personal background and a few points on your positive personal characteristics. Don't talk for an hour- make it short and to-the-point. Also, don't overemphasize your personal details.

6. *What are your strengths and weaknesses?*

Answer: This is a question asked to check how you look about yourself and also how your strength's can contribute to the team.

So, be honest and tell what you consider as your strengths ('I learn new skills fast,' 'I am an effective team player,' "I have good leadership skills etc.) Provide supporting details for your strengths like 'I learn new skills fast. In my previous job, I had to learn scripting. I started to do Java programming from the next day itself, and I did it!'. For weakness, don't elaborate too much; some weakness can cost you your job ('I can't resist stealing if I see costly mobiles!')

7. *What do you know about our Company?*

Answer: To answer this question you should prepare before attending the interview. Visit the company's website in About us section, get help from Google, contact anyone working in that company to get idea about company works on, which countries or state its has presence in, the kind of projects or products they are working on, etc An overview is more than enough.

8. *Why are you planning to leave your current Job?*

Answer: Be careful in answering this question. Usually acceptable answers are: Looking for better pay, looking for better role and growth opportunities, got married and had to shift to this city. And the Bad answers are " I don't like my old Boss !" "I don't want to work on that project" etc.

9. *Tell us about some challenges you faced in your previous job and how you overcome them.*

Answer: This is asked to check how confidence you are in handling your day-to-day work and also your confidence in sticky situations. So, you can explain some of the challenges that you faced in your earlier jobs, how you dealt with them, how you successfully overcame the problem, don't forget!! Avoid talking about bad experiences; also avoid blaming any one or team. So it is better to talk about technical challenges and Problems.

10. *Why should we hire you?*

Answer: This is a question that every interviewer has, they want to justification on why they should select you. The interviewer just bounces this ball to you and checks how you give the reason for hiring you! So, tell them about your professional and personal strengths, relevant job experience, or academic background, your suitability for current job requirements, etc., and give your view on why they should hire you, and Bad Answer: "Because I am desperate for a job;" "I have searched for jobs for more than a year and I didn't get any- you should help me!"

11. *How much salary hike are you looking for?*

Answer: If you are honest and say "Double the current salary" you won't get the job. If you say that I am fine getting even the old salary, you might actually end up getting it! A safe answer is same as the industry average hike one gets while moving to a new job. Or you can say: same as the salary that a person with similar experience and skills will get in your company and throw the ball back in the interviewers court.

12. *How should I dress?*

Answer: Generally, candidates should dress one small step above the average employee in their position, or as nice as the nicest dressed employees in their position In most software firms, this means that jeans (nice jeans with no holes) or slacks with a nice shirt or sweater is fine In a bank or another more formal institution, avoid jeans and stick with slacks.

13. *What language should I use?*

Answer: Many people will tell you "whatever language you're most comfortable with," but ideally you want to use a language that your interviewer is comfortable with I'd usually recommend coding in either C, C++ or Java, as the vast majority of interviewers will be comfortable in one of these languages My personal preference for interviews is Java (unless it's a question requiring C / C++), because it's quick to write and almost everyone can read and understand Java, even if they code mostly in C++ (Almost all the solutions in this book are written in Java for this reason)

How to Prepare for Technical Questions

You've purchased this book, so you've already gone a long way towards good preparation Nice work! That said, there are better and worse ways to prepare many candidates just read through problems and solutions don't do that!

Memorizing or trying to learn specific questions won't help you! Rather, do this:

1. Try to solve the problem on your own I mean, really try to solve it Many questions are designed to be tough - that's ok! When you're solving a problem, make sure to think about the space and time efficiency Ask yourself if you could improve the time efficiency by reducing the space efficiency, or vice versa.

2. Write the code for the algorithm on paper You've been coding all your life on a computer, and you've gotten used to the many nice things about it But, in your interview, you won't have the luxury of syntax highlighting, code completion, or compiling Mimic this situation by coding on paper.

3. Type your paper code as-is into a computer You'll probably have made a bunch of mistakes Start a list of all the mistakes you made, so that you can keep these in mind in the real interview.

Technical Preparation:

What You Need To Know - Most interviewers won't ask about specific algorithms for binary tree balancing or other complex algorithms Frankly, they probably don't remember these algorithms either You're usually only expected to know the basics Here's a list of the absolute must-have knowledge.

Data Structures	Algorithms	Concepts
Linked Lists	Breadth First Search	Bit Manipulation
Binary Trees	Depth First Search	Singleton Design Pattern
Tries	Binary Search	Factory Design Pattern
Stacks	Merge Sort	Memory (Stack vs Heap)
Queues	Quick Sort	Recursion
Vectors / ArrayLists	Tree Insert / Find / etc	Big-O Time
Hash Tables		

This is not, of course, an all-inclusive list Questions may be asked on areas outside of these topics this is merely a "must know" list.

For each of the topics, make sure you understand how to implement / use them, and (where applicable) the space and time complexity.

Practicing implementing the data structures and algorithms you might be asked to implement them in your interview, or you might be asked to implement a modification of them either way, the more comfortable you are with implementations the better.

Do you need to know details of C++, Java, etc?

While I personally never liked asking these sorts of questions (e g, "what is a v table?"), many interviewers regretfully do ask them for big companies like Microsoft, Google, Amazon, etc, you can try "Core Java Professional"

I wouldn't stress too much about these questions Look up the most common questions and make sure you have answers to them, but I would focus on data structures and algorithms preparation. At smaller companies, or non-software companies, these questions can be more important.

Handling Technical Questions
General Advice for Technical Questions

Interviews are supposed to be difficult If you don't get every or any answer immediately, that's ok! In fact, in my experience, maybe only 10 people out of the 120+ that I've interviewed have gotten the question right instantly So when you get a hard question, don't panic Just start talking aloud about how you would solve it

And, one more thing: you're not done until the interviewer says that you're done! What I mean here is that when you come up with an algorithm, start thinking about the problems accompanying it When you write code, start trying to find bugs If you're anything like the other 110 candidates that I've interviewed, you probably made some mistakes.

Five Steps to a Technical Question-

A technical interview question can be solved utilizing a five step approach:

1. Ask your interviewer questions to resolve ambiguity.
2. Design an Algorithm.
3. Write pseudo-code first, but make sure to tell your interviewer that you're writing pseudo-code! Otherwise, he/she may think that you're never planning to write "real" code, and many interviewers will hold that against you.
4. Write your code, not too slow and not too fast.
5. Test your code and carefully fix any mistakes.

Step 1: *Ask Questions -*

Technical problems are more ambiguous than they might appear, so make sure to ask questions to resolve anything that might be unclear or ambiguous You may eventually wind up with a very different – or much easier – problem than you had initially thought In fact, many interviewers (especially at Microsoft) will specifically test to see if you ask good questions. Good questions might be things like:

What are the data types? How much data is there?

What assumptions do you need to solve the problem? Who is the user?

Example: "Design an algorithm to sort a list "

Question: *What sort of list? An array? A linked list?*

Answer: An array.

Question: *What does the array hold? Numbers? Characters? Strings?*

Answer: Numbers.

Question: *And are the numbers integers?*

Answer: Yes.

Question: *Where did the numbers come from? Are they IDs? Values of something?*

Answer: They are the ages of customers.

Question: *And how many customers are there?*

Answer: About a million.

We now have a pretty different problem:

Sort an array containing a million integers between 0 and 130 How do we solve this? Just create an array with 130 elements and count the number of ages at each value.

Step 2: Design an Algorithm-

- Designing an algorithm can be tough, but our five approaches to algorithms can help you out While you're designing your algorithm, don't forget to think about:
- What are the space and time complexities?
- What happens if there is a lot of data?
- Does your design cause other issues? (i e , if you're creating a modified version of a binary search tree, did your design impact the time for insert / find / delete?)
- If there are other issues, did you make the right trade-offs?
- If they gave you specific data (e g , mentioned that the data is ages, or in sorted order), have you leveraged that information? There's probably a reason that you're given it.

Step 3: Pseudo-Code-

Writing pseudo-code first can help you outline your thoughts clearly and reduce the number of mistakes you commit But, make sure to tell your interviewer that you're writing pseudo code first and that you'll follow it up with "real" code Many candidates will write pseudo code in order to 'escape' writing real code, and you certainly don't want to be confused with those candidates.

Step 4: Code-

You don't need to rush through your code; in fact, this will most likely hurt you just go at a nice, slow methodical pace also, remember this advice:

Use Data Structures Generously: Where relevant, use a good data structure or define your own.

For example, if you're asked a problem involving finding the minimum age for a group of people, consider defining a data structure to represent a Person This shows your interviewer that you care about good object oriented design.

Don't Crowd Your Coding: This is a minor thing, but it can really help When you're writing code on a whiteboard, start in the upper left hand corner not in the middle This will give you plenty of space to write your answer.

Step 5: Test-

- Yes, you need to test your code! Consider testing for:
- Extreme cases: 0, negative, null, maximums, etc.
- User error: What happens if the user passes in null or a negative value?
- General cases: Test the normal case.

If the algorithm is complicated or highly numerical (bit shifting, arithmetic, etc), consider testing while you're writing the code rather than just at the end.

Also, when you find mistakes (which you will), carefully think through why the bug is occurring One of the worst things I saw while interviewing was candidates who recognized a mistake and tried making "random" changes to fix the error.

For example, Imagine a candidate writes a function that returns a number When he tests his code with the number '5' he notices that it returns 0 when it should be returning 1 So, he changes the last line from "return ans" to "return ans+1," without thinking through why this would resolve the issue Not only does this look bad, but it also sends the candidate on an endless string of bugs and bug fixes. When you notice problems in your code, really think deeply about why your code failed before fixing the mistake.

Top Ten Mistakes Candidates Make:

#1 | Practicing on a Computer

If you were training for a serious bike race in the mountains, would you practice only by biking on the streets? I hope not the air is different the terrain is different Yeah, I bet you'd practice in the mountains Using a compiler to practice interview questions is like this - and you've basically been biking on the streets your entire life Put away the compiler and get out the old pen and paper Use a compiler only to verify your solutions.

#2 | Not Rehearsing Behavioral Questions

Many candidates spend all their time prepping for technical questions and overlook the behavioral questions Guess what? Your interviewer is judging those too! And, not only that your performance on behavioral questions might bias your interviewer's perception of your technical performance Behavioral prep is relatively easy and well-worth your time Looking over your projects and positions.

#3 | Not Doing a Mock Interview

Imagine you're preparing for a big speech Your whole school, or company, or whatever will be there Your future depends on this And all you do to prepare is read the speech to yourself Silently In your head Crazy, right?

Not doing a mock interview to prepare for your real interview is just like this If you're an engineer, you must know other engineers Grab a buddy and ask him/her to do a mock interview for you, You can even return the favor!

#4 | Trying to Memorize Solutions

Quality beats quantity Try to struggle through and solve questions yourself; don't flip directly to the solutions when you get stuck Memorizing how to solve specific problem isn't going to help you much in an interview Real preparation is about learning how to approach new problems.

#5 | Talking Too Much

I can't tell you how many times I've asked candidates a simple question like "what was the hardest bug on Project Pod?", only to have them ramble on and on about things I don't understand Five minutes later, when they finally come up for air, I've learned nothing - except that they're a poor communicator When asked a question, break your answer into three parts (Situation / Action / Response, Issue 1 / Issue 2 / Issue 3, etc) and speak for just a couple sentences about each If I want more details, I'll ask!

#6 | Talking Too Little

let me tell you a secret: I don't know what's going on in your head So if you aren't talking, I don't know what you're thinking If you don't talk for a long time, I'll assume that you aren't making any progress Speak up often, and try to talk your way through a solution This shows your interviewer that you're tackling the problem and aren't stuck And it lets them guide you when you get off-track, helping you get to the answer faster And it shows your awesome communication skills What's not to love?

#7 | Rushing

Coding is not a race, and neither is interviewing Take your time in a coding problem - don't rush! Rushing leads to mistakes, and reveals you to be careless go slowly and methodically, testing often and thinking through the problem thoroughly you'll finish the problem in less time in the end, and with fewer mistakes.

#8 | Not Debugging

Would you ever write code and not run it or test it? I would hope not! So why do that in an interview? When you finish writing code in an interview, "run" (or walk through) the code to test it or, on more complicated problems, test the code while writing it.

#9 | Sloppy Coding

Did you know that you can write bug-free code while still doing horribly on a coding question? It's true! Duplicated code, messy data structures (i e , lack of object oriented design), etc Bad, bad, bad! When you write code, imagine you're writing for real-world maintainability Break code into sub-routines, and design data structures to link appropriate data.

#10 | Giving Up

Have you ever taken a computer adaptive test? These are tests that give you harder questions the better you do Take it from me - they're not fun Regardless of how well you're actually doing, you suddenly find yourself stumbling through problems Yikes!

Interviewing is sort of like this If you whiz through the easy problems, you're going to get more and harder problems or, the questions might have just started out hard to begin with!

Either way, struggling on a question does not mean that you're doing badly so don't give up or get discouraged you're doing great!

Special Advice for Software Design Engineers in Test (SDETs)

Not only must SDETs master testing, but they also have to be great coders Thus, we recommend the follow preparation process:

- Prepare the Core Testing Problems: For example, how would you test a light bulb? A pen? A cash register? Microsoft Word? The Testing topics will give you more background on these problems.

- Practice the Coding Questions: The #1 thing that SDETs get rejected for is coding skills Make sure that you prepare for all the same coding and algorithm questions that a regular developer would get.

- Practice Testing the Coding Questions: A very popular format for SDET question is "Write code to do X," followed up by "OK, now test it " So, even when the question doesn't specifically ask for this, you should ask yourself, "how would you test this?" Remember: any problem can be an SDET problem!

The 16 Most Revealing Interview Questions.

Tell me about the people you hired in your last position? How long did they stay? What percentage worked out?

Tests knowledge of turn-over, training and honesty too (since no one has a 100% success rate).

What adjectives would your references use to describe you?

Keep it short and can be compared to actual reference comments to see how self-aware they are about their strengths and weaknesses?

What are the biggest strengths you will bring to this organization? (A classic but important)

Purposely open ended to all them to sell their abilities. Looking for specifics and past accomplishments.

What are the things you do not like to do, or not want to work on?

A test for honesty and self-awareness. Also a less threatening way to ask about weaknesses. We all have weaknesses, are they willing to take a risk, be honest and explain where they might need help? Are there requirements of this position that require certain personality types or traits that they may, or may not have?

The "Anti-refs" Question (One of the BEST and most revealing spend some time digging in.)

Question : *Think of someone you have had problems with in your career, as we all do, who you would NEVER use as a reference. Tell me the adjectives (to keep short) they might use to describe you and why they had this perception? Then we can discuss how you dealt with the situation.*

This is a great backdoor to the weaknesses questions and far more effective. It is very open-ended and often brings them to deal with a hidden event or problem. Gets potential reference points they will not volunteer and companies or environments where they may struggle. Test honesty? Tests their ability to deal with difficult situations? Tests their impressions of the resolution of the problem(s) and if the company's mission still got done in spite of personal issues. This also gives you specific things to ask references about, with implied disclosure, which force more honest answers.

Question : *Tell me what are the first five things you would do if you got this position?*

Tests the level they think at, how they go about solving problems, how quickly they will dig in. How much research and investigation they will do before implementing changes to be sensitive to the organization, history and other company specific issues.

Question : *What accomplishment in your career to date are you most proud of?*

What level is the accomplishment at? Is it big or small?

Question : *Where would you like to be in 3-5years in your career? What would you like to be earning?*

Shows ambition, ability to think ahead and plan and tests their plans against the companies goals for the person and position.

Question : *Tell me how you would go about (installing a new system, implement a new procedure)?*

This is a position specific question to test specific technical or managerial knowledge. Too many people do not ask specific deep technical questions, because they do not know them or are worried about offending. You need a few domain knowledge questions that are deep, technical and esoteric enough to prove they understand their technical landscape.

Question : *What do you think, are the most important five things for you to be successful in this position?*

Candidate will most often site what they believe to be their strengths, which may or may not agree with your corporate priorities and goals.

Question : *What are some things your current employer could do differently to be more successful?*

Sour grapes or constructive criticism? What is the level they are thinking at small or large ideas? If nothing but complaints they could be a malcontent, who took no action to improve the situation, or would have a negative impact on company morale.

Question : *Why are you interested in this job? What do you know about our company?*

Genuine interest here or just another job? Shows knowledge of your company Did they do their homework on your company what level of information did they focus on and consider important? Do they talk about a career path that makes sense within your company?

Question : *What have been the biggest failure and frustrations in your career?*

Brings out attitudes about failure, risk, and self-responsibility versus just blaming others and outside factors.

Question : *Why have you decided to leave your current/previous position?*

Dig deeply into this with follow-up questions on their answers? Whatever is driving this person is critical to how they see the world. What did they do to try to correct what was driving them away? Was it out of their control, or possibly projection of their own issues and weaknesses?

Question : *What risks did you take in your last position?*

Studies indicate that people who take risk are generally more successful than those who do not! Discussion on this can be very revealing. In early-stage organizations you will not want to hire people who are not too risk averse, as they may jump at the first new opportunity after learning how up and down things can be.

In my opinion these are some of the best and most revealing interviewing questions. More should be added with job or industry specific questions and this can be done with a forty-five minute interview. Use the small question for people in the same position and process so you can compare apples to apples and have some consistency.

I also always note the number of employees and/or revenue of each company on their resume, as skills are often company size specific. Someone in a small company inevitably has more scope and responsibility for a task than at a big company, where the duties are more likely divided up between several specialists. Claim of success need to be understood in terms of actual contribution. ("Every success has many mothers/fathers & Fckrs, but failure is an orphan".) Ha ha ha ha ! ☺

Always understand their salary requirements and commute distance if they are a strong candidate, as these can vary enormously by candidate and be major factors visa vie your ability to close the deal.

Remember salary is more often a function of ego and background than value or effectiveness. A high salary request does not make a better candidate, though the best candidate's know their value in the marketplace. No decision has more impact than a hiring decision, as they will make many, many decision for you and the organization from that point forward. It has been estimated that the cost of a bad hiring decision can be as high as three times the salary in senior positions.

So take your time and do it right never compromise due to time constraints, but get a temporary solution until you have the best candidate available.

PART - I

350+ JAVA
INTERVIEW
QUES & ANS

Advise Drill – If you thinking that you are weak in Java Programming Then Try this Java book "*Core Java Professional*" Authored By Harry. H. Chaudhary.

Purchase Only Paperback Edition from Amazon, Digital PDF Edition (7.99 USD) from Google Books & Google Play. (800-1000 Pages Deep Core Java)

Why Java -

Like all other computer languages, the elements of Java do not exist in isolation. Rather, they work together to form the language as a whole. However, this interrelatedness can make it difficult to describe one aspect of Java without involving several others. Often a discussion of one feature implies prior knowledge of another.

For this reason, this book presents a quick overview of several key features of Java. The material described here will give you a foothold that will allow you to write and understand simple & typical programs. Most of the topics discussed will be examined in greater detail in upcoming chapters.

As we know in the past few years document the following fact: The Web has irrevocably recast the face of computing and programmers unwilling to master its environment will be left behind. The preceding is a strong statement. It is also true.

More and more, applications must interface to the Web. It no longer matters much what the application is, near universal Web access is dragging, pushing, and coaxing programmers to program for the online world, and Java is the language that many will use to do it.

Frankly, fluency in Java is no longer an option for the professional programmer, it is a requirement. This book will help you acquire it.

Aside from being the preeminent language of the Internet, Java is important for another reason: it has altered the course of computer language development. Many of the features first mainstreamed by Java are now finding their way into other languages.

For example, the new C# language is strongly influenced by Java. Knowledge of Java opens the door to the latest innovations in programming. Put directly, Java is one of the world's most important computer languages.

Story Behind it:

About the time that the details of Java were being worked out, a second, and ultimately more important, factor was emerging that would play a crucial role in the future of Java.

This second force was, of course, the World Wide Web. Had the Web not taken shape at about the same time that Java was being implemented, Java might have remained a useful but obscure language for programming consumer electronics.

However, with the emergence of the World Wide Web, Java was propelled to the forefront of computer language design, because the Web, too, demanded portable programs.

Most programmers learn early in their careers that portable programs are as elusive as they are desirable.

While the quest for a way to create efficient, portable (platform-independent) programs is nearly as old as the discipline of programming itself, it had taken a back seat to other, more pressing problems.

By 1993, it became obvious to members of the Java design team that the problems of portability frequently encountered when creating code for embedded controllers are also found when attempting to create code for the Internet.

In fact, the same problem that Java was initially designed to solve on a small scale could also be applied to the Internet on a large scale. This realization caused the focus of Java to switch from consumer electronics to Internet programming. So, while the desire for an architecture neutral programming language provided the initial spark, the Internet ultimately led to Java's large-scale success.

As mentioned earlier, Java derives much of its character from C and C++. This is by intent. The Java designers knew that using the familiar syntax of C and echoing the object-oriented features of C++ would make their language appealing to the legions of experienced C/C++ programmers.

In addition to the surface similarities, Java shares some of the other attributes that helped make C and C++ successful. First, Java was designed, tested, and refined by real, working programmers. It is a language grounded in the needs and experiences of the people who devised it.

Thus, Java is also a programmer's language. Second, Java is cohesive and logically consistent. Third, except for those constraints imposed by the Internet environment, Java gives you, the programmer, and full control. If you program well, your programs reflect it.

If you program poorly, your programs reflect that, too. Put differently, Java is not a language with training wheels. It is a language for professional programmers.

Introduction-

Java is a powerful object oriented programming language developed by Sun Microsystems Inc. in 1991. Java was developed for consumer electronic devices but later it was shifted towards Internet. Now Java has become the widely used programming language for the Internet. Java is a platform neutral language (Machine Independent). Program developed by Java can run on any hardware or on any operating system in this world.

When the chronicle of computer languages is written, the following will be said: B led to C, C evolved into C++, and C++ set the stage for Java. To understand Java is to understand the reasons that drove its creation, the forces that shaped it, and the legacy that it inherits.

Like the successful computer languages that came before, Java is a blend of the best elements of its rich heritage combined with the innovative concepts required by its unique environment.

While the remaining chapters of this book describe the practical aspects of Java—including its syntax, libraries, and applications—in this chapter, you will learn how and why Java came about, and what makes it so important.

Although Java has become inseparably linked with the online environment of the Internet, it is important to remember that Java is first and foremost a programming language. Computer language innovation and development occurs for two fundamental reasons:

❖ To adapt to changing environments and uses.

❖ To implement refinements and improvements in the art of programming.

❖ As you will see, the creation of Java was driven by both elements in nearly equal measure.

Languages Prior to Java-

First of all a language BCPL (Basic Combined Programming Language) was developed by Martin Richards which influenced a language B which was developed by Ken Thompson after that C was developed by Dennis Ritchie in 1972 at AT & T Bell Laboratories, USA on Unix Operating system.

After a few years C++ was developed by Bjarne Stroustroup in early 1980's because C was unable to handle large programs. Initial name of C++ was "C with Classes" but it was renamed as "C++" in 1983.

Java is related to C++, which is a direct descendent of C. Much of the character of Java is inherited from these two languages. From C, Java derives its syntax. Many of Java's object-oriented features were influenced by C++. In fact, several of Java's defining characteristics come from—or are responses to—its predecessors.

Moreover, the creation of Java was deeply rooted in the process of refinement and adaptation that has been occurring in computer programming languages for the past three decades. For these reasons, this section reviews the sequence of events and forces that led up to Java. As you will see, each innovation in language design was driven by the need to solve a fundamental problem that the preceding languages could not solve. Java is no exception.

History of Java & The Creation of Java-

Basically Java was developed by James Gosling, Patrick Naughton, ChrisWarth, Ed Frank, and Mike Sheridan at Sun Microsystems, Inc. in 1991. Initial name of this language was "Oak" but it was renamed in 1995 as "Java". It took 18 months to develop the first working version. This language was initially called "Oak" but was renamed "Java" in 1995.

Between the initial implementation of Oak in the fall of 1992 and the public announcement of Java in the spring of 1995, many more people contributed to the design and evolution of the language. Bill Joy, Arthur van Hoff, Jonathan Payne, Frank Yellin, and Tim Lindholm were key contributors to the maturing of the original prototype.

Somewhat surprisingly, the original impetus for Java was not the Internet! Instead, the primary motivation was the need for a platform-independent (that is, architecture-neutral) language that could be used to create software to be embedded in various consumer electronic devices, such as microwave ovens and remote controls.

As you can probably guess, many different types of CPUs are used as controllers. The trouble with C and C++ (and most other languages) is that they are designed to be compiled for a specific target. Although it is possible to compile a C++ program for just about any type of CPU, to do so requires a full C++ compiler targeted for that CPU.

The problem is that compilers are expensive and time-consuming to create. An easier and more cost-efficient—solution was needed. In an attempt to find such a solution, Gosling and others began work on a portable, platform-independent language that could be used to produce code that would run on a variety of CPUs under differing environments. This effort ultimately led to the creation of Java.

The Stage Is Set for Java-

By the end of the 1980s and the early 1990s, object-oriented programming using C++ took hold. Indeed, for a brief moment it seemed as if programmers had finally found the perfect language. Because C++ blended the high efficiency and stylistic elements of C with the object-oriented paradigm, it was a language that could be used to create a wide range of programs.

However, just as in the past, forces were brewing that would, once again, drive computer language evolution forward. Within a few years, the World Wide Web and the Internet would reach critical mass. This event would precipitate another revolution in programming.

Need for Java-

Java was developed due to the need for a platform neutral language that could be used to create software to be embedded in various consumer electronic devices, such as microwave ovens and remote controls.

The program written in C and C++ are compiled for a particular piece of hardware and software and that program will not run on any other hardware or software. So we need C/C++ compilers one for each type of hardware to compile a single program. But compilers are expensive and time-consuming to create. So there is a need for platform neutral language. So that program compiled from that compiler can run on any hardware. This need led to the creation of Java.

Java Class Libraries-

Java programs consist of pieces called classes. Classes consist of pieces called methods that perform tasks and return information when they complete their tasks. You can program each piece you may need to form a Java program. However, most Java programmers take advantage of rich collections of existing classes in Java class libraries. The class libraries are also known as the Java APIs (Application Programming Interfaces).

Thus, there are really two pieces to learning the Java "world." The first is learning the Java language itself so that you can program your own classes; the second is learning how to use the classes in the extensive Java class libraries.

Throughout the book, we discuss many library classes. Class libraries are provided primarily by compiler vendors, but many class libraries are supplied by independent software vendors (ISVs). Also, many class libraries are available from the Internet and World Wide Web as freeware or shareware. You can download free ware products and use them for free subject to any restrictions specified by the copyright owner.

You also can download shareware products for free, so you can try the software. Shareware products often are free of charge for personal use. However, for shareware products that you use regularly or use for commercial purposes, you are expected to pay a fee designated by the copyright owner.

Many freeware and shareware products are also open source. The source code for open-source products is freely available on the Internet, which enables you to learn from the source code, validate that the code serves its stated purpose and even modify the code. Often, open-source products require that you publish any enhancements you make so the open-source community can continue to evolve those products. One example of a popular open-source product is the Linux operating system.

Other High-Level Languages-

Hundreds of high-level languages have been developed, but only a few have achieved broad acceptance. FORTRAN (FORMULA TRANSLATOR) was developed by IBM Corporation between 1954 and 1957 to be used for scientific and engineering applications that require complex mathematical computations. FORTRAN is still widely used.

COBOL (Common Business Oriented Language) was developed in 1959 by a group of computer manufacturers and government and industrial computer users. COBOL is used primarily for commercial applications that require precise and efficient manipulation of large amounts of data.

Today, about half of all business software is still programmed in COBOL. Approximately one million people are actively writing COBOL programs. Pascal was designed at about the same time as C. It was created by Professor Nicklaus Wirth and was intended for academic use.

We discuss Pascal further in the next section. Basic was developed in 1965 at Dartmouth College as a simple language to help novices become comfortable with programming. Bill Gates implemented Basic on several early personal computers. Today, Microsoft the company Bill Gates created is the world's leading software-development organization.

Java integrated development environments (IDEs), such as Forte for Java Community Edition, NetBeans, Borland's JBuilder, Symantec's Visual Cafe and IBM's Visual Age have built in editors that are integrated into the programming environment.

We assume the reader knows how to edit a file. Languages such as Java are object-oriented—programming in such a language is called object-oriented programming (OOP) and allows designers to implement the object oriented design as a working system. Languages such as C, on the other hand, are procedural programming languages, so programming tends to be action-oriented.

In C, the unit of programming is the function. In Java, the unit of programming is the class from which objects are eventually instantiated (a fancy term for "created"). Java classes contain methods (that implement class behaviors) and attributes (that implement class data).

C programmers concentrate on writing functions. Groups of actions that perform some common task are formed into functions, and functions are grouped to form programs. Data are certainly important in C, but the view is that data exist primarily in support of the actions that functions perform. The verbs in a system specification help the C programmer determine the set of functions needed to implement that system.

Java programmers concentrate on creating their own user-defined types called classes and components. Each class contains data and the set of functions that manipulate that data. The data components of a Java class are called attributes.

The function components of a Java class are called methods. Just as an instance of a built-in type such as int is called a variable, an instance of a user-defined type (i.e., a class) is called an object. The programmer uses built-in types as the "building blocks" for constructing user-defined types.

The focus in Java is on classes (out of which we make objects) rather than on functions. The nouns in a system specification help the Java programmer determine the set of classes from which objects will be created that will work together to implement the system.

Classes are to objects as blueprints are to houses. We can build many houses from one blueprint, and we can instantiate many objects from one class. Classes can also have relationships with other classes.

For example, in an object-oriented design of a bank, the "bank teller" class needs to relate to the "customer" class. These relationships are called associations.

We will see that, when software is packaged as classes, these classes can be reused in future software systems. Groups of related classes are often packaged as reusable components.

Just as real-estate brokers tell their clients that the three most important factors affecting the price of real estate are "location, location and location," many people in the software community believe that the three most important factors affecting the future of software development are "reuse, reuse and reuse."

Indeed, with object technology, we can build much of the software we will need by combining "standardized, interchangeable parts" called classes. This book teaches you how to "craft valuable classes" for reuse.

Each new class you create will have the potential to become a valuable software asset that you and other programmers can use to speed and enhance the quality of future software-development efforts—an exciting possibility.

Relation of Java with C, C++, & C#

From C Java derives its syntax and from C++ it derives object oriented features. It is not an enhanced version of C++. Java is neither upwardly nor downwardly compatible with C++.

One important thing that I want to tell you is that Java language was not designed to replace C++ and C#. Another language developed by Microsoft to support the .NET Framework, C# is closely related to Java because both share C++ and C style syntax, support distributed programming, and utilize the same object model.

Primary Objective of Java is to achieve:-

1. **Security: -**

   There is no threat of virus infection when we use Java compatible Web Browser. Also there is no threat of malicious programs that can gather private information, such as credit card numbers, bank account balances and passwords from local machine.

   Java provides a firewall between a networked application and our computer.

2. **Portability: -**

   Java programs are portable from one computer to another computer running different types of operating systems and having different hardware.

Java Bytecode:-

The output of a Java compiler is bytecode not the machine code (".class" file). Bytecode is a highly optimized set of instructions designed to be executed by the Java run-time system, which is called as JVM (Java Virtual Machine).

JVM is the interpreter which interprets the bytecode. Compiled program runs faster but still Java uses interpreter to achieve portability so Java programs runs a little slower.

Now a program compiled through a Java compiler can run in any environment but JVM needs to be implemented for each platform. Java programs are interpreted. This also helps to make it secure because the execution of every Java program is under the control of JVM.

JIT (Just In Time):-

JIT is a translator used by JVM to translate bytecode into actual machine code. It does not translate entire bytecodes rather it translates piece by piece on demand basis.

Type of applications Java can develop:-

1. **Standalone Applications-** A standalone application is a program that runs on our local computer under the operating system of that computer just like a C or a C++ program.

2. **Applets-** An applet is a small program which travel across the Internet and executed by a Java-Compatible web browser, such as Internet Explorer or Netscape Navigator, on the client machine.

   An applet is actually a tiny Java program, dynamically downloaded across the network. Applet programs are stored on a web server and they travels to client machine on request from the client machine.

   An applet cannot be executed like standalone application. Applet can be executed only by embedding it into an HTML page like a sound file or a image file or a video clip.

   Now this HTML page which has applet embedded into it can be run after downloading such HTML page by a web browser on a local machine. An applet is a program that can react to user input and can change dynamically. It does not run the same animation or sound over and over.

3. **Web Applications-** These are the programs which run on Web Server. When we access a web site by specifying the URL (Universal Resource Locator) in a web browser then the web browser sends a request to the web server for a particular Web site. After receiving this request server runs a program and this program is called as Web Application. We use Java Servlets and JSP (Java Server Pages) to write such programs.

    These programs run on the server and then send the result/response to the client. JSP pages can be thought of as a combination of HTML and Java Code. The Web Server converts JSP pages into Java Servlets before execution. When a client request for a particular URL and the URL corresponds to an HTML page the web server simply returns the HTML page to the client, which then displays it. If the URL corresponds to the servlet or JSP then it is executed on the Server and the result/response is returned to the client, which is then displayed by the client.

4. **Distributed Applications-** Java application is divided into small programs which can run on separate machines. The objects used in these programs can communicate with each other. These applications are known as Distributed Applications. This allowed objects on two different computers to execute procedure remotely. For this RMI (Remote Method Invocation) is used.

Characteristics of Java:-

1. **Simple-** The syntax of Java is almost similar to C and C++ so that a programmer is familiar with C/C++ does not have to learn the syntax from scratch. But many features of C/C++, which are either complex or result in ambiguity have been removed in Java.

    a. Java does not support multiple inheritance, as the concept is a bit complex and may result in ambiguity.

    b. Java does not support global variables, which also lead to many bugs in C/C++ programs.

    c. Java does not use pointers and does not allow pointer arithmetic, which is cause of most of the bugs in C/C++ programs due to inherent complexity.

    d. Java does not support operator overloading as it may lead to confusion.

    e. There is no concept of garbage value in Java. We have to initialize variables before use.

2. **Secure-** Java programs run within the JVM (Java Virtual Machine) and they are inaccessible to other parts. This greatly improves the security. A Java program rarely hangs due to this feature. It is quite unlike C/C++ programs, which hang frequently. Java's security model has three primary components:

   a. *Class loader.*
   b. *Bytecode Verifier.*
   c. *Security Manager.*

   Java uses different class loaders to load class files (executable files) from local machine and remote machines. The classes loaded from remote machines like Applet classes are not allowed to read or write files on the local machine. This prevents a malicious program from damaging the local file system.

   Bytecode verifier verifies the bytecode as soon as class loader completes its work. It ensures that bytecode is valid Java code. It almost eliminates the possibility of Java program doing some malicious activity like accessing the memory outside the JVM.

   The Security Manager controls many critical operations like file deletion, creation of threads etc. These operations are allowed only if the Java programs have sufficient permissions otherwise Security Manager does not allow the operations and generates Security Exception.

3. **Portable-** Java programs are platform independent. They follow the policy of write-once-run-anywhere. A Java program written for Windows Platform can run on any other platform (Unix, Linux, Sun Solaris etc.) simply by copying the bytecode (".class" files).

   There is no need to copy the source code and compile it again as in case of a C/C++ program. This feature has made the Java a powerful language. We can run bytecode on any machine provided that the machine has the JVM. JVM is itself is platform dependent but it makes the Java code platform independent. It is actually JVM which converts the bytecode into machine code and executes them.

So we can say that Java is a portable language. One more feature which makes Java highly portable is that primitive data types are of fixed length irrespective of the platform. For example an int will always be 4 bytes in Java. This is unlike C/C++ where size of int can be 2 bytes on some machines and 4 bytes on other machines.

4.   **Object Oriented-** Java is almost pure object-oriented language but it supports primitive data types like byte, short, int, long, float, double, char, boolean for the performance reasons.

5.   **Robust:-** Most programs fail one of the two reasons:

a.   Memory Management.
b.   Exceptional conditions at run time.

While designing the language one of the aim was to ensure that Java programs are as robust as possible i.e. they should rarely fail. So due importance was given to the above two factors in the Java.

In Java memory allocation and de-allocation is handled in the language itself, which eliminates many problems caused due to dynamic memory management features in C/C++. Java also supports object oriented exceptional handling features to handle exceptional conditions, which occur at run-time. This allows a Java program to recover and continue execution even after an exceptional condition occurs.

6.   **Multithreaded:-** Java was designed to meet the real world requirement of creating interactive, networked programs. Java provides support for writing multi-threaded programs to achieve this. This allows the programmer to write programs that can do many things concurrently.

For example a GUI (Graphical User Interface) based application might be listening to user events and taking appropriate action, a separate thread might be doing printing and a separate thread might be downloading a file from some machine across the network, all of this being done concurrently. This results in better performance and better CPU utilization.

It is possible to write multi-threaded programs in other languages also but it is achieved only by making use of System calls while in case of Java it can be achieved by using features of the language itself.

7. **Architecture-neutral-** One of the main problems facing programmers is that no guarantee exists that if we write a program today, it will run tomorrow-even on the same machine. Operating system upgrades, processor upgrades, and changes in core system resources can all combine to make a program malfunction. But the goal of Java programs is "write once run anywhere".

8. **Interpreted and High Performance-** Java programs are interpreted but still they run fast as compared to other interpreters.

9. **Distributed-** Java is designed for distributed environment of the Internet. Java has built-in support for various TCP/IP based protocols for this purpose. In fact accessing a resource using a URL is similar to accessing a file on the local machine. Java also has features for Remote Method Invocation, which is somewhat similar to Remote Procedure Calls (RPC). This allows objects on different computers to execute procedures remotely. Java has built-in API's for this purpose called as RMI.

10. **Dynamic-** Every Java class is a separate unit of execution. A class is loaded at the run time only when it is needed. Default mechanism for binding methods in Java is also dynamic (run-time binding).

Learning Programming Strategies:

A programming course is quite different from other courses. In a programming course, you learn from examples, from practice, and from mistakes. You need to devote a lot of time to writing programs, testing them, and fixing errors.

For first-time programmers, learning Java is like learning any high-level programming language. The fundamental point is to develop the critical skills of formulating programmatic solutions for real problems and translating them into programs using selection statements, loops, methods, and arrays.

Once you acquire the basic skills of writing programs using loops, methods, and arrays, you can begin to learn how to develop large programs and GUI programs using the object oriented approach.

When you know how to program and you understand the concept of object-oriented programming, learning Java becomes a matter of learning the Java API. The Java API establishes a framework for programmers to develop applications using Java.

You have to use the classes and interfaces in the API and follow their conventions and rules to create applications. The best way to learn the Java API is to imitate examples and do exercises.

The Java Language Specification, API, JDK, and IDE -

Computer languages have strict rules of usage. If you do not follow the rules when writing a program, the computer will be unable to understand it. The Java language specification and Java API define the Java standard.

The Java language specification is a technical definition of the language that includes the syntax and semantics of the Java programming language. The complete Java language specification can be found at java.sun.com/docs/books/jls.

The application program interface (API) contains predefined classes and interfaces for developing Java programs. The Java language specification is stable, but the API is still expanding. At the Sun Java Website (java.sun.com), you can view and download the latest version of the Java API.

Java is a full-fledged and powerful language that can be used in many ways. It comes in three editions: Java Standard Edition(Java SE),Java Enterprise Edition(Java EE), and Java Micro Edition(Java ME).

Java SE can be used to develop client-side standalone applications or applets. Java EE can be used to develop server-side applications, such as Java servlets and Java Server Pages. Java ME can be used to develop applications for mobile devices, such as cell phones.

JDK consists of a set of separate programs, each invoked from a command line, for developing and testing Java programs. Besides JDK, you can use a Java development tool (e.g., Net Beans, Eclipse, and TextPad)—software that provides an integrated development environment

(IDE) for rapidly developing Java programs. Editing, compiling, building, debugging, and online help are integrated in one graphical user interface. Just enter source code in one window or open an existing file in a window, then click a button, menu item, or function key to compile and run the program.

Creating, Compiling, and Executing a Java Program:

You have to create your program and compile it before it can be executed. This process is repetitive, as shown in Figure 1.1. If your program has compilation errors, you have to modify the program to fix them, and then recompile it. If your program has runtime errors or does not produce the correct result, you have to modify the program, recompile it, and execute it again.

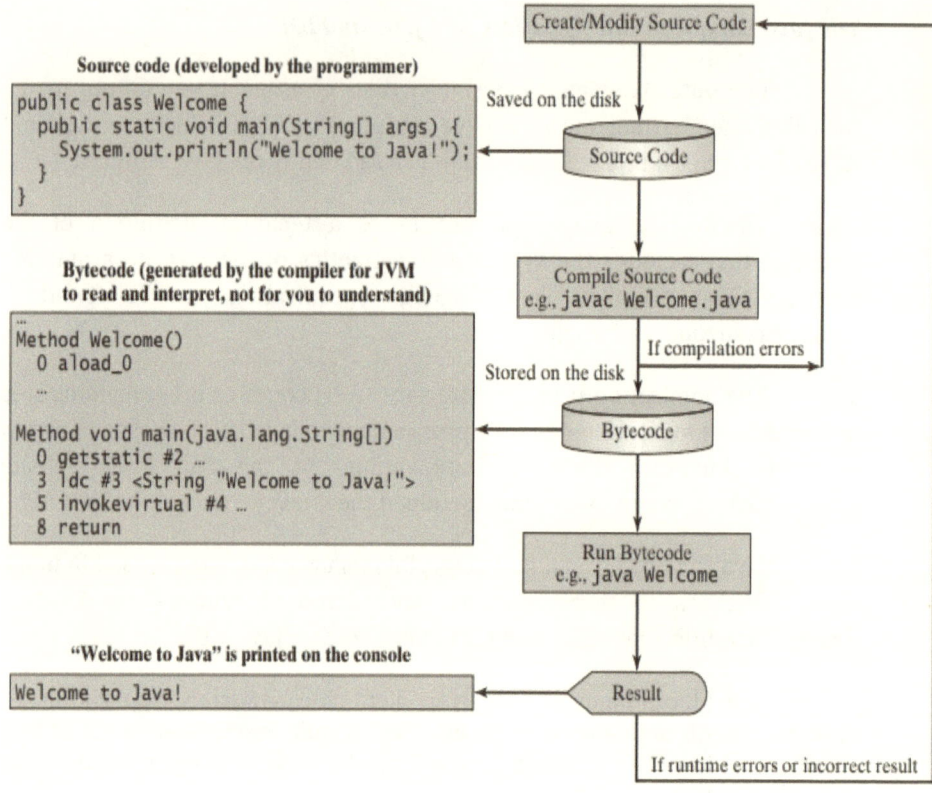

Question Can we define private and protected modifiers for variables in interfaces? (Core Java)

Answer No.

Question What is the query used to display all tables names in SQL Server (Query analyzer)? (JDBC)

Answer select * from information_schema.tables

Question *What is Externalizable? (Core Java)*

Answer Externalizable is an Interface that extends Serializable Interface. And sends data into Streams in Compressed Format. It has two methods, writeExternal(ObjectOuput out) and readExternal(ObjectInput in)

Question *What modifiers are allowed for methods in an Interface? (Core Java)*

Answer Only public and abstract modifiers are allowed for methods in interfaces.

Question *What is a local, member and a class variable? (Core Java)*

Answer Variables declared within a method are "local" variables. Variables declared within the class i.e not within any methods are "member" variables (global variables). Variables declared within the class i.e not within any methods and are defined as "static" are class variables.

Question *How many types of JDBC Drivers are present and what are they? (JDBC)*

Answer There are 4 types of JDBC Drivers

Type 1: JDBC-ODBC Bridge Driver

Type 2: Native API Partly Java Driver

Type 3: Network protocol Driver

Type 4: JDBC Net pure Java Driver

Question *Can we implement an interface in a JSP? (JSP)*

Answer No

Question *What is the difference between ServletContext and PageContext? (JSP)*

Answer ServletContext: Gives the information about the container PageContext: Gives the information about the Request

Question *What is the difference in using request.getRequestDispatcher() and context.getRequestDispatcher()? (JSP)*

Answer request.getRequestDispatcher(path): In order to create it we need to give the relative path of the resource context.getRequestDispatcher(path): In order to create it we need to give the absolute path of the resource.

Question *How to pass information from JSP to included JSP? (JSP)*

Answer Using <%jsp:param> tag.

Question *What is the difference between directives include and jsp include? (JSP)*

Answer <%@ include> : Used to include static resources during translation time. : Used to include dynamic content or static content during.

Question *What are Predefined variables or implicit objects?*

Answer To simplify code in JSP expressions and scriptlets, we can use eight automatically defined variables, sometimes called implicit objects. They are request, response, out, session, application, config, pageContext, and page.

Question *What is BDK?*

Answer BDK, Bean Development Kit is a tool that enables to create, configure and connect a set of set of Beans and it can be used to test Beans without writing a code.

Question *What is a Jar file?*

Answer Jar file allows to efficiently deploying a set of classes and their associated resources. The elements in a jar file are compressed, which makes downloading a Jar file much faster than separately downloading several uncompressed files. The package java. util. zip contains classes that read and write jar files.

Question *Explain the methods, rebind() and lookup() in Naming class?*

Answer rebind() of the Naming class(found in java. rmi) is used to update the RMI registry on the server machine. Naming. rebind("AddSever", AddServerImpl); lookup() of the Naming class accepts one argument, the rmi URL and returns a reference to an object of type AddServerImpl.

Question *what is UnicastRemoteObject?*

Answer All remote objects must extend UnicastRemoteObject, which provides functionality that is needed to make objects available from remote machines.

Question *What is RMI architecture?*

Answer RMI architecture consists of four layers and each layer performs specific functions:
a) Application layer - contains the actual object definition.
b) Proxy layer - consists of stub and skeleton.
c) Remote Reference layer - gets the stream of bytes from the transport layer and sends it to the proxy layer.
d) Transportation layer - responsible for handling the actual machine-to-machine communication.

Question What steps are involved in developing an RMI object?

Answer The steps involved in developing an RMI object are:
a) Define the interfaces.
b) Implementing these interfaces.
c) Compile the interfaces and their implementations with the java compiler.
d) Compile the server implementation with RMI compiler.
e) Run the RMI registry.
f) Run the application.

Question *What is RMI?*

Answer Remote Method Invocation (RMI) allows java object that executes on one machine and to invoke the method of a Java object to execute on another machine.

Question *How do servlets handle multiple simultaneous requests?*

Answer The server has multiple threads that are available to handle requests. When a request comes in, it is assigned to a thread, which calls a service method (for example: doGet(), doPost() and service()) of the servlet. For this reason, a single servlet object can have its service methods called by many threads at once.

Question *What is Servlet chaining?*

Answer Servlet chaining is a technique in which two or more servlets can cooperate in servicing a single request. In servlet chaining, one servlet's output is piped to the next servlet's input. This process continues until the last servlet is reached. Its output is then sent back to the client.

Question *Is it possible to call servlet with parameters in the URL?*

Answer Yes. You can call a servlet with parameters in the syntax as

(?Param1 = xxx || m2 = yyy).

Question *Why should we go for interservlet communication?*

Answer Servlets running together in the same server communicate with each other in several ways. The three major reasons to use interservlet communication are:

a) Direct servlet manipulation - allows to gain access to the other currently loaded servlets and perform certain tasks (through the ServletContext object)

b) Servlet reuse - allows the servlet to reuse the public methods of another servlet.

c) Servlet collaboration - requires to communicate with each other by sharing specific information (through method invocation)

Question *What is connection pooling?*

Answer With servlets, opening a database connection is a major bottleneck because we are creating and tearing down a new connection for every page request and the time taken to create connection will be more. Creating a connection pool is an ideal approach for a complicated servlet.

With a connection pool, we can duplicate only the resources we need to duplicate rather than the entire servlet. A connection pool can also intelligently manage the size of the pool and make sure each connection remains valid. A number of connection pool packages are currently available. Some like DbConnectionBroker are freely available from Java Exchange Works by creating an object that dispenses connections and connection Ids on request.

The ConnectionPool class maintains a Hastable, using Connection objects as keys and Boolean values as stored values. The Boolean value indicates whether a connection is in use or not. A program calls getConnection() method of the ConnectionPool for getting Connection object it can use; it calls returnConnection() to give the connection back to the pool.

Question *Is it possible to communicate from an applet to servlet and how many ways and how?*

Answer Yes, there are three ways to communicate from an applet to servlet and they are:

a) HTTP Communication(Text-based and object-based)
b) Socket Communication
c) RMI Communication

Question *What are cookies and how will you use them?*

Answer Cookies are a mechanism that a servlet uses to have a client hold a small amount of state-information associated with the user.

a) Create a cookie with the Cookie constructor: public Cookie(String name, String value)
b) A servlet can send a cookie to the client by passing a Cookie object to the addCookie() method of HttpServletResponse: public void HttpServletResponse. addCookie(Cookie cookie)
c) A servlet retrieves cookies by calling the getCookies() method of HttpServletRequest: public Cookie[ ] HttpServletRequest. getCookie().

Question *What is Server-Side Includes (SSI)?*

Answer Server-Side Includes allows embedding servlets within HTML pages using a special servlet tag. In many servlets that support servlets, a page can be processed by the server to include output from servlets at certain points inside the HTML page.

This is accomplished using a special internal SSINCLUDE, which processes the servlet tags. SSINCLUDE servlet will be invoked whenever a file with an. shtml extension is requested. So HTML files that include server-side includes must be stored with an . shtml extension.

Question *What is session tracking and how do you track a user session in servlets?*

Answer Session tracking is a mechanism that servlets use to maintain state about a series requests from the same user across some period of time. The methods used for session tracking are:

a) User Authentication - occurs when a web server restricts access to some of its resources to only those clients that log in using a recognized username and password.

b) Hidden form fields - fields are added to an HTML form that are not displayed in the client's browser. When the form containing the fields is submitted, the fields are sent back to the server.

c) URL rewriting - every URL that the user clicks on is dynamically modified or rewritten to include extra information. The extra information can be in the form of extra path information, added parameters or some custom, server-specific URL change.

d) Cookies - a bit of information that is sent by a web server to a browser and which can later be read back from that browser.

e) HttpSession- places a limit on the number of sessions that can exist in memory. This limit is set in the session. maxresidents property.

Question How many ways can we track client and what are they?

Answer The servlet API provides two ways to track client state and they are:

a) Using Session tracking and

b) Using Cookies.

Question What is the difference between doPost and doGet methods?

Answer

a) doGet() method is used to get information, while doPost() method is used for posting information.

b) doGet() requests can't send large amount of information and is limited to 240-255 characters. However, doPost()requests passes all of its data, of unlimited length.

c) A doGet() request is appended to the request URL in a query string and this allows the exchange is visible to the client, whereas a doPost() request passes directly over the socket connection as part of its HTTP request body and the exchange are invisible to the client.

Question *How to create and call stored procedures?*

Answer To create stored procedures:

Create procedure procedurename (specify in, out and in out parameters) BEGIN Any multiple SQL statement; END;

To call stored procedures: CallableStatement csmt = con. prepareCall("{call procedure name(?,?)}"); csmt. registerOutParameter(column no. , data type); csmt. setInt(column no. , column name) csmt. execute();

Question *What is stored procedure?*

Answer Stored procedure is a group of SQL statements that forms a logical unit and performs a particular task. Stored Procedures are used to encapsulate a set of operations or queries to execute on database. Stored procedures can be compiled and executed with different parameters and results and may have any combination of input/output parameters.

Question *What are the types of statements in JDBC?*

Answer Statement: to be used createStatement() method for executing single SQL statement PreparedStatement — To be used preparedStatement() method for executing same SQL statement over and over. CallableStatement To be used prepareCall() method for multiple SQL statements over and over.

Question *What are the steps involved for making a connection with a database or how do you connect to a database?*
Answer

a) Loading the driver : To load the driver, Class. forName() method is used. Class. forName("sun. jdbc. odbc. JdbcOdbcDriver"); When the driver is loaded, it registers itself with the java. sql. DriverManager class as an available database driver.

b) Making a connection with database: To open a connection to a given database, DriverManager. getConnection() method is used. Connection con = DriverManager. getConnection ("jdbc:odbc:somedb", "user", "password");

c) Executing SQL statements : To execute a SQL query, java. sql. statements class is used. createStatement() method of Connection to obtain a new Statement object. Statement stmt = con. createStatement();

A query that returns data can be executed using the executeQuery() method of Statement. This method executes the statement and returns a java. sql. ResultSet that encapsulates the retrieved data: ResultSet rs = stmt. executeQuery("SELECT * FROM some table");

d) Process the results : ResultSet returns one row at a time. Next() method of ResultSet object can be called to move to the next row. The getString() and getObject() methods are used for retrieving column values: while(rs. next()) { String event = rs. getString("event"); Object count = (Integer) rs. getObject("count");

Question What are the types of JDBC Driver Models and explain them?
Answer

There are two types of JDBC Driver Models and they are:
a) Two tier model and
b) Three tier model.

Two Tier model: In this model, Java applications interact directly with the database. A JDBC driver is required to communicate with the particular database management system that is being accessed. SQL statements are sent to the database and the results are given to user.

This model is referred to as client/server configuration where user is the client and the machine that has the database is called as the server. Three tier model: A middle tier is introduced in this model. The functions of this model are:

a) Collection of SQL statements from the client and handing it over to the database,

b) Receiving results from database to the client and c) Maintaining control over accessing and updating of the above.

Question What is the difference between JDBC and ODBC?
Answer

a) OBDC is for Microsoft and JDBC is for Java applications.

b) ODBC can't be directly used with Java because it uses a C interface.

c) ODBC makes use of pointers which have been removed totally from Java.

d) ODBC mixes simple and advanced features together and has complex options for simple queries. But JDBC is designed to keep things simple while allowing advanced capabilities when required.

e) ODBC requires manual installation of the ODBC driver manager and driver on all client machines. JDBC drivers are written in Java and JDBC code is automatically installable, secure, and portable on all platforms.

f) JDBC API is a natural Java interface and is built on ODBC. JDBC retains some of the basic features of ODBC.

Question *What is JDBC?*
Answer JDBC is a set of Java API for executing SQL statements. This API consists of a set of classes and interfaces to enable programs to write pure Java Database applications.

Question *What is serialization and deserialization?*

Answer Serialization is the process of writing the state of an object to a byte stream. Deserialization is the process of restoring these objects.

Question *What is the difference between Reader/Writer and InputStream/Output Stream?*

Answer The Reader/Writer class is character-oriented and the InputStream/OutputStream class is byte-oriented.

Question *What is a stream and what are the types of Streams and classes of the Streams?*
Answer A Stream is an abstraction that either produces or consumes information. There are two types of Streams and they are:

Byte Streams: Provide a convenient means for handling input and output of bytes. Character Streams: Provide a convenient means for handling input & output of characters.

Byte Streams classes: Are defined by using two abstract classes, namely InputStream and OutputStream.

Character Streams classes: Are defined by using two abstract classes, namely Reader and Writer.

Question *What are Vector, Hashtable, LinkedList and Enumeration?*
Answer

Vector : The Vector class provides the capability to implement a growable array of objects.

Hashtable : The Hashtable class implements a Hashtable data structure. A Hashtable indexes and stores objects in a dictionary using hash codes as the object's keys. Hash codes are integer values that identify objects.

LinkedList: Removing or inserting elements in the middle of an array can be done using LinkedList. A LinkedList stores each object in a separate link whereas an array stores object references in consecutive locations.

Enumeration: An object that implements the Enumeration interface generates a series of elements, one at a time. It has two methods, namely hasMoreElements() and nextElement(). HasMoreElemnts() tests if this enumeration has more elements and nextElement method returns successive elements of the series.

Question *How are the elements of different layouts organized?*
Answer

FlowLayout: The elements of a FlowLayout are organized in a top to bottom, left to right fashion.

BorderLayout: The elements of a BorderLayout are organized at the borders (North, South, East and West) and the center of a container.

CardLayout: The elements of a CardLayout are stacked, on top of the other, like a deck of cards.

GridLayout: The elements of a GridLayout are of equal size and are laid out using the square of a grid.

GridBagLayout: The elements of a GridBagLayout are organized according to a grid. However, the elements are of different size and may occupy more than one row or column of the grid. In addition, the rows and columns may have different sizes.

Question *What is a layout manager and what are different types of layout managers available in java AWT?*

Answer A layout manager is an object that is used to organize components in a container. The different layouts are available are FlowLayout, BorderLayout, CardLayout, GridLayout and GridBagLayout.

Question *What is the difference between scrollbar and scrollpane?*

Answer A Scrollbar is a Component, but not a Container whereas Scrollpane is a Conatiner and handles its own events and perform its own scrolling.

Question *What is source and listener ?*

Answer Source : A source is an object that generates an event. This occurs when the internal state of that object changes in some way.

Listener : A listener is an object that is notified when an event occurs. It has two major requirements. First, it must have been registered with one or more sources to receive notifications about specific types of events. Second, it must implement methods to receive and process these notifications.

Question *How do you set security in applets?*

Answer using setSecurityManager() method.

Question *What is the lifecycle of an applet?*

Answer init() method - Can be called when an applet is first loaded start() method - Can be called each time an applet is started. paint() method - Can be called when the applet is minimized or maximized. stop() method - Can be used when the browser moves off the applet's page. destroy() method - Can be called when the browser is finished with the applet.

Question *When do you use codebase in applet?*

Answer When the applet class file is not in the same directory, codebase is used.

Question *How does applet recognize the height and width?*

Answer Using getParameters() method.

Question *Are there any global variables in Java, which can be accessed by other part of your program?*

Answer No, it is not the main method in which you define variables. Global variables is not possible because concept of encapsulation is eliminated here.

Question *What is daemon thread and which method is used to create the daemon thread?*

Answer Daemon thread is a low priority thread which runs intermittently in the back ground doing the garbage collection operation for the java runtime system. setDaemon method is used to create a daemon thread.

Question *When you will synchronize a piece of your code?*

Answer When you expect your code will be accessed by different threads and these threads may change a particular data causing data corruption.

Question *What is synchronization?*

Answer Synchronization is the mechanism that ensures that only one thread is accessed the resources at a time.

Question *What is the class and interface in java to create thread and which is the most advantageous method?*

Answer Thread class and Runnable interface can be used to create threads and using Runnable interface is the most advantageous method to create threads because we need not extend thread class here.

Question *What are the methods for inter-thread communication and what is the class in which these methods are defined?*

Answer wait (), notify () and notifyAll() methods can be used for inter-thread communication and these methods are in Object class. wait() :

When a thread executes a call to wait() method, it surrenders the object lock and enters into a waiting state. notify() or notifyAll() : To remove a thread from the waiting state, some other thread must make a call to notify() or notifyAll() method on the same object.

Question *What is multithreading?*

Answer Multithreading is the mechanism in which more than one thread run independent of each other within the process.

Question *What is the difference between process and thread?*

Answer Process is a program in execution whereas thread is a separate path of execution in a program.

Question *What is the difference between Array and vector?*

Answer Array is a set of related data type and static whereas vector is a growable array of objects and dynamic.

Question *What is the difference between String and String Buffer?*

Answer

    a) String objects are constants and immutable whereas StringBuffer objects are not.

b) String class supports constant strings whereas StringBuffer class supports growable and modifiable strings.

Question *Can you have an inner class inside a method and what variables can you access?*

Answer Yes, we can have an inner class inside a method and final variables can be accessed.

Question *What is a cloneable interface and how many methods does it contain?*

Answer It is not having any method because it is a TAGGED or MARKER interface.

Question *What is the difference between Integer and int?*

Answer

A. Integer is a class defined in the java.lang package, whereas int is a primitive data type defined in the Java language itself. Java does not automatically convert from one to the other.

B. Integer can be used as an argument for a method that requires an object, whereas int can be used for calculations.

Question *What are inner class and anonymous class?*

Answer Inner class : classes defined in other classes, including those defined in methods are called inner classes. An inner class can have any accessibility including private. Anonymous class : Anonymous class is a class defined inside a method without a name and is instantiated and declared in the same place and cannot have explicit constructors.

Question *What modifiers may be used with top-level class?*

Answer public, abstract and final can be used for top-level class.

Question What is meant by Pre-initialization of Servlet?

Answer When servlet container is loaded, all the servlets defined in the web.xml file does not initialized by default. But the container receives the request it loads the servlet. But in some cases if you want your servlet to be initialized when context is loaded, you have to use a concept called pre-initialization of Servlet. In case of Pre-initialization, the servlet is loaded when context is loaded. You can specify 1 in between the tag.

Question *What is ServletContext?*

Answer ServletContext is an Interface that defines a set of methods that a servlet uses to communicate with its servlet container, for example, to get the MIME type of a file, dispatch requests, or write to a log file. There is one context per "web application" per Java Virtual Machine. (A "web application" is a collection of servlets and content installed under a specific subset of the server's URL namespace such as /catalog and possibly installed via a .war file.)

Question *What is a Servlet?*

Answer Java Servlets are server side components that provides a powerful mechanism for developing server side of web application. Earlier CGI was developed to provide server side capabilities to the web applications. Although CGI played a major role in the explosion of the Internet, its performance, scalability and reusability issues make it less than optimal solutions. Java Servlets changes all that. Built from ground up using Sun's write once run anywhere technology java servlets provide excellent framework for server side processing.

Question *Where the CardLayout is used ?*

Answer CardLayout manages two or more components that share the same display space. It lets you use one container (usually a panel) to display one out of many possible component children (like flipping cards on a table). A program can use this layout to show a different child component to different users.

For example, the interface shown to an administrator might have additional functionality from the interface shown to a regular user. With card layout, our program can show the appropriate interface depending on the type of user using the program. Another typical use of card layout would be to let end user toggle among different displays and choose the one they prefer. In this case, the program must provide a GUI for the user to make the selection.

Question *What is JFC ?*

Answer Java Foundation Classes include:

- Standard AWT 1.1
- Accessibility interface
- Lightweight components: which are user interface components that do not subclass an existing AWT interface element. They do not use native interface elements as provided by the underlying windowing

system. This means that they are less limiting than standard AWT components.

+ Java look and feel
+ Support for native look and feel
+ Services such as Java2D and Drag and Drop
+ How do you communicate in between Applets & Servlets ?

We can use the java.net.URLConnection and java.net.URL classes to open a standard HTTP connection and "tunnel" to the web server. The server then passes this information to the servlet in the normal way. Basically, the applet pretends to be a web browser, and the servlet doesn't know the difference. As far as the servlet is concerned, the applet is just another HTTP client.

Question *How will you communicate between two Applets ?*

Answer The simplest method is to use the static variables of a shared class since there's only one instance of the class and hence only one copy of its static variables. A slightly more reliable method relies on the fact that all the applets on a given page share the same AppletContext. We obtain this applet context as follows:

<font><font size="2" face="Verdana, Arial"> AppletContext ac = getAppletContext(); </font></font>
AppletContext provides applets with methods such as getApplet(name), getApplets(),getAudioClip, getImage, showDocument and showStatus().

Question *When is update method called ?*

Answer Whenever a screen needs redrawing (e.g., upon creation, resizing, validating) the update method is called. By default, the update method clears the screen and then calls the paint method, which normally contains all the drawing code.

Question *What is the order of method invocation in an Applet ?*

Answer

+ *public void init()* : Initialization method called once by browser.

+ *public void start()* : Method called after init() and contains code to start processing. If the user leaves the page and returns without killing the current browser session, the start () method is called without being preceded by init ().

- *public void stop()* : Stops all processing started by start (). Done if user moves off page.
- *public void destroy()* : Called if current browser session is being terminated. Frees all resources used by applet.

Question *What's the difference between notify() and notifyAll()?*

Answer notify() is used to unblock one waiting thread; notifyAll() is used to unblock all of them. Using notify() is preferable (for efficiency) when only one blocked thread can benefit from the change (for example, when freeing a buffer back into a pool). notifyAll() is necessary (for correctness) if multiple threads should resume (for example, when releasing a "writer"□ lock on a file might permit all "readers"□ to resume).

Question *What is meant by time slicing?*

Answer Its a task scheduling method. With time slicing, or "Round-Robin Systems", several processes are executed sequentially to completion. Each executable task is assigned a fixed-time quantum called a time slice in which to execute.

Question *How does thread synchronization occurs inside a monitor ?*

Answer The JVM uses locks in conjunction with monitors. A monitor is basically a guardian in that it watches over a sequence of code, making sure only one thread at a time executes the code. Each monitor is associated with an object reference. When a thread arrives at the first instruction in a block of code it must obtain a lock on the referenced object. The thread is not allowed to execute the code until it obtains the lock. Once it has obtained the lock, the thread enters the block of protected code. When the thread leaves the block, no matter how it leaves the block, it releases the lock on the associated object.

Question *What is Model 1?*

Answer Using JSP technology alone to develop Web page. Such term is used in the earlier JSP specification. Model 1 architecture is suitable for applications that have very simple page flow, have little need for centralized security control or logging, and change little over time.

Model 1 applications can often be refactored to Model 2 when application requirements change.

Question *What is Model 2?*

Answer Using JSP and Servlet together to develop Web page. Model 2 applications are easier to maintain and extend, because views do not refer to each other directly.

Question *What will be the default values of all the elements of an array defined as an instance variable?*

Answer If the array is an array of primitive types, then all the elements of the array will be initialized to the default value corresponding to that primitive type. e.g. All the elements of an array of int will be initialized to 0, while that of boolean type will be initialized to false. Whereas if the array is an array of references (of any type), all the elements will be initialized to null.

Question *When a thread blocks on I/O, what state does it enter?*

Answer A thread enters the waiting state when it blocks on I/O.

Question *Why do threads block on I/O ?*

Answer Threads block on i/o (that is enters the waiting state) so that other threads may execute while the i/o Operation is performed.

Question *What is the difference between JSP and JSF?*

Answer JSP simply provides a Page which may contain markup, embedded Java code, and "tags" which encapsulate more complicated logic /html.

JSF may use JSP as its template, but provides much more. This includes validation, rich component model and life cycle, more sophisticated EL, separation of data, navigation handling, different view technologies (instead of JSP), ability to provide more advanced features such as AJAX, etc.

Question *What is JSF?*

Answer JavaServer Faces (JSF) is a new standard Java framework for building Web applications. It simplifies development by providing a component-centric approach to developing Java Web user interfaces. JavaServer Faces also appeals to a diverse audience of Java/Web developers. "Corporate developers" and Web designers will find that JSF development can be as simple as dragging and dropping user interface (UI) components onto a page, while "systems developers" will find that the rich and robust JSF API offers them unsurpassed power and programming flexibility.

JSF also ensures that applications are well designed with greater maintainability by integrating the well established Model-View-Controller (MVC) design pattern into it's architecture. Finally, since JSF is a Java standard developed through Java Community Process (JCP), development tools vendors are fully empowered to provide easy to use, visual, and productive develop environments for JavaServer Faces.

Question *What is the difference between superclass and subclass?*

Answer A super class is a class that is inherited whereas sub class is a class that does the inheriting.

Question *What is difference between overloading and overriding?*
Answer

a) In overloading, there is a relationship between methods available in the same class whereas in overriding, there is relationship between a superclass method and subclass method.

b) Overloading does not block inheritance from the superclass whereas overriding blocks inheritance from the superclass.

c) In overloading, separate methods share the same name whereas in overriding, subclass method replaces the superclass.

d) Overloading must have different method signatures whereas overriding must have same signature.

Question *What is method overloading and method overriding?*

Answer Method Overloading: When a method in a class having the same method name with different arguments is said to be method overloading.Method Overriding: When a method in a class having the same method name with same arguments is said to be method overriding.

Question *What is finalize() method?*

Answer finalize() method is used just before an object is destroyed and can be called just prior to garbage collection.

Question *What are Unicode characters?*

Answer Unicode is used for internal representation of characters and strings and it uses 16 bits to represent each other.

Question *What is final, finalize() and finally?*

Answer

final : final keyword can be used for class, method and variables. A final class cannot be subclassed and it prevents other programmers from subclassing a secure class to invoke insecure methods. A final method can't be overridden. A final variable can't change from its initialized value.

finalize() : finalize() method is used just before an object is destroyed and can be called just prior to garbage collection.

finally : finally, a key word used in exception handling, creates a block of code that will be executed after a try/catch block has completed and before the code following the try/catch block. The finally block will execute whether or not an exception is thrown. For example, if a method opens a file upon exit, then you will not want the code that closes the file to be bypassed by the exception-handling mechanism. This finally keyword is designed to address this contingency.

Question *What are different types of access modifiers in Java?*

Answer

Public: Any thing declared as public can be accessed from anywhere.

Private: Any thing declared as private can't be seen outside of its class.

Protected: Any thing declared as protected can be accessed by classes in the same package and subclasses in the other packages.

Default Modifier: Can be accessed only to classes in the same package.

Question *How many ways can an argument be passed to a subroutine?*

Answer An argument can be passed in two ways. They are Pass by Value and Passing by Reference.

Passing by value: This method copies the value of an argument into the formal parameter of the subroutine.

Passing by reference: In this method, a reference to an argument (not the value of the argument) is passed to the parameter.

Question *What is the use of "bin" and "lib" in JDK?*

Answer "bin" contains all tools such as javac, appletviewer, awt tool, etc. whereas "lib" contains API and all packages.

Question *What are different types of Transaction Isolation Levels?*

Answer The isolation level describes the degree to which the data being updated is visible to other transactions.

This is important when two transactions are trying to read the same row of a table. Imagine two transactions: A and B. Here three types of inconsistencies can occur:

* **Dirty-read**: A has changed a row, but has not committed the changes. B reads the uncommitted data but his view of the data may be wrong if A rolls back his changes and updates his own changes to the database.

* **Non-repeatable read**: B performs a read, but A modifies or deletes that data later. If B reads the same row again, he will get different data.

* **Phantoms**: A does a query on a set of rows to perform an operation. B modifies the table such that a query of A would have given a different result. The table may be inconsistent.

Question *What do you mean by multiple inheritance in C++ ?*

Answer Multiple inheritance is a feature in C++ by which one class can be of different types. Say class teachingAssistant is inherited from two classes say *teacher and Student.*

Question *What do you mean by virtual methods?*

Answer Virtual Methods are used to use the polymorphisms feature in C++. Say class A is inherited from class B. If we declare say function f() as virtual in class B and override the same function in class A then at runtime appropriate method of the class will be called depending upon the type of the object.

Question *What do you mean by static methods?*

Answer By using the static method there is no need creating an object of that class to use that method. We can directly call that method on that class. For example, say class A has static function f(), then we can call f() function as A.f(). There is no need of creating an object of class A.

Question *What are the advantages of OOPL?*

Answer

Object oriented programming languages directly represent the real life objects. The features of OOPL as inhreitance, polymorphism, encapsulation makes it powerful.

Question *Are there any predefined file filters for a JFileChooser?*

Answer Apart from the accept all filter, until Java 6, there were no predefined filters. Java 6 introduces the FileNameExtensionFilter, allowing you to define one or more types of files for the user to select.

```
FileFilter filter = new FileNameExtensionFilter("JPEG file", "jpg", "jpeg");
JFileChooser fileChooser = ...;
fileChooser.addChoosableFileFilter(filter);
```

Question *Why can't my applet read or write to files?*

Answer Applets execute under the control of a web browser. Netscape and Internet Explorer impose a security restriction, that prohibits access to the local filesystem by applets. While this may cause frustration for developers, this is an important security feature for the end-user. Without it, applets would be free to modify the contents of a user's hard-drive, or to read its contents and send this information back over a network.

Digitally signed applets can request permission to access the local file system, but the easiest way around the problem is to read and write to remote files located on a network drive. For example, in conjunction with a CGI script or servlet, you could send HTTP requests to store and retrieve data.

Question *How can I call a Java method from Javascript?*

Answer Direct Web Remoting is an open source Java library which allows for easy integration of AJAX into your web site. It allows you to call Java methods directly from Javascript.

Question *How do I find whether a parameter exists in the request object?*

Answer

```
boolean hasFoo = !(request.getParameter("foo") == null
|| request.getParameter("foo").equals(""));
```

or

```
boolean hasParameter =
request.getParameterMap().contains(theParameter); //(which works in
Servlet 2.3+)
```

Question *What is the difference between RequestDispatcher and sendRedirect?*

Answer RequestDispatcher: server-side redirect with request and response objects. sendRedirect : Client-side redirect with new request and response objects.

Question *What is the difference between directive include and jsp include?*

Answer <%@ include>: Used to include static resources during translation time. JSP include: Used to include dynamic content or static content during runtime.

Question *What is the difference in using request.getRequestDispatcher() and context.getRequestDispatcher()?*

Answer request.getRequestDispatcher(path): In order to create it we need to give the relative path of the resource, context.getRequestDispatcher(path): In order to create it we need to give the absolute path of the resource.

Question *What is the difference between ServletContext and PageContext?*

Answer ServletContext: Gives the information about the container. PageContext: Gives the information about the Request.

Question *How many types of JDBC Drivers are present and what are they?*

Answer   There are 4 types of JDBC Drivers

- JDBC-ODBC Bridge Driver.
- Native API Partly Java Driver.
- Network protocol Driver.
- JDBC Net pure Java Driver .

Question *What is the query used to display all tables names in SQL Server (Query analyzer)?*

Answer select * from information_schema.tables

Question *How do you call a stored procedure from JDBC?*

Answer The first step is to create a CallableStatement object. As with Statement an and PreparedStatement objects, this is done with an open onnection object. A CallableStatement object contains a call to a stored procedure.

```
CallableStatement cs = con.prepareCall("{call SHOW_SUPPLIERS}");
ResultSet rs = cs.executeQuery();
```

Question *How can you use PreparedStatement?*

Answer This special type of statement is derived from class Statement.If you need a Statement object to execute many times, it will normally make sense to use a PreparedStatement object instead.

The advantage to this is that in most cases, this SQL statement will be sent to the DBMS right away, where it will be compiled. As a result, the PreparedStatement object contains not just an SQL statement, but an SQL statement that has been precompiled. This means that when the PreparedStatement is executed, the DBMS can just run the PreparedStatement's SQL statement without having to compile it first.

PreparedStatement updateSales = con.prepareStatement("UPDATE COFFEES SET SALES = ? WHERE COF_NAME =

Question *What are the different types of Statements?*

Answer Regular statement (use createStatement method), prepared statement (use prepareStatement method) and callable statement (use prepareCall)

Question *How can you retrieve data from the ResultSet?*

Answer JDBC returns results in a ResultSet object, so we need to declare an instance of the class ResultSet to hold our results. The following code demonstrates declaring the ResultSet object rs.

ResultSet rs = stmt.executeQuery("SELECT COF_NAME, PRICE FROM COFFEES");
String s = rs.getString("COF_NAME");

The method getString is invoked on the ResultSet object rs, so getString() will retrieve (get) the value stored in the column COF_NAME in the current row of rs.

Question *How can you create JDBC statements and what are they?*

Answer A Statement object is what sends your SQL statement to the DBMS. You simply create a Statement object and then execute it, supplying the appropriate execute method with the SQL statement you want to send.

For a SELECT statement, the method to use is executeQuery. For statements that create or modify tables, the method to use is executeUpdate.

It takes an instance of an active connection to create a Statement object. In the following example, we use our Connection object con to create the Statement object Statement stmt = con.createStatement();

Question *What will Class.forName do while loading drivers?*

Answer It is used to create an instance of a driver and register it with the DriverManager. When you have loaded a driver, it is available for making a connection with a DBMS.

Question *How can you load the drivers?*

Answer Loading the driver or drivers you want to use is very simple and involves just one line of code. If, for example, you want to use the JDBC-ODBC Bridge driver, the following code will load it:

```
Class.forName("sun.jdbc.odbc.JdbcOdbcDriver");
```

Your driver documentation will give you the class name to use. For instance, if the class name is jdbc.DriverXYZ, you would load the driver with the following line of code:

```
Class.forName("jdbc.DriverXYZ");
```

Question *What are the steps involved in establishing a JDBC connection?*

Answer This action involves two steps: loading the JDBC driver and making the connection.

Question *What is a data source?*

Answer A DataSource class brings another level of abstraction than directly using a connection object.

Data source can be referenced by JNDI. Data Source may point to RDBMS, file System , any DBMS etc.

Question *What is 2 phase commit ?*

Answer A 2-phase commit is an algorithm used to ensure the integrity of a committing transaction.

In Phase 1, the transaction coordinator contacts potential participants in the transaction. The participants all agree to make the results of the transaction permanent but do not do so immediately. The participants log information to disk to ensure they can complete.

In phase 2 f all the participants agree to commit, the coordinator logs that agreement and the outcome is decided. The recording of this agreement in the log ends in Phase 2, the coordinator informs each participant of the decision, and they permanently update their resources.

Question What is Metadata and why should I use it?

Answer Metadata ('data about data') is information about one of two things: Database information (java.sql.DatabaseMetaData), or Information about a specific ResultSet (java.sql.ResultSetMetaData).

Use DatabaseMetaData to find information about your database, such as its capabilities and structure. Use ResultSetMetaData to find information about the results of an SQL query, such as size and types of columns

Question What is a "dirty read"?

Answer Quite often in database processing, we come across the situation wherein one transaction can change a value, and a second transaction can read this value before the original change has been committed or rolled back.

This is known as a dirty read scenario because there is always the possibility that the first transaction may rollback the change, resulting in the second transaction having read an invalid value.

While you can easily command a database to disallow dirty reads, this usually degrades the performance of your application due to the increased locking overhead. Disallowing dirty reads also leads to decreased system concurrency.

Question *What is the advantage of using PreparedStatement?*

Answer If we are using PreparedStatement the execution time will be less. The PreparedStatement object contains not just an SQL statement, but the SQL statement that has been precompiled. This means that when the PreparedStatement is executed,the RDBMS can just run the PreparedStatement's Sql statement without having to compile it first.

Question *When we will Denormalize data?*

Answer Data denormalization is reverse procedure, carried out purely for reasons of improving performance. It maybe efficient for a high-throughput system to replicate data for certain data.

Question *What is cold backup, hot backup, warm backup recovery?*

Answer Cold backup (All these files must be backed up at the same time, before the databaseis restarted). Hot backup (official name is 'online backup') is a backup taken of each tablespace while the database is running and is being accessed by the users.

Question *Is the JDBC-ODBC Bridge multi-threaded?*

Answer

No, The JDBC-ODBC Bridge does not support concurrent access from different threads. The JDBC-ODBC Bridge uses synchronized methods to serialize all of the calls that it makes to ODBC. Multi-threaded Java programs may use the Bridge, but they won't get the advantages of multi-threading.

Question *What is an Applet? Should applets have constructors?*

Answer Applets are small programs transferred through Internet, automatically installed and run as part of web-browser. Applets implements functionality of a client.

Applet is a dynamic and interactive program that runs inside a Web page displayed by a Java-capable browser. We don't have the concept of Constructors in Applets. Applets can be invoked either through browser or through Appletviewer utility provided by JDK.

Question *Can main method be declared final?*

Answer Yes, the main method can be declared final, in addition to being public static.

Question *Can a public class MyClass be defined in a source file named YourClass.java?*

Answer No the source file name, if it contains a public class, must be the same as the public class name itself with a .java extension.

Question *What is the default value of the local variables?*

Answer The local variables are not initialized to any default value, neither primitives nor object references. If you try to use these variables without initializing them explicitly, the java compiler will not compile the code. It will complain abt the local varaible not being initilized.

Question *What are the different scopes for Java variables?*

Answer The scope of a Java variable is determined by the context in which the variable is declared. Thus a java variable can have one of the three scopes at any given point in time.

1. *Instance* : - These are typical object level variables, they are initialized to default values at the time of creation of object, and remain accessible as long as the object accessible.

2. Local : - These are the variables that are defined within a method. They remain accessbile only during the course of method excecution. When the method finishes execution, these variables fall out of scope.

3. Static: - These are the class level variables. They are initialized when the class is loaded in JVM for the first time and remain there as long as the class remains loaded. They are not tied to any particular object instance.

Question *What will be the initial value of an object reference which is defined as an instance variable?*

Answer The object references are all initialized to null in Java. However in order to do anything useful with these references, you must set them to a valid object, else you will get NullPointerExceptions everywhere you try to use such default initialized references.

Question What happens if you dont initialize an instance variable of any of the primitive types in Java?

Answer Java by default initializes it to the default value for that primitive type. Thus an int will be initialized to 0, a boolean will be initialized to false.

Question *Are main, next delete, exit keywords in Java?*

Answer No, they are not keywords in Java. delete is not a keyword in Java. Java does not make use of explicit destructors the way C++ does. To exit a program explicitly you use exit method in System object.

Question *Is String a primitive data type in Java?*

Answer No String is not a primitive data type in Java, even though it is one of the most extensively used object. Strings in Java are instances of String class defined in java.lang package.

Question *Can a .java file contain more than one java classes?*

Answer Yes, a .java file contain more than one java classes, provided at the most one of them is a public class.

Question *Is Empty.java file a valid source file?*

Answer Yes, an empty .java file is a perfectly valid source file.

Question *What does it mean that a method or field is "static"?*

Answer Static variables and methods are instantiated only once per class. In other words they are class variables, not instance variables. If you change the value of a static variable in a particular object, the value of that variable changes for all instances of that class.

Static methods can be referenced with the name of the class rather than the name of a particular object of the class (though that works too). That's how library methods like System.out.println() work out is a static field in the java.lang.System class.

Question *What modifiers are allowed for methods in an Interface?*

Answer Only public and abstract modifiers are allowed for methods in interfaces.

Question *What is Externalizable?*

Answer Externalizable is an Interface that extends Serializable Interface. And sends data into Streams in Compressed Format. It has two methods, writeExternal(ObjectOuput out) and readExternal(ObjectInput in)

Question *What method must be implemented by all threads?*

Answer All tasks must implement the run() method, whether they are a subclass of Thread or implement the Runnable interface.

Question *What are synchronized methods and synchronized statements?*

Answer Synchronized methods are methods that are used to control access to an object. A thread only executes a synchronized method after it has acquired the lock for the method's object or class.

Synchronized statements are similar to synchronized methods. A synchronized statement can only be executed after a thread has acquired the lock for the object or class referenced in the synchronized statement.

Question *Can an unreachable object become reachable again?*

Answer An unreachable object may become reachable again. This can happen when the object's finalize() method is invoked and the object performs an operation which causes it to become accessible to reachable objects.

Question *How do I serialize an object to a file?*

Answer The class whose instances are to be serialized should implement an interface Serializable. Then you pass the instance to the ObjectOutputStream which is connected to a fileoutputstream. This will save the object to a file.

Question *Which methods of Serializable interface should I implement?*

Answer The serializable interface is an empty interface, it does not contain any methods. So we do not implement any methods.

Question *How can I customize the seralization process? i.e. how can one have a control over the serialization process?*

Answer Yes it is possible to have control over serialization process. The class should implement Externalizable interface. This interface contains two methods namely readExternal and writeExternal. You should implement these methods and write the logic for customizing the serialization process.

Question *What is the common usage of serialization?*

Answer Whenever an object is to be sent over the network, objects need to be serialized. Moreover if the state of an object is to be saved, objects need to be serilazed.

Question *When you serialize an object, what happens to the object references included in the object?*

Answer The serialization mechanism generates an object graph for serialization. Thus it determines whether the included object references are serializable or not. This is a recursive process. Thus when an object is serialized, all the included objects are also serialized alongwith the original obect.

Question *What one should take care of while serializing the object?*

Answer One should make sure that all the included objects are also serializable. If any of the objects is not serializable then it throws a NotSerializableException.

Question *What happens to the static fields of a class during serialization?*

Answer There are three exceptions in which serialization doesnot necessarily read and write to the stream. These are -

- ✓ Serialization ignores static fields, because they are not part of any particular state state.

- ✓ Base class fields are only hendled if the base class itself is serializable

- ✓ Transient fields.

Question *Does importing a package imports the subpackages as well?*

Answer No you will have to import the subpackages explicitly.

For eg: Importing com.MyTest.* will import classes in the package MyTest only. It will not import any class in any of it's subpackage.

Question *What is the sequence for calling the methods by AWT for applets?*

Answer When an applet begins, the AWT calls the following methods, in this sequence:

> init()
>
> start()
>
> paint()

When an applet is terminated, the following sequence of method calls takes place -

> stop()
>
> destroy()

Question *What are the Applet's Life Cycle methods? Explain them?*

Answer Following are methods in the life cycle of an Applet:

init() method - called when an applet is first loaded. This method is called only once in the entire cycle of an applet. This method usually intialize the variables to be used in the applet-

start() method - called each time an applet is started.

paint() method - called when the applet is minimized or refreshed. This method is used for drawing different strings, figures, and images on the applet window.

stop() method - called when the browser moves off the applet's page.

destroy() method - called when the browser is finished with the applet .

Question *What are some alternatives to inheritance?*

Answer Delegation is an alternative to inheritance. Delegation means that you include an instance of another class as an instance variable, and forward messages to the instance.

It is often safer than inheritance because it forces you to think about each message you forward, because the instance is of a known class, rather than a new class, and because it doesn't force you to accept all the methods of the super class: you can provide only the methods that really make sense. On the other hand, it makes you write more code, and it is harder to re-use (because it is not a subclass).

Question *If I write return at the end of the try block, will the finally block still execute?*

Answer Yes even if you write return as the last statement in the try block and no exception occurs, the finally block will execute. The finally block will execute and then the control return.

Question *Is it necessary that each try block must be followed by a catch block?*
Answer It is not necessary that each try block must be followed by a catch block. It should be followed by either a catch block OR a finally block. And whatever exceptions are likely to be thrown should be declared in the throws clause of the method.

Question *What are the different ways to handle exceptions?*

Answer There are two ways to handle exceptions,
1. By wrapping the desired code in a try block followed by a catch block to catch the exceptions. And

2. List the desired exceptions in the throws clause of the method and let the caller of the method hadle those exceptions.

Question *How does an exception permeate through the code?*

Answer An unhandled exception moves up the method stack in search of a matching When an exception is thrown from a code which is wrapped in a try block followed by one or more catch blocks, a search is made for matching catch block. If a matching type is found then that block will be invoked. If a matching type is not found then the exception moves up the method stack and reaches the caller method. Same procedure is repeated if the caller method is included in a try catch block. This process continues until a catch block handling the appropriate type of exception is found. If it does not find such a block then finally the program terminates.

Question *What are runtime exceptions?*

Answer Runtime exceptions are those exceptions that are thrown at runtime because of either wrong input data or because of wrong business logic etc. These are not checked by the compiler at compile time.

Question *What are checked exceptions?*

Answer Checked exception are those which the Java compiler forces you to catch. e.g. IOException are checked Exceptions.

Question *Does Java provide any construct to find out the size of an object?*

Answer No there is not sizeof operator in Java. So there is not direct way to determine the size of an object directly in Java.

Question *What is Externalizable interface?*

Answer Externalizable is an interface which contains two methods readExternal and writeExternal. These methods give you a control over the serialization mechanism. Thus if your class implements this interface, you can customize the serialization process by implementing these methods.

Question *What type of parameter passing does Java support?*

Answer In Java the arguments are always passed by value .

Question *Can a top level class be private or protected?*

Answer No, a top level class can not be private or protected. It can have either "public" or no modifier. If it does not have a modifier it is supposed to have a default access. If a top level class is declared as private the compiler will complain that the "modifier private is not allowed here". This means that a top level class can not be private. Same is the case with protected.

Question *What is the difference between declaring a variable and defining a variable?*

Answer In declaration we just mention the type of the variable and it's name. We do not initialize it. But defining means declaration + initialization.

e.g String s; is just a declaration while String s = new String ("abcd"); Or String s = "abcd"; are both definitions.

Question *What are different types of inner classes?*

Answer Nested top-level classes, Member classes, Local classes, Anonymous classes Nested top-level classes- If you declare a class within a class and specify the static modifier, the compiler treats the class just like any other top-level class.

Any class outside the declaring class accesses the nested class with the declaring class name acting similarly to a package.

eg, outer.inner. Top-level inner classes implicitly have access only to static variables.There can also be inner interfaces. All of these are of the nested top-level variety.

- **Member classes** - Member inner classes are just like other member methods and member variables and access to the member class is restricted, just like methods and variables. This means a public member class acts similarly to a nested top-level class. The primary difference between member classes and nested top-level classes is that member classes have access to the specific instance of the enclosing class.

- **Local classes** - Local classes are like local variables, specific to a block of code. Their visibility is only within the block of their declaration. In order for the class to be useful beyond the declaration block, it would need to implement a more publicly available interface.Because local classes are not members, the modifiers public, protected, private, and static are not usable.

- **Anonymous classes** - Anonymous inner classes extend local inner classes one level further. As anonymous classes have no name, you cannot provide a constructor.

Question *What is Overriding?*

Answer When a class defines a method using the same name, return type, and arguments as a method in its superclass, the method in the class overrides the method in the superclass.

When the method is invoked for an object of the class, it is the new definition of the method that is called, and not the method definition from superclass. Methods may be overridden to be more public, not more private.

Question *What are Checked and UnChecked Exception?*

Answer A checked exception is some subclass of Exception (or Exception itself), excluding class RuntimeException and its subclasses.

Making an exception checked forces client programmers to deal with the possibility that the exception will be thrown. eg, IOException thrown by java.io.FileInputStream's read() method.

Unchecked exceptions are RuntimeException and any of its subclasses. Class Error and its subclasses also are unchecked. With an unchecked exception, however, the compiler doesn't force client programmers either to catch the exception or declare it in a throws clause. In fact, client programmers may not even know that the exception could be thrown. eg, StringIndexOutOfBoundsException thrown by String's charAt() method. Checked exceptions must be caught at compile time. Runtime exceptions do not need to be. Errors often cannot be.

Question *How can one prove that the array is not null but empty using one line of code?*

Answer Print args.length. It will print 0. That means it is empty. But if it would have been null then it would have thrown a NullPointerException on attempting to print args.length.

Question *What is the first argument of the String array in main method?*

Answer The String array is empty. It does not have any element. This is unlike C/C++ where the first element by default is the program name.

Question *What is an Iterator?*

Answer Some of the collection classes provide traversal of their contents via a java.util.Iterator interface. This interface allows you to walk through a collection of objects, operating on each object in turn. Remember when using Iterators that they contain a snapshot of the collection at the time the Iterator was obtained; generally it is not advisable to modify the collection itself while traversing an Iterator.

Question *Difference between Vector and ArrayList?*

Answer Vector is synchronized whereas arraylist is not.

Question *Difference between HashMap and HashTable?*

Answer The HashMap class is roughly equivalent to Hashtable, except that it is unsynchronized and permits nulls. (HashMap allows null values as key and value whereas Hashtable doesnt allow).

HashMap does not guarantee that the order of the map will remain constant over time. HashMap is unsynchronized and Hashtable is synchronized.

Question *What is HashMap and Map?*

Answer Map is Interface and Hashmap is class that implements that.

Question *What are pass by reference and pass by value?*

Answer Pass By Reference means the passing the address itself rather than passing the value. Pass by Value means passing a copy of the value to be passed.

Question *Describe synchronization in respect to multithreading.*

Answer With respect to multithreading, synchronization is the capability to control the access of multiple threads to shared resources. Without synchonization, it is possible for one thread to modify a shared variable while another thread is in the process of using or updating same shared variable. This usually leads to significant errors.

Question *What is the purpose of garbage collection in Java, and when is it used?*

Answer The purpose of garbage collection is to identify and discard objects that are no longer needed by a program so that their resources can be reclaimed and reused. A Java object is subject to garbage collection when it becomes unreachable to the program in which it is used.

Question *What is the difference between a constructor and a method?*

Answer A constructor is a member function of a class that is used to create objects of that class. It has the same name as the class itself, has no return type, and is invoked using the new operator.

A method is an ordinary member function of a class. It has its own name, a return type (which may be void), and is invoked using the dot operator.

Question *What is final?*

Answer A final class can't be extended ie., final class may not be subclassed. A final method can't be overridden when its class is inherited. You can't change value of a final variable (is a constant).

Question *What is static in java?*

Answer Static means one per class, not one for each object no matter how many instance of a class might exist. This means that you can use them without creating an instance of a class.Static methods are implicitly final, because overriding is done based on the type of the object, and static methods are attached to a class, not an object.

A static method in a superclass can be shadowed by another static method in a subclass, as long as the original method was not declared final. However, you can't override a static method with a nonstatic method. In other words, you can't change a static method into an instance method in a subclass.

Question *What if the main method is declared as private?*

Answer The program compiles properly but at runtime it will give "Main method not public." message.

Question *What is the difference between HttpServlet and GenericServlet?*

Answer A GenericServlet has a service() method aimed to handle requests.

HttpServlet extends GenericServlet and adds support for doGet(), doPost(), doHead() methods (HTTP 1.0) plus doPut(), doOptions(), doDelete(), doTrace() methods (HTTP 1.1).
Both these classes are abstract

Question *What is preinitialization of a servlet?*

Answer A container doesnot initialize the servlets ass soon as it starts up, it initializes a servlet when it receives a request for that servlet first time. This is called lazy loading. The servlet specification defines the element, which can be specified in the deployment descriptor to make the servlet container load and initialize the servlet as soon as it starts up. The process of loading a servlet before any request comes in is called preloading or preinitializing a servlet.

Question *What is the difference between ServletContext and ServletConfig?*

Answer

ServletContext: Defines a set of methods that a servlet uses to communicate with its servlet container, for example, to get the MIME type of a file, dispatch requests, or write to a log file. The ServletContext object is contained within the ServletConfig object, which the Web server provides the servlet when the servlet is initialized

ServletConfig: The object created after a servlet is instantiated and its default constructor is read. It is created to pass initialization information to the servlet.

Question *Explain ServletContext.*

Answer ServletContext interface is a window for a servlet to view it's environment. A servlet can use this interface to get information such as initialization parameters for the web applicationor servlet container's version.

Every web application has one and only one ServletContext and is accessible to all active resource of that application.

Question *What is the difference between the getRequestDispatcher(String path) method of javax.servlet.ServletRequest interface and javax.servlet.ServletContext interface?*

Answer The getRequestDispatcher(String path) method of javax.servlet.ServletRequest interface accepts parameter the path to the resource to be included or forwarded to, which can be relative to the request of the calling servlet. If the path begins with a "/" it is interpreted as relative to the current context root.

The getRequestDispatcher(String path) method of javax.servlet.ServletContext interface cannot accepts relative paths. All path must sart with a "/" and are interpreted as relative to curent context root.

Question *Explain the life cycle methods of a Servlet.*

Answer The javax.servlet.Servlet interface defines the three methods known as life-cycle method.

public void init(ServletConfig config) throws ServletException
public void service(ServletRequest req, ServletResponse res) throws
ServletException, IOException
public void destroy()

First the servlet is constructed, then initialized wih the init() method. Any request from client are handled initially by the service() method before delegating to the doXxx() methods in the case of HttpServlet.

The servlet is removed from service, destroyed with the destroy() methid, then garbaged collected and finalized.

Question *What is an Iterator interface?*

Answer The Iterator interface is used to step through the elements of a Collection :

Question *Describe the Garbage Collection process in Java ?*

Answer The JVM spec mandates automatic garbage collection outside of the programmers control. The System.gc() or Runtime.gc() is merely a suggestion to the JVM to run the GC process but is NOT guaranteed.

Question How many static init can you have ?

Answer As many as you want, but the static initializers and class variable initializers are executed in textual order and may not refer to class variables declared in the class whose declarations appear textually after the use, even though these class variables are in scope.

Question *What is constructor chaining and how is it achieved in Java ?*

Answer A child object constructor always first needs to construct its parent (which in turn calls its parent constructor.). In Java it is done via an implicit call to the no-args constructor as the first statement.

Question *What methods can be overridden in Java?*

Answer In C++ terminology, all public methods in Java are virtual. Therefore, all Java methods can be overwritten in subclasses except those that are declared final, static, and private.

Question *Describe java's security model.*

Answer Java's security model is one of the most interesting and unique aspects of the language. For the most part it's broken into two pieces: the user adjustable security manager that checks various API operations like file access, and the byte code verifier that asserts the validity of compiled byte code. public abstract class SecurityManager java.lang.SecurityManager is an abstract class which different applications subclass to implement a particular security policy. It allows an application to determine whether or not a particular operation will generate a security exception.

Question *What is daemon thread and which method is used to create the daemon thread?*

Answer Daemon thread is a low priority thread which runs intermittently in the back ground doing the garbage collection operation for the java runtime system. setDaemon method is used to create a daemon thread.

Question *What are Transient and Volatile Modifiers?*

Answer

Transient: The transient modifier applies to variables only and it is not stored as part of its object's Persistent state. Transient variables are not serialized. *Volatile:* Volatile modifier applies to variables only and it tells the compiler that the variable modified by volatile can be changed unexpectedly by other parts of the program.

Question *What is preemptive and Non-preemptive Time Scheduling?*

Answer Preemptive: Running tasks are given small portions of time to execute by using time-slicing.

Non-Preemptive: One task doesn't give another task a chance to run until its finished or has normally yielded its time.

Question *What is runnable?*

Answer Its an Interface through which Java implements Threads.The class can extend from any class but if it implements Runnable,Threads can be used in that particular application.

Question *What is the difference between set and list?*
Answer Set stores elements in an unordered way but does not contain duplicate elements, whereas list stores elements in an ordered way but may *contain duplicate elements.*

Question *What is a layout manager?*
Answer A layout manager is an object that is used to organize components in a container.

Question *What is the difference between a public and a non-public class?*
Answer A public class may be accessed outside of its package. A non-public class may not be accessed outside of its package.

Question *What is the difference between instanceof and isInstance?*

Answer *instanceof* is used to check to see if an object can be cast into a specified type without throwing a cast classexception. isInstance() Determines if the specified Object is assignment-compatible with the object represented by this Class. This method is the dynamic equivalent of the Java language instanceof operator. The method returns true if the specified Object argument is non-null and can be cast to the reference type represented by this Class object without raising a ClassCastException. It returns false otherwise.

Question *What does the "abstract" keyword mean in front of a method? A class?*

Answer Abstract keyword declares either a method or a class. If a method has a abstract keyword in front of it,it is called abstract method.Abstract method hs no body.It has only arguments and return type.Abstract methods act as placeholder methods that are implemented in the subclasses.

Abstract classes can't be instantiated.If a class is declared as abstract,no objects of that class can be created.If a class contains any abstract method it must be declared as abstract.

Question *What is JDBC? Describe the steps needed to execute a SQL query using JDBC.*

Answer The JDBC is a pure Java API used to execute SQL statements. It provides a set of classes and interfaces that can be used by developers to write database applications.

The steps needed to execute a SQL query using JDBC:
1. Open a connection to the database.
2. Execute a SQL statement.
3. Process th results.
4. Close the connection to the database.

Question *What is RMI?*

Answer RMI stands for Remote Method Invocation. Traditional approaches to executing code on other machines across a network have been confusing as well as tedious and error-prone to implement. The nicest way to think about this problem is that some object happens to live on another machine, and that you can send a message to the remote object and get a result as if the object lived on your local machine. This simplification is exactly what Java Remote Method Invocation (RMI) allows you to do.

Question *What are native methods? How do you use them?*

Answer Native methods are methods that are defined as public static methods within a java class, but whose implementation is provided in another programming language such as C.

Question *What does the keyword "synchronize" mean in java. When do you use it?*

Answer Synchronize is used when u want to make ur methods thread safe. The disadvantage of synchronise is it will end up in slowing down the program. Also if not handled properly it will end up in dead lock.

1. Only use (and minimize it's use)synchronization when writing multithreaded code as there is a speed (up to five to six time slower, depending on the execution time of the synchronized/non-synchronized method) cost associated with its use.

2. In case of syncronized method modifier, the byte code generated is the exact same as non-syncronized method. The only difference is that a flag called ACC_SYNCRONIZED property flag in method's method_info structure is set if the syncronized method modifier is present.

3. Also, syncronized keyword can make the code larger in size if used in the body of the method as bytecode for monitorenter/monitorexit is generated in addition to any exception handling.

Question *What is the difference between a Vector and an Array. Discuss the advantages and disadvantages*

Answer The vector container class generalizes the concept of an ordinary C array. Like an array, a vector is an indexed data structure, with index values that range from 0 to one less than the number of elements contained in the structure.

Also like an array, values are most commonly assigned to and extracted from the vector using the subscript operator. However, the vector differs from an array in the following important The size of the vector can change dynamically. New elements can be inserted on to the end of a vector, or into the middle. It is important to note, however, that while these abilities are provided, insertion into the middle of a vector is not as efficient as insertion into the middle of a list. A vector has more "self-knowledge" than an ordinary array.

In particular, a vector can be queried about its size, about the number of elements it can potentially hold (which may be different from its current size), and so on. A vector can only hold references to objects and not primitive types. Vector Implementaions are usually slower then array because of all the functionality that comes with them. As implemented in Java, vector is a thread-safe class and hence all methods are synchronous methods, which makes them considerably slow.

Question *Java says "write once, run anywhere". What are some ways this isn't quite true?*

Answer Any time you use system calls specific to one operating system and do not create alternative calls for another operating system, your program will not function correctly. *Solaris systems and Intel systems* order the bits of an integer differently. (You may have heard of little endian vs. big endian) If your code uses bit shifting, or other binary operators, they will not work on systems that have opposite endianism.

Question *What is the difference between an Applet and an Application?*
Answer

1. Applets can be embedded in HTML pages and downloaded over the Internet whereas Applications have no special support in HTML for embedding or downloading.

2. Applets can only be executed inside a java compatible container, such as a browser or appletviewer whereas Applications are executed at command line by java.exe or jview.exe.

3. Applets execute under strict security limitations that disallow certain operations(sandbox model security) whereas Applications have no inherent security restrictions.

4. Applets don't have the main() method as in applications. Instead they operate on an entirely different mechanism where they are initialized by init(),started by start(),stopped by stop() or destroyed by destroy().

Question How can you force all derived classes to implement a method present in the base class?

Answer Creating and implementing an interface would be the best way for this situation. Just create an interface with empty methods which forces a programmer to implement all the methods present under it. Another way of achieving this task is to declare a class as abstract with all its methods abstract.

Question What are abstract classes, abstract methods?

Answer Simply speaking a class or a method qualified with "abstract" keyword is an abstract class or abstract method. You create an abstract class when you want to manipulate a set of classes through a common interface. All derived-class methods that match the signature of the base-class declaration will be called using the dynamic binding mechanism. An abstract method is an incomplete method. It has only a declaration and no method body. Here is the syntax for an abstract method declaration: abstract void f();

Question What's the difference between == and equals method?

Answer The equals method can be considered to perform a deep comparison of the value of an object, whereas the == operator performs a shallow comparison. The equals() method compares the characters inside a string object. == operator compares two object references to check whether they refer to the same instances or not.

Question Describe, in general, how java's garbage collector works?

Answer The Java runtime environment deletes objects when it determines that they are no longer being used.

This process is known as garbage collection. The Java runtime environment supports a garbage collector that periodically frees the memory used by objects that are no longer needed.

The Java garbage collector is a mark-sweep garbage collector that scans Java's dynamic memory areas for objects, marking those that are referenced. After all possible paths to objects are investigated, those objects that are not marked (i.e. are not referenced) are known to be garbage and are collected.

Question What is the difference between StringBuffer and String class?

Answer A string buffer implements a mutable sequence of characters. A string buffer is like a String, but can be modified. At any point in time it contains some particular sequence of characters, but the length and content of the sequence can be changed through certain method calls. The String class represents character strings. All string literals in Java programs, such as "abc" are constant and implemented as instances of this class; their values cannot be changed after they are created.

Question How can you achieve Multiple Inheritance in Java?

Answer Java's interface mechanism can be used to implement multiple inheritance, with one important difference from c++ way of doing MI: the inherited interfaces must be abstract. This obviates the need to choose between different implementations, as with interfaces there are no implementations.

Question What are interfaces?

Answer Interfaces provide more sophisticated ways to organize and control the objects in your system. The interface keyword takes the abstract concept one step further. You could think of it as a "pure" abstract class. It allows the creator to establish the form for a class: method names, argument lists, and return types, but no method bodies.

An interface can also contain fields, but The interface keyword takes the abstract concept one step further. You could think of it as a "pure" abstract class. It allows the creator to establish the form for a class: method names, argument lists, and return types, but no method bodies. An interface can also contain fields, but An interface says: "This is what all classes that implement this particular interface will look like." Thus, any code that uses a particular interface knows what methods might be called for that interface, and that's all. So the interface is used to establish a "protocol" between classes.

Question *How to make application thread-safe ?*

Answer You should use the word synchronized to mark the critical section of code. You may also use other methods of thread synchronization (see wait(), notify(), notifyAll() etc.

Question *What do you know about networking support in Java ?*

Answer Java supports "low-level" and "high-level" classes. "Low-level" classes provide support for socket programming: Socket, DatagramSocket, and ServerSocket classes. "High-level" classes provide "Web programming": URL, URLEncoder, and URLConnection classes.

Networking programming classes ease the programming of network applications, but do not substitute your knowledge of networking. Java networking like anything else in Java is platform-independent.

Question *What are the problems faced by Java programmers who don't use layout managers?*

Answer Without layout managers, Java programmers are faced with determining how their GUI will be displayed across multiple windowing systems and finding a common sizing and positioning that will work within the constraints imposed by each windowing system.

Question *What are the two basic ways in which classes that can be run as threads may be defined?*

Answer A thread class may be declared as a subclass of Thread, or it may implement the Runnable interface.

Question *What is the purpose of a statement block?*

Answer A statement block is used to organize a sequence of statements as a single statement group.

Question *What is the purpose of garbage collection?*

Answer The purpose of garbage collection is to identify and discard objects that are no longer needed by a program so that their resources may be *reclaimed and reused.*

Question *How are this and super used?*

Answer This is used to refer to the current object instance. super is used to refer to the variables and methods of the superclass of the current object instance.

Question What an I/O filter?

Answer An I/O filter is an object that reads from one stream and writes to another, usually altering the data in some way as it is passed from one stream to another.

Question *How are the elements of a GridLayout organized?*

Answer The elements of a GridBad layout are of equal size and are laid out using the squares of a grid.

Question *How are this() and super() used with constructors?*

Answer this() is used to invoke a constructor of the same class. super() is used to invoke a superclass constructor.

Question *How can the Checkbox class be used to create a radio button?*
Answer By associating Checkbox objects with a CheckboxGroup

Question *If a method is declared as protected, where may the method be accessed?*

Answer A protected method may only be accessed by classes or interfaces of the same package or by subclasses of the class in which it is declared.

Question *When does the compiler supply a default constructor for a class?*

Answer The compiler supplies a default constructor for a class if no other constructors are provided.

Question *What is the highest-level event class of the event-delegation model?*

Answer The java.util.EventObject class is the highest-level class in the event-delegation class hierarchy.

Question *What restrictions are placed on the values of each case of a switch statement?*

Answer During compilation, the values of each case of a switch statement must evaluate to a value that can be promoted to an int value.

Question *How are the elements of a CardLayout organized?*

Answer The elements of a CardLayout are stacked, one on top of the other, like a deck of cards.

Question *For which statements does it make sense to use a label?*

Answer The only statements for which it makes sense to use a label are those statements that can enclose a break or continue statement.

Question *How is rounding performed under integer division?*

Answer The fractional part of the result is truncated. This is known as rounding toward zero.

Question *Can an object be garbage collected while it is still reachable?*

Answer A reachable object cannot be garbage collected. Only unreachable objects may be garbage collected.

Question *What is the difference between a Window and a Frame?*

Answer The Frame class extends Window to define a main application window that can have a menu bar.

Question *When can an object reference be cast to an interface reference?*

Answer An object reference be cast to an interface reference when the object implements the referenced interface.

Question *What is the Dictionary class?*

Answer The Dictionary class provides the capability to store key-value pairs.

Question *What are the high-level thread states?*

Answer The high-level thread states are ready, running, waiting, and dead.

Question *What is the argument type of a program's main() method?*

Answer A program's main() method takes an argument of the String[] type.

Question *What invokes a thread's run() method?*

Answer After a thread is started, via its start() method or that of the Thread class, the JVM invokes the thread's run() method when the thread is initially executed.

Question *What are order of precedence and associativity, and how are they used?*

Answer Order of precedence determines the order in which operators are evaluated in expressions. Associatity determines whether an expression is evaluated left-to-right or right-to-left

Question *What is clipping?*

Answer Clipping is the process of confining paint operations to a limited area or shape. Which characters may be used as the second character of an identifier, but not as the first The digits 0 through 9 may not be used as the first character of an identifier but they may be used after the first character of an identifier

Question *What is CTS (Common Type System)?*

Answer It defines about how Objects should be declard, defined and used within .NET. CLS is the subset of CTS.

Question *What is a policy?.*

Answer It's an abstract class for representing the system security policy for a Java application environment(specifying which permissions are available for code from various sources). Java security properties file resides in /lib/security/java.security directory. Value of "policy.provider" should be changed.

Question *What are the restrictions imposed by a Security Manager on Applets?.*
Answer

i) Cannot read or write files on the host that's executing it.
ii) Cannot load libraries or define native methods.
iii) Cannot make network connections except to the host that it came from
iv) Cannot start any program on the host that's executing it.
v) Cannot read certain system properties.
vi) Windows that an applet brings up look different than windows that an application brings up.

Question *Scope and lifetime of variables ?*
Answer Scope of variables is only to that particular blocklifetime will be till the block ends.variables declared above the block within the class are valid to that inner block also.

Question *What is Object class and java.lang ?*

Answer Object class is the superclass of all the classes and means that reference variable of type object can refer to an object of any other class. and also defines methods like finalise,wait.java.lang contains all the basic language functions and is imported in all the programs implicitly.

Question *What are packages and why? how 2 execute a program in a package ?*

Answer Package is a set of classes, which can be accessed by themselves and cannot be accessed outside the package. and can be defined as package .Package name and the directory name must be the same.And the execution of programs in package is done by : java mypack.account where mypack is directory name and account is program name.

Question *What is a StringTokenizer ?*

Answer String Tokenizer provide parsing process in which it identifies the delimiters provided by the user , by default delimiters are spaces, tab, newline etc. and separates them from the tokens. Tokens are those which are separated by delimiters.

Question *What are nested classes ?*

Answer There are two types- static and non-static. static class means the members in its enclosing class (class within class) can be accessed by creating an object and cannot be accessed directly without creating the object. non-static class means inner class and can be accessed directly with the object created for the outer class no need to create again an object like static class.

Question *What are methods and how are they defined?*

Answer Methods are functions that operate on instances of classes in which they are defined. Objects can communicate with each other using methods and can call methods in other classes.Method definition has four parts.
They are name of the method, type of object or primitive type the method returns, a list of parameters and the body of the method. A method's signature is a combination of the first three parts mentioned above.

Question *What is Garbage Collection and how to call it explicitly?*

Answer When an object is no longer referred to by any variable, java automatically reclaims memory used by that object. This is known as garbage collection.System.gc() method may be used to call it explicitly.

Question *What is interface and its use?*

Answer Interface is similar to a class which may contain method's signature only but not bodies and it is a formal set of method and constant declarations that must be defined by the class that implements it. Interfaces are useful for:

Declaring methods that one or more classes are expected to implement Capturing similarities between unrelated classes without forcing a class relationship. Determining an object's programming interface without revealing the actual body of the class.

Question *What is the difference between abstract class and interface?*
Answer

a) All the methods declared inside an interface are abstract whereas abstract class must have at least one abstract method and others may be concrete or abstract.

b) In abstract class, key word abstract must be used for the methodsWhereas interface we need not use that keyword for the methods. c)Abstract class must have subclasses whereas interface can't have subclasses.

Question *What is the difference between exception and error?*

Answer The exception class defines mild error conditions that your program encounters.

Ex: Arithmetic Exception, FilenotFound exception Exceptions can occur when try to open the file, which does not exist,the network connection is disrup,operands being manipulated are out of prescribed range,the class file you are interested in loading is missing The error class defines serious error conditions that you should not attempt to recover from. In most cases it is advisable to let the program terminate when such an error is encountered.Ex: Running out of memory error, Stack overflow error.

Question *What is the difference between applications and applets?*
Answer

a) Application must be run on local machine whereas applet needs no explicit installation on local machine.

b) Application must be run explicitly within a java-compatible virtual machine whereas applet loads and runs itself automatically in a java-enabled browser.

c) Application starts execution with its main method whereas applet starts execution with its init method.

d) Application can run with or without graphical user interface whereas applet must run within a graphical user interface.

Question *What is an event and what are the models available for event handling?*

Answer An event is an event object that describes a state of change in a source. In other words, event occurs when an action is generated, like pressing button, clicking mouse, selecting a list, etc. There are two types of models for handling events and they are: a) event-inheritance model and b) event-delegation model

Question *What is adapter class?*
Answer An adapter class provides an empty implementation of all methods in an event listener interface. Adapter classes are useful when you want to receive and process only some of the events that are handled by a particular event listener interface. You can define a new class to act listener by extending one of the adapter classes and implementing only those events in which you are interested.

Question *What is meant by controls and what are different types of controls in AWT?*

Answer Controls are components that allow a user to interact with your application and the AWT supports the following types of controls:Labels, Push Buttons, Check Boxes, Choice Lists, Lists, Scrollbars, Text Components. These controls are subclasses of Component.

Question *What is the difference between choice and list?*

Answer A Choice is displayed in a compact form that requires you to pull it down to see the list of available choices and only one item may be selected from a choice.A List may be displayed in such a way that several list items are visible and it supports the selection of one or more list items.

Question *What is a Java package and how is it used?*
Answer A Java package is a naming context for classes and interfaces. A package is used to create a separate name space for groups of classes and interfaces. Packages are also used to organize related classes and interfaces into a single API unit and to control accessibility to these classes and interfaces.

Question *What is the difference between the prefix and postfix forms of the ++ operator?*

Answer The prefix form performs the increment operation and returns the value of the increment operation. The postfix form returns the current value all of the expression and then performs the increment operation on that value.

Question *What is numeric promotion?*

Answer Numeric promotion is the conversion of a smaller numeric type to a larger numeric type, so that integer and floating-point operations may take place. In numerical promotion, byte, char, and short values are converted to int values. The int values are also converted to long values, if necessary. The long and float values are converted to double values, as required.

Question *What are three ways in which a thread can enter the waiting state?*

Answer A thread can enter the waiting state by invoking its sleep() method, by blocking on I/O, by unsuccessfully attempting to acquire an object's lock, or by invoking an object's wait() method. It can also enter the waiting state by invoking its (deprecated) suspend() method.

Question *What happens if an exception is not caught?*

Answer An uncaught exception results in the uncaughtException() method of the thread's ThreadGroup being invoked, which eventually results in the termination of the program in which it is thrown.

Question *What restrictions are placed on method overriding?*

Answer Overridden methods must have the same name, argument list, and return type. The overriding method may not limit the access of the method it overrides. The overriding method may not throw any exceptions that may not be thrown by the overridden method.

Question *What is your platform's default character encoding?*

Answer If you are running Java on English Windows platforms, it is probably Cp1252. If you are running Java on English Solaris platforms, it is most likely 8859_1..

Question *What is the difference between the File and RandomAccessFile classes?*

Answer The File class encapsulates the files and directories of the local file system. The RandomAccessFile class provides the methods needed to directly access data contained in any part of a file.

Question *What is the purpose of the enableEvents() method?*

Answer The enableEvents() method is used to enable an event for a particular object. Normally, an event is enabled when a listener is added to an object for a particular event. The enableEvents() method is used by objects that handle events by overriding their event-dispatch methods.

Question *What is the difference between the JDK 1.02 event model and the event-delegation*

Answer The JDK 1.02 event model uses an event inheritance or bubbling approach. In this model, components are required to handle their own events. If they do not handle a particular event, the event is inherited by (or bubbled up to) the component's container. The container then either handles the event or it is bubbled up to its container and so on, until the highest-level container has been tried. In the event-delegation model, specific objects are designated as event handlers for GUI components. These objects implement event-listener interfaces. The event-delegation model is more efficient than the event-inheritance model because it eliminates the processing required to support the bubbling of unhandled events.

Question *What is the difference between a Choice and a List?*

Answer A Choice is displayed in a compact form that requires you to pull it down to see the list of available choices. Only one item may be selected from a Choice. A List may be displayed in such a way that several List items are visible. A List supports the selection of one or more List items.

Question *What is casting?*

Answer There are two types of casting, casting between primitive numeric types and casting between object references. Casting between numeric types is used to convert larger values, such as double values, to smaller values, such as byte values. Casting between object references is used to refer to an object by a compatible class, interface, or array type reference.

Question *When is the finally clause of a try-catch-finally statement executed?*

Answer The finally clause of the try-catch-finally statement is always executed unless the thread of execution terminates or an exception occurs within the execution of the finally clause.

Question *How does multithreading take place on a computer with a single CPU?*

Answer The operating system's task scheduler allocates execution time to multiple tasks. By quickly switching between executing tasks, it creates the impression that tasks execute sequentially.

Question *What is the difference between static and non-static variables?*

Answer A static variable is associated with the class as a whole rather than with specific instances of a class. Non-static variables take on unique values with each object instance.

Question *What advantage do Java's layout managers provide over traditional windowing systems?*

Answer Java uses layout managers to lay out components in a consistent manner across all windowing platforms. Since Java's layout managers aren't tied to absolute sizing and positioning, they are able to accomodate platform-specific differences among windowing systems.

Question *How are the elements of a GridBagLayout organized?*

Answer The elements of a GridBagLayout are organized according to a grid. However, the elements are of different sizes and may occupy more than one row or column of the grid. In addition, the rows and columns may have different sizes.

Question *What is the difference between a while statement and a do statement?*

Answer A while statement checks at the beginning of a loop to see whether the next loop iteration should occur. A do statement checks at the end of a loop to see whether the next iteration of a loop should occur. The do statement will always execute the body of a loop at least once.

Question *What is the relationship between an event-listener interface and an event adapter ?*

Answer An event-listener interface defines the methods that must be implemented by an event handler for a particular kind of event. An event adapter provides a default implementation of an event-listener interface.

Question *If a class is declared without any access modifiers, where may the class be accessed?*

Answer A class that is declared without any access modifiers is said to have package access. This means that the class can only be accessed by other classes and interfaces that are defined within the same package.

Question *What classes of exceptions may be caught by a catch clause?*

Answer A catch clause can catch any exception that may be assigned to the Throwable type. This includes the Error and Exception types.

Question *What happens when a thread cannot acquire a lock on an object?*

Answer If a thread attempts to execute a synchronized method or synchronized statement and is unable to acquire an object's lock, it enters the waiting state until the lock becomes available.

Question *What is the difference between the Font and FontMetrics classes?*

Answer The FontMetrics class is used to define implementation-specific properties, such as ascent and descent, of a Font object.

Question *What is the difference between a Window and a Frame?*

Answer The Frame class extends Window to define a main application window that can have a menu bar.

Question *What is the % operator?*

Answer It is referred to as the modulo or remainder operator. It returns the remainder of dividing the first operand by the second operand.

Question *What is an object's lock and which object's have locks?*
Answer An object's lock is a mechanism that is used by multiple threads to obtain synchronized access to the object. A thread may execute a synchronized method of an object only after it has acquired the object's lock. All objects and classes have locks. A class's lock is acquired on the class's Class object.

Question *What is the difference between a static and a non-static inner class?*

Answer A non-static inner class may have object instances that are associated with instances of the class's outer class. A static inner class does not have any object instances.

Question *How are Java source code files named?*

Answer A Java source code file takes the name of a public class or interface that is defined within the file. A source code file may contain at most one public class or interface.

If a public class or interface is defined within a source code file, then the source code file must take the name of the public class or interface. If no public class or interface is defined within a source code file, then the file must take on a name that is different than its classes and interfaces. Source code files use the .java extension.

Question *What is the purpose of the wait(), notify(), and notifyAll() methods?*

Answer The wait(),notify(), and notifyAll() methods are used to provide an efficient way for threads to wait for a shared resource. When a thread executes an object's wait() method, it enters the waiting state. It only enters the ready state after another thread invokes the object's notify() or notifyAll() methods..

Question *What is the advantage of the event-delegation model over the earlier event-inheritance model?*

Answer The event-delegation model has two advantages over the event-inheritance model. First, it enables event handling to be handled by objects other than the ones that generate the events (or their containers). This allows a clean separation between a component's design and its use. The other advantage of the event-delegation model is that it performs much better in applications where many events are generated. This performance improvement is due to the fact that the event-delegation model does not have to repeatedly process unhandled events, as is the case of the event-inheritance model.

Question *What must a class do to implement an interface?*

Answer It must provide all of the methods in the interface and identify the interface in its implements clause.

Question *What is the difference between a break statement and a continue statement?*

Answer A break statement results in the termination of the statement to which it applies (switch, for, do, or while). A continue statement is used to end the current loop iteration and return control to the loop statement.

Question *What is the Locale class?*

Answer The Locale class is used to tailor program output to the conventions of a particular geographic, political, or cultural region.

Question *What is the purpose of the finally clause of a try-catch-finally statement?*

Answer The finally clause is used to provide the capability to execute code no matter whether or not an exception is thrown or caught.

Question *What is the purpose of the Runtime class?*

Answer The purpose of the Runtime class is to provide access to the Java runtime system.

Question *What is the difference between the Boolean & operator and the && operator?*

Answer If an expression involving the Boolean & operator is evaluated, both operands are evaluated. Then the & operator is applied to the operand. When an expression involving the && operator is evaluated, the first operand is evaluated. If the first operand returns a value of true then the second operand is evaluated.

The && operator is then applied to the first and second operands. If the first operand evaluates to false, the evaluation of the second operand is skipped.

Question *What is the purpose of finalization?*

Answer The purpose of finalization is to give an unreachable object the opportunity to perform any cleanup processing before the object is garbage collected.

Question *In which package are most of the AWT events that support the event-delegation?*

Answer Most of the AWT-related events of the event-delegation model are defined in the java.awt.event package. The AWTEvent class is defined in the java.awt package.

Question *Can an anonymous class be declared as implementing an interface and extending a class?*

Answer An anonymous class may implement an interface or extend a superclass, but may not be declared to do both.

Question *What class is the top of the AWT event hierarchy?*

The java.awt.AWTEvent class is the highest-level class in the AWT event-class hierarchy.

Question *What is a task's priority and how is it used in scheduling?*

Answer A task's priority is an integer value that identifies the relative order in which it should be executed with respect to other tasks. The scheduler attempts to schedule higher priority tasks before lower priority tasks.

Question *What is the catch or declare rule for method declarations?*

Answer If a checked exception may be thrown within the body of a method, the method must either catch the exception or declare it in its throws clause.

Question *What are order of precedence and associativity, and how are they used?*

Answer Order of precedence determines the order in which operators are evaluated in expressions. Associatity determines whether an expression is evaluated left-to-right or right-to-left.

Question *What is the difference between preemptive scheduling and time slicing?*

Answer Under preemptive scheduling, the highest priority task executes until it enters the waiting or dead states or a higher priority task comes into existence. Under time slicing, a task executes for a predefined slice of time and then reenters the pool of ready tasks. The scheduler then determines which task should execute next, based on priority and other factors.

Question *Does garbage collection guarantee that a program will not run out of memory?*

Answer Garbage collection does not guarantee that a program will not run out of memory. It is possible for programs to use up memory resources faster than they are garbage collected. It is also possible for programs to create objects that are not subject to garbage collection.

Question *Which java.util classes and interfaces support event handling?*

Answer The EventObject class and the EventListener interface support event processing.

Question *What is the difference between yielding and sleeping?*

Answer When a task invokes its yield() method, it returns to the ready state. When a task invokes its sleep() method, it returns to the waiting state.

Question *How many bits are used to represent Unicode, ASCII, UTF-16, and UTF-8 characters?*

Answer Unicode requires 16 bits and ASCII require 7 bits. Although the ASCII character set uses only 7 bits, it is usually represented as 8 bits. UTF-8 represents characters using 8, 16, and 18 bit patterns. UTF-16 uses 16-bit and larger bit patterns.

Question *What is the Vector class?*

Answer The Vector class provides the capability to implement a growable array of objects.

Question *What is the List interface?*

Answer The List interface provides support for ordered collections of objects.

Question *What is the Collections API?*

Answer The Collections API is a set of classes and interfaces that support operations on collections of objects.

Question *What is the preferred size of a component?*

Answer The preferred size of a component is the minimum component size that will allow the component to display normally.

Question *Can a lock be acquired on a class?*

Answer Yes, a lock can be acquired on a class. This lock is acquired on the class's Class object..

Question *What is synchronization and why is it important?*

Answer With respect to multithreading, synchronization is the capability to control the access of multiple threads to shared resources. Without synchronization, it is possible for one thread to modify a shared object while another thread is in the process of using or updating that object's value. This often leads to significant errors.

Question *How are Observer and Observable used?*

Answer Objects that subclass the Observable class maintain a list of observers. When an Observable object is updated it invokes the update() method of each of its observers to notify the observers that it has changed state. The Observer interface is implemented by objects that observe Observable objects.

Question *what is a transient variable?*

Answer A transient variable is a variable that may not be serialized.

PART - II

350+ JAVA
INTERVIEW
QUES & ANS

Advise Drill – If you thinking that you are weak in Java Programming Then Try this Java book *"Core Java Professional"* Authored By Harry. H. Chaudhary.

Purchase Only Paperback Edition from Amazon, Digital PDF Edition (7.99 USD) from Google Books & Google Play. (800-1000 Pages Deep Core Java)

Question *Can there be an abstract class with no abstract methods in it?*

Answer: Yes

Question *Can an Interface be final? (Core Java)*

Answer: No

Question *Can an Interface have an inner class? (Core Java)*

Answer: Yes.

```
public interface abc {
static int i=0;
void dd();
class a1 {
a1() {
int j;
System.out.println("in interfia"); };
public static void main(String a1[]) {
System.out.println("in interfia"); } } }
```

Question *Can we define private and protected modifiers for variables in interfaces? (Core Java)*

Answer No.

Question *What is the query used to display all tables names in SQL Server (Query analyzer)? (JDBC)*

Answer select * from information_schema.tables

Question *What is Externalizable? (Core Java)*

Answer Externalizable is an Interface that extends Serializable Interface. And sends data into Streams in Compressed Format. It has two methods, writeExternal(ObjectOuput out) and readExternal(ObjectInput in)

Question *What modifiers are allowed for methods in an Interface?*

Answer Only public and abstract modifiers are allowed for methods in interfaces.

Question *What is a local, member and a class variable? (Core Java)*

Answer Variables declared within a method are "local" variables. Variables declared within the class i.e not within any methods are "member" variables (global variables). Variables declared within the class i.e not within any methods and are defined as "static" are class variables.

Question *How many types of JDBC Drivers are present and what are they?*

Answer There are 4 types of JDBC Drivers

Type 1: JDBC-ODBC Bridge Driver.

Type 2: Native API Partly Java Driver.

Type 3: Network protocol Driver.

Type 4: JDBC Net pure Java Driver.

Question *Can we implement an interface in a JSP? (JSP)*

Answer *No*

Question *What is the difference between ServletContext and PageContext?*

Answer ServletContext: Gives the information about the container PageContext: Gives the information about the Request

Question *What is the difference in using request.getRequestDispatcher() and context.getRequestDispatcher()? (JSP)*

Answer request.getRequestDispatcher(path): In order to create it we need to give the relative path of the resource context.getRequestDispatcher(path): In order to create it we need to give the absolute path of the resource.

Question *How to pass information from JSP to included JSP? (JSP)*

Answer Using <%jsp:param> tag.

Question *What is the difference between directive include and jsp include?*

Answer <%@ include> : Used to include static resources during translation time. : Used to include dynamic content or static content during runtime.

Question *What is the difference between RequestDispatcher and sendRedirect?*

Answer RequestDispatcher: server-side redirect with request and response objects. sendRedirect : Client-side redirect with new request and response objects.

Question *How does JSP handle runtime exceptions? (JSP)*

Answer Using errorPage attribute of page directive and also we need to specify isErrorPage=true if the current page is intended to URL redirecting of a JSP.

Question *How do you delete a Cookie within a JSP? (JSP)*

Answer

Cookie mycook = new Cookie("name","value");

response.addCookie(mycook);

Cookie killmycook = new Cookie("mycook","value");

killmycook.setMaxAge(0);

killmycook.setPath("/");

killmycook.addCookie(killmycook);

Question *How do I mix JSP and SSI #include? (JSP)*

Answer If you're just including raw HTML, use the #include directive as usual inside your .jsp file.

<!--#include file="data.inc"-->

But it's a little trickier if you want the server to evaluate any JSP code that's inside the included file. Ronel Sumibcay

(ronel@LIVESOFTWARE.COM) says: If your data.inc file contains jsp code you will have to use -

<%@ vinclude="data.inc" %>

The <!--#include file="data.inc"--> is used for including non-JSP files.

Question *I made my class Cloneable but I still get 'Can't access protected method clone. Why? (Core Java)*

Answer Yeah, some of the Java books, in particular "The Java Programming Language", imply that all you have to do in order to have your class support clone() is implement the Cloneable interface.

Note: Not so. Perhaps that was the intent at some point, but that's not the way it works currently. As it stands, you have to implement your own public clone() method, even if it doesn't do anything special and just calls super.clone().

Question *why is XML such an important development? (XML)*

Answer It removes two constraints which were holding back Web developments:

1. Dependence on a single, inflexible document type (HTML) which Was being much abused for tasks it was never designed for;

2. The complexity of full SGML, whose syntax allows many powerful

But hard-to-program options. XML allows the flexible development of user-defined document types. It provides a robust, non-proprietary, persistent, and verifiable file format for the storage and transmission of text and data both on and off the Web; and it removes the more complex options of SGML, making it easier to program for.

Question *Are enterprise beans allowed to use Thread.sleep()? (EJB)*

Answer Enterprise beans make use of the services provided by the EJB container, such as life-cycle management. To avoid conflicts with these services, enterprise beans are restricted from performing certain operations: Managing or synchronizing threads

Question *Is it possible to write two EJB's that share the same Remote and Home interfaces, and have different bean classes? if so, what are the advantages/disadvantages? (EJB)*

Answer It's certainly possible. In fact, there's an example that ships with the Inprise Application Server of an Account interface with separate implementations for CheckingAccount and SavingsAccount, one of which was CMP and one of which was BMP.

Question *Is it possible to specify multiple JNDI names when deploying an EJB?*

Answer No. To achieve this you have to deploy your EJB multiple times each specifying a different JNDI name.

Question *Is there any way to force an Entity Bean to store itself to the db? I don't wanna wait for the container to update the db, I want to do it NOW! Is it possible? (EJB)*

Answer Specify the transaction attribute of the bean as RequiresNew. Then as per section 11.6.2.4 of the EJB v 1.1 spec EJB container automatically starts a new transaction before the method call. The container also performs the commit protocol before the method result is sent to the client.

Question *I am developing a BMP Entity bean. I have noticed that whenever the create method is invoked, the ejbLoad() and the ejbStore() methods are also invoked. I feel that once my database insert is done, having to do a select and update SQL queries is major overhead. is this behavior typical of all EJB containers? Is there any way to suppress these invocations? (EJB)*

Answer This is the default behaviour for EJB. The specification states that ejbLoad() will be called before every transaction and ejbStore() after every transaction. Each Vendor has optimizations, which are proprietary for this scenario.

Question Can an EJB send asynchronous notifications to its clients? (EJB)

Answer Asynchronous notification is a known hole in the first versions of the EJB spec. The recommended solution to this is to use JMS, which is becoming available in J2EE-compliant servers. The other option, of course, is to use client-side threads and polling. This is not an ideal solution, but it's workable for many scenarios.

Question How can I access EJB from ASP? (EJB)

Answer You can use the Java 2 Platform, Enterprise Edition Client Access Services (J2EETM CAS) COM Bridge 1.0, currently downloadable from

http://developer.java.sun.com/developer/earlyAccess/j2eecas/

Question Is there a guarantee of uniqueness for entity beans? (EJB)

Answer There is no such guarantee. The server (or servers) can instantiate as many instances of the same underlying Entity Bean (with the same PK) as it wants. However, each instance is guaranteed to have up-to-date data values, and be transactionally consistent, so uniqueness is not required. This allows the server to scale the system to support multiple threads, multiple concurrent requests, and multiple hosts.

Question How do the six transaction attributes map to isolation levels like "dirty read"? Will an attribute like "Required" lock out other readers until I'm finished updating? (EJB)

Answer The Transaction Attributes in EJB do not map to the Transaction Isolation levels used in JDBC. This is a common misconception. Transaction Attributes specify to the container when a Transaction should be started, suspended(paused) and committed between method invocations on Enterprise JavaBeans. For more details and a summary of Transaction Attributes refer to section 11.6 of the EJB 1.1 specification.

Question I have created a remote reference to an EJB in FirstServlet. Can I put the reference in a servlet session and use that in SecondServlet? (EJB)

Answer Yes. The EJB client (in this case your servlet) acquires a remote reference to an EJB from the Home Interface; that reference is serializable and can be passed from servlet to servlet. If it is a session bean, then the EJB server will consider your web client's servlet session to correspond to a single EJB session, which is usually (but not always) what you want.

Question *Can the primary key in the entity bean be a Java primitive type such as int? (EJB)*

Answer The primary key can't be a primitive type--use the primitive wrapper classes, instead. For example, you can use java.lang.Integer as the primary key *class, but not int (it has to be a class, not a primitive)*

Question *What's new in the EJB 2.0 specification? (EJB)*

Answer Following are the main features supported in EJB 2.0 * Integration of EJB with JMS * Message Driven Beans * Implement additional Business methods in Home interface which are not specific for bean instance. * EJB QL.

Question *How many types of protocol implementations does RMI have? (RMI)*

Answer RMI has at least three protocol implementations: Java Remote Method Protocol(JRMP), Internet Inter ORB Protocol(IIOP), and Jini Extensible Remote Invocation(JERI).

These are alternatives, not part of the same thing, All three are indeed layer 6 protocols for those who are still speaking OSI reference model.

Question *What are the different identifier states of a Thread? (Core Java)*

Answer The different identifiers of a Thread are:

R - Running or runnable thread.

S - Suspended thread.

CW - Thread waiting on a condition variable.

MW - Thread waiting on a monitor lock.

MS - Thread suspended waiting on a monitor lock.

Question *What is the need of Remote and Home interface. Why cant it be in one? (EJB)*

Answer

In a few words, I would say that the main reason is because there is a clear division of roles and responsibilities between the two interfaces. The home interface is your way to communicate with the container, that is who is responsible of creating, locating even removing one or more beans.

The remote interface is your link to the bean, that will allow you to remotely access to all its methods and members. As you can see there are two distinct elements (the container and the beans) and you need two different interfaces for accessing to both of them.

Question *What is the difference between Java Beans and EJB?s? (EJB)*

Answer Java Beans are client-side objects and EJBs are server side object, and they have completely different development, lifecycle, purpose.

Question *QuestionWith regard to Entity Beans, what happens if both my EJB Server and Database crash, what will happen to unsaved changes? Is there any transactional log file used? (EJB)*

Answer Actually, if your EJB server crashes, you will not even be able to make a connection to the server to perform a bean lookup, as the server will no longer be listening on the port for incoming JNDI lookup requests. You will lose any data that wasn't committed prior to the crash. This is where you should start looking into clustering your EJB server.

Another Answer -

Any unsaved and uncommitted changes are lost the moment your EJB Server crashes. If your database also crashes, then all the saved changes are also lost unless you have some backup or some recovery mechanism to retrieve the data. So consider database replication and EJB Clustering for such scenarios, though the occurrence of such a thing is very very rare. All database have the concept of log files(for example oracle have redo log files concept). So if data bases crashes then on starting up they fill look up the log files to perform all pending jobs. But is EJB crashes, It depend upon the container how frequently it passivates or how frequently it refreshes the data with Database.

Question *Can you control when passivation occurs? (EJB)*

Answer The developer, according to the specification, cannot directly control when passivation occurs. Although for Stateful Session Beans, the container cannot passivate an instance that is inside a transaction. So using transactions can be a a strategy to control passivation. The ejbPassivate() method is called during passivation, so the developer has control over what to do during this exercise and can implement the require optimized logic. Some EJB containers, such as BEA WebLogic, provide the ability to tune the container to minimize passivation calls. Taken from the WebLogic 6.0 DTD -

"The passivation-strategy can be either "default" or "transaction". With the default setting the container will attempt to keep a working set of beans in the cache. With the "transaction" setting, the container will passivate the bean after every transaction (or method call for a non-transactional invocation)."

Question *Does RMI-IIOP support dynamic downloading of classes? (RMI)*

Answer No, RMI-IIOP doesn't support dynamic downloading of the classes as it is done with CORBA in DII (Dynamic Interface Invocation).Actually RMI-IIOP combines the usability of Java Remote Method Invocation (RMI)with the interoperability of the Internet InterORB Protocol (IIOP).So in order to attain this interoperability between RMI and CORBA,some of the features that are supported by RMI but not CORBA and vice versa are eliminated from the RMI-IIOP specification.

Question *Does EJB 1.1 support mandate the support for RMI-IIOP ? What is the meaning of "the client API must support the Java RMI-IIOP programming model for portability, but the underlying protocol can be anything"? (EJB)*

Answer EJB1.1 does mandate the support of RMI-IIOP. OK, to Answer the second Question:

There are 2 types of implementations that an EJB Server might provide: CORBA-based EJB Servers and Proprietry EJB Servers. Both support the RMI-IIOP API but how that API is implemented is a different story. (NB: By API we mean the interface provided to the client by the stub or proxy). A CORBA-based EJB Server actually implements its EJB Objects as CORBA Objects (it therefore encorporates an ORB and this means that EJB's can be contacted by CORBA clients (as well as RMI-IIOP clients)

A proprietry EJB still implements the RMI-IIOP API (in the client's stub) but the underlying protocol can be anything. Therefore your EJB's CANNOT be contacted by CORBA clients. The difference is that in both cases, your clients see the same API (hence, your client portability) BUT how the stubs communicate with the server is different.

Question *The EJB specification says that we cannot use Bean Managed Transaction in Entity Beans. Why? (EJB)*

Answer The short, practical Answeris... because it makes your entity beans useless as a reusable component. Also, transaction management is best left to the application server - that's what they're there for. It's all about atomic operations on your data. If an operation updates more than one entity then you want the whole thing to succeed or the whole thing to fail, nothing in between. If you put commits in the entity beans then it's very difficult to rollback if an error occurs at some point late in the operation.

Question *Can I invoke Runtime.gc() in an EJB? (EJB)*

Answer You shouldn't. What will happen depends on the implementation, but the call will most likely be ignored. You should leave system level management like garbage collection for the container to deal with. After all, that's part of the benefit of using EJBs, you don't have to manage resources yourself.

Question *What is clustering? What are the different algorithms used for clustering? (EJB)*

Answer Clustering is grouping machines together to transparantly provide enterprise services.The client does not now the difference between approaching one server or approaching a cluster of servers.Clusters provide two benefits: scalability and high availability. Further information can be found in the JavaWorld article J2EE Clustering.

Question *What is the advantage of using Entity bean for database operations, over directly using JDBC API to do database operations? When would I use one over the other? (EJB)*

Answer Entity Beans actually represents the data in a database. It is not that Entity Beans replaces JDBC API. There are two types of Entity Beans Container Managed and Bean Mananged. In Container Managed Entity Bean - Whenever the instance of the bean is created the container automatically retrieves the data from the DB/Persistance storage and assigns to the object variables in bean for user to manipulate or use them.

For this the developer needs to map the fields in the database to the variables in deployment descriptor files (which varies for each vendor).

In the Bean Managed Entity Bean - The developer has to specifically make connection, retrive values, assign them to the objects in the ejbLoad() which will be called by the container when it instatiates a bean object. Similarly in the ejbStore() the container saves the object values back the the persistance storage.

ejbLoad and ejbStore are callback methods and can be only invoked by the container. Apart from this, when you use Entity beans you dont need to worry about database transaction handling, database connection pooling etc.

which are taken care by the ejb container. But in case of JDBC you have to explicitly do the above features. what suresh told is exactly perfect. ofcourse, this comes under the database transations, but i want to add this. the great thing about the entity beans of container managed, whenever the connection is failed during the transaction processing, the database consistancy is mantained automatically.

The container writes the data stored at persistant storage of the entity beans to the database again to provide the database consistancy. where as in jdbc api, we, developers has to do manually.

Question *What is the role of serialization in EJB? (EJB)*

Answer A big part of EJB is that it is a framework for underlying RMI: remote method invocation. You're invoking methods remotely from JVM space 'A' on objects which are in JVM space 'B' -- possibly running on another machine on the network.

To make this happen, all arguments of each method call must have their current state plucked out of JVM 'A' memory, flattened into a byte stream which can be sent over a TCP/IP network connection, and then deserialized for reincarnation on the other end in JVM 'B' where the actual method call takes place. If the method has a return value, it is serialized up for streaming back to JVM A. Thus the requirement that all EJB methods arguments and return values must be serializable. The easiest way to do this is to make sure all your classes implement java.io.Serializable.

Question *What is EJB QL? (EJB)*

Answer EJB QL is a Query Language provided for navigation across a network of enterprise beans and dependent objects defined by means of container managed persistence. EJB QL is introduced in the EJB 2.0 specification.

The EJB QL query language defines finder methods for entity beans with container managed persistenceand is portable across containers and persistence managers. EJB QL is used for queries of two types of finder methods: Finder methods that are defined in the home interface of an entity bean and which return entity objects. Select methods, which are not exposed to the client, but which are used by the Bean Provider to select persistent values that are maintained by the Persistence Manager or to select entity objects that are related to the entity bean on which the query is defined.

Question *What is the fastest type of JDBC driver? (JDBC)*

Answer JDBC driver performance will depend on a number of issues:

(a) The quality of the driver code,   **(b)** the size of the driver code,

(c) The database server and its load, **(d)** network topology,

(e) The number of times your request is translated to a different API. In general, all things being equal, you can assume that the more your request and response change hands, the slower it will be. This means that Type 1 and Type 3 drivers will be slower than Type 2 drivers (the database calls are make at least three translations versus two), and Type 4 drivers are the fastest (only one translation).

Question *Request parameter How to find whether a parameter exists in the request object? (Servlets)*

Answer

1.boolean hasFoo = !(request.getParameter("foo") ==

null || request.getParameter("foo").equals(""));

2. boolean hasParameter =

request.getParameterMap().contains(theParameter);

(which works in Servlet 2.3+)

Question *How can I send user authentication information while makingURLConnection? (Servlets)*

Answer You'll want to use HttpURLConnection.setRequestProperty and set all the appropriate headers to HTTP authorization.

Question *What are some alternatives to inheritance? (Core Java)*

Answer Delegation is an alternative to inheritance. Delegation means that you include an instance of another class as an instance variable, and forward messages to the instance.

It is often safer than inheritance because it forces you to think about each message you forward, because the instance is of a known class, rather than a new class, and because it doesn't force you to accept all the methods of the super class: you can provide only the methods that really make sense. On the other hand, it makes you write more code, and it is harder to re-use (because it is not a subclass).

Question *Why isn't there operator overloading? (Core Java)*

Answer Because C++ has proven by example that operator overloading makes code almost impossible to maintain. In fact there very nearly wasn't even method overloading in Java, but it was thought that this was too useful for some very basic methods like print(). Note that some of the classes like DataOutputStream have unoverloaded methods like writeInt() and writeByte().

Question *What does it mean that a method or field is "static"? (Core Java)*

Answer Static variables and methods are instantiated only once per class. In other words they are class variables, not instance variables. If you change the value of a static variable in a particular object, the value of that variable changes for all instances of that class. Static methods can be referenced with the name of the class rather than the name of a particular object of the class (though that works too). That's how library methods like System.out.println() work. out is a static field in the java.lang.System class.

Question *How do I convert a numeric IP address like 192.18.97.39 into a hostname like java.sun.com? (Networking)*

Answer String hostname = InetAddress.getByName("192.18.97.39").getHostName();

Question *Difference between JRE And JVM AND JDK (Core Java)*

Answer: Read Above in Introduction at Beginning of this chapter.

Question *Why do threads block on I/O? (Core Java)*

Answer Threads block on i/o (that is enters the waiting state) so that other threads may execute while the i/o Operation is performed.

Question *What is synchronization and why is it important? (Core Java)*

Answer With respect to multithreading, synchronization is the capability to control the access of multiple threads to shared resources. Without synchronization, it is possible for one thread to modify a shared object while another thread is in the process of using or updating that object's value. This often leads to significant errors.

Question *Is null a keyword? (Core Java)*

Answer The null value is not a keyword.

Question *Which characters may be used as the second character of an identifier,but not as the first character of an identifier? (Core Java)*

Answer The digits 0 through 9 may not be used as the first character of an identifier but they may be used after the first character of an identifier

Question *What modifiers may be used with an inner class that is a member of an outer class? (Core Java)*

Answer A (non-local) inner class may be declared as public, protected, private, static, final, or abstract.

Question *How many bits are used to represent Unicode, ASCII, UTF-16, and UTF-8 characters? (Core Java)*

Answer Unicode requires 16 bits and ASCII require 7 bits. Although the ASCII character set uses only 7 bits, it is usually represented as 8 bits. UTF-8 represents characters using 8, 16, and 18 bit patterns. UTF-16 uses 16-bit and larger bit patterns.

Question *What are wrapped classes? (Core Java)*

Answer Wrapped classes are classes that allow primitive types to be accessed as objects.

Question *What restrictions are placed on the location of a package statement within a source code file? (Core Java)*

Answer A package statement must appear as the first line in a source code file (excluding blank lines and comments).

Question *What is the difference between preemptive scheduling and time slicing? (Core Java)*

Answer Under preemptive scheduling, the highest priority task executes until it enters the waiting or dead states or a higher priority task comes into existence.

Under time slicing, a task executes for a predefined slice of time and then reenters the pool of ready tasks. The scheduler then determines which task should execute next, based on priority and other factors.

Question *What is a native method? (Core Java)*

Answer A native method is a method that is implemented in a language other than Java.

Question *What are order of precedence and associativity, & how are they used?*

Answer Order of precedence determines the order in which operators are evaluated in expressions. Associatity determines whether an expression is evaluated left-to-right or right-to-left Question What is the catch or declare rule for method declarations? (Core Java)Answer If a checked exception may be thrown within the body of a method, the method must either catch the exception or declare it in its throws clause.

Question *Can an anonymous class be declared as implementing an interface and extending a class? (Core Java)*

Answer An anonymous class may implement an interface or extend a superclass, but may not be declared to do both.

Question *What is the range of the char type? (Core Java)*

Answer The range of the char type is 0 to $2^{16} - 1$.

Question *What is the purpose of finalization? (Core Java)*

Answer The purpose of finalization is to give an unreachable object the opportunity to perform any cleanup processing before the object is garbage collected.

Question *What is the difference between the Boolean & operator and the && operator? (Core Java)*

Answer If an expression involving the Boolean & operator is evaluated, both operands are evaluated. Then the & operator is applied to the operand. When an expression involving the && operator is evaluated, the first operand is evaluated. If the first operand returns a value of true then the second operand is evaluated. The && operator is then applied to the first and second operands. If the first operand evaluates to false, the evaluation of the second operand is skipped.

Question *How many times may an object's finalize() method be invoked by the garbage collector? (Core Java)*

Answer An object's finalize() method may only be invoked once by the garbage collector.

Question *What is the purpose of the finally clause of a try-catchfinally statement? (Core Java)*

Answer The finally clause is used to provide the capability to execute code no matter whether or not an exception is thrown or caught.

Question *What is the argument type of a program's main() method? (Core)*

Answer A program's main() method takes an argument of the String[] type.

Question *Which Java operator is right associative? (Core Java)*

Answer The = operator is right associative.

Question *Can a double value be cast to a byte? (Core Java)*

Answer Yes, a double value can be cast to a byte.

Question *What is the difference between a break statement and a continue statement? (Core Java)*

Answer A break statement results in the termination of the statement to which it applies (switch, for, do, or while). A continue statement is used to end the current loop iteration and return control to the loop statement.

Question *What must a class do to implement an interface? (Core Java)*

Answer It must provide all of the methods in the interface and identify the interface in its implements clause.

Question *What is the advantage of the event-delegation model over the earlier event-inheritance model? (Core Java)*

Answer The event-delegation model has two advantages over the event-inheritance model. First, it enables event handling to be handled by objects other than the ones that generate the events (or their containers).

This allows a clean separation between a component's design and its use. The other advantage of the eventdelegation model is that it performs much better in applications where many events are generated.

This performance improvement is due to the fact that the event-delegation model does not have to repeatedly process unhandled events, as is the case of the event-inheritance model.

Question *How are commas used in the intialization and iteration parts of a for statement? (Core Java)*

Answer Commas are used to separate multiple statements within the initialization and iteration parts of a for statement.

Question *What is an abstract method? (Core Java)*

Answer An abstract method is a method whose implementation is deferred to a subclass.

Question *What value does read() return when it has reached the end of a file? (Core Java)*

Answer The read() method returns -1 when it has reached the end of a file.

Question *Can a Byte object be cast to a double value? (Core Java)*

Answer No, an object cannot be cast to a primitive value.

Question *What is the difference between a static and a non-static inner class? (Core Java)*

Answer A non-static inner class may have object instances that are associated with instances of the class's outer class. A static inner class does not have any object instances.

Question *If a variable is declared as private, where may the variable be accessed? (Core Java)*

Answer A private variable may only be accessed within the class in which it is declared.

Question *What is an object's lock and which object's have locks? (Core Java)*

Answer An object's lock is a mechanism that is used by multiple threads to obtain synchronized access to the object. A thread may execute a synchronized method of an object only after it has acquired the object's lock. All objects and classes have locks. A class's lock is acquired on the class's Class object.

Question *What is the % operator? (Core Java)*

Answer It is referred to as the modulo or remainder operator. It returns the remainder of dividing the first operand by the second operand.

Question *When can an object reference be cast to an interface reference?*

Answer An object reference be cast to an interface reference when the object implements the referenced interface.

Question *Which class is extended by all other classes? (Core Java)*

Answer The Object class is extended by all other classes.

Question *Can an object be garbage collected while it is still reachable?*

Answer A reachable object cannot be garbage collected. Only unreachable objects may be garbage collected.

Question *Is the ternary operator written x : y ? z or x ? y : z ? (Core Java)*

Answer It is written x ? y : z.

Question *How is rounding performed under integer division? (Core Java)*

Answer The fractional part of the result is truncated. This is known as rounding toward zero.

Question *What is the difference between the Reader/Writer class hierarchy and the InputStream/OutputStream class hierarchy? (Core Java)*

Answer The Reader/Writer class hierarchy is character-oriented, and the InputStream/OutputStream class hierarchy is byte-oriented.

Question What classes of exceptions may be caught by a catch clause?

Answer A catch clause can catch any exception that may be assigned to the Throwable type. This includes the Error and Exception types.

Question If a class is declared without any access modifiers, where may the class be accessed? (Core Java)

Answer A class that is declared without any access modifiers is said to have package access. This means that the class can only be accessed by other classes and interfaces that are defined within the same package.

Question Does a class inherit the constructors of its superclass? (Core Java)

Answer A class does not inherit constructors from any of its superclasses.

Question What is the purpose of the System class? (Core Java)

Answer The purpose of the System class is to provide access to system resources.

Question Name the eight primitive Java types. (Core Java)

Answer The eight primitive types are byte, char, short, int, long, float, double, and boolean.

Question Which class should you use to obtain design information about an object? (Core Java)

Answer The Class class is used to obtain information about an object's design.

Question Is "abc" a primitive value? (Core Java)

Answer The String literal "abc" is not a primitive value. It is a String object.

Question What restrictions are placed on the values of each case of a switch statement? (Core Java)

Answer During compilation, the values of each case of a switch statement must evaluate to a value that can be promoted to an int value.

Question What modifiers may be used with an interface declaration?

Answer An interface may be declared as public or abstract.

Question Is a class a subclass of itself? (Core Java)

Answer A class is a subclass of itself.

Question What is the difference between a while statement and a do statement?

Answer A while statement checks at the beginning of a loop to see whether the next loop iteration should occur.

A do statement checks at the end of a loop to see whether the next iteration of a loop should occur. The do statement will always execute the body of a loop at least once.

Question *What modifiers can be used with a local inner class? (Core Java)*

Answer A local inner class may be final or abstract.

Question *What is the purpose of the File class? (Core Java)*

Answer The File class is used to create objects that provide access to the files and directories of a local file system.

Question *Can an exception be rethrown? (Core Java)*

Answer Yes, an exception can be rethrown.

Question *When does the compiler supply a default constructor for a class?*

Answer The compiler supplies a default constructor for a class if no other constructors are provided.

Question *If a method is declared as protected, where may the method be accessed?*

Answer A protected method may only be accessed by classes or interfaces of the same package or by subclasses of the class in which it is declared.

Question *Which non-Unicode letter characters may be used as the first character of an identifier? (Core Java)*

Answer The non-Unicode letter characters $ and _ may appear as the first character of an identifier.

Question *What restrictions are placed on method overloading? (Core Java)*

Answer Two methods may not have the same name and argument list but different return types.

Question *What is casting? (Core Java)*

Answer There are two types of casting, casting between primitive numeric types and casting between object references. Casting between numeric types is used to convert larger values, such as double values, to smaller values, such as byte values. Casting between object references is used to refer to an object by a compatible class, interface, or array type reference.

Question *What is the return type of a program's main() method? (Core Java)*

Answer A program's main() method has a void return type.

Question *What class of exceptions are generated by the Java runtime system?*

Answer The Java runtime system generates RuntimeException and Error exceptions.

Question *What class allows you to read objects directly from a stream?*

Answer The ObjectInputStream class supports the reading of objects from input streams.

Question *What is the difference between a field variable and a local variable?*

Answer A field variable is a variable that is declared as a member of a class. A local variable is a variable that is declared local to a method.

Question *How are this() and super() used with constructors? (Core Java)*

Answer this() is used to invoke a constructor of the same class. super() is used to invoke a superclass constructor.

Question *What is the relationship between a method's throws clause and the exceptions that can be thrown during the method's execution? (Core Java)*

Answer A method's throws clause must declare any checked exceptions that are not caught within the body of the method.

Question *Why are the methods of the Math class static?   (Core Java)*

Answer So they can be invoked as if they are a mathematical code library.

Question *What are the legal operands of the instanceof operator? (Core Java)*

Answer The left operand is an object reference or null value and the right operand is a class, interface, or array type.

Question *What an I/O filter? (Core Java)*

Answer An I/O filter is an object that reads from one stream and writes to another, usually altering the data in some way as it is passed from one stream to another.

Question *If an object is garbage collected, can it become reachable again?*
Answer Once an object is garbage collected, it ceases to exist. It can no longer become reachable again.

Question *What are E and PI? (Core Java)*

Answer E is the base of the natural logarithm and PI is mathematical value pi.

Question *Are true and false keywords? (Core Java)*

Answer The values true and false are not keywords.

Question *What is the difference between the File and RandomAccessFile classes?   (Core Java)*

Answer The File class encapsulates the files and directories of the local file system. The RandomAccessFile class provides the methods needed to directly access data contained in any part of a file.

Question *What happens when you add a double value to a String? (Core Java)*

Answer The result is a String object.

Question What is your platform's default character encoding? (Core Java)

Answer If you are running Java on English Windows platforms, it is probably Cp1252. If you are running Java on English Solaris platforms, it is most likely 8859_1.

Question Which package is always imported by default? (Core Java)

Answer The java.lang package is always imported by default.

Question What interface must an object implement before it can be written to a stream as an object? (Core Java)

Answer An object must implement the Serializable or Externalizable interface before it can be written to a stream as an object.

Question How can my application get to know when a HttpSession is removed?

Answer Define a Class HttpSessionNotifier which implements HttpSessionBindingListener and implement the functionality what you need in valueUnbound() method. Create an instance of that class and put that instance in HttpSession.

Question Whats the difference between notify() and notifyAll()? (Core Java)

Answer notify() is used to unblock one waiting thread; notifyAll() is used to unblock all of them. Using notify() is preferable (for efficiency) when only one blocked thread can benefit from the change (for example, when freeing a buffer back into a pool). notifyAll() is necessary (for correctness) if multiple threads should resume (for example, when releasing a "writer" lock on a file might permit all "readers" to resume).

Question Why can't I say just abs() or sin() instead of Math.abs() and Math.sin()? (Core Java)

Answer The import statement does not bring methods into your local name space. It lets you abbreviate class names, but not get rid of them altogether. That's just the way it works, you'll get used to it. It's really a lot safer this way.
 However, there is actually a little trick you can use in some cases that gets you what you want.

If your top-level class doesn't need to inherit from anything else, make it inherit from java.lang.Math. That *does* bring all the methods into your local name space. But you can't use this trick in an applet, because you have to inherit from java.awt.Applet. And actually, you can't use it on java.lang.Math at all, because Math is a "final" class which means it can't be extended.

Question Is is possible for an EJB client to marshall an object of class java.lang.Class to an EJB? (EJB)

Answer Technically yes, spec. compliant NO! - The enterprise bean must not attempt to query a class to obtain information about the declared members that are not otherwise accessible to the enterprise bean because of the security rules of the Java language.

Question *Is it legal to have static initializer blocks in EJB? (EJB)*

Answer Although technically it is legal, static initializer blocks are used to execute some piece of code before executing any constructor or method while instantiating a class.

Static initializer blocks are also typically used to initialize static fields - which may be illegal in EJB if they are read/write - In EJB this can be achieved by including the code in either the ejbCreate(), setSessionContext() or setEntityContext() methods.

Question *How can I implement a thread-safe JSP page? (JSP)*

Answer You can make your JSPs thread-safe by having them implement the SingleThreadModel interface. This is done by adding the directive <%@ page isThreadSafe="false" % > within your JSP page.

Question *Is it possible to stop the execution of a method before completion in a SessionBean? (EJB)*

Answer Stopping the execution of a method inside a Session Bean is not possible without writing code inside the Session Bean. This is because you are not allowed to access Threads inside an EJB.

Question *What is the default transaction attribute for an EJB? (EJB)*

Answer There is no default transaction attribute for an EJB. Section 11.5 of EJB v1.1 spec says that the deployer must specify a value for the transaction attribute for those methods having container managed transaction. In weblogic, the default transaction attribute for EJB is SUPPORTS.

Question *What is the difference between session and entity beans? When should I use one or the other? (EJB)*

Answer An entity bean represents persistent global data from the database; a session bean represents transient user-specific data that will die when the user disconnects (ends his session). Generally, the session beans implement business methods (e.g. Bank.transferFunds) that call entity beans (e.g. Account.deposit, Account.withdraw)

Question *Is there any default cache management system with Entity beans ? In other words whether a cache of the data in database will be maintained in EJB ?*

Answer Caching data from a database inside the Application Server are what Entity EJB's are used for.The ejbLoad() and ejbStore() methods are used to synchronize the Entity Bean state with the persistent storage(database).

Transactions also play an important role in this scenario. If data is removed from the database, via an external application - your Entity Bean can still be "alive" the EJB container. When the transaction commits, ejbStore() is called and the row will not be found, and the transcation rolled back.

Question *Why is ejbFindByPrimaryKey mandatory? (EJB)*

Answer An Entity Bean represents persistent data that is stored outside of the EJB Container/Server. The ejbFindByPrimaryKey is a method used to locate and load an Entity Bean into the container, similar to a SELECT statement in SQL. By making this method mandatory, the client programmer can be assured that if they have the primary key of the Entity Bean, then they can retrieve the bean without having to create a new bean each time - which would mean creating duplications of persistent data and break the integrity of EJB.

Question *Why do we have a remove method in both EJBHome and EJBObject?*
Answer With the EJBHome version of the remove, you are able to delete an entity bean without first instantiating it (you can provide a PrimaryKey object as a parameter to the remove method). The home version only works for entity beans. On the other hand, the Remote interface version works on an entity bean that you have alreadyinstantiated. In addition, the remote version also works on session beans (stateless and statefull) to inform the container of your loss of interest in this bean.

Question *How can I call one EJB from inside of another EJB? (EJB)*

Answer EJBs can be clients of other EJBs. It just works. Use JNDI to locate the Home Interface of the other bean, then acquire an instance reference, and so forth.

Question *What is the difference between a Server, a Container, and a Connector? (EJB)*

Answer An EJB server is an application, usually a product such as BEA WebLogic, that provides (or should provide) for concurrent client connections and manages system resources such as threads, processes, memory, database connections, network connections, etc. An EJB container runs inside (or within) an EJB server, and provides deployed EJB beans with transaction and security management, etc.

The EJB container insulates an EJB bean from the specifics of an underlying EJB server by providing a simple, standard API between the EJB bean and its container.A Connector provides the ability for any Enterprise Information System (EIS) to plug into any EJB server which supports the Connector architecture. See http://java.sun.com/j2ee/connector/ for more indepth information on Connectors.

Question *How is persistence implemented in enterprise beans? (EJB)*

Answer Persistence in EJB is taken care of in two ways, depending on how you implement your beans: container managed persistence (CMP) or bean managed persistence (BMP) For CMP, the EJB container which your beans run under takes care of the persistence of the fields you have declared to be persisted with the database - this declaration is in the deployment descriptor.

So, anytime you modify a field in a CMP bean, as soon as the method you have executed is finished, the new data is persisted to the database by the container. For BMP, the EJB bean developer is responsible for defining the persistence routines in the proper places in the bean, for instance, the ejbCreate(), ejbStore(), ejbRemove() methods would be developed by the bean developer to make calls to the database.

The container is responsible, in BMP, to call the appropriate method on the bean. So, if the bean is being looked up, when the create() method is called on the Home interface, then the container is responsible for calling the ejbCreate() method in the bean, which should have functionality inside for going to the database and looking up the data.

Question What is an EJB Context? (EJB)

Answer EJBContext is an interface that is implemented by the container, and it is also a part of the bean-container contract. Entity beans use a subclass of EJBContext called EntityContext. Session beans use a subclass called SessionContext. These EJBContext objects provide the bean class with information about its container, the client using the bean and the bean itself. They also provide other functions. See the API docs and the spec for more details.

Question Is method overloading allowed in EJB? (EJB)

Answer Yes you can overload methods

Question Should synchronization primitives be used on bean methods? (EJB)

Answer No. The EJB specification specifically states that the enterprise bean is not allowed to use thread primitives. The container is responsible for managing concurrent access to beans at runtime.

Question Are we allowed to change the transaction isolation property in middle of a transaction? (EJB)

Answer No. You cannot change the transaction isolation level in the middle of transaction.

Question For Entity Beans, What happens to an instance field not mapped to any persistent storage,when the bean is passivated? (EJB)

Answer The specification infers that the container never serializes an instance of an Entity bean (unlike stateful session beans). Thus passivation simply involves moving the bean from the "ready" to the "pooled" bin.

So what happens to the contents of an instance variable is controlled by the programmer. Remember that when an entity bean is passivated the instance gets logically disassociated from it's remote object.

Be careful here, as the functionality of passivation/activation for Stateless Session, Stateful Session and Entity beans is completely different. For entity beans the ejbPassivate method notifies the entity bean that it is being disassociated with a particular entity prior to reuse or for dereferenc.

Question *What is a Message Driven Bean, What functions does a message driven bean have and how do they work in collaboration with JMS? (EJB)*

Answer: Message driven beans are the latest addition to the family of component bean types defined by the EJB specification.

The original bean types include session beans, which contain business logic and maintain a state associated with client sessions, and entity beans, which map objects to persistent data. Message driven beans will provide asynchrony to EJB based applications by acting as JMS message consumers.

A message bean is associated with a JMS topic or queue and receives JMS messages sent by EJB clients or other beans. Unlike entity beans and session beans, message beans do not have home or remote interfaces. Instead, message driven beans are instantiated by the container as required.

Like stateless session beans, message beans maintain no client-specific state, allowing the container to optimally manage a pool of message-bean instances. Clients send JMS messages to message beans in exactly the same manner as they would send messages to any other JMS destination.

This similarity is a fundamental design goal of the JMS capabilities of the new specification. To receive JMS messages, message driven beans implement the javax.jms.MessageListener interface, which defines a single "onMessage()" method.

When a message arrives, the container ensures that a message bean corresponding to the message topic/queue exists (instantiating it if necessary), and calls its onMessage method passing the client's message as the single argument. The message bean's implementation of this method contains the business logic required to process the message.

Note that session beans and entity beans are not allowed to function as message beans.

Question *Does RMI-IIOP support code downloading for Java objects sent by value across an IIOP connection in the same way as RMI does across a JRMP connection? (RMI)*

Answer Yes. The JDK 1.2 supports the dynamic class loading.

Question *The EJB container implements the EJBHome and EJBObject classes. For every request from a unique client, does the container create a separate instance of the generated EJBHome and EJBObject classes? (EJB)*

Answer The EJB container maintains an instance pool. The container uses these instances for the EJB Home reference irrespective of the client request. while refering the EJB Object classes the container creates a separate instance for each client request.

Another Answer

The instance pool maintainence is up to the implementation of the container. If the container provides one, it is available otherwise it is not mandatory for the provider to implement it.

Having said that, yes most of the container providers implement the pooling functionality to increase the performance of the app server. How it is implemented, it is again up to the implementer.

Question *What is the advantage of puttting an Entity Bean instance from the "Ready State" to "Pooled state"? (EJB)*

Answer The idea of the "Pooled State" is to allow a container to maintain a pool of entity beans that has been created, but has not been yet "synchronized" or assigned to an EJBObject. This mean thatthe instances do represent entity beans, but they can be used only for serving Home methods (create or findBy), since those methods do not relay on the specific values of the bean.

All these instances are, in fact, exactly the same, so, they do not have meaningful state. Jon Thorarinsson has also added:

It can be looked at it this way: If no client is using an entity bean of a particular type there is no need for cachig it (the data is persisted in the database). Therefore, in such cases, the container will, after some time, move the entity bean from the "Ready State" to the "Pooled state" to save memory.

Then, to save additional memory, the container may begin moving entity beans from the "Pooled State" to the "Does Not Exist State", because even though the bean's cache has been cleared, the bean still takes up some memory just being in the "Pooled State".

Question *Can a Session Bean be defined without ejbCreate() method? (EJB)*

Answer The ejbCreate() methods is part of the bean's lifecycle, so, the compiler will not return an error because there is no ejbCreate() method. However, the J2EE spec is explicit: the home interface of a Stateless Session Bean must have a single create() method with no arguments, while the session bean class must contain exactly one ejbCreate() method, also without arguments.

Stateful Session Beans can have arguments (more than one create method) stateful beans can contain multiple ejbCreate() as long as they match with the home interface definition You need a reference to your EJBObject to startwith. For that Sun insists on putting a method for creating that reference (create methodin the home interface). The EJBObject does matter here. Not the actual bean.

Question *Is it possible to share an HttpSession between a JSP and EJB? What happens when I change a value in the HttpSession from inside an EJB? (EJB)*

Answer You can pass the HttpSession as parameter to an EJB method, only if all objects in session are serializable.This has to be consider as "passed-by-value", that means that it's read-only in the EJB. If anything is altered from inside the EJB, it won't be reflected back to the HttpSession of the Servlet Container.The "pass-byreference" can be used between EJBs Remote Interfaces, as they are remote references.

While it IS possible to pass an HttpSession as a parameter to an EJB object, it is considered to be "bad practice (1)" in terms of object oriented design. This is because you are creating an unnecessary coupling between back-end objects (ejbs) and frontend objects (HttpSession).

Create a higher-level of abstraction for your ejb's api. Rather than passing the whole, fat, HttpSession (which carries with it a bunch of http semantics), create a class that acts as a value object (or structure) that holds all the data you need to pass back and forth between front-end/back-end.

Consider the case where your ejb needs to support a non-http-based client. This higher level of abstraction will be flexible enough to support it. (1) Core J2EE design patterns (2001)

Question *Is there any way to read values from an entity bean without locking it for the rest of the transaction (e.g. read-only transactions)? We have a key-value map bean which deadlocks during some concurrent reads. Isolation levels seem to affect the database only, and we need to work within a transaction. (EJB)*

Answer The only thing that comes to (my) mind is that you could write a 'group accessor' - a method that returns a single object containing all of your entity bean's attributes (or all interesting attributes). This method could then be placed in a 'Requires New' transaction.

This way, the current transaction would be suspended for the duration of the call to the entity bean and the entity bean's fetch/operate/commit cycle will be in a separate transaction and any locks should be released immediately. Depending on the granularity of what you need to pull out of the map, the group accessor might be overkill.

Question *What is the difference between a "Coarse Grained" Entity Bean and a "Fine Grained" Entity Bean? (EJB)*

Answer A 'fine grained' entity bean is pretty much directly mapped to one relational table, in third normal form. A 'coarse grained' entity bean is larger and more complex, either because its attributes include values or lists from other tables, or because it 'owns' one or more sets of dependent objects.

Note that the coarse grained bean might be mapped to a single table or flat file, but that single table is going to be pretty ugly, with data copied from other tables, repeated field groups, columns that are dependent on non-key fields, etc.

Fine grained entities are generally considered a liability in large systems because they will tend to increase the load on several of the EJB server's subsystems (there will be more objects exported through the distribution layer, more objects participating in transactions, more skeletons in memory, more EJB Objects in memory, etc.)

The other side of the coin is that the 1.1 spec doesn't mandate CMP Error! No index entries found.support for dependent objects (or even indicate how they should be supported), which makes it more difficult to do coarse grained objects with CMP. The EJB 2.0 specification improves this in a huge way.

Question What is EJBDoclet? (EJB)

Answer EJBDoclet is an open source JavaDoc doclet that generates a lot of the EJB related source files from custom JavaDoc comments tags embedded in the EJB source file.

Question What is the output from System.out.println("Hello"+null);

Answer Hellonull

Question Can we use the constructor, instead of init(), to initialize servlet? (Servlets)

Answer Yes , of course you can use the constructor instead of init(). There's nothing to stop you. But you shouldn't. The original reason for init() was that ancient versions of Java couldn't dynamically invoke constructors with arguments, so there was no way to give the constructur a ServletConfig. That no longer applies, but servlet containers still will only call your no-arg constructor. So you won't have access to a ServletConfig or ServletContext.

Question How can a servlet refresh automatically if some new data has entered the database? (Servlets)

Answer You can use a client-side Refresh or Server Push.

Question The code in a finally clause will never fail to execute, right? (Servlets)

Answer Using System.exit(1); in try block will not allow finally code to execute.

Question *Why are there no global variables in Java? (Core Java)*

Answer Global variables are considered bad form for a variety of reasons:

Adding state variables breaks referential transparency (you no longer can understand a statement or expression on its own: you need to understand it in the context of the settings of the global variables). State variables lessen the cohesion of a program: you need to know more to understand how something works. A major point of ObjectOriented programming is to break up global state into more easily understood collections of local state. When you add one variable, you limit the use of your program to one instance. What you thought was global, someone else might think of as local: they may want to run two copies of your program at once. For these reasons, Java decided to ban global variables.

Question *What does it mean that a class or member is final? (Core Java)*

Answer A final class can no longer be subclassed. Mostly this is done for security reasons with basic classes like String and Integer. It also allows the compiler to make some optimizations, and makes thread safety a little easier to achieve. Methods may be declared final as well. This means they may not be overridden in a subclass.

Fields can be declared final, too. However, this has a completely different meaning. A final field cannot be changed after it's initialized, and it must include an initializer statement where it's declared. For example,

public final double c = 2.998;

It's also possible to make a static field final to get the effect of C++'s const statement or some uses of C's #define, e.g. public static final double c = 2.998;

Question *What does it mean that a method or class is abstract? (Core Java)*

Answer An abstract class cannot be instantiated. Only its subclasses can be instantiated. You indicate that a class is abstract with the abstract keyword like this: public abstract class Container extends Component { Abstract classes may contain abstract methods. A method declared abstract is not actually implemented in the current class. It exists only to be overridden in subclasses. It has no body. For example,

public abstract float price();

Abstract methods may only be included in abstract classes. However, an abstract class is not required to have any abstract methods, though most of them do.Each subclass of an abstract class must override the abstract methods of its superclasses or itself be declared abstract.

Question *what is a transient variable? (Core Java)*

Answer transient variable is a variable that may not be serialized.

Question *How are Observer and Observable used? (Core Java)*

Answer Objects that subclass the Observable class maintain a list of observers. When an Observable object is updated it invokes the update() method of each of its observers to notify the observers that it has changed state. The Observer interface is implemented by objects that observe Observable objects.

Question *Can a lock be acquired on a class? (Core Java)*

Answer Yes, a lock can be acquired on a class. This lock is acquired on the class's Class object.

Question *What state does a thread enter when it terminates its processing?*

Answer When a thread terminates its processing, it enters the dead state.

Question *How does Java handle integer overflows and underflows?*

Answer It uses those low order bytes of the result that can fit into the size of the type allowed by the operation.

Question *What is the difference between the >> and >>> operators?*

Answer The >> operator carries the sign bit when shifting right. The >>> zero-fills bits that have been shifted out.

Question *Is sizeof a keyword? (Core Java)*

Answer The sizeof operator is not a keyword.

Question *Does garbage collection guarantee that a program will not run out of memory? (Core Java)*

Answer Garbage collection does not guarantee that a program will not run out of memory. It is possible for programs to use up memory resources faster than they are garbage collected. It is also possible for programs to create objects that are not subject to garbage collection.

Question *Can an object's finalize() method be invoked while it is reachable?*
Answer An object's finalize() method cannot be invoked by the garbage collector while the object is still reachable. However, an object's finalize() method may be invoked by other objects.

Question *What value does readLine() return when it has reached the end of a file? (Core Java)*

Answer The readLine() method returns null when it has reached the end of a file.

Question *Can a for statement loop indefinitely? (Core Java)*

Answer Yes, a for statement can loop indefinitely. For example, consider the following: for(;;) ;

Question *To what value is a variable of the String type automatically initialized? (Core Java)*

Answer The default value of an String type is null.

Question *What is a task's priority and how is it used in scheduling?*

Answer A task's priority is an integer value that identifies the relative order in which it should be executed with respect to other tasks. The scheduler attempts to schedule higher priority tasks before lower priority tasks.

Question *What is the range of the short type? (Core Java)*

Answer The range of the short type is $-(2^{15})$ to $2^{15} - 1$.

Question *What is the purpose of garbage collection? (Core Java)*

Answer The purpose of garbage collection is to identify and discard objects that are no longer needed by a program so that their resources may be reclaimed and reused.

Question *How may messaging models do JMS provide for and what are they?*

Answer JMS provide for two messaging models, publish-andsubscribe and point-to-point queuing.

Question *What information is needed to create a TCP Socket? (Networking)*

Answer The Local System?s IP Address and Port Number. And the Remote System's IPAddress and Port Number.

Question *What Class.forName will do while loading drivers? (JDBC)*

Answer It is used to create an instance of a driver and register it with the DriverManager. When you have loaded a driver, it is available for making a connection with a DBMS.

Question *How to Retrieve Warnings? (JDBC)*

Answer SQLWarning objects are a subclass of SQLException that deal with database access warnings. Warnings do not stop the execution of an application, as exceptions do; they simply alert the user that something did not happen as planned.

A warning can be reported on a Connection object, a Statement object (including PreparedStatement and CallableStatement objects), or a ResultSet object. Each of these classes has a getWarnings method, which you must invoke in order to see the first warning reported on the calling object *E.g.*

```
SQLWarning warning = stmt.getWarnings();

if (warning != null) {

while (warning != null) {

System.out.println("Message: " +

warning.getMessage());

System.out.println("SQLState: " +

warning.getSQLState());

System.out.print("Vendor error code: ");

System.out.println(warning.getErrorCode());

warning = warning.getNextWarning();

} }
```

Question *How many JSP scripting elements are there and what are they?(JSP)*

Answer There are three scripting language elements:

declarations

scriptlets

expressions

Question *In the Servlet 2.4 specification SingleThreadModel has been deprecates, why? (JSP)*

Answer Because it is not practical to have such model. Whether you set isThreadSafe to true or false, you should take care of concurrent client requests to the JSP page by synchronizing access to any shared objects defined at the page level.

Question *what are stored procedures? How is it useful? (JDBC)*

Answer A stored procedure is a set of statements/commands which reside in the database. The stored procedure is precompiled and saves the database the effort of parsing and compiling sql statements everytime a query is run.

Each Database has it's own stored procedure language, usually a variant of C with a SQL preproceesor. Newer versions of db's support writing stored procs in Java and Perl too.

Before the advent of 3-tier/n-tier architecture it was pretty common for stored procs to implement the business logic(A lot of systems still do it). The biggest advantage is of course speed. Also certain kind of data manipulations are not achieved in SQL.

Stored procs provide a mechanism to do these manipulations. Stored procs are also useful when you want to do Batch updates/exports/houseKeeping kind of stuff on the db. The overhead of a JDBC Connection may be significant in these cases.

Question *What do you understand by private, protected and public?*

Answer These are accessibility modifiers. Private is the most restrictive, while public is the least restrictive. There is no real difference between protected and the default type (also known as package protected) within the context of the same package, however the protected keyword allows visibility to a derived class in a different package

Question *What is Downcasting ? (Core Java)*

Answer Downcasting is the casting from a general to a more specific type, i.e. casting down the hierarchy

Question *Can a method be overloaded based on different return type but same argument type? (Core Java)*

Answer No, because the methods can be called without using their return type in which case there is ambiquity for the compiler.

Question *What happens to a static var that is defined within a method of a class ? (Core Java)*

Answer Can't do it. You'll get a compilation error.

Question *How many static init can you have? (Core Java)*

Answer As many as you want, but the static initializers and class variable initializers are executed in textual order and may not refer to class variables declared in the class whose declarations appear textually after the use, even though these class variables are in scope.

Question *What is the difference amongst JVM Spec, JVM Implementation, JVM Runtime ? (Core Java)*

Answer The JVM spec is the blueprint for the JVM generated and owned by Sun. The JVM implementation is the actual implementation of the spec by a vendor and the JVM runtime is the actual running instance of a JVM implementation

Question *Describe what happens when an object is created in Java?*

Answer Several things happen in a particular order to ensure the object is constructed properly:

1. Memory is allocated from heap to hold all instance variables and implementation-specific data of the object and its superclasses. Implemenation-specific data includes pointers to class and method data.

2. The instance variables of the objects are initialized to their default values.

3. The constructor for the most derived class is invoked. The first thing a constructor does is call the consctructor for its superclasses. This process continues until the constrcutor for java.lang.Object is called, as java.lang.Object is the base class for all objects in java.

4. Before the body of the constructor is executed, all instance variable initializers and initialization blocks are executed. Then the body of the constructor is executed. Thus, the constructor for the base class completes first and constructor for the most derived class completes last.

Question *What does the "final" keyword mean in front of a variable? A method? A class? (Core Java)*

Answer FINAL for a variable : value is constant.

FINAL for a method : cannot be overridden.

FINAL for a class : cannot be derived .

Question *What is the difference between instanceof and isInstance?*

Answer instanceof is used to check to see if an object can be cast into a specified type without throwing a cast class exception. isInstance() Determines if the specified Object is assignment-compatible with the object represented by this Class. This method is the dynamic equivalent of the Java language instanceof operator. The method returns true if the specified Object argument is non-null and can be cast to the reference type represented by this Class object without raising a ClassCastException. It returns false otherwise.

Question *Why does it take so much time to access an Applet having Swing Components the first time? (Swing)*

Answer Because behind every swing component are many Java objects and resources. This takes time to create them in memory. JDK 1.3 from Sun has some improvements which may lead to faster execution of Swing applications.

Question *How do I include static files within a JSP page? (JSP)*

Answer Static resources should always be included using the JSP include directive. This way, the inclusion is performed just once during the translation phase. The following example shows the syntax: Do note that you should always supply a relative URL for the file attribute. Although you can also include static resources using the action, this is not advisable as the inclusion is then performed for each and every request.

Question Why does JComponent have add() and remove() methods but Component does not? (Swing)

Answer because JComponent is a subclass of Container, and can contain other components and jcomponents.

Question How would you create a button with rounded edges? (Swing)

Answer There are 2 ways. The first thing is to know that a JButton?s edges are drawn by a Border. so you can override the Button?s paintComponent(Graphics) method and draw a circle or rounded rectangle (whatever), and turn off the border. Or you can create a custom border that draws a circle or rounded rectangle around any component and set the button?s border to it.

Question How would you detect a keypress in a JComboBox? (Swing)

Answer Add a KeyListener to the JComboBox?s editor component instead of adding a KeyListener to the JComboBox itself.

Question Why should the implementation of any Swing callback (like a listener) execute quickly? (Swing)

Answer Because callbacks are invoked by the event dispatch thread which will be blocked processing other events for as long as your method takes to execute.

Question Why would you use SwingUtilities.invokeAndWait or SwingUtilities.invokeLater? (Swing)

Answer I want to update a Swing component but I?m not in a callback. If I want the update to happen immediately (perhaps for a progress bar component) then I?d use invokeAndWait. If I don?t care when the update occurs, I?d use invokeLater.

Question If your UI seems to freeze periodically, what might be a likely reason?
Answer A callback implementation like ActionListener.actionPerformed or MouseListener.mouseClicked is taking a long time to execute thereby blocking the event dispatch thread from processing other UI events.

Question Which Swing methods are thread-safe? (Swing)

Answer The only thread-safe methods are repaint(), revalidate(), and invalidate()

Question Why won?t the JVM terminate when I close all the application windows? (Swing)

Answer The AWT event dispatcher thread is not a daemon thread. You must explicitly call System.exit to terminate the JVM.

Question *JFrame is a heavy weight component. Since it extends an awt Frame, is it Thread Safe? (Swing)*

Answer JFrame itself is, since it is just a java.awt.Frame in essence, but the root pane/content pane is not, so it effectively follows the same rules for Swing containers and is not considered thread safe.

Question *What is the difference between invokeAndWait() and invokeLater()? (Swing)*

Answer invokeAndWait() blocks until the Runnable task is complete; it's synchronous. invokeLater() posts an action event to the event queue and returns immediately; it's asynchronous.

Question *Why is not recommended to have instance variables in Interface.*
Answer By Default, All data members and methods in an Interface are public. Having public variables in a class that will be implementing it will be violation of the Encapsulation principal. I hope that's pretty ok..

Question *What is the diffrence between inner class and nested class?*

Answer When a class is defined within a scope od another class, then it becomes inner class. If the access modifier of the inner class is static, then it becomes nested class.

Question *What is a compilation unit? (Core Java)*

Answer A compilation unit is a Java source code file.

Question *What restrictions are placed on method overriding? (Core Java)*

Answer Overridden methods must have the same name, argument list, and return type. The overriding method may not limit the access of the method it overrides. The overriding method may not throw any exceptions that may not be thrown by the overridden method.

Question *How can a dead thread be restarted? (Core Java)*

Answer A dead thread cannot be restarted.

Question *What happens if an exception is not caught? (Core Java)*

Answer An uncaught exception results in the uncaughtException() method of the thread's ThreadGroup being invoked, which eventually results in the termination of the program in which it is thrown.

Question *Which arithmetic operations can result in the throwing of an ArithmeticException? (Core Java)*

Answer Integer / and % can result in the throwing of an ArithmeticException

Question *Can an abstract class be final? (Core Java)*

Answer An abstract class may not be declared as final

Question *What happens if a try-catch-finally statement does not have a catch clause to handle an exception that is thrown within the body of the try statement? (Core Java)*

Answer The exception propagates up to the next higher level trycatch statement (if any) or results in the program's termination

Question *What is numeric promotion? (Core Java)*

Answer Numeric promotion is the conversion of a smaller numeric type to a larger numeric type, so that integer and floatingpoint operations may take place. In numerical promotion, byte, char, and short values are converted to int values. The int values are also converted to long values, if necessary. The long and float values are converted to double values, as required.

Question *What is the difference between a public and a non-public class?*

Answer A public class may be accessed outside of its package. A non-public class may not be accessed outside of its package.

Question *To what value is a variable of the boolean type automatically initialized? (Core Java)*

Answer The default value of the boolean type is false.

Question *Can try statements be nested? (Core Java)*

Answer Yes

Question *What is the difference between the prefix and postfix forms of the ++ operator? (Core Java)*

Answer The prefix form performs the increment operation and returns the value of the increment operation. The postfix form returns the current value all of the expression and then performs the increment operation on that value.

Question *What is the purpose of a statement block? (Core Java)*

Answer A statement block is used to organize a sequence of statements as a single statement group.

Question *What is a Java package and how is it used? (Core Java)*

Answer A Java package is a naming context for classes and interfaces. A package is used to create a separate name space forgroups of classes and interfaces. Packages are also used to organize related classes and interfaces into a single API unit and to control accessibility to these classes and interfaces.

Question *What modifiers may be used with a top-level class? (Core Java)*

Answer A top-level class may be public, abstract, or final.

Question *What are the Object and Class classes used for? (Core Java)*

Answer The Object class is the highest-level class in the Java class hierarchy. The Class class is used to represent the classes and interfaces that are loaded by a Java program.

Question *How does a try statement determine which catch clause should be used to handle an exception? (Core Java)*

Answer When an exception is thrown within the body of a try statement, the catch clauses of the try statement are examined in the order in which they appear. The first catch clause that is capable of handling the exception is executed. The remaining catch clauses are ignored.

Question *What are synchronized methods and synchronized statements?*

Answer Synchronized methods are methods that are used to control access to an object. A thread only executes a synchronized method after it has acquired the lock for the method's object or class. Synchronized statements are similar to synchronized methods. A synchronized statement can only be executed after a thread has acquired the lock for the object or class referenced in the synchronized statement.

Question *What is the difference between an if statement and a switch statement? (Core Java)*

Answer The if statement is used to select among two alternatives. It uses a boolean expression to decide which alternative should be executed. The switch statement is used to select among multiple alternatives. It uses an int expression to determine which alternative should be executed.

Question *which containers use a border Layout as their default layout? (AWT)*

Answer The window, Frame and Dialog classes use a border layout as their default layout.

Question *What is the preferred size of a component? (AWT)*

Answer The preferred size of a component is the minimum component size that will allow the component to display normally.

Question *Which containers use a FlowLayout as their default layout? (AWT)*

Answer The Panel and Applet classes use the FlowLayout as their default layout.

Question *What is the immediate superclass of the Applet class? (AWT)*

Answer Panel.

Question *Name three Component subclasses that support painting (AWT)*

Answer The Canvas, Frame, Panel, and Applet classes support painting.

Question *what is the immediate superclass of the Dialog class? (AWT)*

Answer Window.

Question *what is clipping? (AWT)*

Answer Clipping is the process of confining paint operations to a limited area or shape.

Question *What is the difference between a MenuItem and a CheckboxMenuItem? (AWT)*

Answer The CheckboxMenuItem class extends the MenuItem class to support a menu item that may be checked or unchecked.

Question *What class is the top of the AWT event hierarchy? (AWT)*

Answer The java.awt.AWTEvent class is the highest-level class in the AWT event-class hierarchy.

Question *In which package are most of the AWT events that support the event-delegation model defined? (AWT)*

Answer Most of the AWT-related events of the event-delegation model are defined in the java.awt.event package. The AWTEvent class is defined in the java.awt package.

Question *Which class is the immediate superclass of the MenuComponent class (AWT)*

Answer Object.

Question *Which containers may have a MenuBar? (AWT)*

Answer Frame.

Question *What is the relationship between the Canvas class and the Graphics class? (AWT)*

Answer A Canvas object provides access to a Graphics object via its paint() method.

Question *How are the elements of a BorderLayout organized? (AWT)*

Answer The elements of a BorderLayout are organized at the borders (North, South, East, and West) and the center of a container.

Question *What is the difference between a Window and a Frame? (AWT)*

Answer The Frame class extends Window to define a main application window that can have a menu bar.

Question *What is the difference between the Font and FontMetrics classes?*

Answer The FontMetrics class is used to define implementationspecific properties, such as ascent and descent, of a Font object.

Question *How are the elements of a CardLayout organized? (AWT)*

Answer The elements of a CardLayout are stacked, one on top of the other, like a deck of cards.

Question *What is the relationship between clipping and repainting? (AWT)*

Answer When a window is repainted by the AWT painting thread, it sets the clipping regions to the area of the window that requires repainting.

Question *What is the relationship between an event-listener interface and an event-adapter class? (AWT)*

Answer An event-listener interface defines the methods that must be implemented by an event handler for a particular kind of event. An event adapter provides a default implementation of an event-listener interface.

Question *How can a GUI component handle its own events? (AWT)*

Answer A component can handle its own events by implementing the required event-listener interface and adding itself as its own event listener.

Question *How are the elements of a GridBagLayout organized? (AWT)*

Answer The elements of a GridBagLayout are organized according to a grid. However, the elements are of different sizes and may occupy more than one row or column of the grid. In addition, the rows and columns may have different sizes.

Question *What advantage do Java's layout managers provide over traditional windowing systems? (AWT)*

Answer Java uses layout managers to lay out components in a consistent manner across all windowing platforms. Since Java's layout managers aren't tied to absolute sizing and positioning, they are able to accommodate platform-specific differences among windowing systems.

Question *What is the difference between the paint() and repaint() methods? (AWT)*

Answer The paint() method supports painting via a Graphics object. The repaint() method is used to cause paint() to be invoked by the AWT painting thread.

Question *How can the Checkbox class be used to create a radio button? (AWT)*

Answer By associating Checkbox objects with a CheckboxGroup

Question *What is the difference between a Choice and a List? (AWT)*

Answer A Choice is displayed in a compact form that requires you to pull it down to see the list of available choices. Only one item may be selected from a Choice. A List may be displayed in such a way that several List items are visible. A List supports the selection of one or more List items.

Question *What interface is extended by AWT event listeners? (AWT)*

Answer All AWT event listeners extend the java.util.EventListener interface.

Question *What is a layout manager? (AWT)*

Answer A layout manager is an object that is used to organize components in a container.

Question *Which Component subclass is used for drawing and painting? (AWT)*

Answer Canvas.

Question *What are the problems faced by Java programmers who dont use layout managers? (AWT)*

Answer Without layout managers, Java programmers are faced with determining how their GUI will be displayed across multiple windowing systems and finding a common sizing and positioning that will work within the constraints imposed by each windowing system.

Question *What is the difference between a Scrollbar and a ScrollPane? (Swing)*

Answer A Scrollbar is a Component, but not a Container. A ScrollPane is a Container. A ScrollPane handles its own events and performs its own scrolling.

Question *What is the Collections API? (Java util)*

Answer The Collections API is a set of classes and interfaces that support operations on collections of objects.

Question *What is the List interface? (Java util)*

Answer The List interface provides support for ordered collections of objects.

Question *What is the Vector class? (Java util)*

Answer The Vector class provides the capability to implement a growable array of objects.

Question *What is an Iterator interface? (Java util)*

Answer The Iterator interface is used to step through the elements of a Collection.

Question *Which java.util classes and interfaces support event handling?*

Answer The EventObject class and the EventListener interface support event processing.

Question *What is the GregorianCalendar class? (Java util)*

Answer The GregorianCalendar provides support for traditional Western calendars.

Question *What is the Locale class? (Java util)*

Answer The Locale class is used to tailor program output to the conventions of a particular geographic, political, or cultural region.

Question *What is the SimpleTimeZone class? (Java util)*

Answer The SimpleTimeZone class provides support for a Gregorian calendar.

Question *What is the Map interface? (Java util)*

Answer The Map interface replaces the JDK 1.1 Dictionary class and is used associate keys with values.

Question *What is the highest-level event class of the eventdelegation model?*

Answer The java.util.EventObject class is the highest-level class in the event-delegation class hierarchy.

Question *What is the Collection interface? (Java util)*

Answer The Collection interface provides support for the implementation of a mathematical bag - an unordered collection of objects that may contain duplicates.

Question *What is the Set interface? (Java util)*

Answer The Set interface provides methods for accessing the elements of a finite mathematical set. Sets do not allow duplicate elements.

Question *What is the purpose of the enableEvents() method? (Java util)*

Answer The enableEvents() method is used to enable an event for a particular object. Normally, an event is enabled when a listener is added to an object for a particular event. The enableEvents() method is used by objects that handle events by overriding their event-dispatch methods.

Question *What is the ResourceBundle class? (Java util)*

Answer The ResourceBundle class is used to store localespecific resources that can be loaded by a program to tailor the program's appearance to the particular locale in which it is being run.

Question *What is the difference between yielding and sleeping? (Threads)*

Answer When a task invokes its yield() method, it returns to the ready state. When a task invokes its sleep() method, it returns to the waiting state.

Question *When a thread blocks on I/O, what state does it enter? (Threads)*

Answer A thread enters the waiting state when it blocks on I/O.

Question *When a thread is created and started, what is its initial state? (Threads)*

Answer A thread is in the ready state after it has been created and started.

Question *What invokes a thread's run() method? (Threads)*

Answer After a thread is started, via its start() method or that of the Thread class, the JVM invokes the thread's run() method when the thread is initially executed.

Question *What method is invoked to cause an object to begin executing as a separate thread? (Threads)*

Answer The start() method of the Thread class is invoked to cause an object to begin executing as a separate thread.

Question *What is the purpose of the wait(), notify(), and notifyAll() methods? (Threads)*

Answer The wait(),notify(), and notifyAll() methods are used to provide an efficient way for threads to wait for a shared resource. When a thread executes an object's wait() method, it enters the waiting state. It only enters the ready state after another thread invokes the object's notify() or notifyAll() methods.

Question *What are the high-level thread states? (Threads)*

Answer The high-level thread states are ready, running, waiting, and dead.

Question *What happens when a thread cannot acquire a lock on an object? (Threads)*

Answer If a thread attempts to execute a synchronized method or synchronized statement and is unable to acquire an object's lock, it enters the waiting state until the lock becomes available.

Question *How does multithreading take place on a computer with a single CPU? (Threads)*

Answer The operating system's task scheduler allocates execution time to multiple tasks. By quickly switching between executing tasks, it creates the impression that tasks execute sequentially.

Question *What happens when you invoke a thread's interrupt method while it is sleeping or waiting? (Threads)*

Answer When a task's interrupt() method is executed, the task enters the ready state. The next time the task enters the running state, an InterruptedException is thrown.

Question *What state is a thread in when it is executing? (Threads)*

Answer An executing thread is in the running state.

Question *What are three ways in which a thread can enter the waiting state? (Threads)*

Answer A thread can enter the waiting state by invoking its sleep() method, by blocking on I/O, by unsuccessfully attempting to acquire an object's lock, or by invoking an object's wait() method.

It can also enter the waiting state by invoking its (deprecated) suspend() method.

Question *What method must be implemented by all threads? (Threads)*

Answer All tasks must implement the run() method, whether they are a subclass of Thread or implement the Runnable interface.

Question *What are the two basic ways in which classes that can be run as threads may be defined? (Threads)*

Answer A thread class may be declared as a subclass of Thread, or it may implement the Runnable interface.

Question *How can you store international / Unicode characters into a cookie? (JSP)*

Answer One way is, before storing the cookie URLEncode it. URLEnocder.encoder(str); And use URLDecoder.decode(str) when you get the stored cookie.

Question *What is the difference between URL instance and URLConnection instance? (Networking)*

Answer A URL instance represents the location of a resource, and a URLConnection instance represents a link for accessing or communicating with the resource at the location.

Question *What are the two important TCP Socket classes? (Networking)*

Answer Socket and ServerSocket. ServerSocket is used for normal two-way socket communication. Socket class allows us to read and write through the sockets. getInputStream() and getOutputStream() are the two methods available in Socket class.

Question *How to call a Stored Procedure from JDBC? (JDBC)*

Answer The first step is to create a CallableStatement object. As with Statement an and PreparedStatement objects, this is done with an open Connection object. A CallableStatement object contains a call to a stored procedure. *E.g.*

CallableStatement cs = con.prepareCall("{call

SHOW_SUPPLIERS}");

ResultSet rs = cs.executeQuery();

Question *What are the implicit objects? (JSP)*

Answer Implicit objects are objects that are created by the web container and contain information related to a particular request, page, or application. They are:

- ✓ request
- ✓ response
- ✓ pageContext
- ✓ session
- ✓ application
- ✓ out
- ✓ config
- ✓ page
- ✓ exception

Question *Is JSP technology extensible? (JSP)*

Answer YES. JSP technology is extensible through the development of custom actions, or tags, which are encapsulated in tag libraries

Question *What gives java it's "write once and run anywhere" nature?*

Answer Java is compiled to be a byte code which is the intermediate language between source code and machine code. This byte code is not platorm specific and hence can be fed to any platform. After being fed to the JVM, which is specific to a particular operating system, the code platform specific machine code is generated thus making java platform independent.

Question *What are the four corner stones of OOP ? (Core Java)*

Answer Abstraction, Encapsulation, Polymorphism and Inheritance.

Question *Difference between a Class and an Object ? (Core Java)*

Answer A class is a definition or prototype whereas an object is an instance or living representation of the prototype.

Question *What is the difference between method overriding and overloading? (Core Java)*

Answer Overriding is a method with the same name and arguments as in a parent, whereas overloading is the same method name but different arguments.

Question *What is a "stateless" protocol ? (Core Java)*

Answer Without getting into lengthy debates, it is generally accepted that protocols like HTTP are stateless i.e. there is no retention of state between a transaction which is a single request response combination.

Question What is constructor chaining and how is it achieved in Java ?

Answer A child object constructor always first needs to construct its parent (which in turn calls its parent constructor.). In Java it is done via an implicit call to the no-args constructor as the first statement.

Question What is passed by ref and what by value ? (Core Java)

Answer All Java method arguments are passed by value. However, Java does manipulate objects by reference, and all object variables themselves are references.

Question Can RMI and Corba based applications interact ? (RMI)

Answer Yes they can. RMI is available with IIOP as the transport protocol instead of JRMP.

Question You can create a String object as String str = "abc"; Why cant a button object be created as Button bt = "abc";? Explain (Core Java)

Answer The main reason you cannot create a button by Button bt1= "abc"; is because "abc" is a literal string (something slightly different than a String object, by-the-way) and bt1 is a Button object. The only object in Java that can be assigned a literal String is java.lang.String. Important to note that you are NOT calling a java.lang.String constuctor when you type String s = "abc";

Question What does the "abstract" keyword mean in front of a method? A class?   (Core Java)

Answer Abstract keyword declares either a method or a class. If a method has a abstract keyword in front of it,it is called abstract method.Abstract method hs no body.It has only arguments and return type.Abstract methods act as placeholder methods that are implemented in the subclasses. Abstract classes can't be instantiated.If a class is declared as abstract,no objects of that class can be created.If a class contains any abstract method it must be declared as abstract.

Question How many methods do u implement if implement the Serializable Interface? (Core Java)

Answer The Serializable interface is just a "marker" interface, with no methods of its own to implement. Other 'marker' interfaces are java.rmi.Remote java.util.EventListener

Question What are the practical benefits, if any, of importing a specific class rather than an entire package (e.g. import java.net. versus import java.net.Socket)? (Core Java)*

Answer It makes no difference in the generated class files since only the classes that are actually used are referenced by the generated class file. There is another practical benefit to importing single classes, and this arises when two (or more) packages have classes with the same name. Take java.util.Timer and javax.swing.Timer, for example. If I import java.util.* and javax.swing.* and then try to use "Timer", I get an error while compiling (the class name is ambiguous between both packages).

Let's say what you really wanted was the javax.swing.Timer class, and the only classes you plan on using in java.util are Collection and HashMap. In this case, some people will prefer to import java.util.Collection and import java.util.HashMap instead of importing java.util.*. This will now allow them to use Timer, Collection, HashMap, and other javax.swing classes without using fully qualified class names in.

Question *What is the difference between logical data independence and physical data independence? (Core Java)*

Answer Logical Data Independence - meaning immunity of external schemas to changeds in conceptual schema. Physical Data Independence - meaning immunity of conceptual schema to changes in the internal schema.

Question What is user defined exception? (Core Java)

Answer Apart from the exceptions already defined in Java package libraries, user can define his own exception classes by extending Exception class.

PART - III

350+ JAVA
INTERVIEW
QUES & ANS

Serious Note Drill –

Some (Very Little) Questions are Repetitive, Don't Worry about them, I mentioned them with relation of some other topics. For random brain storm.

1. What is a transient variable?

Answer A transient variable is a variable that may not be serialized.

2. Which containers use a border Layout as their default layout?

Answer The window, Frame and Dialog classes use a border layout as their default layout.

3. Why do threads block on I/O?

Answer Threads block on I/O (that is enters the waiting state) so that other threads may execute while the I/O Operation is performed.

4. How are Observer and Observable used?

Answer Objects that subclass the Observable class maintain a list of observers. When an Observable object is updated it invokes the update() method of each of its observers to notify the observers that it has changed state. The Observer interface is implemented by objects that observe Observable objects.

5. What is synchronization and why is it important?

Answer With respect to multithreading, synchronization is the capability to control the access of multiple threads to shared resources. Without synchronization, it is possible for one thread to modify a shared object while another thread is in the process of using or updating that object's value. This often leads to significant errors.

6. Can a lock be acquired on a class?

Answer Yes, a lock can be acquired on a class. This lock is acquired on the class's Class object.

7. What's new with the stop(), suspend() and resume() methods in JDK 1.2?

Answer The stop(), suspend() and resume() methods have been deprecated in JDK 1.2.

8. Is null a keyword?

Answer The null value is not a keyword.

9. What is the preferred size of a component?

Answer The preferred size of a component is the minimum component size that will allow the component to display normally.

10. What method is used to specify a container's layout?

Answer The setLayout() method is used to specify a container's layout.

11. Which containers use a FlowLayout as their default layout?

Answer The Panel and Applet classes use the FlowLayout as their default layout.

12. What state does a thread enter when it terminates its processing?

Answer When a thread terminates its processing, it enters the dead state.

13. What is the Collections API?

Answer The Collections API is a set of classes and interfaces that support operations on collections of objects.

14. which characters may be used as the second character of an identifier, but not as the first character of an identifier?

Answer The digits 0 through 9 may not be used as the first character of an identifier but they may be used after the first character of an identifier.

15. What is the List interface?

Answer The List interface provides support for ordered collections of objects.

16. How does Java handle integer overflows and underflows?

Answer It uses those low order bytes of the result that can fit into the size of the type allowed by the operation.

17. What is the Vector class?

Answer The Vector class provides the capability to implement a growable array of objects.

18. What modifiers may be used with an inner class that is a member of an outer class?

Answer A (non-local) inner class may be declared as public, protected, private, static, final, or abstract.

19. What is an Iterator interface?

Answer The Iterator interface is used to step through the elements of a Collection.

20. What is the difference between the >> and >>> operators?

Answer The >> operator carries the sign bit when shifting right. The >>> zero-fills bits that have been shifted out.

21. Which method of the Component class is used to set the position and size of a component?

Answer setBounds()

22. How many bits are used to represent Unicode, ASCII, UTF-16, and UTF-8 characters?

Answer Unicode requires 16 bits and ASCII require 7 bits. Although the ASCII character set uses only 7 bits, it is usually represented as 8 bits. UTF-8 represents characters using 8, 16, and 18 bit patterns. UTF-16 uses 16-bit and larger bit patterns.

23 What is the difference between yielding and sleeping?

Answer When a task invokes its yield() method, it returns to the ready state. When a task invokes its sleep() method, it returns to the waiting state.

24. Which java.util classes and interfaces support event handling?

Answer The EventObject class and the EventListener interface support event processing.

25. Is sizeof a keyword?

Answer The sizeof operator is not a keyword.

26. What are wrapper classes?

Answer Wrapper classes are classes that allow primitive types to be accessed as objects.

27. Does garbage collection guarantee that a program will not run out of memory?

Answer Garbage collection does not guarantee that a program will not run out of memory. It is possible for programs to use up memory resources faster than they are garbage collected. It is also possible for programs to create objects that are not subject to garbage collection.

28. What restrictions are placed on the location of a package statement within a source code file?

Answer A package statement must appear as the first line in a source code file (excluding blank lines and comments).

29. Can an object's finalize() method be invoked while it is reachable?

Answer An object's finalize() method cannot be invoked by the garbage collector while the object is still reachable. However, an object's finalize() method may be invoked by other objects.

30. What is the immediate superclass of the Applet class?

Answer Panel.

31. What is the difference between preemptive scheduling and time slicing?

Answer Under preemptive scheduling, the highest priority task executes until it enters the waiting or dead states or a higher priority task comes into existence. Under time slicing, a task executes for a predefinedslice of time and then reenters the pool of ready tasks. The scheduler then determines which task should execute next, based on priority and other factors.

32. Name three Component subclasses that support painting.

Answer The Canvas, Frame, Panel, and Applet classes support painting.

33. What value does readLine() return when it has reached the end of a file?

Answer The readLine() method returns null when it has reached the end of a file.

34. What is the immediate superclass of the Dialog class?

Answer Window.

35. What is clipping?

Answer Clipping is the process of confining paint operations to a limited area or shape.

36. What is a native method?

Answer A native method is a method that is implemented in a language other than Java.

37. Can a for statement loop indefinitely?

Answer Yes, a for statement can loop indefinitely. For example, consider the following: for(;;) ;

38. What are order of precedence and associativity, and how are they used?

Answer Order of precedence determines the order in which operators are evaluated in expressions. Associatity determines whether an expression is evaluated left-to-right or right-to-left.

39. When a thread blocks on I/O, what state does it enter?

Answer A thread enters the waiting state when it blocks on I/O.

40. To what value is a variable of the String type automatically initialized?

Answer The default value of a String type is null.

41. What is the catch or declare rule for method declarations?

Answer If a checked exception may be thrown within the body of a method, the method must either catch the exception or declare it in its throws clause.

42. What is the difference between a MenuItem and a CheckboxMenuItem?

Answer The CheckboxMenuItem class extends the MenuItem class to support a menu item that may be checked or unchecked.

43. What is a task's priority and how is it used in scheduling?

Answer A task's priority is an integer value that identifies the relative order in which it should be executed with respect to other tasks. The scheduler attempts to schedule higher priority tasks before lower priority tasks.

44. What class is the top of the AWT event hierarchy?

Answer The java.awt.AWTEvent class is the highest-level class in the AWT event-class hierarchy.

45. When a thread is created and started, what is its initial state?

Answer A thread is in the ready state after it has been created and started.

46. Can an anonymous class be declared as implementing an interface and extending a class?

Answer An anonymous class may implement an interface or extend a superclass, but may not be declared to do both.

47. What is the range of the short type?

Answer The range of the short type is $-(2^{15})$ to $2^{15} - 1$.

48. What is the range of the char type?

Answer The range of the char type is 0 to $2^{16} - 1$.

49. In which package are most of the AWT events that support the event-delegation model defined?

Answer Most of the AWT-related events of the event-delegation model are defined in the java.awt.event package. The AWTEvent class is defined in the java.awt package.

50. What is the immediate superclass of Menu?

Answer MenuItem.

51. What is the purpose of finalization?

Answer The purpose of finalization is to give an unreachable object the opportunity to perform any cleanup processing before the object is garbage collected.

52. Which class is the immediate superclass of the MenuComponent

Answer class.Object

53. What invokes a thread's run() method?

Answer After a thread is started, via its start() method or that of the Thread class, the JVM invokes the thread's run() method when the thread is initially executed.

54. What is the difference between the Boolean & operator and the && operator?

Answer If an expression involving the Boolean & operator is evaluated, both operands are evaluated. Then the & operator is applied to the operand. When an expression involving the && operator is evaluated, the first operand is evaluated. If the first operand returns a value of true then the second operand is evaluated. The && operator is then applied to the first and second operands. If the first operand evaluates to false, the evaluation of the second operand is skipped.

55. Name three subclasses of the Component class.

Answer Box.Filler, Button, Canvas, Checkbox, Choice, Container, Label, List, Scrollbar, or TextComponent

56. What is the GregorianCalendar class?

Answer The GregorianCalendar provides support for traditional Western calendars.

57. Which Container method is used to cause a container to be laid out and redisplayed?

Answer validate()

58. What is the purpose of the Runtime class?

Answer The purpose of the Runtime class is to provide access to the Java runtime system.

59. How many times may an object's finalize() method be invoked by the garbage collector?

Answer An object's finalize() method may only be invoked once by the garbage collector.

60. What is the purpose of the finally clause of a try-catch-finally statement?

Answer The finally clause is used to provide the capability to execute code no matter whether or not an exception is thrown or caught.

61. What is the argument type of a program's main() method?

Answer A program's main() method takes an argument of the String[] type.

62. Which Java operator is right associative?

Answer The = operator is right associative.

63. What is the Locale class?

Answer The Locale class is used to tailor program output to the conventions of a particular geographic, political, or cultural region.64. Can a double value be cast to a byte?

Answer Yes, a double value can be cast to a byte.

65. What is the difference between a break statement and a continue statement?

Answer A break statement results in the termination of the statement to which it applies (switch, for, do, or while). A continue statement is used to end the current loop iteration and return control to the loop statement.

66. What must a class do to implement an interface?

Answer It must provide all of the methods in the interface and identify the interface in its implements clause.

67. What method is invoked to cause an object to begin executing as a separate thread?

Answer The start() method of the Thread class is invoked to cause an object to begin executing as a separate thread.

68. Name two subclasses of the TextComponent class.

Answer TextField and TextArea

69. What is the advantage of the event-delegation model over the earlier event-inheritance model?

Answer The event-delegation model has two advantages over the event-inheritance model. First, it enables event handling to be handled by objects other than the ones that generate the events (or their containers). This allows a clean separation between a component's design and its use. The other advantage of the event-delegation model is that it performs much better in applications where many events are generated. This performance improvement is due to the fact that the event-delegation model does not have to repeatedly process unhandled events, as is the case of the event-inheritance model.

70. Which containers may have a MenuBar?

Answer Frame.

71. How are commas used in the initialization and iteration parts of a for statement?

Answer Commas are used to separate multiple statements within the initialization and iteration parts of a for statement.

72. What is the purpose of the wait(), notify(), and notifyAll() methods?

Answer The wait(),notify(), and notifyAll() methods are used to provide an efficient way for threads to wait for a shared resource. When a thread executes an object's wait() method, it enters the waiting state. It only enters the ready state after another thread invokes the object's notify() or notifyAll() methods.

73. What is an abstract method?

Answer An abstract method is a method whose implementation is deferred to a subclass.

74. How are Java source code files named?

Answer A Java source code file takes the name of a public class or interface that is defined within the file. A source code file may contain at most one public class or interface. If a public class or interface is defined within a source code file, then the source code file must take the name of the public class or interface. If no public class or interface is defined within a source code file, then the file must take on a namethat is different than its classes and interfaces. Source code files use the .java extension.

75. What is the relationship between the Canvas class and the Graphics class?

Answer A Canvas object provides access to a Graphics object via its paint() method.

76. What are the high-level thread states?

Answer The high-level thread states are ready, running, waiting, and dead.

77. What value does read() return when it has reached the end of a file?

Answer The read() method returns -1 when it has reached the end of a file.

78. Can a Byte object be cast to a double value?

Answer No, an object cannot be cast to a primitive value.

79. What is the difference between a static and a non-static inner class?

Answer A non-static inner class may have object instances that are associated with instances of the class's outerclass. A static inner class does not have any object instances.

80. What is the difference between the String and StringBuffer classes?

Answer String objects are constants. StringBuffer objects are not.

81. If a variable is declared as private, where may the variable be accessed?

Answer A private variable may only be accessed within the class in which it is declared.

82. What is an object's lock and which objects have locks?

Answer An object's lock is a mechanism that is used by multiple threads to obtain synchronized access to the object. A thread may execute a synchronized method of an object only after it has acquired the object's lock. All objects and classes have locks. A class's lock is acquired on the class's Class object.

83. What is the Dictionary class?

Answer The Dictionary class provides the capability to store key-value pairs.

84. How are the elements of a BorderLayout organized?

Answer The elements of a BorderLayout are organized at the borders (North, South, East, and West) and the center of a container.

85. What is the % operator?

Answer It is referred to as the modulo or remainder operator. It returns the remainder of dividing the first operand by the second operand.

86. When can an object reference be cast to an interface reference?

Answer An object reference be cast to an interface reference when the object implements the referenced interface.

87. What is the difference between a Window and a Frame?

Answer The Frame class extends Window to define a main application window that can have a menu bar.

88. Which class is extended by all other classes?

Answer The Object class is extended by all other classes.

89. Can an object be garbage collected while it is still reachable?

Answer A reachable object cannot be garbage collected. Only unreachable objects may be garbage collected..

90. Is the ternary operator written x : y ? z or x ? y : z ?

Answer It is written x ? y : z.

91. What is the difference between the Font and FontMetrics classes?

Answer The FontMetrics class is used to define implementation-specific properties, such as ascent and descent, of a Font object.

92. How is rounding performed under integer division?

Answer The fractional part of the result is truncated. This is known as rounding toward zero.

93. What happens when a thread cannot acquire a lock on an object?

Answer If a thread attempts to execute a synchronized method or synchronized statement and is unable to acquire an object's lock, it enters the waiting state until the lock becomes available.

94. What is the difference between the Reader/Writer class hierarchy and the InputStream/OutputStream class hierarchy?

Answer The Reader/Writer class hierarchy is character-oriented, and the InputStream/OutputStream class hierarchy is byte-oriented.

95. What classes of exceptions may be caught by a catch clause?

Answer A catch clause can catch any exception that may be assigned to the Throwable type. This includes theError and Exception types.

96. If a class is declared without any access modifiers, where may the class be accessed?

Answer A class that is declared without any access modifiers is said to have package access. This means that the class can only be accessed by other classes and interfaces that are defined within the same package.

97. What is the SimpleTimeZone class?

Answer The SimpleTimeZone class provides support for a Gregorian calendar.

98. What is the Map interface?

Answer The Map interface replaces the JDK 1.1 Dictionary class and is used associate keys with values.

99. Does a class inherit the constructors of its superclass?

Answer A class does not inherit constructors from any of its super classes.

100. For which statements does it make sense to use a label?

Answer The only statements for which it makes sense to use a label are those statements that can enclose a break or continue statement.

101. What is the purpose of the System class?

Answer The purpose of the System class is to provide access to system resources.

102. Which TextComponent method is used to set a TextComponent to the read-only state?

Answer setEditable()

103. How are the elements of a CardLayout organized?

Answer The elements of a CardLayout are stacked, one on top of the other, like a deck of cards.

104. Is &&= a valid Java operator?

Answer No, it is not.

105. Name the eight primitive Java types.

Answer The eight primitive types are byte, char, short, int, long, float, double, and boolean.

106. Which class should you use to obtain design information about an object?

Answer The Class class is used to obtain information about an object's design.

107. What is the relationship between clipping and repainting?

Answer When a window is repainted by the AWT painting thread, it sets the clipping regions to the area of the window that requires repainting.

108. Is "abc" a primitive value?

Answer The String literal "abc" is not a primitive value. It is a String object.

109. What is the relationship between an event-listener interface and an event-adapter class?

Answer An event-listener interface defines the methods that must be implemented by an event handler for a particular kind of event. An event adapter provides a default implementation of an event-listener interface.

110. What restrictions are placed on the values of each case of a switch statement?

Answer During compilation, the values of each case of a switch statement must evaluate to a value that can be promoted to an int value.

111. What modifiers may be used with an interface declaration?

Answer An interface may be declared as public or abstract.

112. Is a class a subclass of itself?

Answer A class is a subclass of itself.

113. What is the highest-level event class of the event-delegation model?

Answer The java.util.EventObject class is the highest-level class in the event-delegation class hierarchy.

114. What event results from the clicking of a button?

Answer The ActionEvent event is generated as the result of the clicking of a button.

115. How can a GUI component handle its own events?

Answer A component can handle its own events by implementing the required event-listener interface and adding itself as its own event listener.

116. What is the difference between a while statement and a do statement?

Answer A while statement checks at the beginning of a loop to see whether the next loop iteration should occur.

A do statement checks at the end of a loop to see whether the next iteration of a loop should occur. The do statement will always execute the body of a loop at least once.

117. How are the elements of a GridBagLayout organized?

Answer The elements of a GridBagLayout are organized according to a grid. However, the elements are of different sizes and may occupy more than one row or column of the grid. In addition, the rows and columns may have different sizes.

118. What advantage do Java's layout managers provide over traditional windowing systems?

Answer Java uses layout managers to lay out components in a consistent manner across all windowing platforms. Since Java's layout managers aren't tied to absolute sizing and positioning, they are able to accommodate platform-specific differences among windowing systems.

119. What is the Collection interface?

Answer The Collection interface provides support for the implementation of a mathematical bag - an unordered collection of objects that may contain duplicates.

120. What modifiers can be used with a local inner class?

Answer A local inner class may be final or abstract.

121. What is the difference between static and non-static variables?

Answer A static variable is associated with the class as a whole rather than with specific instances of a class. Non-static variables take on unique values with each object instance.

122. What is the difference between the paint() and repaint() methods?

Answer The paint() method supports painting via a Graphics object. The repaint() method is used to cause paint() to be invoked by the AWT painting thread.

123. What is the purpose of the File class?

Answer The File class is used to create objects that provide access to the files and directories of a local file system.

124. Can an exception be rethrown?

Answer Yes, an exception can be rethrown.

125. Which Math method is used to calculate the absolute value of a number?

Answer The abs() method is used to calculate absolute values.

126. How does multithreading take place on a computer with a single CPU?

Answer The operating system's task scheduler allocates execution time to multiple tasks. By quickly switching between executing tasks, it creates the impression that tasks execute sequentially.

127. When does the compiler supply a default constructor for a class?

Answer The compiler supplies a default constructor for a class if no other constructors are provided.

128. When is the finally clause of a try-catch-finally statement executed?

Answer The finally clause of the try-catch-finally statement is always executed unless the thread of execution terminates or an exception occurs within the execution of the finally clause.

129. Which class is the immediate superclass of the Container class?

Answer Component.

130. If a method is declared as protected, where may the method be accessed?

Answer A protected method may only be accessed by classes or interfaces of the same package or by subclasses of the class in which it is declared.

131. How can the Checkbox class be used to create a radio button?

Answer By associating Checkbox objects with a CheckboxGroup.

132. Which non-Unicode letter characters may be used as the first character of an identifier?

Answer The non-Unicode letter characters $ and _ may appear as the first character of an identifier.

133. What restrictions are placed on method overloading?

Answer Two methods may not have the same name and argument list but different return types.

134. What happens when you invoke a thread's interrupt method while it is sleeping or waiting?

Answer When a task's interrupt() method is executed, the task enters the ready state. The next time the task enters the running state, an InterruptedException is thrown.

135. What is casting?

Answer There are two types of casting, casting between primitive numeric types and casting between object references. Casting between numeric types is used to convert larger values, such as double values, to smaller values, such as byte values. Casting between object references is used to refer to an objectby a compatible class, interface, or array type reference.

136. What is the return type of a program's main() method?

Answer A program's main() method has a void return type.

137. Name four Container classes.

Answer Window, Frame, Dialog, FileDialog, Panel, Applet, or ScrollPane

138. What is the difference between a Choice and a List?

Answer A Choice is displayed in a compact form that requires you to pull it down to see the list of available choices. Only one item may be selected from a Choice. A List may be displayed in such a way that several List items are visible. A List supports the selection of one or more List items.

139. What class of exceptions are generated by the Java run-time system?

Answer The Java runtime system generates RuntimeException and Error exceptions.

140. What class allows you to read objects directly from a stream?

The ObjectInputStream class supports the reading of objects from input streams.

141. What is the difference between a field variable and a local variable?

Answer A field variable is a variable that is declared as a member of a class. A local variable is a variable that is declared local to a method.

142. Under what conditions is an object's finalize() method invoked by the garbage collector?

Answer The garbage collector invokes an object's finalize() method when it detects that the object has become unreachable.

143. How are this () and super () used with constructors?

Answer this() is used to invoke a constructor of the same class. super() is used to invoke a superclass constructor.

144. What is the relationship between a method's throws clause and the exceptions that can be thrown during the method's execution?

Answer A method's throws clause must declare any checked exceptions that are not caught within the body of the method.

145. What is the difference between the JDK 1.02 event model and the event-delegation model introduced with JDK 1.1?

Answer The JDK 1.02 event model uses an event inheritance or bubbling approach. In this model, components are required to handle their own events. If they do not handle a particular event, the event is inherited by (or bubbled up to) the component's container. The container then either handles the event or it is bubbled up to its container and so on, until the highest-level container has been tried.In the event-delegation model, specific objects are designated as event handlers for GUI components.

These objects implement event-listener interfaces. The event-delegation model is more efficient than the event-inheritance model because it eliminates the processing required to support the bubbling of unhandled events.

146. How is it possible for two String objects with identical values not to be equal under the == operator?

Answer The == operator compares two objects to determine if they are the same object in memory. It is possible. for two String objects to have the same value, but located indifferent areas of memory.

147. Why are the methods of the Math class static?

Answer So they can be invoked as if they are a mathematical code library.

148. What Checkbox method allows you to tell if a Checkbox is checked?

Answer getState()

149. What state is a thread in when it is executing?

Answer An executing thread is in the running state.

150. What are the legal operands of the instanceof operator?

Answer The left operand is an object reference or null value and the right operand is a class, interface, or array type.

151. How are the elements of a GridLayout organized?

Answer The elements of a GridBad layout are of equal size and are laid out using the squares of a grid.

152. What an I/O filter?

Answer An I/O filter is an object that reads from one stream and writes to another, usually altering the data in some way as it is passed from one stream to another.

153. If an object is garbage collected, can it become reachable again?

Answer Once an object is garbage collected, it ceases to exist. It can no longer become reachable again.

154. What is the Set interface?

Answer The Set interface provides methods for accessing the elements of a finite mathematical set. Sets do not allow duplicate elements.

155. What classes of exceptions may be thrown by a throw statement?

Answer A throw statement may throw any expression that may be assigned to the Throwable type.

156. What are E and PI?

Answer E is the base of the natural logarithm and PI is mathematical value pi.

157. Are true and false keywords?

Answer The values true and false are not keywords.

158. What is a void return type?

Answer A void return type indicates that a method does not return a value.

159. What is the purpose of the enableEvents() method?

Answer The enableEvents() method is used to enable an event for a particular object. Normally, an event is enabled when a listener is added to an object for a particular event. The enableEvents() method is used by objects that handle events by overriding their event-dispatch methods.

160. What is the difference between the File and RandomAccessFile classes?

Answer The File class encapsulates the files and directories of the local file system. The RandomAccessFile class provides the methods needed to directly access data contained in any part of a file.

161. What happens when you add a double value to a String?

Answer The result is a String object.162. What is your platform's default character encoding?If you are running Java on English Windows platforms, it is probably Cp1252. If you are running Javaon English Solaris platforms, it is most likely 8859_1..

163. Which package is always imported by default?

Answer The java.lang package is always imported by default.

164. What interface must an object implement before it can be written to a stream as an object?

Answer An object must implement the Serializable or Externalizable interface before it can be written to a stream as an object.

165. How are this and super used?

Answer this is used to refer to the current object instance. super is used to refer to the variables and methods of the superclass of the current object instance.

166. What is the purpose of garbage collection?

Answer The purpose of garbage collection is to identify and discard objects that are no longer needed by a program so that their resources may be reclaimed and reused.

167. What is a compilation unit?

Answer A compilation unit is a Java source code file.

168. What interface is extended by AWT event listeners?

Answer All AWT event listeners extend the java.util.EventListener interface.

169. What restrictions are placed on method overriding?

Answer Overridden methods must have the same name, argument list, and return type. The overriding method may not limit the access of the method it overrides. The overriding method may not throw any exceptions that may not be thrown by the overridden method.

170. How can a dead thread be restarted?

Answer A dead thread cannot be restarted.

171. What happens if an exception is not caught?

Answer An uncaught exception results in the uncaughtException() method of the thread's ThreadGroup being invoked, which eventually results in the termination of the program in which it is thrown.

172. What is a layout manager?

Answer A layout manager is an object that is used to organize components in a container.

173. Which arithmetic operations can result in the throwing of an ArithmeticException?

Answer Integer / and % can result in the throwing of an ArithmeticException.

174. What are three ways in which a thread can enter the waiting state?

Answer A thread can enter the waiting state by invoking its sleep() method, by blocking on I/O, by unsuccessfully attempting to acquire an object's lock, or by invoking an object's wait() method. It can also enter the waiting state by invoking its (deprecated) suspend() method.

175. Can an abstract class be final?

Answer An abstract class may not be declared as final.176. What is the ResourceBundle class?The ResourceBundle class is used to store locale-specific resources that can be loaded by a program to tailor the program's appearance to the particular locale in which it is being run.

177. What happens if a try-catch-finally statement does not have a catch clause to handle an exception that is thrown within the body of the try statement?

Answer The exception propagates up to the next higher level try-catch statement (if any) or results in the program's termination.

178. What is numeric promotion?

Answer Numeric promotion is the conversion of a smaller numeric type to a larger numeric type, so that integer and floating-point operations may take place. In numerical promotion, byte, char, and short values are converted to int values. The int values are also converted to long values, if necessary. The long and float values are converted to double values, as required.

179. What is the difference between a Scrollbar and a ScrollPane?

Answer A Scrollbar is a Component, but not a Container. A ScrollPane is a Container. A ScrollPane handles its own events and performs its own scrolling.

180. What is the difference between a public and a non-public class?

Answer A public class may be accessed outside of its package. A non-public class may not be accessed outside of its package.

181. To what value is a variable of the boolean type automatically initialized?

Answer The default value of the boolean type is false.

182. Can try statements be nested?

Answer Try statements may be tested.

183. What is the difference between the prefix and postfix forms of the ++ operator?

Answer The prefix form performs the increment operation and returns the value of the increment operation. The postfix form returns the current value all of the expression and then performs the increment operation on that value.

184. What is the purpose of a statement block?

Answer A statement block is used to organize a sequence of statements as a single statement group.

185. What is a Java package and how is it used?

Answer A Java package is a naming context for classes and interfaces. A package is used to create a separate name space for groups of classes and interfaces. Packages are also used to organize related classes and interfaces into a single API unit and to control accessibility to these classes and interfaces.

186. What modifiers may be used with a top-level class?

Answer A top-level class may be public, abstract, or final.

187. What are the Object and Class classes used for?

Answer The Object class is the highest-level class in the Java class hierarchy. The Class class is used to represent the classes and interfaces that are loaded by a Java program.

188. How does a try statement determine which catch clause should be used to handle an exception?

Answer When an exception is thrown within the body of a try statement, the catch clauses of the try statement are examined in the order in which they appear. The first catch clause that is capable of handling the exception is executed. The remaining catch clauses are ignored.

189. Can an unreachable object become reachable again?

Answer An unreachable object may become reachable again. This can happen when the object's finalize() method is invoked and the object performs an operation which causes it to become accessible to reachable objects.

190. When is an object subject to garbage collection?

Answer An object is subject to garbage collection when it becomes unreachable to the program in which it issued.

191. What method must be implemented by all threads?

Answer All tasks must implement the run() method, whether they are a subclass of Thread or implement the Runnable interface.

192. What methods are used to get and set the text label displayed by a Button object?

Answer getLabel() and setLabel()

193. Which Component subclass is used for drawing and painting?

Answer Canvas.

194. What are synchronized methods and synchronized statements?

Answer Synchronized methods are methods that are used to control access to an object. A thread only executes a synchronized method after it has acquired the lock for the method's object or class. Synchronized statements are similar to synchronized methods. A synchronized statement can only be executed after a thread has acquired the lock for the object or class referenced in the synchronized statement

195. What are the two basic ways in which classes that can be run as threads may be defined?

Answer A thread class may be declared as a subclass of Thread, or it may implement the Runnable interface.

196. What are the problems faced by Java programmers who don't use layout managers?

Answer Without layout managers, Java programmers are faced with determining how their GUI will be displayedacross multiple windowing systems and finding a common sizing and positioning that will work within the constraints imposed by each windowing system.

197. What is the difference between an if statement and a switch statement?

The if statement is used to select among two alternatives. It uses a boolean expression to decide which alternative should be executed. The switch statement is used to select among multiple alternatives. It uses an int expression to determine which alternative should be executed.

198. *Describe what happens when an object is created in Java ?*

Answer: Several things happen in a particular order to ensure the object is constructed properly:

- ❖ Memory is allocated from heap to hold all instance variables and implementation-specific data of the object and its super classes. Implementation-specific data includes pointers to class and method data.

- ❖ The instance variables of the objects are initialized to their default values.

- ❖ The constructor for the most derived class is invoked. The first thing a constructor does is call the constructor for its super classes. This process continues until the constructor for java.lang.Object is called, as java.lang.Object is the base class for all objects in java.

❖ Before the body of the constructor is executed, all instance variable initializers and initialization blocks are executed. Then the body of the constructor is executed. Thus, the constructor for the base class completes first and constructor for the most derived class completes last. The methods of the class and its parent hierarchy are made available. Lastly, the address of the object is returned.

199. Question: *In Java, You can create a String object as below :*

String str = "abc"; & String str = new String ("abc");

Why can't a button object be created as: Button bt = "abc". Why is it compulsory to create a button object as:

Button bt = new Button ("abc")

Answer: String is not just another class in Java. There are a lot of special cases in String class. If you notice carefully, String is an Immutable class where as that's not true for Button or most of the other classes.

Java compiler as well as '+' and '+=' operators convert quoted characters in to String. I believe Java designers wanted to treat Strings as close to primitive types as possible and hence some of the differences. Important to not that you are NOT calling a java.lang.String constructor when you type String s = "abc";

for example:

String x = "abc";

String y = "abc";

refer to the same object.

While

String x1 = new String ("abc");

String x2 = new String ("abc");

refer to two different objects.

200. Question: *What is the advantage of OOP?*

Answer: You will get varying answers to this question depending on whom you ask. Major advantages of OOP are:

➕ **Simplicity:** software objects model real world objects, so the complexity is reduced and the program structure is very clear;

- **Modularity:** each object forms a separate entity whose internal workings are decoupled from other parts of the system;

- **Modifiability:** it is easy to make minor changes in the data representation or the procedures in an OO program. Changes inside a class do not affect any other part of a program, since the only public interface that the external world has to a class is through the use of methods;

- **Extensibility:** adding new features or responding to changing operating environments can be solved by introducing a few new objects and modifying some existing ones;

- **Maintainability:** objects can be maintained separately, making locating and fixing problems easier;

- **Re-usability:** objects can be reused in different programs.

201. Question: *What are the main differences between Java and C++?*
Answer: Main differences between C++ and Java are:

- ✓ Everything is an object in Java(Single root hierarchy as everything gets derived from java.lang.Object)

- ✓ Java does not have all the complicated aspects of C++ (For ex: Pointers, templates, unions, operator overloading, structures etc...)

- ✓ The Java language promoters initially said "No pointers!", but when many programmers questioned how you can work without pointers, the promoters began saying "Restricted pointers." You can make up your mind whether it's really a pointer or not. In any event, there's no pointer arithmetic.

- ✓ There are no destructors in Java (automatic garbage collection).

- ✓ Java does not support conditional compile (#ifdef/#ifndef type).

- ✓ Thread support is built into java but not in C++.

- ✓ Java does not support default arguments.

- ✓ There's no scope resolution operator: in Java. Java uses the dot for everything, but can get away with it since you can define elements only within a class. Even the method definitions must always occur within a class, so there is no need for scope resolution there either.

✓ There's no "goto" statement in Java.

✓ Java doesn't provide multiple inheritance (MI), at least not in the same sense that C++ does.

✓ Exception handling in Java is different because there are no destructors.

✓ Java has method overloading, but no operator overloading. The String class does use the + and += operators to concatenate strings and String expressions use automatic type conversion, but that's a special built-in case.

✓ Java is interpreted for the most part and hence platform independent.

202. Question: *What are interfaces?*
Answer: Interfaces provide more sophisticated ways to organize and control the objects in your system. The interface keyword takes the abstract concept one step further. You could think of it as a "pure" abstract class.

It allows the creator to establish the form for a class: method names, argument lists, and return types, but no method bodies. An interface can also contain fields. An interface says:

"This is what all classes that implement this particular interface will look like." Thus, any code that uses a particular interface knows what methods might be called for that interface, and that's all.

So the interface is used to establish a "protocol" between classes (some object-oriented programming languages have a keyword called protocol to do the same thing).

A typical example is listed below (from "Coe Java Professional"):

```
import java.util.*;
interface Instrument {
        int i = 5; // static & final
        // Cannot have method definitions:
        void play(); // Automatically public
        String what();
        void adjust();
}

class Wind implements Instrument {
        public void play() {
        System.out.println("Wind.play()");
        }
        public String what() { return "Wind"; }
        public void adjust() {}
}
```

203. Question: *How can you achieve Multiple Inheritance in Java?*

Answer: Java's interface mechanism can be used to implement multiple inheritances, with one important difference from c++ way of doing MI: the inherited interfaces must be abstract. This obviates the need to choose between different implementations, as with interfaces there are no implementations.

```
Example:
    interface CanFight {
        void fight();
    }

    interface CanSwim {
        void swim();
    }
    interface CanFly {
        void fly();
    }
    class ActionCharacter {
        public void fight() {}
    }
    class Hero extends ActionCharacter implements CanFight, CanSwim,
    CanFly {
        public void swim() {}
        public void fly() {}
    }
```

```
interface A {
   void methodA();
}

class AImpl implements A {
   void methodA() { //do stuff }
}

interface B {
   void methodB();
}

class BImpl implements B {
   void methodB() { //do stuff }
}

class Multiple implements A, B {
   private A a = new AImpl();
   private B b = new BImpl();
   void methodA() { a.methodA(); }
   void methodB() { b.methodB(); }
}
```

See Above, You can even achieve a form of multiple inheritance where you can use the *functionality* of classes rather than just the interface:

This completely solves the traditional problems of multiple inheritance in C++ where name clashes occur between multiple base classes. The coder of the derived class will have to explicitly resolve any clashes.

204. Question: *What is the difference between String Buffer and String class?*

Answer: A string buffer implements a mutable sequence of characters. A string buffer is like a String, but can be modified. At any point in time it contains some particular sequence of characters, but the length and content of the sequence can be changed through certain method calls.

The String class represents character strings. All string literals in Java programs, such as "abc" are constant and implemented as instances of this class; their values cannot be changed after they are created.

205. Question: *Describe, in general, how java's garbage collector works?*

Answer: The Java runtime environment deletes objects when it determines that they are no longer being used. This process is known as garbage collection. The Java runtime environment supports a garbage collector that periodically frees the memory used by objects that are no longer needed. The Java garbage collector is a mark-sweep garbage collector that scans Java's dynamic memory areas for objects, marking those that are referenced.

After all possible paths to objects are investigated, those objects that are not marked (i.e. are not referenced) are known to be garbage and are collected (A more complete description of our garbage collection algorithm might be "A compacting, marks weep collector with some conservative scanning").

The garbage collector run synchronously when the system runs out of memory, or in response to a request from a Java program. Your Java program can ask the garbage collector to run at any time by calling System.gc().

The garbage collector requires about 20 milliseconds to complete its task so, your program should only run the garbage collector when there will be no performance impact and the program anticipates an idle period long enough for the garbage collector to finish its job.

Note:

Asking the garbage collection to run does not guarantee that your objects will be garbage collected.

The Java garbage collector runs asynchronously when the system is idle on systems that allow the Java runtime to note when a thread has begun and to interrupt another thread (such as Windows 95).

As soon as another thread becomes active, the garbage collector is asked to get to a consistent state and then terminate. (From "from "Coe Java Professional" by Harry").

206. Question: What are some of the main differences between == operatorand equals method?

Answer: The equals method can be considered to perform a deep comparison of the value of an object, whereas the == operator performs a shallow comparison. The equal's method compares what an object points to rather than the pointer itself (if we can admit that Java has pointers). This indirection may appear clear to C++ programmers.

Remember to override the toString() method provided by java.lang.Object when you want to use equals() method on custom objects as for an Object the toString method simply returns the memory address and comparing two memory address is not what you want when checking for Object equality.

String class comes with an implementation of toString () which does the character by character comparison, so you don't have to worry about toString () while using equals on string objects.

207. Question: *What are abstract classes and abstract methods?*

Answer: Simply speaking a class or a method qualified with "abstract" keyword is an abstract class or abstract method. You create an abstract class when you want to manipulate a set of classes through a common interface. All derived-class methods that match the signature of the base-class declaration will be called using the dynamic binding mechanism.

If you have an abstract class, objects of that class almost always have no meaning. That is, abstract class is meant to express only the interface and sometimes some default method implementations, and not a particular implementation, so creating an abstract class object makes no sense and are not allowed (compile will give you an error message if you try to create one). An abstract method is an incomplete method. It has only a declaration and no method body. Here is the syntax for an abstract method declaration:

$$abstract\ void\ f();$$

If a class contains one or more abstract methods, the class must be qualified an abstract. (Otherwise, the compiler gives you an error message.). It's possible to create a class as abstract without including any abstract methods. This is useful when you've got a class in which it doesn't make sense to have any abstract methods, and yet you want to prevent any instances of that class. Abstract classes and methods are created because they make the abstractness of a class explicit, and tell both the user and the compiler how it was intended to be used.

For example:

```
abstract class Instrument
{
    int i; // storage allocated for each
    public abstract void play();
    public String what()
    {
        return "Instrument";
    }

    public abstract void adjust();
}
class Wind extends Instrument
{
    public void play()
    {
        System.out.println("Wind.play()");
    }
    public String what()
    {
        return "Wind";
    }
    public void adjust()
    {
    }
}
```

208. Question: *How can you force all derived classes to implement a method present in the base class?*

Answer: An abstract Class is the way to go. An Interface is absolutely the wrong way to go. The best way to think of an Interface is just as what it is, a completely abstract class. One main difference between an interface and an abstract class is that in an abstract class you can define some methods but not all (though you still can't instantiate an abstract class).

In an interface you can only declare methods, but you cannot define them. In sum, an abstract class is the way to go. This will allow you to leave the single method in question as an abstract class and allow it to be defined by a subclass.

209. Question: *Java says "write once, run anywhere". What are some ways this isn't quite true?*

Answer: There are some issues that require you to spend some effort porting a system written for one OS to run on another OS:

- You have the ability to use JNI, which will use native libraries, which can work differently on different systems.
- You have the ability to make system calls with Runtime.getRuntime ().exec ("<system command>") which can make the code hardware dependent, e.g. "ls" will not work on Windows.
- You have the ability to use XY coordinates in Pixels instead of specifying a Layout Manager in Swing, which will change the way the GUI looks on different systems.
- There are also some bugs in VM implementations on different systems which may cause your program to run well on Sun but crash on HP if your program runs into a bug on the HP VM that is not in the SUN implementation. I have personally run into this.
- You have to perform separate performance tuning, e.g. garbage collection parameters, initial heap size, etc. for each OS you run your system on, depending on the performance of each OS and the hardware it runs on.
- Threads are implemented differently on each system. For example, on Windows even low priority threads will get a few time slices, while on UNIX a low priority thread will never run if high priority threads do not yield to it.

There are other minor operating differences as well, e.g. you send a kill -S SIGQUIT command on UNIX to see a thread dump, and on Windows you press the Break key.

210. Question: *What is the difference between a Vector and an Array? Discuss the advantages and disadvantages of both?*

Answer: Main differences between Vector and Arrays are:

- Vector can contain objects of different types whereas array can contain objects only of a single type.
- Vector can expand at run-time, while array length is fixed.
- Vector methods are synchronized while Array methods are not.

Use ArrayList if you want functionality similar to a vector, but do not need synchronization..

211. Question: *What does the keyword "synchronize" mean in Java? When do you use it? What are the disadvantages of synchronization*

Answer: Synchronize is used when u want to make your methods thread safe. The disadvantage of synchronize is it will end up in slowing down the program. Also if not handled properly it will end up in dead lock.

There are few more things one should know about synchronization:

- Only use (and minimize its use) synchronization when writing multithreaded code as there is a speed (up to five to six time slower, depending on the execution time of the synchronized/non-synchronized method) cost associated with its use.

- In case of synchronized method modifier, the byte code generated is the exact same as non synchronized method. The only difference is that a flag called ACC_SYNCRONIZED property flag in method's method_info structure is set if the synchronized method modifier is present.

- Also, synchronized keyword can make the code larger in size if used in the body of the method as bytecode for monitorenter/monitorexit is generated in addition to any exception handling.

So, bottom line is use synchronization very carefully, understand the performance implications, and prefer synchronize method modifier to synchronized blocks.

212. Question: *What is JDBC? Describe the steps needed to execute a SQL query using JDBC.*

Answer: JDBC is java based API for accessing data from the relational databases.JDBC provides a set of classes and interfaces for doing various database operations.

The steps are:

- Register/load the jdbc driver with the driver manager.
- Establish the connection thru DriverManager.getConnection();
- Fire a SQL thru conn.executeStatement()
- Fetch the results in a result set
- Process the results
- Close statement/result set and connection object.

213. Question: *Are constructors inherited? Can a subclass call the parent classe's constructor? When?*

Answer: Constructors are not inherited. The first statement in the constructor of the sub-class should be the call to the constructor of the super class.

```
Ex:
class A
{
        int i;
        A(int a)
        {
            i=a;
        }
}
class B extends A
{
        B()
        {
            super(10);//This is must.
        }
}
```

The first statement in the constructor of the sub-class should be a call to the constructor of the super class, only and only if, the base-class constructor has arguments. However if your base-class constructor does not have arguments, then the base-class constructor is automatically called in the sub-class.

214. Question: *Describe java's security model*

Answer: Java has a "sand-box" security model, where un-trusted code can be kept away from data that it should not be able to touch, using a fine-grained analysis of individual operations.

This is as opposed to a "trusted user" security model, which is what Microsoft has been pushing with ActiveX, etc. In this model, the emphasis is on obtaining a chain of certificates of trusted users. Once something is trusted, it has full access to do all operations.

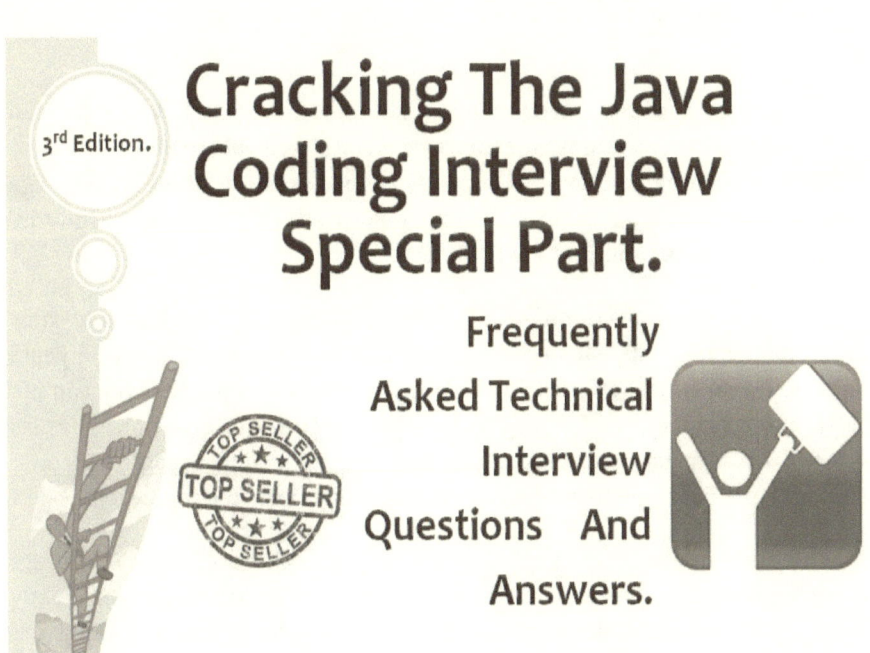

3rd Edition.

Cracking The Java Coding Interview Special Part.

Frequently Asked Technical Interview Questions And Answers.

TOP SELLER

10 Advanced core Java interview questions for senior and experienced programmer

Java interview questions for Senior and Experienced programmer -

As you know, Java is very big and there is no way to prepare completely for any core java interview but there is a level of question depends upon your experience, if you are fresher than questions asked in Java interview are mostly based on fundamentals like Iterator vs Enumeration in Java, Why main is public static and void or may be ArrayList vs LinkedList in Java.

Things changes when you apply for senior developer, Technical lead or Team Lead Java positions, questions asked on that level are more advanced and less popular among Java circles, you may be asked questions from design pattern, questions from multi-threading, Collections and even asked to write code, design classes and prepare JUnit tests.

In this Java Section I will share some advanced Core Java interview questions which is appear in Senior level interviews mostly on 4 to 6 years and 6 to 8 years of experience. One important thing to note is that you can not clear interview by just mugging answers of these question because interviewer is most likely asked you follow-up question based upon your response and only way to get through it is to understand the topic well.

Here are my list of questions which is worth preparing if you are going for core java interview for senior position, these questions are mostly based upon Garbage collection , Concurrency, Collections, design, Coding and testing.How does ConcurrentHashMap works in Java ?

Question : is ConcurrentHashMap is thread-safe?

Question : Can we replace Hashtable to ConcurrentHashMap without external synchronization?

As you see there are multiple question in this category, those are mostly followup and can be answered if you understand ConcurrentHashMap well.

Question : What is CountDownLatch in Java?

Question : What is CyclicBarrier in Java?

Question : What is difference between CountDownLatch and CyclicBarrier in Java?

Concurrency is favorite topic on advanced core java interviews and its expected from experienced and senior Java developers to have good understanding of multi-threading and concurrency API in Java.

Question : What is Race condition ? Have you faced any race condition?

Question : What is deadLock in Java? Write code to avoid deadlock in Java

Raced conditions and deadlock are major challenges while writing high performance concurrent Java applications and hands on experience of dealing with synchronization and concurrency issue expected from a senior and experience Java programmer. Refer how to avoid deadlock in Java and What is race condition in Java for more details.

Question : What is PermGen space ?

Question : What is memory leak in Java?

Question : What is OutOfMemoryError in PermGen mens?

Question : What is difference between NoClassDefFoundError and ClassNotFoundException in Java?

These are some questions related to Errors and Exceptions in Java, OutOfMemoryError and NoclassDefFoundError are most common yet dreaded errors in Java.

Question : What skills are you expected to have as a senior Java developer?

Skill #1: Good "software craftsmanship" skills. In other words have good handle on the 16 technical key areas listed below. You should have the ability to ask the right questions (e.g. should I use aspect oriented programming (i.e. AOP) here?, should I favor optimistic or pessimistic locking here? should the method call made within a transactional context?) and solve problems (e.g. memory leaks, thread safety, SQL injection attacks, performance, etc) relating to these 16 technical key areas.

What are these 16 key areas?

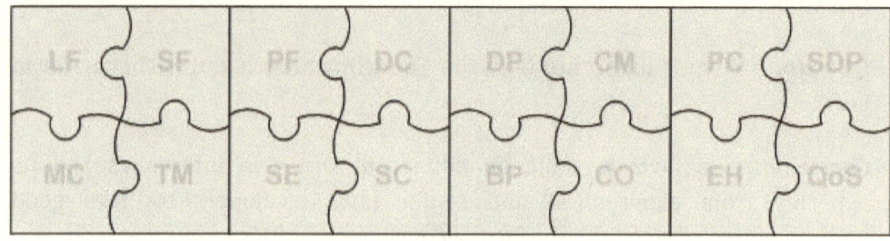

1) Language Fundamentals (LF)

2) Specification Fundamentals (SF)

3) Platform Fundamentals (PF)

4) Design Considerations (DC)

5) Design Patterns (DP)

6) Concurrency Management (CM)

7) Performance Considerations (PC)

8) Memory/Resource Considerations (MC)

9) Transaction Management (TM)

10) Security (SE)

11) Scalability (SC)

12) Best Practices (BP)

13) Coding (CO)

14) Exception Handling (EH)

15) Software Development Processes (SDP)

16) Quality of Service (QoS)

How to get an entry level Java developer job?

Entry level Java developers and career changers get caught in the vicious cycle where "you can't get a job without some hands-on experience, but the employers are not keen to hire you without some experience". Employers are looking for entry level developers who can start contributing from the day they join. This does not mean that employers are not going to provide you training and support, but rather looking for skills outside academic qualifications like -- working independently, quick learner, passion for the chosen profession, understanding of the industry, ability to communicate your thoughts/capabilities and some much needed "**hands-on experience**". There is no other magic formula. Most employers don't care where you got that experience from.

So, if you are stuck in this vicious cycle, the key is to get some experience to break this cycle via **self-taught projects**, **open-source contribution**, and **volunteer work in Java** (e.g. charity organizations and local community projects). It does not matter what avenue you take, and every experience counts. You need to demonstrate your passion & understanding of the chosen profession, and ability to work independently and as a team. Here are some step by step guide to get the ball rolling.

Things that do not make a real difference in securing a job:

1) Thinking that piling up of your certifications can help.

2) Thinking that a post-graduate qualification can increase your chances.

3) Thinking that reading a Java book from cover to cover can help. It is very important to learn the fundamentals, but mix learning the fundamentals with gaining the much needed hands-on experience. Can you drive a car by just learning how the controls work?

1) **Things you should do to make a break as a Java developer**: Only way to learn to drive a car is by getting behind the wheels. So, 3 things you should do in a nutshell.

2) Invest in improving your job hunting skills encompassing interviewing, networking, and resume writing skills.

3) Keep applying for jobs via both **published & hidden job markets**.

4) Follow the tips outlined below to enhance your hands-on experience while keeping at points 1 & 2.

All the above 3 points should go hand-in-hand. That is your full-time or part-time job of "**finding a job**"

Getting the much needed hands-on experience

Tip #1:

Java is very accessible and all the following are available for free. The steps you take may slightly vary depending on your familiarity with Java and its tools.

1) A computer -- desk top or lap top.
2) Download latest version of Java (JDK and JRE).
3) Download latest version of eclipse IDE.
4) Dowload Tomcat or JBoss to deploy your applications.
5) Download and install MySQL database. All non trivial applications need information to be persisted to a database.
6) Set up Maven as a build and dependency management tool so that you can download sought after frameworks like Spring and Hibernate.

Tip #2:

Start with the basics first. Enterprise Java has hundreds of frameworks and libraries and it is easy for the beginners to get confused. Once you get to a certain point, you will get a better handle on them, but to get started, stick to the following basic steps. Feel free to make changes as you see fit.

❖ Core Java fundamentals. Write simple stand alone Java programs using OO concepts. Write unit tests with JUnit.

❖ Learn SQL and write stand alone Java programs that connect to MySQL database via JDBC.

❖ Write simple web applications using Servelts and JSPs using enterprise Java. The application needs to persist data to the MySQL database. Deploy your application to Tomcat or JBoss server and run them as an enterprise application. Use Maven for build and dependency management.

❖ Expand your project created with JSPs, Servlets, and JDBC to use sought after frameworks. Learn the concept of "dependency injection". Start wiring up sought after frameworks like Spring. Spring is very vast, and start with spring core and spring jdbc. Spring core is used for dependency injection and Spring jdbc is to connect to databases and to execute SQL queries.

❖ Learn the MVC (Model View Controller) design pattern for web development. Convert your JSPs and Servlets to Spring-mvc based web application.

- ❖ Write RESTFul web services using Spring MVC.

- ❖ Get a working knowledge in HTML, JavaScript/jQuery/JSON, ajax, and CSS. This is imperative as more and more organizations are moving towards JavaScript based MVC frameworks like angularjs or backbone. These frameworks make RESTFul web service calls to get data in JSON format and populate the front end. It will be handy to learn node.js as well if time permits.

- ❖ Make sure that you write unit tests for your code with JUnit and mocking frameworks like Mockito.

Tip #3:

Once you have some familiarity and experience with developing enterprise applications with Java, try contributing to open source projects or if your self-taught project is non trivial, try to opensource your self-taught project. You can learn a lot by looking at others' code.

Tip #4:

Look for volunteer work to enhance your hands-on experience. Don't over commit yourself. Allocate say 2 to 3 days to build a website for a charity or community organization.

Tip #5:

Share your hands-on experience gained via tips 1-4 in your resume and through blogging (can be kept private initially). It is vital to capture your experience via blogging. Improve your resume writing and interviewing skills via many handy posts found in this blog or elseware on the internet. It is essential that while you are working on the tips 1-5, keep applying for the paid jobs as well.

Tip #6:

Voluntary work and other networking opportunities via Java User Groups (JUGs) and graduate trade fairs can put you in touch with the professionals in the industry and open more doors for you. The tips 1-5 will also differentiate you from the other entry level developers. My books and blog has covered lots of Java interview questions and answers.

Practice those questions and answers as many employers have initial phone screening and technical tests to ascertain your Java knowledge, mainly in core Java and web development (e.g. stateless HTTP protocol, sessions, cookies, etc).

All it takes is to learn 10 Q&A each day while gaining hands-on experience and applying for entry level jobs. Top 20 Java technical interview questions and answers for experienced Java developers.

Getting a good handle on the 16 technical key areas and handy tools to improve your productivity as a Java developer.

Do you want to become a front-end developer, and confused about where to start?

The new trend is to use JavaScript based frameworks like AngularJS. So, learning JavaScript, HTML(5), and CSS is a must. AngularJS is growing fast. The current JEE standard is JSF. Newer projects are moving towards client side MVW (Model View Whatever) frameworks using AngularJS, Backbone, ExtJs, etc. If you end up enhancing an existing application, you have a good chance of working on one of the following Web frameworks JSF, Spring MVC, Struts(2), and GWT.

Finding an entry level Java developer job itself a full-time job

You have the 8 hour+ work cut out for you. Regularly review your progress, and fine tune your approach. Sometimes you may require 360 degree turn (e.g. shift from piling up certifications to gaining much needed hands-on experience, shift from reading Java books from cover to cover to taking up a volunteer work, turning your job hunting from 2 hours a day to a 8 hour a day, etc) to your approach.

It is really important to do variety of things to keep it interesting and keep you motivated. It is easy to lose motivation. Share your experience with your fellow entry level Java developers. It is vital that you keep applying for a paid job whilst working on the above tips.

PART - IV

50+ JAVA
INTERVIEW
QUES & ANS

**Top 50 Java Multi-threading & Concurrency
Interview Questions Answers
for Freshers, Experienced Programmers.**

You go to any Java interview, senior or junior, experience or freshers, you are bound to see couple of questions from thread, concurrency and multi-threading. In fact this built-in concurrency support is one of the strongest point of Java programming language and helped it to gain popularity among enterprise world and programmers equally. Most of lucrative Java developer position demands excellent core Java multi-threading skills and experience on developing, debugging and tuning high performance low latency concurrent Java applications.

This is the reason, it is one of the most sought after skill on interviews. In a typical Java interview, Interviewer slowly starts from basic concepts of Thread by asking questions like, why you need threads, how to create threads, which one is better way to create threads e.g.

By extending thread class or implementing Runnable and then slowly goes into Concurrency issues, challenges faced during development of concurrent Java applications, Java memory model, higher order concurrency utilities introduced in JDK 1.5, principles and design patterns of concurrent Java applications, classical multi-threading problems e.g. producer consumer, dining philosopher, reader writer or simply bounded buffer problems. Since its not enough just to know basics of threading, you must know how to deal with concurrency problems e.g. deadlock, race conditions, memory inconsistency and various thread safety related issues.

These skills are thoroughly get tested by presenting various multi-threading and concurrency problems. Many Java developers are used to only look and read interview questions before going for interview, which is not bad but you should not be too far away.

Also collecting questions and going through same exercise is too much time consuming, that's why I have created this list of top 50 Java multi-threading and concurrency related questions, collected from various interviews. I am only going to add new and recent interview questions as and when I am going to discover them.

By the way, I have not provided answers of this questions here, Why? because I expect most of Java developer to know the answers of this question and if not, Here is my list of top questions from Java thread, concurrency and multi-threading. You can use this list to prepare well for your Java interview.

1) What is Thread in Java?

Thread is an independent path of execution. It's way to take advantage of multiple CPU available in a machine. By employing multiple threads you can speed up CPU bound task. For example, if one thread takes 100 millisecond to do a job, you can use 10 thread to reduce that task into 10 millisecond. Java provides excellent support for multi-threading at language level, and its also one of strong selling point.

2) Difference between Thread and Process in Java?

Thread is subset of Process, in other words one process can contain multiple threads. Two process runs on different memory space, but all threads share same memory space. Don't confuse this with stack memory, which is different for different thread and used to store local data to that thread.

3) How do you implement Thread in Java?

At language level, there are two ways to implement Thread in Java. An instance of java.lang.Thread represent a thread but it need a task to execute, which is instance of interface java.lang.Runnable. Since Thread class itself implement Runnable, you can override run() method either by extending Thread class or just implementing Runnable interface. For detailed answer and discussion see this article.

4) When to use Runnable vs Thread in Java?

This is follow-up of previous multi-threading interview question. As we know we can implement thread either by extending Thread class or implementing Runnable interface, question arise, which one is better and when to use one? This question will be easy to answer, if you know that Java programming language doesn't support multiple inheritance of class, but it allows you to implement multiple interface. Which means, its better to implement Runnable than extends Thread, if you also want to extend another class e.g. Canvas or CommandListener.

6) Difference between start() and run() method of Thread class?

One of trick Java question from early days, but still good enough to differentiate between shallow understanding of Java threading model start() method is used to start newly created thread, while start() internally calls run() method, there is difference calling run() method directly. When you invoke run() as normal method, its called in the same thread, no new thread is started, which is the case when you call start() method.

7) Difference between Runnable and Callable in Java?

Both Runnable and Callable represent task which is intended to be executed in separate thread. Runnable is there from JDK 1.0, while Callable was added on JDK 1.5. Main difference between these two is that Callable's call() method can return value and throw Exception, which was not possible with Runnable's run() method. Callable return Future object, which can hold result of computation.

8) Difference between CyclicBarrier and CountDownLatch in Java?

Though both CyclicBarrier and CountDownLatch wait for number of threads on one or more events, main difference between them is that you can not re-use CountDownLatch once count reaches to zero, but you can reuse same CyclicBarrier even after barrier is broken.

9) *What is Java Memory model?*

Java Memory model is set of rules and guidelines which allows Java programs to behave deterministically across multiple memory architecture, CPU, and operating system. It's particularly important in case of multi-threading. Java Memory Model provides some guarantee on which changes made by one thread should be visible to others, one of them is happens-before relationship.

This relationship defines several rules which allows programmers to anticipate and reason behaviour of concurrent Java programs. For example, happens-before relationship guarantees :

- ✓ Each action in a thread happens-before every action in that thread that comes later in the program order, this is known as program order rule.

- ✓ An unlock on a monitor lock happens-before every subsequent lock on that same monitor lock, also known as Monitor lock rule.

- ✓ A write to a volatile field happens-before every subsequent read of that same field, known as Volatile variable rule.

- ✓ A call to Thread.start on a thread happens-before any other thread detects that thread has terminated, either by successfully return from Thread.join() or by Thread.isAlive() returning false, also known as Thread start rule.

- ✓ A thread calling interrupt on another thread happens-before the interrupted thread detects the interrupt(either by having InterruptedException thrown, or invoking isInterrupted or interrupted), popularly known as Thread Interruption rule.

- ✓ The end of a constructor for an object happens-before the start of the finalizer for that object, known as Finalizer rule.

If A happens-before B, and B happens-before C, then A happens-before C, which means happens-before guarantees Transitivity.

10) *What is volatile variable in Java?*

volatile is a special modifier, which can only be used with instance variables. In concurrent Java programs, changes made by multiple threads on instance variables is not visible to other in absence of any synchronizers e.g. synchronized keyword or locks. Volatile variable guarantees that a write will happen before any subsequent read, as stated "volatile variable rule" in previous question.

11) *What is thread-safety? is Vector a thread-safe class? (Yes, see details)*

Thread-safety is a property of an object or code which guarantees that if executed or used by multiple thread in any manner e.g. read vs write it will behave as expected. For example, a thread-safe counter object will not miss any count if same instance of that counter is shared among multiple threads.

Apparently, you can also divide collection classes in two category, thread-safe and non-thread-safe. Vector is indeed a thread-safe class and it achieves thread-safety by synchronizing methods which modifies state of Vector, on the other hand, its counterpart ArrayList is not thread-safe.

12) What is race condition in Java? Given one example?

Race condition are cause of some subtle programming bugs when Java programs are exposed to concurrent execution environment. As name suggests, race condition occurs due to race between multiple threads, if a thread which is supposed to execute first lost the race and executed second, behaviour of code changes, which surface as non-deterministic bugs. This is one of the hardest bugs to find and re-produce because of random nature of racing between threads. One example of race condition is out-of-order processing.

13) How to stop thread in Java?

I always said that Java provides rich APIs for everything but ironically Java doesn't provide a sure shot way of stopping thread. There was some control methods in JDK 1.0 e.g. stop(), suspend() and resume() which was deprecated in later releases due to potential deadlock threats, from then Java API designers has not made any effort to provide a consistent, thread-safe and elegant way to stop threads. Programmers mainly rely on the fact that thread stops automatically as soon as they finish execution of run() or call() method. To manually stop, programmers either take advantage of volatile boolean variable and check in every iteration if run method has loops or interrupt threads to abruptly cancel tasks.

14) What happens when an Exception occurs in a thread?

This is one of the good tricky Java question I have seen on interviews. In simple words, If not caught thread will die, if an uncaught exception handler is registered then it will get a call back. Thread.UncaughtExceptionHandler is an interface, defined as nested interface for handlers invoked when a Thread abruptly terminates due to an uncaught exception. When a thread is about to terminate due to an uncaught exception the Java Virtual Machine will query the thread for its UncaughtExceptionHandler using Thread.getUncaughtExceptionHandler() and will invoke the handler's uncaughtException() method, passing the thread and the exception as arguments.

15) How do you share data between two thread in Java?

You can share data between threads by using shared object, or concurrent data-structure like BlockingQueue. See this tutorial to learn inter thread communication in Java. It implements Producer consumer pattern using wait and notify methods, which involves sharing objects between two threads.

16) *Difference between notify and notifyAll in Java?*

This is another tricky questions from core Java interviews, since multiple threads can wait on single monitor lock, Java API designer provides method to inform only one of them or all of them, once waiting condition changes, but they provide half implementation.

There notify() method doesn't provide any way to choose a particular thread, that's why its only useful when you know that there is only one thread is waiting. On the other hand, notifyAll() sends notification to all threads and allows them to compete for locks, which ensures that at-least one thread will proceed further.

17) *Why wait, notify and notifyAll are not inside thread class?*

This is a design related question, which checks what candidate thinks about existing system or does he ever thought of something which is so common but looks in-appropriate at first. In order to answer this question, you have to give some reasons why it make sense for these three method to be in Object class, and why not on Thread class.

One reason which is obvious is that Java provides lock at object level not at thread level. Every object has lock, which is acquired by thread. Now if thread needs to wait for certain lock it make sense to call wait() on that object rather than on that thread. Had wait() method declared on Thread class, it was not clear that for which lock thread was waiting. In short, since wait, notify and notifyAll operate at lock level, it make sense to defined it on object class because lock belongs to object.

18) *What is ThreadLocal variable in Java?*

ThreadLocal variables are special kind of variable available to Java programmer. Just like instance variable is per instance, ThreadLocal variable is per thread. It's a nice way to achieve thread-safety of expensive-to-create objects, for example you can make SimpleDateFormat thread-safe using ThreadLocal. Since that class is expensive, its not good to use it in local scope, which requires separate instance on each invocation.

By providing each thread their own copy, you shoot two birds in one arrow. First, you reduce number of instance of expensive object by reusing fixed number of instances, and Second, you achieve thread-safety without paying cost of synchronization or immutability. Another good example of thread local variable is ThreadLocalRandom class, which reduces number of instances of expensive-to-create Random object in multi-threading environment.

19) *What is FutureTask in Java?*

FutureTask represents a cancellable asynchronous computation in concurrent Java application.

This class provides a base implementation of Future, with methods to start and cancel a computation, query to see if the computation is complete, and retrieve the result of the computation. The result can only be retrieved when the computation has completed; the get methods will block if the computation has not yet completed. A FutureTask object can be used to wrap a Callable or Runnable object. Since FutureTask also implements Runnable, it can be submitted to an Executor for execution.

20) Difference between interrupted and isInterrupted method in Java?

Main difference between interrupted() and isInterrupted() is that former clears the interrupt status while later does not. The interrupt mechanism in Java multi-threading is implemented using an internal flag known as the interrupt status. Interrupting a thread by calling Thread.interrupt() sets this flag. When interrupted thread checks for an interrupt by invoking the static method Thread.interrupted(), interrupt status is cleared. The non-static isInterrupted() method, which is used by one thread to query the interrupt status of another, does not change the interrupt status flag. By convention, any method that exits by throwing an InterruptedException clears interrupt status when it does so. However, it's always possible that interrupt status will immediately be set again, by another thread invoking interrupt

21) Why wait and notify method are called from synchronized block?

Main reason for calling wait and notify method from either synchronized block or method is that it made mandatory by Java API. If you don't call them from synchronized context, your code will throw IllegalMonitorStateException. A more subtle reason is to avoid race condition between wait and notify calls.

22) Why you should check condition for waiting in a loop?

Its possible for a waiting thread to receive false alerts and spurious wake up calls, if it doesn't check the waiting condition in loop, it will simply exit even if condition is not met. As such, when a waiting thread wakes up, it cannot assume that the state it was waiting for is still valid. It may have been valid in the past, but the state may have been changed after the notify() method was called and before the waiting thread woke up. That's why it always better to call wait() method from loop, you can even create template for calling wait and notify in Eclipse.

23) Difference between synchronized and concurrent collection in Java?

Though both synchronized and concurrent collection provides thread-safe collection suitable for multi-threaded and concurrent access, later is more scalable than former. Before Java 1.5, Java programmers only had synchronized collection which becomes source of contention if multiple thread access them concurrently, which hampers scalability of system. Java 5 introduced concurrent collections like ConcurrentHashMap, which not only provides thread-safety but also improves scalability by using modern techniques like lock stripping and partitioning internal table.

24) Difference between Stack and Heap in Java?

Why do someone this question as part of multi-threading and concurrency? because Stack is a memory area which is closely associated with threads. To answer this question, both stack and heap are specific memories in Java application. Each thread has their own stack, which is used to store local variables, method parameters and call stack. Variable stored in one Thread's stack is not visible to other. On other hand, heap is a common memory area which is shared by all threads. Objects whether local or at any level is created inside heap. To improve performance thread tends to cache values from heap into their stack, which can create problems if that variable is modified by more than one thread, this is where volatile variables comes in picture. volatile suggest threads to read value of variable always from main memory.

25) What is thread pool? Why should you thread pool in Java?

Creating thread is expensive in terms of time and resource. If you create thread at time of request processing it will slow down your response time, also there is only a limited number of threads a process can create. To avoid both of these issue, a pool of thread is created when application starts-up and threads are reused for request processing. This pool of thread is known as "thread pool" and threads are known as worker thread. From JDK 1.5 release, Java API provides Executor framework, which allows you to create different types of thread pools e.g. single thread pool, which process one task at a time, fixed thread pool (a pool of fixed number of thread) or cached thread pool (an expandable thread pool suitable for applications with many short lived tasks).

26) Write code to solve Producer Consumer problem in Java?

Most of the threading problem you solved in real world are of category of Producer consumer pattern, where one thread is producing task and other thread is consuming that. You must know how to do inter thread communication to solve this problem. At lowest level, you can use wait and notify to solve this problem, and at high level you can leverage Semaphore or BlockingQueue to implement Producer consumer pattern.

27) How do you check if a Thread holds a lock or not?

I didn't even know that you can check if a Thread already holds lock before this question hits me in a telephonic round of Java interview. There is a method called holdsLock() on java.lang.Thread, it returns true if and only if the current thread holds the monitor lock on the specified object.

28) How do you avoid deadlock in Java? Write Code?

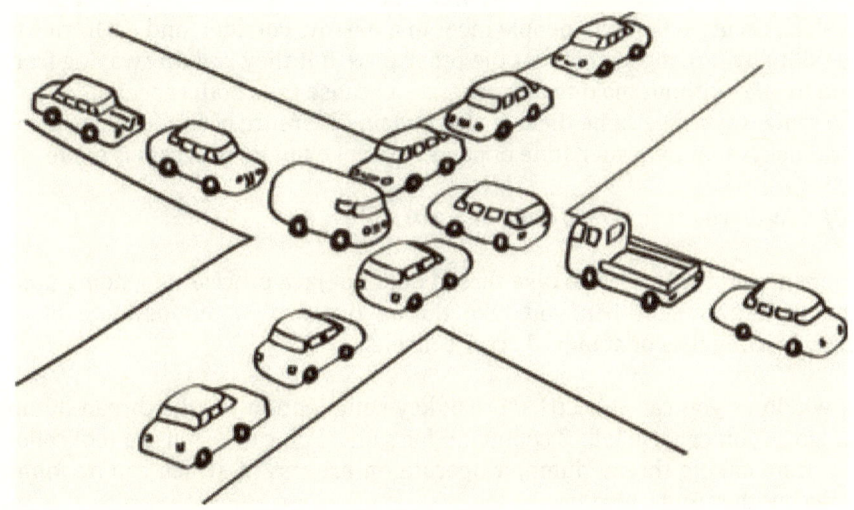

Deadlock is a condition in which two threads wait for each other to take action which allows them to move further. It's a serious issue because when it happen your program hangs and doesn't do the task it is intended for. In order for deadlock to happen, following four condition must be true :

- Mutual Exclusion : At least one resource must be held in a non-shareable mode. Only one process can use the resource at any given instant of time.

- Hold and Wait : A process is currently holding at least one resource and requesting additional resources which are being held by other processes.

- No Pre-emption : The operating system must not de-allocate resources once they have been allocated; they must be released by the holding process voluntarily.

- Circular Wait : A process must be waiting for a resource which is being held by another process, which in turn is waiting for the first process to release the resource.

Easiest way to avoid deadlock is to prevent Circular wait, and this can be done by acquiring locks in a particular order and releasing them in reverse order, so that a thread can only proceed to acquire a lock if it held the other one.

29) *Difference between livelock and deadlock in Java?*

This question is extension of previous interview question. A livelock is similar to a deadlock, except that the states of the threads or processes involved in the livelock constantly change with regard to one another, without any one progressing further.

Livelock is a special case of resource starvation. A real-world example of livelock occurs when two people meet in a narrow corridor, and each tries to be polite by moving aside to let the other pass, but they end up swaying from side to side without making any progress because they both repeatedly move the same way at the same time. In short, main difference between livelock and deadlock is that in former state of process change but no progress is made.

30) How do you take thread dump in Java?

There are multiple ways to take thread dump of Java process depending upon operating system. When you take thread dump, JVM dumps state of all threads in log files or standard error console.

In windows you can use Ctrl + Break key combination to take thread dump, on Linux you can use kill -3 command for same. You can also use a tool called jstack for taking thread dump, it operate on process id, which can be found using another tool called jps.

31) Which JVM parameter is used to control stack size of thread?

This is the simple one, -Xss parameter is used to control stack size of Thread in Java.

32) Difference between synchronized and ReentrantLock in Java?

There were days when only way to provide mutual exclusion in Java was via synchronized keyword, but it has several shortcomings e.g. you can not extend lock beyond a method or block boundary, you can not give up trying for a lock etc. Java 5 solves this problem by providing more sophisticated control via Lock interface.

ReentrantLock is a common implementation of Lock interface and provides re-entrant mutual exclusion Lock with the same basic behaviour and semantics as the implicit monitor lock accessed using synchronized methods and statements, but with extended capabilities.

33) There are three threads T1, T2 and T3? How do you ensure sequence T1, T2, T3 in Java?

Sequencing in multi-threading can be achieved by different means but you can simply use join() method of thread class to start a thread when another one is finished its execution. To ensure three threads execute you need to start the last one first e.g. T3 and then call join methods in reverse order e.g. T3 calls T2. join, and T2 calls T1.join, this ways T1 will finish first and T3 will finish last.

34) *What does yield method of Thread class do?*

Yield method is one way to request current thread to relinquish CPU so that other thread can get chance to execute. Yield is a static method and only guarantees that current thread will relinquish the CPU but doesn't say anything about which other thread will get CPU. Its possible for same thread to get CPU back and start its execution again.

35) *What is concurrence level of ConcurrentHashMap in Java?*

ConcurrentHashMap achieves it's scalability and thread-safety by partitioning actual map into number of sections. This partitioning is achieved using concurrency level. It's optional parameter of ConcurrentHashMap constructor and it's default value is 16. The table is internally partitioned to try to permit the indicated number of concurrent updates without contention.

36) *What is Semaphore in Java?*

Semaphore in Java is a new kind of synchronizer. It's a counting semaphore. Conceptually, a semaphore maintains a set of permits. Each acquire() blocks if necessary until a permit is available, and then takes it. Each release() adds a permit, potentially releasing a blocking acquirer. However, no actual permit objects are used; the Semaphore just keeps a count of the number available and acts accordingly. Semaphore is used to protect expensive resource which is available in fixed number e.g. database connection in pool. learn more about counting Semaphore in Java.

37) *What happens if you submit task, when queue of thread pool is already fill?*

This is another tricky question in my list. Many programmer will think that it will block until a task is cleared but its true. ThreadPoolExecutor's submit() method throws RejectedExecutionException if the task cannot be scheduled for execution.

38) *Difference between submit() and execute() method thread pool in Java?*

Both method are ways to submit task to thread pools but there is slight difference between them. execute(Runnable command) is defined in Executor interface and executes given task in future, but more importantly it does not return anything. It's return type is void. On other hand submit() is overloaded method, it can take either Runnable or Callable task and can return Future object which can hold pending result of computation. This method is defined on ExecutorService interface, which extends Executor interface, and every other thread pool class e.g. ThreadPoolExecutor or ScheduledThreadPoolExecutor gets these methods.

39) *What is blocking method in Java?*

A blocking method is a method which blocks until task is done, for example accept() method of ServerSocket blocks until a client is connected. here blocking means control will not return to caller until task is finished. On the other hand there are asynchronous or non-blocking method which returns even before task is finished.

40) *Is Swing thread-safe? What do you mean by Swing thread-safe?*
You can simply this question as No, Swing is not thread-safe, but you have to explain what you mean by that even if interviewer doesn't ask about it. When we say swing is not thread-safe we usually refer its component, which can not be modified in multiple threads. All update to GUI components has to be done on AWT thread, and Swing provides synchronous and asynchronous callback methods to schedule such updates. You can also read my article to learn more about swing and thread-safety to better answer this question. Even next two questions are also related to this concept.

41) *Difference between invokeAndWait and invokeLater in Java?*

These are two methods Swing API provides Java developers to update GUI components from threads other than Event dispatcher thread. InvokeAndWait() synchronously update GUI component, for example a progress bar, once progress is made, bar should also be updated to reflect that change.

If progress is tracked in a different thread, it has to call invokeAndWait() to schedule an update of that component by Event dispatcher thread. On other hand, invokeLater() is asynchronous call to update components.

42) *Which method of Swing API are thread-safe in Java?*

This question is again related to swing and thread-safety, though components are not thread-safe there are certain method which can be safely call from multiple threads.

I know about repaint(), and revalidate() being thread-safe but there are other methods on different swing components e.g. setText() method of JTextComponent, insert() and append() method of JTextAreaclass.

43) *How to create Immutable object in Java?*

This question might not look related to multi-threading and concurrency, but it is. Immutability helps to simplify already complex concurrent code in Java. Since immutable object can be shared without any synchronization its very dear to Java developers.

Core value object, which is meant to be shared among thread should be immutable for performance and simplicity. Unfortunately there is no @Immutable annotation in Java, which can make your object immutable, hard work must be done by Java developers. You need to keep basics like initializing state in constructor, no setter methods, no leaking of reference, keeping separate copy of mutable object to create Immutable object.

44) What is ReadWriteLock in Java?

In general, read write lock is result of lock stripping technique to improve performance of concurrent applications. In Java, ReadWriteLock is an interface which was added in Java 5 release. A ReadWriteLock maintains a pair of associated locks, one for read-only operations and one for writing. The read lock may be held simultaneously by multiple reader threads, so long as there are no writers. The write lock is exclusive. If you want you can implement this interface with your own set of rules, otherwise you can use ReentrantReadWriteLock, which comes along with JDK and supports a maximum of 65535 recursive write locks and 65535 read locks.

45) What is busy spin in multi-threading?

Busy spin is a technique which concurrent programmers employ to make a thread wait on certain condition. Unlike traditional methods e.g. wait(), sleep() or yield() which all involves relinquishing CPU control, this method does not relinquish CPU, instead it just runs empty loop. Why would someone do that? to preserve CPU caches. In multi core system, its possible for a paused thread to resume on different core, which means rebuilding cache again. To avoid cost of rebuilding cache, programmer prefer to wait for much smaller time doing busy spin.

46) Difference between volatile and atomic variable in Java?

This is an interesting question for Java programmer, at first, volatile and atomic variable look very similar, but they are different. Volatile variable provides you happens-before guarantee that a write will happen before any subsequent write, it doesn't guarantee atomicity. For example count++ operation will not become atomic just by declaring count variable as volatile. On the other hand AtomicInteger class provides atomic method to perform such compound operation atomically e.g. getAndIncrement() is atomic replacement of increment operator. It can be used to atomically increment current value by one. Similarly you have atomic version for other data type and reference variable as well.

47) What happens if a thread throws an Exception inside synchronized block?

This is one more tricky question for average Java programmer, if he can bring the fact about whether lock is released or not is key indicator of his understanding. To answer this question, no matter how you exist synchronized block, either normally by finishing execution or abruptly by throwing exception, thread releases the lock it acquired while entering that synchronized block. This is actually one of the reason I like synchronized block over lock interface, which requires explicit attention to release lock, generally this is achieved by releasing lock in finally block.

48) *What is double checked locking of Singleton?*

This is one of the very popular question on Java interviews, and despite its popularity, chances of candidate answering this question satisfactory is only 50%. Half of the time, they failed to write code for double checked locking and half of the time they failed how it was broken and fixed on Java 1.5. This is actually an old way of creating thread-safe singleton, which tries to optimize performance by only locking when Singleton instance is created first time, but because of complexity and the fact it was broken for JDK 1.4, I personally don't like it. Anyway, even if you not prefer this approach its good to know from interview point of view.

49) *How to create thread-safe Singleton in Java?*

This question is actually follow-up of previous question. If you say you don't like double checked locking then Interviewer is bound to ask about alternative ways of creating thread-safe Singleton class. There are actually man, you can take advantage of class loading and static variable initialization feature of JVM to create instance of Singleton, or you can leverage powerful enumeration type in Java to create Singleton.

50) *List down 3 multi-threading best practice you follow?*

This is my favourite question, because I believe that you must follow certain best practices while writing concurrent code which helps in performance, debugging and maintenance. Following are three best practices, I think an average Java programmer should follow :

- Always give meaningful name to your threadThis goes a long way to find a bug or trace an execution in concurrent code. OrderProcessor, QuoteProcessor or TradeProcessor is much better than Thread-1. Thread-2 and Thread-3. Name should say about task done by that thread. All major framework and even JDK follow this best practice.

- Avoid locking or Reduce scope of Synchronization Locking is costly and context switching is even more costlier. Try to avoid synchronization and locking as much as possible and at bare minimum, you should reduce critical section.

  That's why I prefer synchronized block over synchronized method, because it gives you absolute control on scope of locking.

- Prefer Synchronizers over wait and notify Synchronizers like CountDownLatch, Semaphore, CyclicBarrier or Exchanger simplif ies coding. It's very difficult to implement complex control flow right using wait and notify. Secondly, these classes are written and maintained by best in business and there is good chance that they are optimized or replaced by better performance code in subsequent JDK releases. By using higher level synchronization utilities, you automatically get all these benefits.

- Prefer Concurrent Collection over Synchronized Collection This is another simple best practice which is easy to follow but reap good benefits. Concurrent collection are more scalable than their synchronized counterpart, that's why its better to use them while writing concurrent code. So next time if you need map, think about ConcurrentHashMap before thinking Hashtable.

51) How do you force start a Thread in Java?

This question is like how do you force garbage collection in Java, their is no way, though you can make request using System.gc() but its not guaranteed. On Java multi-threading their is absolute no way to force start a thread, this is controlled by thread scheduler and Java exposes no API to control thread schedule. This is still a random bit in Java.

52) What is fork join framework in Java?

The fork join framework, introduced in JDK 7 is a powerful tool available to Java developer to take advantage of multiple processors of modern day servers. It is designed for work that can be broken into smaller pieces recursively.

The goal is to use all the available processing power to enhance the performance of your application. One significant advantage of The fork/join framework is that it uses a work-stealing algorithm. Worker threads that run out of things to do can steal tasks from other threads that are still busy.

53) What is difference between calling wait() and sleep() method in Java multi-threading?

Though both wait and sleep introduce some form of pause in Java application, they are tool for different needs.

Wait method is used for inter thread communication, it relinquish lock if waiting condition is true and wait for notification when due to action of another thread waiting condition becomes false. On the other hand sleep() method is just to relinquish CPU or stop execution of current thread for specified time duration. Calling sleep method doesn't release the lock held by current thread.

PART - V

Java Multi-Threading and Concurrency

Interview Questions with Answers

250+ RANDOM ALL-IN-ONE JAVA INTERVIEW QUESTIONS & ANSWERS.

250+ JAVA INTERVIEW QUES & ANS

Multithreading or Concurrency is one of the popular topic in java interview questions. Here I am listing down most of the important questions from interview perspective, but you should have good knowledge on **java threads** to deal with follow up questions.

1. What is the difference between Process and Thread?

A process is a self contained execution environment and it can be seen as a program or application whereas Thread is a single task of execution within the process. Java runtime environment runs as a single process which contains different classes and programs as processes. Thread can be called lightweight process. Thread requires less resources to create and exists in the process, thread shares the process resources.

2. What are the benefits of multi-threaded programming?

In Multi-Threaded programming, multiple threads are executing concurrently that improves the performance because CPU is not idle incase some thread is waiting to get some resources. Multiple threads share the heap memory, so it's good to create multiple threads to execute some task rather than creating multiple processes. For example, Servlets are better in performance than CGI because Servlet support multi-threading but CGI doesn't.

3. What is difference between user Thread and daemon Thread?

When we create a Thread in java program, it's known as user thread. A daemon thread runs in background and doesn't prevent JVM from terminating. When there are no user threads running, JVM shutdown the program and quits. A child thread created from daemon thread is also a daemon thread.

4. How can we create a Thread in Java?

There are two ways to create Thread in Java – first by implementing Runnable interface and then creating a Thread object from it and second is to extend the Thread Class.

5. What are different states in lifecycle of Thread?

When we create a Thread in java program, its state is New. Then we start the thread that change it's state to Runnable. Thread Scheduler is responsible to allocate CPU to threads in Runnable thread pool and change their state to Running. Other Thread states are Waiting, Blocked and Dead.

6. *Can we call run() method of a Thread class?*

Yes, we can call run() method of a Thread class but then it will behave like a normal method. To actually execute it in a Thread, we need to start it using **Thread.start()** method.

7. *How can we pause the execution of a Thread for specific time?*

We can use Thread class sleep() method to pause the execution of Thread for certain time. Note that this will not stop the processing of thread for specific time, once the thread awake from sleep, it's state gets changed to runnable and based on thread scheduling, it gets executed.

8. *What do you understand about Thread Priority?*

Every thread has a priority, usually higher priority thread gets precedence in execution but it depends on Thread Scheduler implementation that is OS dependent. We can specify the priority of thread but it doesn't guarantee that higher priority thread will get executed before lower priority thread. Thread priority is an INT whose value varies from 1 to 10 where 1 is the lowest priority thread and 10 is the highest priority thread.

9. *What is Thread Scheduler and Time Slicing?*

Thread Scheduler is the Operating System service that allocates the CPU time to the available runnable threads. Once we create and start a thread, it's execution depends on the implementation of Thread Scheduler. Time Slicing is the process to divide the available CPU time to the available runnable threads. Allocation of CPU time to threads can be based on thread priority or the thread waiting for longer time will get more priority in getting CPU time. Thread scheduling can't be controlled by java, so it's always better to control it from application itself.

10. *What is context-switching in multi-threading?*

Context Switching is the process of storing and restoring of CPU state so that Thread execution can be resumed from the same point at a later point of time. Context Switching is the essential feature for multitasking operating system and support for multi-threaded environment.

---

11. *How can we make sure main() is the last thread to finish in Java Program?*

We can use Thread join() method to make sure all the threads created by the program is dead before finishing the main function. Here is an article about **Thread join method**.

12. *How does thread communicate with each other?*

When threads share resources, communication between Threads is important to coordinate their efforts. Object class wait(), notify() and notifyAll() methods allows threads to communicate about the lock status of a resource.

13. *Why thread communication methods wait(), notify() and notifyAll() are in Object class?*

In Java every Object has a monitor and wait, notify methods are used to wait for the Object monitor or to notify other threads that Object monitor is free now. There is no monitor on threads in java and synchronization can be used with any Object, that's why it's part of Object class so that every class in java has these essential methods for inter thread communication.

14. *Why wait(), notify() and notifyAll() methods have to be called from synchronized method or block?*

When a Thread calls wait() on any Object, it must have the monitor on the Object that it will leave and goes in wait state until any other thread call notify() on this Object. Similarly when a thread calls notify() on any Object, it leaves the monitor on the Object and other waiting threads can get the monitor on the Object. Since all these methods require Thread to have the Object monitor, that can be achieved only by synchronization, they need to be called from synchronized method or block.

15. *Why Thread sleep() and yield() methods are static?*

Thread sleep() and yield() methods work on the currently executing thread. So there is no point in invoking these methods on some other threads that are in wait state. That's why these methods are made static so that when this method is called statically, it works on the current executing thread and avoid confusion to the programmers who might think that they can invoke these methods on some non-running threads.

16. How can we achieve thread safety in Java?

There are several ways to achieve thread safety in java – synchronization, atomic concurrent classes, implementing concurrent Lock interface, using volatile keyword, using immutable classes and Thread safe classes. Learn more at **thread safety tutorial**.

17. What is volatile keyword in Java

When we use volatile keyword with a variable, all the threads read it's value directly from the memory and don't cache it. This makes sure that the value read is the same as in the memory.

18. Which is more preferred – Synchronized method or Synchronized block?

Synchronized block is more preferred way because it doesn't lock the Object, synchronized methods lock the Object and if there are multiple synchronization blocks in the class, even though they are not related, it will stop them from execution and put them in wait state to get the lock on Object.

19. How to create daemon thread in Java?

Thread class setDaemon(true) can be used to create daemon thread in java. We need to call this method before calling start() method else it will throw IllegalThreadStateException.

20. What is ThreadLocal?

Java ThreadLocal is used to create thread-local variables. We know that all threads of an Object share it's variables, so if the variable is not thread safe, we can use synchronization but if we want to avoid synchronization, we can use ThreadLocal variables.

Every thread has it's own ThreadLocal variable and they can use it's get() and set() methods to get the default value or change it's value local to Thread.

ThreadLocal instances are typically private static fields in classes that wish to associate state with a thread.

21. *What is Thread Group? Why it's advised not to use it?*

ThreadGroup is a class which was intended to provide information about a thread group. ThreadGroup API is weak and it doesn't have any functionality that is not provided by Thread. Two of the major feature it had are to get the list of active threads in a thread group and to set the uncaught exception handler for the thread. But Java 1.5 has added SETUNCAUGHTEXCEPTIONHANDLER(UNCAUGHTEXCEPTIONHANDL ER EH) method using which we can add uncaught exception handler to the thread. So ThreadGroup is obsolete and hence not advised to use anymore.

```
t1.setUncaughtExceptionHandler(new UncaughtExceptionHandler(){

    @Override
    public void uncaughtException(Thread t, Throwable e) {
        System.out.println("exception occured:"+e.getMessage());
    }

});
```

22. *What is Java Thread Dump, How can we get Java Thread dump of a Program?*

Thread dump is list of all the threads active in the JVM, thread dumps are very helpful in analyzing bottlenecks in the application and analyzing deadlock situations. There are many ways using which we can generate Thread dump – Using Profiler, Kill -3 command, jstack tool etc. I prefer jstack tool to generate thread dump of a program because it's easy to use and comes with JDK installation. Since it's a terminal based tool, we can create script to generate thread dump at regular intervals to analyze it later on.

23. *What is Deadlock? How to analyze and avoid deadlock situation?*

Deadlock is a programming situation where two or more threads are blocked forever, this situation arises with at least two threads and two or more resources.

To analyze a deadlock, we need to look at the java thread dump of the application, we need to look out for the threads with state as BLOCKED and then the resources it's waiting to lock, every resource has a unique ID using which we can find which thread is already holding the lock on the object. Avoid Nested Locks, Lock Only What is Required and Avoid waiting indefinitely are common ways to avoid deadlock situation,

24. What is Java Timer Class? How to schedule a task to run after specific interval?

java.util.Timer is a utility class that can be used to schedule a thread to be executed at certain time in future. Java Timer class can be used to schedule a task to be run one-time or to be run at regular intervals.

java.util.TimerTask is an abstract class that implements Runnable interface and we need to extend this class to create our own TimerTask that can be scheduled using java Timer class.

25. What is Thread Pool? How can we create Thread Pool in Java?

A thread pool manages the pool of worker threads, it contains a queue that keeps tasks waiting to get executed. A thread pool manages the collection of Runnable threads and worker threads execute Runnable from the queue.

java.util.concurrent.Executors provide implementation of java.util.concurrent.Executor interface to create the thread pool in java. **Thread Pool Example** program shows how to create and use Thread Pool in java. Or read **ScheduledThreadPoolExecutor Example** to know how to schedule tasks after certain delay.

Java Concurrency Interview Questions Answers-

1. What is atomic operation? What are atomic classes in Java Concurrency API?

Atomic operations are performed in a single unit of task without interference from other operations. Atomic operations are necessity in multi-threaded environment to avoid data inconsistency. int++ is not an atomic operation. So by the time one threads read it's value and increment it by one, other thread has read the older value leading to wrong result. To solve this issue, we will have to make sure that increment operation on count is atomic, we can do that using Synchronization but Java 5 java.util.concurrent.atomic provides wrapper classes for int and long that can be used to achieve this atomically without usage of Synchronization. Go to this article to learn more about **atomic concurrent classes**.

2. What is Lock interface in Java Concurrency API? What are it's benefits over synchronization?

Lock interface provide more extensive locking operations than can be obtained using synchronized methods and statements. They allow more flexible structuring, may have quite different properties, and may support multiple   associated   Condition   objects. The advantages of a lock are-

- it's possible to make them fair
- it's possible to make a thread responsive to interruption while waiting on a Lock object.
- it's possible to try to acquire the lock, but return immediately or after a timeout if the lock can't be acquired
- it's possible to acquire and release locks in different scopes, and in different orders

3. What is Executors Framework?

In   Java   5,   Executor   framework   was   introduced   with   the java.util.concurrent.Executor   interface.   The   Executor   framework   is   a framework for standardizing invocation, scheduling, execution, and control of asynchronous tasks according to a set of execution policies.

Creating a lot many threads with no bounds to the maximum threshold can cause application to run out of heap memory. So, creating a ThreadPool is a better solution as a finite number of threads can be pooled and reused. Executors framework facilitate process of creating Thread pools in java.

4. What is BlockingQueue? How can we implement Producer-Consumer problem using Blocking Queue?

java.util.concurrent.BlockingQueue is a Queue that supports operations that wait for the queue to become non-empty when retrieving and removing an element, and wait for space to become available in the queue when adding an element. BlockingQueue doesn't accept null values and throw NullPointerException if you try to store null value in the queue. BlockingQueue implementations are thread-safe. All queuing methods are atomic in nature and use internal locks or other forms of concurrency control.

BlockingQueue interface is part of java collections framework and it's primarily used for implementing producer consumer problem.

5. What is Callable and Future?

Java 5 introduced java.util.concurrent.Callable interface in concurrency package that is similar to Runnable interface but it can return any Object and able to throw Exception. Callable interface use Generic to define the return type of Object. Executors class provide useful methods to execute Callable in a thread pool. Since callable tasks run in parallel, we have to wait for the returned Object. Callable tasks return java.util.concurrent.Future object. Using Future we can find out the status of the Callable task and get the returned Object. It provides get() method that can wait for the Callable to finish and then return the result.

6. What is FutureTask Class?

FutureTask is the base implementation class of Future interface and we can use it with Executors for asynchronous processing.

Most of the time we don't need to use FutureTask class but it comes real handy if we want to override some of the methods of Future interface and want to keep most of the base implementation. We can just extend this class and override the methods according to our requirements.

7. *What are Concurrent Collection Classes?*

Java Collection classes are fail-fast which means that if the Collection will be changed while some thread is traversing over it using iterator, the iterator.next() will throw ConcurrentModificationException.

Concurrent Collection classes support full concurrency of retrievals and adjustable expected concurrency for updates. Major classes are ConcurrentHashMap, CopyOnWriteArrayList and CopyOnWriteArraySet,

8. *What is Executors Class?*

Executors class provide utility methods for Executor, ExecutorService, ScheduledExecutorService, ThreadFactory, and Callable classes. Executors class can be used to easily create Thread Pool in java, also this is the only class supporting execution of Callable implementations.

9. *What are some of the improvements in Concurrency API in Java 8?*

Some important concurrent API enhancements are:

+ ConcurrentHashMap compute(), forEach(), forEachEntry(), forEachKey(), forEachValue(), merge(), reduce() and search() methods.

+ CompletableFuture that may be explicitly completed (setting its value and status).

+ Executors newWorkStealingPool() method to create a work-stealing thread pool using all available processors as its target parallelism level.

40 Java Collections Interview
Questions and Answers

Java Collections Framework are the fundamental aspect of java programming language. It's one of the important topic for java interview questions. Here I am listing some important questions and answers for **java collections** framework.

1. *What are Collection related features in Java 8?*

Java 8 has brought major changes in the Collection API. Some of the changes are:

❖ **Java Stream API** for collection classes for supporting sequential as well as parallel processing

❖ **Iterable interface is extended with forEach()** default method that we can use to iterate over a collection. It is very helpful when used with **lambda expressions** because it's argument Consumer is a **function interface**.

❖ Miscellaneous Collection API improvements such as forEachRemaining(Consumer action) method inIterator interface, Map replaceAll(), compute(), merge() methods.

2. What is Java Collections Framework? List out some benefits of Collections framework?

Collections are used in every programming language and initial java release contained few classes for collections: **Vector**, **Stack**, **Hashtable**, **Array**. But looking at the larger scope and usage, Java 1.2 came up with Collections Framework that group all the collections interfaces, implementations and algorithms.

Java Collections have come through a long way with usage of Generics and Concurrent Collection classes for thread-safe operations.

It also includes blocking interfaces and their implementations in java concurrent package. Some of the benefits of collections framework are;

➕ Reduced development effort by using core collection classes rather than implementing our own collection classes.

➕ Code quality is enhanced with the use of well tested collections framework classes.

➕ Reduced effort for code maintenance by using collection classes shipped with JDK.

➕ Reusability and Interoperability

3. What is the benefit of Generics in Collections Framework?

Java 1.5 came with Generics and all collection interfaces and implementations use it heavily. Generics allow us to provide the type of Object that a collection can contain, so if you try to add any element of other type it throws compile time error. This avoids ClassCastException at Runtime because you will get the error at compilation. Also Generics make code clean since we don't need to use casting and INSTANCEOF operator.

4. What are the basic interfaces of Java Collections Framework?

Collection is the root of the collection hierarchy. A collection represents a group of objects known as its elements. The Java platform doesn't provide any direct implementations of this interface.

❖ **Set** is a collection that cannot contain duplicate elements. This interface models the mathematical set abstraction and is used to represent sets, such as the deck of cards.

❖ **List** is an ordered collection and can contain duplicate elements. You can access any element from it's index. List is more like array with dynamic length.

❖ A **Map** is an object that maps keys to values. A map cannot contain duplicate keys: Each key can map to at most one value.

❖ Some other interfaces are Queue, Dequeue, Iterator, SortedSet, SortedMap and ListIterator.

5. Why Collection doesn't extend Cloneable and Serializable interfaces?

Collection interface specifies group of Objects known as elements. How the elements are maintained is left up to the concrete implementations of Collection. For example, some Collection implementations like List allow duplicate elements whereas other implementations like Set don't. A lot of the Collection implementations have a public clone method. However, it does't really make sense to include it in all implementations of Collection. This is because Collection is an abstract representation. What matters is the implementation.

The semantics and the implications of either cloning or serializing come into play when dealing with the actual implementation; so concrete implementation should decide how it should be cloned or serialized, or even if it can be cloned or serialized. So mandating cloning and serialization in all implementations is actually less flexible and more restrictive. The specific implementation should make the decision as to whether it can be cloned or serialized.

6. Why Map interface doesn't extend Collection interface?

Although Map interface and it's implementations are part of Collections Framework, Map are not collections and collections are not Map. Hence it doesn't make sense for Map to extend Collection or vice versa. If Map extends Collection interface, then where are the elements? Map contains key-value pairs and it provides methods to retrieve list of Keys or values as Collection but it doesn't fit into the "group of elements" paradigm.

7. What is an Iterator?

Iterator interface provides methods to iterate over any Collection. We can get iterator instance from a Collection using ITERATOR() method. Iterator takes the place of Enumeration in the Java Collections Framework. Iterators allow the caller to remove elements from the underlying collection during the iteration. Java Collection iterator provides a generic way for traversal through the elements of a collection and implements Iterator Design Pattern.

8. What is difference between Enumeration and Iterator interface?

Enumeration is twice as fast as Iterator and uses very less memory. Enumeration is very basic and fits to basic needs. But Iterator is much safer as compared to Enumeration because it always denies other threads to modify the collection object which is being iterated by it. Iterator takes the place of Enumeration in the Java Collections Framework. Iterators allow the caller to remove elements from the underlying collection that is not possible with Enumeration. Iterator method names have been improved to make it's functionality clear.

9. Why there is not method like Iterator.add() to add elements to the collection?

The semantics are unclear, given that the contract for Iterator makes no guarantees about the order of iteration. Note, however, that ListIterator does provide an add operation, as it does guarantee the order of the iteration.

10. Why Iterator don't have a method to get next element directly without moving the cursor?

It can be implemented on top of current Iterator interface but since it's use will be rare, it doesn't make sense to include it in the interface that everyone has to implement.

11. *What is different between Iterator and ListIterator?*

We can use Iterator to traverse Set and List collections whereas ListIterator can be used with Lists only.

- ↓ Iterator can traverse in forward direction only whereas ListIterator can be used to traverse in both the directions.

- ↓ ListIterator inherits from Iterator interface and comes with extra functionalities like adding an element, replacing an element, getting index position for previous and next elements.

12. *What are different ways to iterate over a list?*

We can iterate over a list in two different ways – using iterator and using for-each loop.

```
1    List<String> strList = new ArrayList<>();
2    //using for-each loop
3    for(String obj : strList){
4        System.out.println(obj);
5    }
6    //using iterator
7    Iterator<String> it = strList.iterator();
8    while(it.hasNext()){
9        String obj = it.next();
10       System.out.println(obj);
11   }
```

Using iterator is more thread-safe because it makes sure that if underlying list elements are modified, it will throw ConcurrentModificationException.

13. *What do you understand by iterator fail-fast property?*

Iterator fail-fast property checks for any modification in the structure of the underlying collection everytime we try to get the next element. If there are any modifications found, it throwsConcurrentModificationException. All the implementations of Iterator in Collection classes are fail-fast by design except the concurrent collection classes like ConcurrentHashMap and CopyOnWriteArrayList.

14. What is difference between fail-fast and fail-safe?

Iterator fail-safe property work with the clone of underlying collection, hence it's not affected by any modification in the collection. By design, all the collection classes in java.util package are fail-fast whereas collection classes in java.util.concurrent are fail-safe. Fail-fast iterators throw ConcurrentModificationException whereas fail-safe iterator never throws ConcurrentModificationException.

15. How to avoid ConcurrentModificationException while iterating a collection?

We can use concurrent collection classes to avoid ConcurrentModificationException while iterating over a collection, for example CopyOnWriteArrayList instead of ArrayList.

16. Why there are no concrete implementations of Iterator interface?

Iterator interface declare methods for iterating a collection but it's implementation is responsibility of the Collection implementation classes. Every collection class that returns an iterator for traversing has it's own Iterator implementation nested class.

This allows collection classes to chose whether iterator is fail-fast or fail-safe. For example ArrayList iterator is fail-fast whereas CopyOnWriteArrayList iterator is fail-safe.

17. What is UnsupportedOperationException?

UnsupportedOperationException is the exception used to indicate that the operation is not supported.

It's used extensively in **JDK** classes, in collections framework java.util.Collections.UnmodifiableCollectionthrows this exception for all add and remove operations.

18. How HashMap works in Java?

HashMap stores key-value pair in Map.Entry static nested class implementation. HashMap works on hashing algorithm and uses hashCode() and equals() method in put and get methods. When we call put method by passing key-value pair, HashMap uses Key hashCode() with hashing to find out the index to store the key-value pair. The Entry is stored in the LinkedList, so if there are already existing entry, it uses equals() method to check if the passed key already exists, if yes it overwrites the value else it creates a new entry and store this key-value Entry.

When we call get method by passing Key, again it uses the hashCode() to find the index in the array and then use equals() method to find the correct Entry and return it's value. Below image will explain these detail clearly.

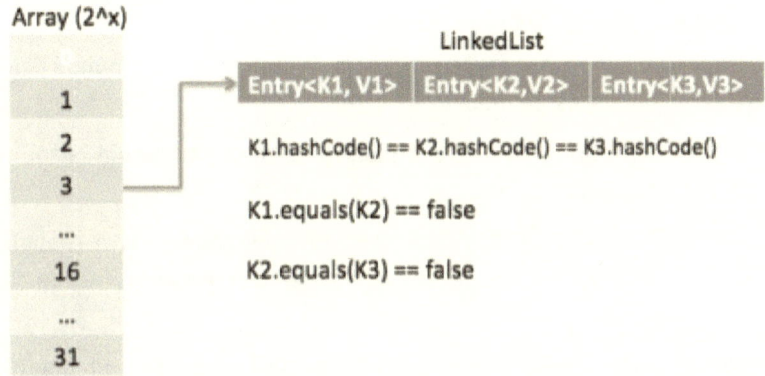

The other important things to know about HashMap are capacity, load factor, threshold resizing. HashMap initial default capacity is 32 and load factor is 0.75. Threshold is capacity multiplied by load factor and whenever we try to add an entry, if map size is greater than threshold, HashMap rehashes the contents of map into a new array with a larger capacity. The capacity is always power of 2, so if you know that you need to store a large number of key-value pairs, for example in caching data from database, it's good idea to initialize the HashMap with correct capacity and load factor.

19. What is the importance of hashCode() and equals() methods?

HashMap uses Key object hashCode() and equals() method to determine the index to put the key-value pair. These methods are also used when we try to get value from HashMap. If these methods are not implemented correctly, two different Key's might produce same hashCode() and equals() output and in that case rather than storing it at different location, HashMap will consider them same and overwrite them.

Similarly all the collection classes that doesn't store duplicate data use hashCode() and equals() to find duplicates, so it's very important to implement them correctly. The implementation of equals() and hashCode() should follow these rules.

If o1.equals(o2), then o1.hashCode() == o2.hashCode()should always be true.

If o1.hashCode() == o2.hashCode is true, it doesn't mean that o1.equals(o2) will be true.

20. Can we use any class as Map key?

We can use any class as Map Key, however following points should be considered before using them.

* ❖ If the class overrides equals() method, it should also override hashCode() method.

* ❖ The class should follow the rules associated with equals() and hashCode() for all instances. Please refer earlier question for these rules.

* ❖ If a class field is not used in equals(), you should not use it in hashCode() method.

* ❖ Best practice for user defined key class is to make it immutable, so that hashCode() value can be cached for fast performance. Also immutable classes make sure that hashCode() and equals() will not change in future that will solve any issue with mutability.

For example, let's say I have a class MyKey that I am using for HashMap key.

```
1    //MyKey name argument passed is used for equals() and hashCode()

2    MyKey key = new MyKey("Pankaj"); //assume hashCode=1234

3    myHashMap.put(key, "Value");

4

5    // Below code will change the key hashCode() and equals()

6    // but it's location is not changed.

7    key.setName("Amit"); //assume new hashCode=7890

8

9    //below will return null, because HashMap will try to look for key

10   //in the same index as it was stored but since key is mutated,

11   //there will be no match and it will return null.

12   myHashMap.get(new MyKey("Pankaj"));
```

This is the reason why String and Integer are mostly used as HashMap keys.

21. What are different Collection views provided by Map interface?

Map interface provides three collection views:

    A. **Set keySet()**: Returns a Set view of the keys contained in this map. The set is backed by the map, so changes to the map are reflected in the set, and vice-versa.

        If the map is modified while an iteration over the set is in progress (except through the iterator's own remove operation), the results of the iteration are undefined. The set supports element removal, which removes the corresponding mapping from the map, via the Iterator.remove, Set.remove, removeAll, retainAll, and clear operations. It does not support the add or addAll operations.

    B. **Collection values()**: Returns a Collection view of the values contained in this map. The collection is backed by the map, so changes to the map are reflected in the collection, and vice-versa.

        If the map is modified while an iteration over the collection is in progress (except through the iterator's own remove operation), the results of the iteration are undefined. The collection supports element removal, which removes the corresponding mapping from the map, via the Iterator.remove, Collection.remove, removeAll, retainAll and clear operations. It does not support the add or addAll operations.

C. **Set<Map.Entry<K, V>> entrySet()**: Returns a Set view of the mappings contained in this map. The set is backed by the map, so changes to the map are reflected in the set, and vice-versa. If the map is modified while an iteration over the set is in progress (except through the iterator's own remove operation, or through the setValue operation on a map entry returned by the iterator) the results of the iteration are undefined.

The set supports element removal, which removes the corresponding mapping from the map, via the Iterator.remove, Set.remove, removeAll, retainAll and clear operations. It does not support the add or addAll operations.

1. What is difference between HashMap and Hashtable?

HashMap and Hashtable both implements Map interface and looks similar, however there are following difference between HashMap and Hashtable.

+ HashMap allows null key and values whereas Hashtable doesn't allow null key and values.

+ Hashtable is synchronized but HashMap is not synchronized. So HashMap is better for single threaded environment, Hashtable is suitable for multi-threaded environment.

+ LinkedHashMap was introduced in Java 1.4 as a subclass of HashMap, so incase you want iteration order, you can easily switch from HashMap to LinkedHashMap but that is not the case with Hashtable whose iteration order is unpredictable.

+ HashMap provides Set of keys to iterate and hence it's fail-fast but Hashtable provides Enumeration of keys that doesn't support this feature.

+ Hashtable is considered to be legacy class and if you are looking for modifications of Map while iterating, you should use ConcurrentHashMap.

2. *How to decide between HashMap and TreeMap?*

For inserting, deleting, and locating elements in a Map, the HashMap offers the best alternative. If, however, you need to traverse the keys in a sorted order, then TreeMap is your better alternative.

Depending upon the size of your collection, it may be faster to add elements to a HashMap, then convert the map to a TreeMap for sorted key traversal.

3. *What are similarities and difference between ArrayList and Vector?*

ArrayList and Vector are similar classes in many ways.

- Both are index based and backed up by an array internally.
- Both maintains the order of insertion and we can get the elements in the order of insertion.
- The iterator implementations of ArrayList and Vector both are fail-fast by design.
- ArrayList and Vector both allows null values and random access to element using index number.

These are the differences between ArrayList and Vector.

- Vector is synchronized whereas ArrayList is not synchronized. However if you are looking for modification of list while iterating, you should use CopyOnWriteArrayList.
- ArrayList is faster than Vector because it doesn't have any overhead because of synchronization.
- ArrayList is more versatile because we can get synchronized list or read-only list from it easily using Collections utility class.

25. *What is difference between Array and ArrayList? When will you use Array over ArrayList?*

Arrays can contain primitive or Objects whereas ArrayList can contain only Objects. Arrays are fixed size whereas ArrayList size is dynamic. Arrays doesn't provide a lot of features like ArrayList, such as addAll, removeAll, iterator etc. Although ArrayList is the obvious choice when we work on list, there are few times when array are good to use.

If the size of list is fixed and mostly used to store and traverse them. For list of primitive data types, although Collections use autoboxing to reduce the coding effort but still it makes them slow when working on fixed size primitive data types. If you are working on fixed multi-dimensional situation, using [ ][ ] is far more easier than List<List<>>

26. What is difference between ArrayList and LinkedList?

ArrayList and LinkedList both implement List interface but there are some differences between them.

- ArrayList is an index based data structure backed by Array, so it provides random access to it's elements with performance as O(1) but LinkedList stores data as list of nodes where every node is linked to it's previous and next node. So even though there is a method to get the element using index, internally it traverse from start to reach at the index node and then return the element, so performance is O(n) that is slower than ArrayList.

- Insertion, addition or removal of an element is faster in LinkedList compared to ArrayList because there is no concept of resizing array or updating index when element is added in middle.

- LinkedList consumes more memory than ArrayList because every node in LinkedList stores reference of previous and next elements.

27. Which collection classes provide random access of it's elements?

ArrayList, HashMap, TreeMap, Hashtable classes provide random access to it's elements. Download **java collections pdf** for more information.

28. What is EnumSet?

java.util.EnumSet is Set implementation to use with enum types. All of the elements in an enum set must come from a single enum type that is specified, explicitly or implicitly, when the set is created. EnumSet is not synchronized and null elements are not allowed. It also provides some useful methods like copyOf(Collection c), of(E first, E... rest) and complementOf(EnumSet s).

29. Which collection classes are thread-safe?

Vector, Hashtable, Properties and Stack are synchronized classes, so they are thread-safe and can be used in multi-threaded environment.

Java 1.5 Concurrent API included some collection classes that allows modification of collection while iteration because they work on the clone of the collection, so they are safe to use in multi-threaded environment.

30. What are concurrent Collection Classes?

Java 1.5 Concurrent package (java.util.concurrent) contains thread-safe collection classes that allow collections to be modified while iterating. By design iterator is fail-fast and throws ConcurrentModificationException. Some of these classes are CopyOnWriteArrayList, ConcurrentHashMap,CopyOnWriteArraySet.

- Avoid ConcurrentModificationException
- CopyOnWriteArrayList Example
- HashMap vs ConcurrentHashMap

31. What is BlockingQueue?

java.util.concurrent.BlockingQueue is a Queue that supports operations that wait for the queue to become non-empty when retrieving and removing an element, and wait for space to become available in the queue when adding an element. BlockingQueue interface is part of java collections framework and it's primarily used for implementing producer consumer problem. We don't need to worry about waiting for the space to be available for producer or object to be available for consumer in BlockingQueue as it's handled by implementation classes of BlockingQueue. Java provides several BlockingQueue implementations such as ArrayBlockingQueue, LinkedBlockingQueue, PriorityBlockingQueue, SynchronousQueue etc.

32. What is Queue and Stack, list their differences?

Both Queue and Stack are used to store data before processing them. java.util.Queue is an interface whose implementation classes are present in java concurrent package. Queue allows retrieval of element in First-In-First-Out (FIFO) order but it's not always the case.

There is also Deque interface that allows elements to be retrieved from both end of the queue.Stack is similar to queue except that it allows elements to be retrieved in Last-In-First-Out (LIFO) order. Stack is a class that extends Vector whereas Queue is an interface.

33. What is Collections Class?

java.util.Collections is a utility class consists exclusively of static methods that operate on or return collections. It contains polymorphic algorithms that operate on collections, "wrappers", which return a new collection backed by a specified collection, and a few other odds and ends.

This class contains methods for collection framework algorithms, such as binary search, sorting, shuffling, reverse etc.

34. What is Comparable and Comparator interface?

Java provides Comparable interface which should be implemented by any custom class if we want to use Arrays or Collections sorting methods. Comparable interface has compareTo(T obj) method which is used by sorting methods. We should override this method in such a way that it returns a negative integer, zero, or a positive integer if "this" object is less than, equal to, or greater than the object passed as argument.

But, in most real life scenarios, we want sorting based on different parameters. For example, as a CEO, I would like to sort the employees based on Salary, an HR would like to sort them based on the age. This is the situation where we need to use Comparator interface because Comparable.compareTo(Object o)method implementation can sort based on one field only and we can't chose the field on which we want to sort the Object.

Comparator interface compare(Object o1, Object o2) method need to be implemented that takes two Object argument, it should be implemented in such a way that it returns negative int if first argument is less than the second one and returns zero if they are equal and positive int if first argument is greater than second one.

35. What is difference between Comparable and Comparator interface?

Comparable and Comparator interfaces are used to sort collection or array of objects. Comparable interface is used to provide the natural sorting of objects and we can use it to provide sorting based on single logic. Comparator interface is used to provide different algorithms for sorting and we can chose the comparator we want to use to sort the given collection of objects.

36. How can we sort a list of Objects?

If we need to sort an array of Objects, we can use Arrays.sort(). If we need to sort a list of objects, we can use Collections.sort(). Both these classes have overloaded sort() methods for natural sorting (using Comparable) or sorting based on criteria (using Comparator). Collections internally uses Arrays sorting method, so both of them have same performance except that Collections take sometime to convert list to array.

37. While passing a Collection as argument to a function, how can we make sure the function will not be able to modify it?

We can create a read-only collection using Collections.unmodifiableCollection(Collection c) method before passing it as argument, this will make sure that any operation to change the collection will throwUnsupportedOperationException.

38. *How can we create a synchronized collection from given collection?*

We can use Collections.synchronizedCollection(Collection c) to get a synchronized (thread-safe) collection backed by the specified collection.

39. *What are common algorithms implemented in Collections Framework?*

Java Collections Framework provides algorithm implementations that are commonly used such as sorting and searching. Collections class contain these method implementations. Most of these algorithms work on List but some of them are applicable for all kinds of collections. Some of them are sorting, searching, shuffling, min-max values.

40. What is Big-O notation? Give some examples?

The Big-O notation describes the performance of an algorithm in terms of number of elements in a data structure. Since Collection classes are actually data structures, we usually tend to use Big-O notation to chose the collection implementation to use based on time, memory and performance.

Example 1: ArrayList get(index i) is a constant-time operation and doesn't depend on the number of elements in the list. So it's performance in Big-O notation is O(1).

Example 2: A linear search on array or list performance is O(n) because we need to search through entire list of elements to find the element.

41. What are best practices related to Java Collections Framework?

Chosing the right type of collection based on the need, for example if size is fixed, we might want to use Array over ArrayList. If we have to iterate over the Map in order of insertion, we need to use TreeMap. If we don't want duplicates, we should use Set.

- Some collection classes allows to specify the initial capacity, so if we have an estimate of number of elements we will store, we can use it to avoid rehashing or resizing.

- Write program in terms of interfaces not implementations, it allows us to change the implementation easily at later point of time.

- Always use Generics for type-safety and avoid ClassCastException at runtime.

- Use immutable classes provided by JDK as key in Map to avoid implementation of hashCode() and equals() for our custom class.

- Use Collections utility class as much as possible for algorithms or to get read-only, synchronized or empty collections rather than writing own implementation. It will enhance code-reuse with greater stability and low maintainability.

42. What is Java Priority Queue?

PriorityQueue is an unbounded queue based on a priority heap and the elements are ordered in their natural order or we can provide **Comparator** for ordering at the time of creation. PriorityQueue doesn't allow null values and we can't add any object that doesn't provide natural ordering or we don't have any comparator for them for ordering. Java PriorityQueue is not **thread-safe** and provided O(log(n)) time for enqueing and dequeing operations.

43. Why can't we write code as List<Number> numbers = new ArrayList<Integer>();?

Generics doesn't support sub-typing because it will cause issues in achieving type safety. That's why List<T> is not considered as a subtype of List<S> where S is the super-type of T.

To understanding why it's not allowed, let's see what could have happened if it has been supported.

```
1   List<Long> listLong = new ArrayList<Long>();
2   listLong.add(Long.valueOf(10));
3   List<Number> listNumbers = listLong; // compiler error
4   listNumbers.add(Double.valueOf(1.23));
```

As you can see from above code that IF generics would have been supporting sub-typing, we could have easily add a Double to the list of Long that would have caused ClassCastException at runtime while traversing the list of Long.

44. *Why can't we create generic array? or write code as List<Integer>[] array = new ArrayList<Integer>[10];*

We are not allowed to create generic arrays because array carry type information of it's elements at runtime. This information is used at runtime to throw ArrayStoreException if elements type doesn't match to the defined type. Since generics type information gets erased at runtime by Type Erasure, the array store check would have been passed where it should have failed. Let's understand this with a simple example code.

```
1   List<Integer>[] intList = new List<Integer>[5]; // compile error
2   Object[] objArray = intList;
3   List<Double> doubleList = new ArrayList<Double>();
4   doubleList.add(Double.valueOf(1.23));
5   objArray[0] = doubleList; // this should fail but it would pass because at
    runtime intList and doubleList both are just List
```

Arrays are covariant by nature i.e S[] is a subtype of T[] whenever S is a subtype of T but generics doesn't support covariance or sub-typing as we saw in last question. So if we would have been allowed to create generic arrays, because of type erasure we would not get array store exception even though both types are not related.

Java Exception Interview
Questions and Answers

Java provides a robust and object-oriented approach to handle exception scenarios known as **Java Exception Handling**.

1. What is Exception in Java?

Exception is an error event that can happen during the execution of a program and disrupts it's normal flow. Exception can arise from different kind of situations such as wrong data entered by user, hardware failure, network connection failure etc.

Whenever any error occurs while executing a java statement, an exception object is created and then JREtries to find exception handler to handle the exception. If suitable exception handler is found then the exception object is passed to the handler code to process the exception, known as **catching the exception**. If no handler is found then application throws the exception to runtime environment and JRE terminates the program.

Java Exception handling framework is used to handle runtime errors only, compile time errors are not handled by exception handling framework.

2. What are the Exception Handling Keywords in Java?

There are four keywords used in java exception handling.

- ✓ **throw**: Sometimes we explicitly want to create exception object and then throw it to halt the normal processing of the program. **throw** keyword is used to throw exception to the runtime to handle it.

- ✓ **throws**: When we are throwing any checked exception in a method and not handling it, then we need to use throws keyword in method signature to let caller program know the exceptions that might be thrown by the method. The caller method might handle these exceptions or propagate it to it's caller method using throws keyword. We can provide multiple exceptions in the throws clause and it can be used with **main()** method also.

- ✓ **try-catch**: We use try-catch block for exception handling in our code. try is the start of the block and catch is at the end of try block to handle the exceptions. We can have multiple catch blocks with a try and try-catch block can be nested also. catch block requires a parameter that should be of type Exception.

- ✓ **finally**: finally block is optional and can be used only with try-catch block. Since exception halts the process of execution, we might have some resources open that will not get closed, so we can use finally block. finally block gets executed always, whether exception occurrs or not.

3. Explain Java Exception Hierarchy?

Java Exceptions are hierarchical and **inheritance** is used to categorize different types of exceptions.Throwable is the parent class of Java Exceptions Hierarchy and it has two child objects – Error andException. Exceptions are further divided into checked exceptions and runtime exception.

- ✓ **Errors** are exceptional scenarios that are out of scope of application and it's not possible to anticipate and recover from them, for example hardware failure, JVM crash or out of memory error.

- ✓ **Checked Exceptions** are exceptional scenarios that we can anticipate in a program and try to recover from it, for example FileNotFoundException. We should catch this exception and provide useful message to user and log it properly for debugging purpose. Exception is the parent class of all Checked Exceptions.

- ✓ **Runtime Exceptions** are caused by bad programming, for example trying to retrieve an element from the Array. We should check the length of array first before trying to retrieve the element otherwise it might throw ArrayIndexOutOfBoundException at runtime. RuntimeException is the parent class of all runtime exceptions.

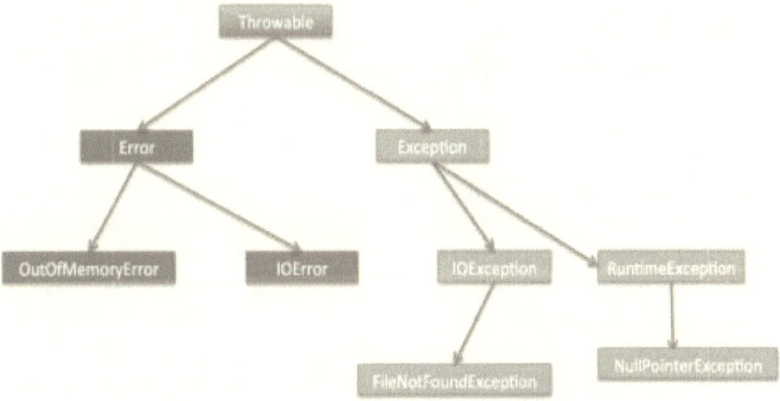

4. What are important methods of Java Exception Class?

Exception and all of it's subclasses doesn't provide any specific methods and all of the methods are defined in the base class Throwable.

1. **String getMessage()** – This method returns the message String of Throwable and the message can be provided while creating the exception through it's constructor.

2. **String getLocalizedMessage()** – This method is provided so that subclasses can override it to provide locale specific message to the

calling program. Throwable class implementation of this method simply use getMessage() method to return the exception message.

3. **synchronized Throwable getCause()** – This method returns the cause of the exception or null id the cause is unknown.

4. **String toString()** – This method returns the information about Throwable in String format, the returned String contains the name of Throwable class and localized message.

5. **void printStackTrace()** – This method prints the stack trace information to the standard error stream, this method is overloaded and we can pass PrintStream or PrintWriter as argument to write the stack trace information to the file or stream.

5. Explain Java 7 ARM Feature and multi-catch block?

If you are catching a lot of exceptions in a single try block, you will notice that catch block code looks very ugly and mostly consists of redundant code to log the error, keeping this in mind Java 7 one of the feature was multi-catch block where we can catch multiple exceptions in a single catch block. The catch block with this feature looks like below:

```
1   catch(IOException | SQLException | Exception ex){
2       logger.error(ex);
3       throw new MyException(ex.getMessage());
4   }
```

Most of the time, we use finally block just to close the resources and sometimes we forget to close them and get runtime exceptions when the resources are exhausted. These exceptions are hard to debug and we might need to look into each place where we are using that type of resource to make sure we are closing it. So java 7 one of the improvement was **try-with-resources** where we can create a resource in the try statement itself and use it inside the try-catch block. When the execution comes out of try-catch block, runtime environment automatically close these resources. Sample of try-catch block with this improvement is:

```
1   try (MyResource mr = new MyResource()) {
2           System.out.println("MyResource created in try-with-resources");
3       } catch (Exception e) {
4           e.printStackTrace();
5       }
```

6. *What is difference between Checked and Unchecked Exception in Java?*

- ✓ Checked Exceptions should be handled in the code using try-catch block or else main() method should use throws keyword to let JRE know about these exception that might be thrown from the program. Unchecked Exceptions are not required to be handled in the program or to mention them in throws clause.

- ✓ Exception is the super class of all checked exceptions whereas RuntimeException is the super class of all unchecked exceptions.

- ✓ Checked exceptions are error scenarios that are not caused by program, for example FileNotFoundException in reading a file that is not present, whereas Unchecked exceptions are mostly caused by poor programming, for example NullPointerException when invoking a method on an object reference without making sure that it's not null.

7. *What is difference between throw and throws keyword in Java?*

throws keyword is used with method signature to declare the exceptions that the method might throw whereas throw keyword is used to disrupt the flow of program and handing over the exception object to runtime to handle it.

8. *How to write custom exception in Java?*

We can extend Exception class or any of it's subclasses to create our custom exception class. The custom exception class can have it's own variables and methods that we can use to pass error codes or other exception related information to the exception handler.

A simple example of custom exception is shown below.

MyException.java

```
package com.journaldev.exceptions;
import java.io.IOException;
public class MyException extends IOException {
    private static final long serialVersionUID = 4664456874499611218L;
    private String errorCode="Unknown_Exception";
    public MyException(String message, String errorCode){
        super(message);
        this.errorCode=errorCode;
}
    public String getErrorCode(){
        return this.errorCode; } }
```

9. What is OutOfMemoryError in Java?

OutOfMemoryError in Java is a subclass of java.lang.VirtualMachineError and it's thrown by JVM when it ran out of heap memory. We can fix this error by providing more memory to run the java application through java options.

$>java   MyProgram   -Xms1024m   -Xmx1024m   -XX:PermSize=64M   -XX:MaxPermSize=256m

10. What are different scenarios causing "Exception in thread main"?

Some of the common main thread exception scenarios are:

Exception in thread main java.lang.UnsupportedClassVersionError: This exception comes when your java class is compiled from another JDK version and you are trying to run it from another java version.

Exception in thread main java.lang.NoClassDefFoundError: There are two variants of this exception. The first one is where you provide the class full name with .class extension. The second scenario is when Class is not found.

Exception in thread main java.lang.NoSuchMethodError: main: This exception comes when you are trying to run a class that doesn't have main method.

Exception in thread "main" java.lang.ArithmeticException: Whenever any exception is thrown from main method, it prints the exception is console. The first part explains that exception is thrown from main method, second part prints the exception class name and then after a colon, it prints the exception message.

11. What is difference between final, finally and finalize in Java?

final and finally are keywords in java whereas finalize is a method. final keyword can be used with class variables so that they can't be reassigned, with class to avoid extending by classes and with methods to avoid overriding by subclasses, finally keyword is used with try-catch block to provide statements that will always gets executed even if some exception arises, usually finally is used to close resources.

finalize() method is executed by Garbage Collector before the object is destroyed, it's great way to make sure all the global resources are closed. Out of the three, only finally is related to java exception handling.

12. What happens when exception is thrown by main method?

When exception is thrown by main() method, Java Runtime terminates the program and print the exception message and stack trace in system console.

13. *Can we have an empty catch block?*

We can have an empty catch block but it's the example of worst programming. We should never have empty catch block because if the exception is caught by that block, we will have no information about the exception and it wil be a nightmare to debug it. There should be at least a logging statement to log the exception details in console or log files.

14. *Provide some Java Exception Handling Best Practices?*

Some of the best practices related to Java Exception Handling are:

- ❖ Use Specific Exceptions for ease of debugging.
- ❖ Throw Exceptions Early (Fail-Fast) in the program.
- ❖ Catch Exceptions late in the program, let the caller handle the exception.
- ❖ Use Java 7 ARM feature to make sure resources are closed or use finally block to close them properly.
- ❖ Always log exception messages for debugging purposes.
- ❖ Use multi-catch block for cleaner close.
- ❖ Use custom exceptions to throw single type of exception from your application API.
- ❖ Follow naming convention, always end with Exception.
- ❖ Document the Exceptions Thrown by a method using @throws in javadoc.
- ❖ Exceptions are costly, so throw it only when it makes sense. Else you can catch them and provide null or empty response.

Random Brain Wash
201 Core Java Interview Questions.

1) What is difference between JDK,JRE and JVM?

JVM- JVM is an acronym for Java Virtual Machine, it is an abstract machine which provides the runtime environment in which java bytecode can be executed. JVMs are available for many hardware and software platforms (so JVM is plateform dependent).

JRE - JRE stands for Java Runtime Environment. It is the implementation of JVM and physically exists.

JDK - JDK is an acronym for Java Development Kit. It physically exists. It contains JRE + development tools.

2) *How many types of memory areas are allocated by JVM?*

Many types:

1. Class(Method) Area
2. Heap
3. Stack
4. Program Counter Register
5. Native Method Stack

3) *What is JIT compiler?*

Just-In-Time(JIT) compiler: It is used to improve the performance. JIT compiles parts of the byte code that have similar functionality at the same time, and hence reduces the amount of time needed for compilation.Here the term "compiler" refers to a translator from the instruction set of a Java virtual machine (JVM) to the instruction set of a specific CPU.

4) *What is platform?*

A platform is basically the hardware or software environment in which a program runs. There are two types of platforms software-based and hardware-based. Java provides software-based platform.

5) *What is the main difference between Java platform and other platforms?*

The Java platform differs from most other platforms in the sense that it's a software-based platform that runs on top of other hardware-based platforms.It has two components:

1. Runtime Environment

2. API(Application Programming Interface)

6) *What gives Java its 'write once and run anywhere' nature?*

The bytecode. Java is compiled to be a byte code which is the intermediate language between source code and machine code. This byte code is not platform specific and hence can be fed to any platform.

7) *What is classloader?*

The classloader is a subsystem of JVM that is used to load classes and interfaces.There are many types of classloaders e.g. Bootstrap classloader, Extension classloader, System classloader, Plugin classloader etc.

8) *Is Empty .java file name a valid source file name?*

Yes, save your java file by .java only, compile it by **javac .java** and run by **java yourclassname** Let's take a simple example:

```
//save by .java only
class A{
public static void main(String args[]){
System.out.println("Hello java");
}
}
//compile by javac .java
//run by    java A
compile it by javac .java
run it by java A
```

9) *Is delete,next,main,exit or null keyword in java?*
No.

10) *If I don't provide any arguments on the command line, then the String array of Main method will be empty or null?*

It is empty. But not null.

11) *What if I write static public void instead of public static void?*

Program compiles and runs properly.

12) *What is the default value of the local variables?*

The local variables are not initialized to any default value, neither primitives nor object references.

Core Java - OOPs Concepts:
Initial OOPs Interview Questions

There is given more than 50 OOPs (Object-Oriented Programming and System) interview questions.

But they have been categorized in many sections such as constructor interview questions, static interview questions, Inheritance Interview questions, Abstraction interview question, Polymorphism interview questions etc. for better understanding.

13) *What is difference between object oriented programming language and object based programming language?*

Object based programming languages follow all the features of OOPs except Inheritance. Examples of object based programming languages are JavaScript, VBScript etc.

14) *What will be the initial value of an object reference which is defined as an instance variable?*

The object references are all initialized to null in Java.

Core Java - OOPs Concepts: Constructor Interview Questions

15) *What is constructor?*

Constructor is just like a method that is used to initialize the state of an object. It is invoked at the time of object creation.

16) *What is the purpose of default constructor?*

The default constructor provides the default values to the objects. The java compiler creates a default constructor only if there is no constructor in the class.more details...

17) *Does constructor return any value?*

Ans:yes, that is current instance (You cannot use return type yet it returns a value).more details...

18) *Is constructor inherited?*

No, constructor is not inherited.

19) *Can you make a constructor final?*

No, constructor can't be final.

Core Java - OOPs Concepts: static keyword Interview Questions

20) *What is static variable?*

static variable is used to refer the common property of all objects (that is not unique for each object) e.g. company name of employees,college name of students etc. static variable gets memory only once in class area at the time of class loading.

21) *What is static method?*

- A static method belongs to the class rather than object of a class.

- A static method can be invoked without the need for creating an instance of a class.

- static method can access static data member and can change the value of it.

22) *Why main method is static?*

Because object is not required to call static method if It were non-static method,jvm creats object first then call main() method that will lead to the problem of extra memory allocation.more details...

23) *What is static block?*

- Is used to initialize the static data member.

- It is excuted before main method at the time of classloading.

24) *Can we execute a program without main() method?*

Ans) Yes, one of the way is static block.

25) *What if the static modifier is removed from the signature of the main method?*

Program compiles. But at runtime throws an error "NoSuchMethodError".

26) *What is difference between static (class) method and instance method?*

static or class method	instance method
1)A method i.e. declared as static is known as static method.	A method i.e. not declared as static is known as instance method.
2)Object is not required to call static method.	Object is required to call instance methods.
3)Non-static (instance) members cannot be accessed in static context (static method, static block and static nested class) directly.	static and non-static variables both can be accessed in instance methods.
4)For example: public static int cube(int n) { return n*n*n;}	For example: public void msg(){...}.

Core Java - OOPs Concepts:
Inheritance Interview Questions

27) *What is this in java?*

It is a keyword that that refers to the current object.

28) *What is Inheritance?*

Inheritance is a mechanism in which one object acquires all the properties and behaviour of another object of another class. It represents IS-A relationship. It is used for Code Resusability and Method Overriding.

29) *Which class is the superclass for every class.*

Object class.

30) *Why multiple inheritance is not supported in java?*

To reduce the complexity and simplify the language, multiple inheritance is not supported in java in case of class.

31) *What is composition?*

Holding the reference of the other class within some other class is known as composition.

32) *What is difference between aggregation and composition?*

Aggregation represents weak relationship whereas composition represents strong relationship. For example: bike has an indicator (aggregation) but bike has an engine (compostion).

33) *Why Java does not support pointers?*

Pointer is a variable that refers to the memory address. They are not used in java because they are unsafe(unsecured) and complex to understand.

34) *What is super in java?*

It is a keyword that refers to the immediate parent class object.

35) *Can you use this() and super() both in a constructor?*

No. Because super() or this() must be the first statement.

36) *What is object cloning?*

The object cloning is used to create the exact copy of an object.

Core Java - OOPs Concepts:
Method Overloading Interview Questions

37) What is method overloading?

If a class have multiple methods by same name but different parameters, it is known as Method Overloading. It increases the readability of the program.

38) Why method overloading is not possible by changing the return type in java?

Becauseof ambiguity.

39) Can we overload main() method?

Yes, You can have many main() methods in a class by overloading the main method.

Core Java - OOPs Concepts:
Method Overriding Interview Questions

40) What is method overriding:

If a subclass provides a specific implementation of a method that is already provided by its parent class, it is known as Method Overriding. It is used for runtime polymorphism and to provide the specific implementation of the method.

41) Can we override static method?

No, you can't override the static method because they are the part of class not object.

42) Why we cannot override static method?

It is because the static method is the part of class and it is bound with class whereas instance method is bound with object and static gets memory in class area and instance gets memory in heap.

43) Can we override the overloaded method?

Yes.

44) Difference between method Overloading and Overriding.

Method Overloading	Method Overriding
1) Method overloading increases the readability of the program.	Method overriding provides the specific implementation of the method that is already provided by its super class.
2) method overlaoding is occurs within the class.	Method overriding occurs in two classes that have IS-A relationship.
3) In this case, parameter must be different.	In this case, parameter must be same.

45) Can you have virtual functions in Java?

Yes, all functions in Java are virtual by default.

46) What is covariant return type?

Now, since java5, it is possible to override any method by changing the return type if the return type of the subclass overriding method is subclass type. It is known as covariant return type.

Core Java - OOPs Concepts:
final keyword Interview Questions

47) *What is final variable?*

If you make any variable as final, you cannot change the value of final variable(It will be constant).

48) *What is final method?*

Final methods can't be overriden.

49) *What is final class?*

Final class can't be inherited.

50) *What is blank final variable?*

A final variable, not initalized at the time of declaration, is known as blank final variable.

51) *Can we intialize blank final variable?*

Yes, only in constructor if it is non-static. If it is static blank final variable, it can be initialized only in the static block.

52) **Can you declare the main method as final?**

Yes, such as, public static final void main(String[] args){}.

OOPs: Polymorphism, Abstraction And Package interview questions

53) *What is Runtime Polymorphism?*

Runtime polymorphism or dynamic method dispatch is a process in which a call to an overridden method is resolved at runtime rather than at compile-time. In this process, an overridden method is called through the reference variable of a super class. The determination of the method to be called is based on the object being referred to by the reference variable.

54) *Can you achieve Runtime Polymorphism by data members?*

No.

55) *What is the difference between static binding and dynamic binding?*

In case of static binding type of object is determined at compile time whereas in dynamic binding type of object is determined at runtime.

Core Java - OOPs Concepts : Abstraction Interview Questions

56) *What is abstraction?*

Abstraction is a process of hiding the implementation details and showing only functionality to the user. Abstraction lets you focus on what the object does instead of how it does it.

57) *What is the difference between abstraction and encapsulation?*

Abstraction hides the implementation details whereas encapsulation wraps code and data into a single unit.

58) *What is abstract class?*

A class that is declared as abstract is known as abstract class. It needs to be extended and its method implemented. It cannot be instantiated.

59) *Can there be any abstract method without abstract class?*

No, if there is any abstract method in a class, that class must be abstract.

60) *Can you use abstract and final both with a method?*

No, because abstract method needs to be overridden whereas you can't override final method.

61) *Is it possible to instantiate the abstract class?*

No, abstract class can never be instantiated.

62) *What is interface?*

Interface is a blueprint of a class that have static constants and abstract methods.It can be used to achieve fully abstraction and multiple inheritance.

63) *Can you declare an interface method static?*

No, because methods of an interface is abstract by default, and static and abstract keywords can't be used together.

64) *Can an Interface be final?*

No, because its implementation is provided by another class.

65) *What is marker interface?*

An interface that have no data member and method is known as a marker interface.For example Serializable, Cloneable etc.

66) *What is difference between abstract class and interface?*

Abstract class	Interface
1) An abstract class can have method body (non-abstract methods).	Interface have only abstract methods.
2) An abstract class can have instance variables.	An interface cannot have instance variables.
3) An abstract class can have constructor.	Interface cannot have constructor.
4) An abstract class can have static methods.	Interface cannot have static methods.
5) You can extends one abstract class.	You can implement multiple interfaces.

67) *Can we define private and protected modifiers for variables in interfaces?*

No, they are implicitly public.

68) *When can an object reference be cast to an interface reference?*

An object reference can be cast to an interface reference when the object implements the referenced interface.

Core Java - OOPs Concepts :
Package Interview Questions

69) *What is package?*

A package is a group of similar type of classes interfaces and sub-packages. It provides access protection and removes naming collision.

70) *Do I need to import java.lang package any time? Why ?*

No. It is by default loaded internally by the JVM.

71) *Can I import same package/class twice? Will the JVM load the package twice at runtime?*

One can import the same package or same class multiple times. Neither compiler nor JVM complains about it.But the JVM will internally load the class only once no matter how many times you import the same class.

72) *What is static import ?*

By static import, we can access the static members of a class directly, there is no to qualify it with the class name.

Java Exception and String
Interview Questions.

73) *What is Exception Handling?*

Exception Handling is a mechanism to handle runtime errors.It is mainly used to handle checked exceptions.

74) *What is difference between Checked Exception and Unchecked Exception?*

1)Checked Exception:

The classes that extend Throwable class except RuntimeException and Error are known as checked exceptions e.g.IOException,SQLException etc. Checked exceptions are checked at compile-time.

2)Unchecked Exception:

The classes that extend RuntimeException are known as unchecked exceptions e.g. ArithmeticException,NullPointerException etc. Unchecked exceptions are not checked at compile-time.

75) *What is the base class for Error and Exception?*

Throwable.

76) *Is it necessary that each try block must be followed by a catch block?*

It is not necessary that each try block must be followed by a catch block. It should be followed by either a catch block OR a finally block. And whatever exceptions are likely to be thrown should be declared in the throws clause of the method.

77) *What is finally block?*

finally block is a block that is always executed.

78) *Can finally block be used without catch?*

Yes, by try block. finally must be followed by either try or catch.

79) *Is there any case when finally will not be executed?*

finally block will not be executed if program exits(either by calling System.exit() or by causing a fatal error that causes the process to abort).

80) *What is difference between throw and throws?*

throw keyword	throws keyword
1)throw is used to explicitly throw an exception.	throws is used to declare an exception.
2)checked exceptions can not be propagated with throw only.	checked exception can be propagated with throws.
3)throw is followed by an instance.	throws is followed by class.
4)throw is used within the method.	throws is used with the method signature.
5)You cannot throw multiple exception	You can declare multiple exception e.g. public void method()throws IOException,SQLException.

81) *Can an exception be rethrown?*

Yes.

82) *Can subclass overriding method declare an exception if parent class method doesn't throw an exception ?*

Yes but only unchecked exception not checked.

83) *What is exception propagation ?*

Forwarding the exception object to the invoking method is known as exception propagation.

Core Java:

String Handling Interview Questions

There is given a list of string handling interview questions with short and pointed answers. If you know any string handling interview question.

84) *What is the meaning of immutable in terms of String?*

The simple meaning of immutable is unmodifiable or unchangeable. Once string object has been created, its value can't be changed.

85) *Why string objects are immutable in java?*

Because java uses the concept of string literal. Suppose there are 5 reference variables,all referes to one object "sachin".If one reference variable changes the value of the object, it will be affected to all the reference variables. That is why string objects are immutable in java.

86) *How many ways we can create the string object?*

There are two ways to create the string object, by string literal and by new keyword.

87) *How many objects will be created in the following code?*

> String s1="Welcome";
> String s2="Welcome";
> String s3="Welcome";
> Only one object.

88) *Why java uses the concept of string literal?*

To make Java more memory efficient (because no new objects are created if it exists already in string constant pool).

89)*How many objects will be created in the following code?*

> String s = **new** String("Welcome");

Two objects, one in string constant pool and other in non-pool(heap).

90) *What is the basic difference between string and stringbuffer object?*

String is an immutable object. StringBuffer is a mutable object.

91) *What is the difference between StringBuffer and StringBuilder ?*

StringBuffer is synchronized whereas StringBuilder is not synchronized.

92) *How can we create immutable class in java ?*

We can create immutable class as the String class by defining final class and

93) *What is the purpose of toString() method in java ?*

The toString() method returns the string representation of any object. If you print any object, java compiler internally invokes the toString() method on the object. So overriding the toString() method, returns the desired output, it can be the state of an object etc. depends on your implementation.

Core Java : Nested classes and Interfaces Interview Questions

94) *What is nested class?*

A class which is declared inside another class is known as nested class. There are 4 types of nested class member inner class, local inner class, annonymous inner class and static nested class.

95) *Is there any difference between nested classes and inner classes?*

Yes, inner classes are non-static nested classes i.e. inner classes are the part of nested classes.

96) *Can we access the non-final local variable, inside the local inner class?*

No, local variable must be constant if you want to access it in local inner class.

97) *What is nested interface ?*

Any interface i.e. declared inside the interface or class, is known as nested interface. It is static by default.

98) *Can a class have an interface?*

Yes, it is known as nested interface.

99) *Can an Interface have a class?*

Yes, they are static implicitely.

Java Garbage Collection, I/O Stream, Serialziation & Networking Interview Questions

***117)** What is Garbage Collection?*

Garbage collection is a process of reclaiming the runtime unused objects.It is performed for memory management.

***118)** What is gc()?*

gc() is a daemon thread.gc() method is defined in System class that is used to send request to JVM to perform garbage collection.

***119)** What is the purpose of finalize() method?*

finalize() method is invoked just before the object is garbage collected.It is used to perform cleanup processing.

***120)** Can an unrefrenced objects be refrenced again?*

Yes.

***121)** What kind of thread is the Garbage collector thread?*

Daemon thread.

***122)** What is difference between final, finally and finalize?*

final: final is a keyword, final can be variable, method or class.You, can't change the value of final variable, can't override final method, can't inherit final class.

finally: finally block is used in exception handling. finally block is always executed.

finalize():finalize() method is used in garbage collection.finalize() method is invoked just before the object is garbage collected.The finalize() method can be used to perform any cleanup processing.

***123)** What is the purpose of the Runtime class?*

The purpose of the Runtime class is to provide access to the Java runtime system.

***124)** How will you invoke any external process in Java?*

By Runtime.getRuntime().exec(?) method.

I/O Interview Questions

125) *What is the difference between the Reader/Writer class hierarchy and the InputStream/OutputStream class hierarchy?*

The Reader/Writer class hierarchy is character-oriented, and the InputStream/OutputStream class hierarchy is byte-oriented.

126) *What an I/O filter?*

An I/O filter is an object that reads from one stream and writes to another, usually altering the data in some way as it is passed from one stream to another.

Serialization Interview Questions

127) *What is serialization?*

Serialization is a process of writing the state of an object into a byte stream.It is mainly used to travel object's state on the network.

128) *What is Deserialization?*

Deserialization is the process of reconstructing the object from the serialized state.It is the reverse operation of serialization.

129) *What is transient keyword?*

If you define any data member as transient,it will not be serialized.

130) *What is Externalizable?*

Externalizable interface is used to write the state of an object into a byte stream in compressed format.It is not a marker interface.

131) *What is the difference between Serializalble and Externalizable interface?*

Serializable is a marker interface but Externalizable is not a marker interface.When you use Serializable interface, your class is serialized automatically by default. But you can override writeObject() and readObject() two methods to control more complex object serailization process. When you use Externalizable interface, you have a complete control over your class's serialization process.

Networking Interview Questions

132) *How do I convert a numeric IP address like 192.18.97.39 into a hostname like java.sun.com?*

By InetAddress.getByName("192.18.97.39").getHostName() where 192.18.97.39 is the IP address.

Reflection Interview Questions

133) What is reflection?

Reflection is the process of examining or modifying the runtime behaviour of a class at runtime.It is used in:

- IDE (Integreted Development Environment) e.g. Eclipse, MyEclipse, NetBeans.
- Debugger
- Test Tools etc.

134) *Can you access the private method from outside the class?*

Yes, by changing the runtime behaviour of a class if the class is not secured.

Java Miscellaneous, AWT and Swing Interview Questions

148) *What are wrapper classes?*

Wrapper classes are classes that allow primitive types to be accessed as objects.

149) *What is a native method?*

A native method is a method that is implemented in a language other than Java.

150) *What is the purpose of the System class?*

The purpose of the System class is to provide access to system resources.

151) *What comes to mind when someone mentions a shallow copy in Java?*

Object cloning.

152) *What is singleton class?*

Singleton class means that any given time only one instance of the class is present, in one JVM.

AWT and SWING Interview Questions

153) *Which containers use a border layout as their default layout?*

The Window, Frame and Dialog classes use a border layout as their default layout.

154) *Which containers use a FlowLayout as their default layout?*

The Panel and Applet classes use the FlowLayout as their default layout.

155) *What are peerless components?*

The peerless components are called light weight components.

156) *is the difference between a Scrollbar and a ScrollPane?*

A Scrollbar is a Component, but not a Container. A ScrollPane is a Container. A ScrollPane handles its own events and performs its own scrolling.

157) *What is a lightweight component?*

Lightweight components are the one which doesn?t go with the native call to obtain the graphical units. They share their parent component graphical units to render them. For example, Swing components.

158) *What is a heavyweight component?*

For every paint call, there will be a native call to get the graphical units.For Example, AWT.

159) *What is an applet?*

An applet is a small java program that runs inside the browser and generates dynamic contents.

160) *Can you write a Java class that could be used both as an applet as well as an application?*

Yes. Add a main() method to the applet.

Internationalization Interview Questions

161) *What is Locale?*

A Locale object represents a specific geographical, political, or cultural region.

162) How will you load a specific locale?

By ResourceBundle.getBundle(?) method.

Java Bean Interview Questions

163) *What is a JavaBean?*

are reusable software components written in the Java programming language, designed to be manipulated visually by a software development environment, like JBuilder or VisualAge for Java.

RMI Interview Questions

164) *Can RMI and Corba based applications interact?*

Yes they can. RMI is available with IIOP as the transport protocol instead of JRMP.

Java Multithreading Interview Questions

Multithreading and Synchronization is considered as the typical chapter in java programming. In game development company, mulithreading related interview questions are asked mostly. A list of frequently asked java multithreading interview questions are given below.

1) *What is multithreading?*

Multithreading is a process of executing multiple threads simultaneously. Its main advantage is:

- Threads share the same address space.
- Thread is lightweight.
- Cost of communication between process is low.

2) *What is thread?*

A thread is a lightweight subprocess.It is a separate path of execution.It is called separate path of execution because each thread runs in a separate stack frame.

3) *What is the difference between preemptive scheduling and time slicing?*

Under preemptive scheduling, the highest priority task executes until it enters the waiting or dead states or a higher priority task comes into existence. Under time slicing, a task executes for a predefined slice of time and then reenters the pool of ready tasks. The scheduler then determines which task should execute next, based on priority and other factors.

4) *What does join() method?*

The join() method waits for a thread to die. In other words, it causes the currently running threads to stop executing until the thread it joins with completes its task.

5) *What is difference between wait() and sleep() method?*

wait()	sleep()
1) The wait() method is defined in Object class.	The sleep() method is defined in Thread class.
2) wait() method releases the lock.	The sleep() method doesn't releases the lock.

6) *Is it possible to start a thread twice?*

No, there is no possibility to start a thread twice. If we does, it throws an exception.

7) *Can we call the run() method instead of start()?*

yes, but it will not work as a thread rather it will work as a normal object so there will not be context-switching between the threads.

8) *What about the daemon threads?*

The daemon threads are basically the low priority threads that provides the background support to the user threads. It provides services to the user threads.

9) *Can we make the user thread as daemon thread if thread is started?*

No, if you do so, it will throw IllegalThreadStateException

10) What is shutdown hook?

The shutdown hook is basically a thread i.e. invoked implicitly before JVM shuts down. So we can use it perform clean up resource.

11) When should we interrupt a thread?

We should interrupt a thread if we want to break out the sleep or wait state of a thread.

12) What is synchronization?

Synchronization is the capabilility of control the access of multiple threads to any shared resource.It is used:

1. To prevent thread interference.
2. To prevent consistency problem.

13) What is the purpose of Synchronized block?

- Synchronized block is used to lock an object for any shared resource.
- Scope of synchronized block is smaller than the method.

14) Can Java object be locked down for exclusive use by a given thread?

Yes. You can lock an object by putting it in a "synchronized" block. The locked object is inaccessible to any thread other than the one that explicitly claimed it.

15) What is static synchronization?

If you make any static method as synchronized, the lock will be on the class not on object.

16) What is the difference between notify() and notifyAll()?

The notify() is used to unblock one waiting thread whereas notifyAll() method is used to unblock all the threads in waiting state.

17) What is deadlock?

Deadlock is a situation when two threads are waiting on each other to release a resource. Each thread waiting for a resource which is held by the other waiting thread.

20 Java Collections Interview Questions

In java, collection interview questions are mostly asked by the interviewers. Here is the list of mostly asked collections interview questions with answers.

1) What is the difference between ArrayList and Vector?

No.	ArrayList	Vector
1)	ArrayList is not synchronized.	Vector is synchronized.
2)	ArrayList is not a legacy class.	Vector is a legacy class.
3)	ArrayList increases its size by 50% of the array size.	Vector increases its size by doubling the array size.

2) What is the difference between ArrayList and LinkedList?

No.	ArrayList	LinkedList
1)	ArrayList uses a dynamic array.	LinkedList uses doubly linked list.
2)	ArrayList is not efficient for manipulation because a lot of shifting is required.	LinkedList is efficient for manipulation.
3)	ArrayList is better to store and fetch data.	LinkedList is better to manipulate data.

3) What is the difference between Iterator and ListIterator?

Iterator traverses the elements in forward direction only whereas ListIterator traverses the elements in forward and backward direction.

No.	Iterator	ListIterator
1)	Iterator traverses the elements in forward direction only.	ListIterator traverses the elements in backward and forward directions both.
2)	Iterator can be used in List, Set and Queue.	ListIterator can be used in List only.

4) What is the difference between Iterator and Enumeration?

No.	Iterator	Enumeration
1)	Iterator can traverse legacy and non-legacy elements.	Enumeration can traverse only legacy elements.
2)	Iterator is fail-fast.	Enumeration is not fail-fast.
3)	Iterator is slower than Enumeration.	Enumeration is faster than Iterator.

5) What is the difference between List and Set?

List can contain duplicate elements whereas Set contains only unique elements.

6) What is the difference between HashSet and TreeSet?

HashSet maintains **no order** whereas TreeSet maintains **ascending order**.

7) What is the difference between Set and Map?

Set contains values only whereas Map contains key and values both.

8) What is the difference between HashSet and HashMap?

HashSet contains only values whereas HashMap contains entry(key,value). HashSet can be iterated but HashMap need to convert into Set to be iterated.

9) What is the difference between HashMap and TreeMap?

HashMap maintains **no order** but TreeMap maintains **ascending order**.

10) What is the difference between HashMap and Hashtable?

No.	HashMap	Hashtable
1)	HashMap is not synchronized.	Hashtable is synchronized.
2)	HashMap can contain one null key and multiple null values.	Hashtable cannot contain any null key or null value.

11) What is the difference between Collection and Collections?

Collection is an interface whereas Collections is a class. Collection interface provides normal functionality of data structure to List, Set and Queue. But, Collections class is to sort and synchronize collection elements.

12) What is the difference between Comparable and Comparator?

No.	Comparable	Comparator
1)	Comparable provides only one sort of sequence.	Comparator provides multiple sort of sequences.
2)	It provides one method named compareTo().	It provides one method named compare().
3)	It is found in java.lang package.	it is found in java.util package.
4)	If we implement Comparable interface, actual class is modified.	Actual class is not modified.

13) What is the advantage of Properties file?

If you change the value in properties file, you don't need to recompile the java class. So, it makes the application easy to manage.

14) What does the hashCode() method?

The hashCode() method returns a hash code value (an integer number).

The hashCode() method returns the same integer number, if two keys (by calling equals() method) are same. But, it is possible that two hash code numbers can have different or same keys.

15) *Why we override equals() method?*

The equals method is used to check whether two objects are same or not. It needs to be overridden if we want to check the objects based on property.

For example, Employee is a class that has 3 data members: id, name and salary. But, we want to check the equality of employee object on the basis of salary. Then, we need to override the equals() method.

16) *How to synchronize List, Set and Map elements?*

Yes, Collections class provides methods to make List, Set or Map elements as synchronized:

public static List synchronizedList(List l){}

public static Set synchronizedSet(Set s){}

public static SortedSet synchronizedSortedSet(SortedSet s){}

public static Map synchronizedMap(Map m){}

public static SortedMap synchronizedSortedMap(SortedMap m){}

17) *What is the advantage of generic collection?*

If we use generic class, we don't need typecasting. It is typesafe and checked at compile time.

18) *What is hash-collision in Hashtable and how it is handled in Java?*

Two different keys with the same hash value is known as hash-collision. Two different entries will be kept in a single hash bucket to avoid the collision.

19) *What is the Dictionary class?*

The Dictionary class provides the capability to store key-value pairs.

20) *What is the default size of load factor in hashing based collection?*

The default size of load factor is **0.75**. The default capacity is computed as initial capacity * load factor. For example, 16 * 0.75 = 12. So, 12 is the default capacity of Map.

JDBC Interview Questions

A list of frequently asked jdbc interview questions with answers are given below.

1) *What is JDBC?*

JDBC is a Java API that is used to connect and execute query to the database. JDBC API uses jdbc drivers to connects to the database.

2) *What is JDBC Driver?*

JDBC Driver is a software component that enables java application to interact with the database.There are 4 types of JDBC drivers:

1. JDBC-ODBC bridge driver
2. Native-API driver (partially java driver)
3. Network Protocol driver (fully java driver)
4. Thin driver (fully java driver)

3) *What are the steps to connect to the database in java?*

- Registering the driver class
- Creating connection
- Creating statement
- Executing queries
- Closing connection

4) *What are the JDBC API components?*

The java.sql package contains interfaces and classes for JDBC API.

Interfaces:

- Connection
- Statement
- PreparedStatement
- ResultSet
- ResultSetMetaData
- DatabaseMetaData
- CallableStatement etc.

Classes:

- DriverManager
- Blob
- Clob
- Types
- SQLException etc.

5) What are the JDBC statements?

There are 3 JDBC statements.

1. Statement
2. PreparedStatement
3. CallableStatement

6) What is the difference between Statement and PreparedStatement interface?

In case of Statement, query is complied each time whereas in case of PreparedStatement, query is complied only once. So performance of PreparedStatement is better than Statement.

7) How can we execute stored procedures and functions?

By using **Callable statement** interface, we can execute procedures and functions.

8) What is the role of JDBC DriverManager class?

The **DriverManager class** manages the registered drivers. It can be used to register and unregister drivers. It provides factory method that returns the instance of Connection.

9) What does the JDBC Connection interface?

The **Connection interface** maintains a session with the database. It can be used for transaction management. It provides factory methods that returns the instance of Statement, PreparedStatement, CallableStatement and DatabaseMetaData.

10) *What does the JDBC ResultSet interface?*

The ResultSet object represents a row of a table. It can be used to change the cursor pointer and get the information from the database.

11) *What does the JDBC ResultSetMetaData interface?*

The ResultSetMetaData interface returns the information of table such as total number of columns, column name, column type etc.

12) *What does the JDBC DatabaseMetaData interface?*

The DatabaseMetaData interface returns the information of the database such as username, driver name, driver version, number of tables, number of views etc.

13) *Which interface is responsible for transaction management in JDBC?*

The **Connection interface** provides methods for transaction management such as commit(), rollback() etc.

14) *What is batch processing and how to perform batch processing in JDBC?*

By using batch processing technique in JDBC, we can execute multiple queries. It makes the performance fast.

15) *How can we store and retrieve images from the database?*

By using PreparedStaement interface, we can store and retrieve images.

PART - VI

Java 8 Features for Developers Lambdas, Functional interface, Stream And Time API

Java 8 is released in 18th March 2014, so it's high time to look for the Java 8 features for the developers. And no enogh material is available for java 8. But here after a lots of hard work i am writing Some of the important features introduced in Java 8 that I am looking forward to are:

1.   forEach() method in Iterable interface.

2.   default and static methods in Interfaces.

3.   Functional Interfaces and Lambda Expressions.

4.   Java Stream API for Bulk Data Operations on Collections.

5.   Java Time API.

6.   Collection API improvements.

7.   Concurrency API improvements.

8.   Java IO improvements.

9.   Miscellaneous Core API improvements.

Let's have a brief look on these Java 8 features. I will provide some code snippets for better understanding, so if you want to run programs in Java 8, you will have to setup Java 8 environment by following steps.

Download JDK8 and install it. Installation is simple like other java versions. JDK installation is required to write, compile and run the program in Java.

NOTE: Current Eclipse IDE doesn't support Java8, so you will have to download it from **efxclipse.org Eclipse for Java 8**. There are different versions for Mac OS, Windows and Linux systems with stable builds, so download the latest one for most features.

I just checked today (28-July-2014) and Eclipse Kepler 4.3.2 SR2 package can be used for Java 8. You need to download it first and then install "Java 8 support for Eclipse Kepler SR2" plugin from Eclipse Marketplace. I have tried this and it seems to be working fine.

1. forEach() method in Iterable interface-

Whenever we need to traverse through a Collection, we need to create an Iterator whose whole purpose is to iterate over and then we have business logic in a loop for each of the elements in the Collection. We might get **ConcurrentModificationException** if iterator is not used properly.

Java 8 has introduced FOREACH method in java.lang.Iterable interface so that while writing code we focus on business logic only. FOREACH method takes java.util.function.Consumer object as argument, so it helps in having our business logic at a separate location that we can reuse. Let's see forEach usage with simple example.

Java8ForEachExample.java

```
package com.journaldev.java8.foreach;

import java.util.ArrayList;
import java.util.Iterator;
import java.util.List;
import java.util.function.Consumer;
```

```java
import java.lang.Integer;
public class Java8ForEachExample {

    public static void main(String[] args) {
        //creating sample Collection
        List<Integer> myList = new ArrayList<Integer>();
        for(int i=0; i<10; i++) myList.add(i);

        //traversing using Iterator
        Iterator<Integer> it = myList.iterator();
        while(it.hasNext()){
            Integer i = it.next();
            System.out.println("Iterator Value::"+i);
        }
    //traversing through forEach method of Iterable with anonymous class
        myList.forEach(new Consumer<Integer>() {

        public void accept(Integer t) {
            System.out.println("forEach anonymous class Value::"+t);
            }
        });
        //traversing with Consumer interface implementation
        MyConsumer action = new MyConsumer();
        myList.forEach(action);

    }
}
//Consumer implementation that can be reused class MyConsumer
implements Consumer<Integer>{
    public void accept(Integer t) {
        System.out.println("Consumer impl Value::"+t);
    }
}
```

The number of lines might increase but forEach method helps in having the logic for iteration and business logic at separate place resulting in higher separation of concern and cleaner code.

2. default and static methods in Interfaces-

If you read forEach method details carefully, you will notice that it's defined in Iterable interface but we know that interfaces can't have method body. From Java 8, interfaces are enhanced to have method with implementation. We can use 'DEFAULT' and 'STATIC' keyword to create interfaces with method implementation.

For each method implementation in Iterable interface is:

```
default void forEach(Consumer<? super T> action) {
    Objects.requireNonNull(action);
    for (T t : this) {
        action.accept(t);
    }
}
```

Remember :

We know that Java doesn't provide **multiple inheritance in Classes** because it leads to **Diamond Problem**. So how it will be handled with interfaces now, since interfaces are now similar to abstract classes.

The solution is that compiler will throw exception in this scenario and we will have to provide implementation logic in the class implementing the interfaces.

Interface1.java

```java
package com.journaldev.java8.defaultmethod;
@FunctionalInterface
public interface Interface1 {
    void method1(String str);
    default void log(String str){
        System.out.println("I1 logging::"+str);
    }
    static void print(String str){
        System.out.println("Printing "+str);
    }
//trying to override Object method gives compile time error as
//"A    default    method    cannot    override    a    method    from
java.lang.Object"
//   default String toString(){
//        return "i1";
//   }
}
```

Interface2.java

```java
package com.journaldev.java8.defaultmethod;


@FunctionalInterface
public interface Interface2 {
    void method2();
    default void log(String str){
        System.out.println("I2 logging::"+str);
    }


}
```

Notice that both the interfaces have a common method log() with implementation logic.

MyClass.java

```
package com.journaldev.java8.defaultmethod;
public class MyClass implements Interface1, Interface2 {

    @Override
    public void method2() {

    }
    @Override
    public void method1(String str) {

    }
    //MyClass won't compile without having it's own log() implementation

    @Override
    public void log(String str){
        System.out.println("MyClass logging::"+str);
        Interface1.print("abc");

    }
}
```

As you can see that Interface1 has static method implementation that is used in MYCLASS.LOG() method implementation. Java 8 uses default and static methods heavily in Collection API and default methods are added so that our code remains backward compatible.

If any class in the hierarchy has a method with same signature, then default methods become irrelevant. Since any class implementing an interface already has Object as superclass, if we have equals(), hashCode() default methods in interface, it will become irrelevant. Thats why for better clarity, interfaces are not allowed to have Object class default methods.

For complete details of interface changes in Java 8, please read *Java 8 interface changes **Below.***

Java 8 Interface Changes – static methods, default methods, functional Interfaces-

One of the biggest design change in Java 8 is with the concept of interfaces. Prior to Java 7, we could have only method declarations in the interfaces. But from Java 8, we can have **default methods** and **static methods** in the interfaces.

Designing interfaces have always been a tough job because if we want to add additional methods in the interfaces, it will require change in all the implementing classes.

As interface grows old, the number of classes implementing it might grow to an extent that it's not possible to extend interfaces. That's why when designing an application, most of the frameworks provide a base implementation class and then we extend it and override methods that are applicable for our application. Let's look into the default and static interface methods and the reasoning of their introduction.

Interface Default Method-

For creating a default method in the interface, we need to use "**default**" keyword with the method signature. For example,

Interface1.java

```
package com.journaldev.java8.defaultmethod;
public interface Interface1 {
  void method1(String str);

  default void log(String str){
    System.out.println("I1 logging::"+str);
    print(str);
  }
}
```

Notice that log(String str) is the default method in the Interface1. Now when a class will implement Interface1, it is not mandatory to provide implementation for default methods. This feature will help us in extending interfaces with additional methods, all we need is to provide a default implementation. Let's say we have another interface with following methods:

Interface2.java

```
package com.journaldev.java8.defaultmethod;
public interface Interface2 {
  void method2();
  default void log(String str){
    System.out.println("I2 logging::"+str);
  }
}
```

We know that Java doesn't allow us to extend multiple classes because it will result in the "Diamond Problem" where compiler can't decide which superclass method to use. With the default methods, the diamond problem would arise for interfaces too.

Because if a class is implementing both Interface1 andInterface2 and doesn't implement the common default method, compiler can't decide which one to chose.

Extending multiple interfaces are an integral part of Java, you will find it in the core java classes as well as in most of the enterprise application and frameworks. So to make sure, this problem won't occur in interfaces, it's made mandatory to provide implementation for common default methods.

So if a class is implementing both the above interfaces, it will have to provide implementation for log() method otherwise compiler will throw error. A simple class that is implementing both Interface1 and Interface2 will be:

MyClass.java

```java
package com.journaldev.java8.defaultmethod;
public class MyClass implements Interface1, Interface2 {
  @Override
  public void method2() {
  }
  @Override
  public void method1(String str) {
  }
  @Override
  public void log(String str){
    System.out.println("MyClass logging::"+str);
    Interface1.print("abc");
  }
}
```

Important points about interface default methods:

- ✓ Default methods will help us in extending interfaces without having the fear of breaking implementation classes.

- ✓ Default methods has bridge down the differences between interfaces and abstract classes.

- ✓ Default methods will help us in avoiding utility classes, such as all the Collections class method can be provided in the interfaces itself.

- ✓ Default methods will help us in removing base implementation classes, we can provide default implementation and the implementation classes can chose which one to override.

- ✓ One of the major reason for introducing default methods is to enhance the Collections API in Java 8 to support lambda expressions.

✓ If any class in the hierarchy has a method with same signature, then default methods become irrelevant. A default method cannot override a method from java.lang.Object.

The reasoning is very simple, it's because Object is the base class for all the java classes. So even if we have Object class methods defined as default methods in interfaces, it will be useless because Object class method will always be used. That's why to avoid confusion, we can't have default methods that are overriding Object class methods.

✓ Default methods are also referred to as Defender Methods or Virtual extension methods.

Interface static methods -

Static methods are similar to default methods except that we can't override them in the implementation classes. This feature helps us in avoiding undesired results incase of poor implementation in child classes. Let's look into this with a simple example.

MyData.java

```
package com.journaldev.java8.staticmethod;
public interface MyData {

  default void print(String str) {
    if (!isNull(str))
      System.out.println("MyData Print::" + str);
  }
  static boolean isNull(String str) {
    System.out.println("Interface Null Check");
    return str == null ? true : "".equals(str) ? true : false;
  }
}
```

Now let's see an implementation class that is having isNull() method with poor implementation.

MyDataImpl.java

```
package com.journaldev.java8.staticmethod;
public class MyDataImpl implements MyData {
  public boolean isNull(String str) {
    System.out.println("Impl Null Check");
    return str == null ? true : false;
  }
  public static void main(String args[]){
    MyDataImpl obj = new MyDataImpl();
    obj.print("");
    obj.isNull("abc");
  }
}
```

Note that isNull(String str) is a simple class method, it's not overriding the interface method.

For example, if we will add **@Override annotation** to the isNull() method, it will result in compiler error. Now when we will run the application, we get following output.

Interface Null Check

Impl Null Check

If we make the interface method from static to default, we will get following output.

1   Impl Null Check

2   MyData Print::

3   Impl Null Check

The static methods are visible to interface methods only, if we remove the isNull() method from theMyDataImpl class, we won't be able to use it for the MyDataImpl object. However like other static methods, we can use interface static methods using class name. For example, a valid statement will be:

```
1    boolean result = MyData.isNull("abc");
```

Important points about interface static methods:

- ❖ Interface static methods are part of interface, we can't use it for implementation class objects.

- ❖ Interface static methods are good for providing utility methods, for example null check, collection sorting etc.

- ❖ Interface static method helps us in providing security by not allowing implementation classes to override them.

- ❖ We can't define static methods for Object class methods, we will get compiler error as "This static method cannot hide the instance method from Object". This is because it's not allowed in java, since Object is the base class for all the classes and we can't have one class level static method and another instance method with same signature.

- ❖ We can use static interface methods to remove utility classes such as Collections and move all of it's static methods to the corresponding interface, that would be easy to find and use.

Functional Interfaces -

Before I conclude the topic, I would like to provide a brief introduction to Functional interfaces. An interface with exactly one abstract method is known as Functional Interface.

A new annotation @FunctionalInterface has been introduced to mark an interface as Functional Interface. @FunctionalInterface annotation is a facility to avoid accidental addition of abstract methods in the functional interfaces. It's optional but good practice to use it.

Functional interfaces are long awaited and much sought out feature of Java 8 because it enables us to use **lambda expressions** to instantiate them. A new package java.util.function with bunch of functional interfaces are added to provide target types for lambda expressions and method references.

3. Functional Interfaces and Lambda Expressions -

If you notice above interfaces code, you will notice @FunctionalInterface **annotation**. Functional interfaces are new concept introduced in Java 8. An interface with exactly one abstract method becomes Functional Interface.

We don't need to use @FunctionalInterface annotation to mark an interface as Functional Interface. @FunctionalInterface annotation is a facility to avoid accidental addition of abstract methods in the functional interfaces.

You can think of it like **@Override annotation** and it's best practice to use it. java.lang.Runnablewith single abstract method run() is a great example of functional interface.

One of the major benefits of functional interface is the possibility to use **lambda expressions** to instantiate them. We can instantiate an interface with **anonymous class** but the code looks bulky.

```
Runnable r = new Runnable(){
        @Override
        public void run() {
            System.out.println("My Runnable");
    }};
```

Since functional interfaces have only one method, lambda expressions can easily provide the method implementation.

We just need to provide method arguments and business logic. For example, we can write above implementation using lambda expression as:

```
Runnable r1 = () -> {
            System.out.println("My Runnable");
    };
```

If you have single statement in method implementation, we don't need curly braces also. For example above Interface1 anonymous class can be instantiated using lambda as follows:

```
Interface1 i1 = (s) -> System.out.println(s);
i1.method1("abc");
```

So lambda expressions are means to create anonymous classes of functional interfaces easily. There are no runtime benefits of using lambda expressions, so I will use it cautiously because I don't mind writing few extra lines of code.

A new package java.util.function has been added with bunch of functional interfaces to provide target types for lambda expressions and method references.

Lambda expressions are a huge topic, I will write a separate + (Note) on that in future (Next Edition of this Book). You can read complete tutorial below **Java 8 Lambda Expressions Tutorial**.

Java 8 Lambda Expressions and Functional Interfaces Tutorial-

Java has always been an **Object Oriented Programming** language. What is means that everything in java programming revolves around Objects (except some primitive types for simplicity). We don't have only functions in java, they are part of Class and we need to use the class/object to invoke any function.

If we look into some other programming languages such as C++, JavaScript; they are called **functional programming language** because we can write functions and use them when required. Some of these languages support Object Oriented Programming as well as Functional Programming.

Being object oriented is not bad, but it brings a lot of verbosity to the program. For example, let's say we have to create an instance of Runnable. Usually we do it using anonymous classes like below.

```
1    Runnable r = new Runnable(){
2        @Override
3        public void run() {
4            System.out.println("My Runnable");
5        }
    };
```

If you look at the above code, the actual part that is of use is the code inside run() method. Rest all of the code is because of the way java programs are structured.

Java 8 brings us the concept of **Functional Interfaces** and **Lambda Expressions** to avoid writing all the useless code that we can easily avoid by making our java compiler intelligent.

Functional Interface -

An interface with exactly one abstract method is called Functional Interface. @FunctionalInterfaceannotation is added so that we can mark an interface as functional interface. It is not mandatory to use it, but it's best practice to use it with functional interfaces to avoid addition of extra methods accidentally. If the interface is annotated with @FunctionalInterface annotation and we try to have more than one abstract method, it throws compiler error.

The major benefit of functional interface is that we can use **lambda expressions** to instantiate them and avoid using bulky anonymous class implementation.

Java 8 Collections API has rewritten and new Stream API is provided that uses a lot of functional interfaces. Java 8 has defined a lot of functional interfaces in java.util.function package, some of the useful ones areConsumer, Supplier, Function and Predicate. You can find more detail about them in **Java 8 Stream Example**.

java.lang.Runnable is a great example of functional interface with single abstract method run().

Below code snippet provides some guidance for functional interfaces:

```
interface Foo { boolean equals(Object obj); }
// Not functional because equals is already an implicit member (Object class)
interface Comparator<T> {
  boolean equals(Object obj);
  int compare(T o1, T o2);
}
// Functional because Comparator has only one abstract non-Object method
interface Foo {
  int m();
  Object clone();
}
// Not functional because method Object.clone is not public
interface X { int m(Iterable<String> arg); }
interface Y { int m(Iterable<String> arg); }
interface Z extends X, Y {}
// Functional: two methods, but they have the same signature
interface X { Iterable m(Iterable<String> arg); }
interface Y { Iterable<String> m(Iterable arg); }
interface Z extends X, Y {}
// Functional: Y.m is a subsignature & return-type-substitutable
interface X { int m(Iterable<String> arg); }
interface Y { int m(Iterable<Integer> arg); }
interface Z extends X, Y {}
// Not functional: No method has a subsignature of all abstract methods
interface X { int m(Iterable<String> arg, Class c); }
interface Y { int m(Iterable arg, Class<?> c); }
```

interface Z extends X, Y {}

// Not functional: No method has a subsignature of all abstract methods

interface X { long m(); }

interface Y { int m(); }

interface Z extends X, Y {}

// Compiler error: no method is return type substitutable

interface Foo<T> { void m(T arg); }

interface Bar<T> { void m(T arg); }

interface FooBar<X, Y> extends Foo<X>, Bar<Y> {}

// Compiler error: different signatures, same erasure

Lambda Expressions -

Lambda Expressions are the way through which we can visualize **functional programming** in the java object oriented world. Objects are the base of java programming language and we can never have a function without an Object, that's why Java language provide support for using lambda expressions only with functional interfaces.

Since there is only one abstract function in the functional interfaces, there is no confusion in applying the lambda expression to the method. Lambda Expressions syntax is **(argument) -> (body)**. Now let's see how we can write above anonymous Runnable using lambda expression.

1   Runnable r1 = () -> System.out.println("My Runnable");

❖   Let's try to understand what is happening in the lambda expression above.

❖   Runnable is a functional interface, that's why we can use lambda expression to create it's instance.

❖   Since run() method takes no argument, our lambda expression also have no argument.

❖   Just like if-else blocks, we can avoid curly braces ({}) since we have a single statement in the method body. For multiple statements, we would have to use curly braces like any other methods.

Why do we need Lambda Expressions -

1. Reduced Lines of Code –

One of the clear benefit of using lambda expression is that the amount of code is reduced, we have already seen that how easily we can create instance of a functional interface using lambda expression rather than using anonymous class.

2. Sequential and Parallel Execution Support -

Another benefit of using lambda expression is that we can benefit from the Stream API sequential and parallel operations support. To explain this, let's take a simple example where we need to write a method to test if a number passed is prime number or not.

Traditionally we would write it's code like below. The code is not fully optimized but good for example purpose, so bear with me on this.

```
1   //Traditional approach
2   private static boolean isPrime(int number) {
3       if(number < 2) return false;
4       for(int i=2; i<number; i++){
5           if(number % i == 0) return false;
6       }
7       return true;
8   }
```

The problem with above code is that it's sequential in nature, if the number is very huge then it will take significant amount of time. Another problem with code is that there are so many exit points and it's not readable. Let's see how we can write the same method using lambda expressions and stream API.

```
1   //Declarative approach
2   private static boolean isPrime(int number) {
3       return number > 1
4           && IntStream.range(2, number - 1).noneMatch(
5               index -> number % index == 0);
6   }
```

IntStream is a sequence of primitive int-valued elements supporting sequential and parallel aggregate operations. This is the int primitive specialization of Stream. For more readability, we can also write the method like below.

```
1   private static boolean isPrime(int number) {
2       IntPredicate isDivisible = index -> number % index == 0;
3       return number > 1
4           && IntStream.range(2, number - 1).noneMatch(
5               isDivisible);
6   }
7
```

If you are not familiar with IntStream, it's range() method returns a sequential ordered IntStream from startInclusive (inclusive) to endExclusive (exclusive) by an incremental step of 1. noneMatch() method returns whether no elements of this stream match the provided predicate.

It may not evaluate the predicate on all elements if not necessary for determining the result.

3. Passing Behaviors into methods -

Let's see how we can use lambda expressions to pass behavior of a method with a simple example. Let's say we have to write a method to sum the numbers in a list if they match a given criteria. We can use Predicate and write a method like below.

```
1   public static int sumWithCondition(List<Integer> numbers,
    Predicate<Integer> predicate) {
2       return numbers.parallelStream()
3           .filter(predicate)
4           .mapToInt(i -> i)
5           .sum();
6   }
```

Sample usage:

```
1   //sum of all numbers
2   sumWithCondition(numbers, n -> true)
3   //sum of all even numbers
4   sumWithCondition(numbers, i -> i%2==0)
5   //sum of all numbers greater than 5
6   sumWithCondition(numbers, i -> i>5)
```

4. Higher Efficiency with Laziness -

One more advantage of using lambda expression is the lazy evaluation, for example let's say we need to write a method to find out the maximum odd number in the range 3 to 11 and return square of it. Usually we will write code for this method like this:

```
1   private static int findSquareOfMaxOdd(List<Integer> numbers) {
2       int max = 0;
3       for (int i : numbers) {
4           if (i % 2 != 0 && i > 3 && i < 11 && i > max) {
5               max = i;
6           }
7       }
8       return max * max;
9   }
```

Above program will always run in sequential order but we can use Stream API to achieve this and get benefit of Laziness-seeking. Let's see how we can rewrite this code in functional programming way using Stream API and lambda expressions.

```java
public static int findSquareOfMaxOdd(List<Integer> numbers) {
    return numbers.stream()
        .filter(NumberTest::isOdd)     //Predicate is functional interface and
        .filter(NumberTest::isGreaterThan3) // we are using lambdas to initialize it
        .filter(NumberTest::isLessThan11)   // rather than anonymous inner classes
        .max(Comparator.naturalOrder())
        .map(i -> i * i)
        .get();
}

public static boolean isOdd(int i) {
    return i % 2 != 0;
}

public static boolean isGreaterThan3(int i){
    return i > 3;
}

public static boolean isLessThan11(int i){
    return i < 11;
}
```

If you are surprised with the double colon (::) operator, it's introduced in Java 8 and used for **method references**. Java Compiler takes care of mapping the arguments to the called method. It's short form of lambda expressions i -> isGreaterThan3(i) or i -> NumberTest.isGreaterThan3(i).

Lambda Expression Examples -

Below I am providing some code snippets for lambda expressions with small comments explaining them.

```
1
2   () -> {}                // No parameters; void result
3   () -> 42                // No parameters, expression body
4   () -> null              // No parameters, expression body
5   () -> { return 42; }    // No parameters, block body with return
6   () -> { System.gc(); }  // No parameters, void block body
7
8   // Complex block body with multiple returns
9   () -> {
10    if (true) return 10;
11    else {
12      int result = 15;
13      for (int i = 1; i < 10; i++)
14        result *= i;
15      return result;
16    }
17  }
18  (int x) -> x+1          // Single declared-type argument
19  (int x) -> { return x+1; } // same as above
20  (x) -> x+1              // Single inferred-type argument, same as below
21  x -> x+1                // Parenthesis optional for single inferred-type case
22  (String s) -> s.length()  // Single declared-type argument
23  (Thread t) -> { t.start(); } // Single declared-type argument
24  s -> s.length()         // Single inferred-type argument
25  t -> { t.start(); }     // Single inferred-type argument
26  (int x, int y) -> x+y   // Multiple declared-type parameters
27  (x,y) -> x+y            // Multiple inferred-type parameters
28  (x, final y) -> x+y     // Illegal: can't modify inferred-type parameters
29  (x, int y) -> x+y       // Illegal: can't mix inferred and declared types
30
```

Method and Constructor References -

A method reference is used to refer to a method without invoking it; a constructor reference is similarly used to refer to a constructor without creating a new instance of the named class or array type.

Examples of method and constructor references:

1 System::getProperty

2 System.out::println

3 "abc"::length

4 ArrayList::new

5 int[]::new

That's all for Functional Interfaces and Lambda Expression Tutorial, I would strongly suggest to look into using it because this syntax is new to Java and it will take some time to grasp it and use it in a better way.

4. Java Stream API for Bulk Data Operations on Collections -

A new java.util.stream has been added in Java 8 to perform filter/map/reduce like operations with the collection. Stream API will allow sequential as well as parallel execution.

This is one of the best feature for me because I work a lot with Collections and usually with Big Data, we need to filter out them based on some conditions. Collection interface has been extended with STREAM() and PARALLELSTREAM() default methods to get the Stream for sequential and parallel execution. Let's see their usage with simple example.

StreamExample.java

```java
package com.journaldev.java8.stream;

import java.util.ArrayList;

import java.util.List;

import java.util.stream.Stream;


public class StreamExample {
    public static void main(String[] args) {

        List<Integer> myList = new ArrayList<>();

        for(int i=0; i<100; i++) myList.add(i);

        //sequential stream
        Stream<Integer> sequentialStream =
myList.stream();


        //parallel stream
        Stream<Integer> parallelStream =
myList.parallelStream();


        //using lambda with Stream API, filter example
        Stream<Integer> highNums =
parallelStream.filter(p -> p > 90);

        //using lambda in forEach
        highNums.forEach(p -> System.out.println("High
Nums parallel="+p));


        Stream<Integer> highNumsSeq =
sequentialStream.filter(p -> p > 90);

        highNumsSeq.forEach(p ->
System.out.println("High Nums sequential="+p));
    }
}
```

If you will run above example code, you will get output like this:

```
High Nums parallel=91
High Nums parallel=96
High Nums parallel=93
High Nums parallel=98
High Nums parallel=94
High Nums parallel=95
High Nums parallel=97
High Nums parallel=92
High Nums parallel=99
High Nums sequential=91
High Nums sequential=92
High Nums sequential=93
High Nums sequential=94
High Nums sequential=95
High Nums sequential=96
High Nums sequential=97
High Nums sequential=98
High Nums sequential=99
```

Notice that parallel processing values are not in order, so parallel processing will be very helpful while working with huge collections. Covering everything about Stream API is not possible in this topic, you can read everything about Stream API at **Java 8 Stream API Example Tutorial**.

Java 8 Stream API Example Tutorial -

In the last topics , we looked into **Java 8 Interface Changes** and **Functional Interfaces and Lambda Expressions**.

Now we will look into one of the major API introduced in Java 8 – **Java Stream API**.

Stream API Overview -

Before we look into Java 8 Stream API Examples, let's see why it was required. Suppose we want to iterate over a list of integers and find out sum of all the integers greater than 10. Prior to Java 8, the approach to do it would be:

```
1    private static int sumIterator(List<Integer> list) {
2       Iterator<Integer> it = list.iterator();
3       int sum = 0;
4       while (it.hasNext()) {
5         int num = it.next();
6         if (num > 10) {
7            sum += num;
8         }
9       }
10      return sum;
11   }
```

There are three major problems with the above approach:

1) We just want to know the sum of integers but we would also have to provide how the iteration will take place, this is also called **external iteration** because client program is handling the algorithm to iterate over the list.

2) The program is sequential in nature, there is no way we can do this in parallel easily.

3) There is a lot of code to do even a simple task.

To overcome all the above shortcomings, Java 8 introduces Stream API. We can use Stream API to implement**internal iteration**, that is better because java framework is in control of the iteration. **Internal iteration** provides several features such as sequential and parallel execution, filtering based on the given criteria, mapping etc.

Most of the Stream API method arguments are functional interfaces, so lambda expressions work very well with them. Let's see how can we write above logic in a single line statement.

```
1  private static int sumStream(List<Integer> list) {
2     return list.stream().filter(i -> i > 10).mapToInt(i -> i).sum();
3  }
```

Notice that above program utilizes java framework iteration strategy, filtering and mapping methods and would increase efficiency. First of all we will look into the core concepts of Stream API and then we will go through some examples for understanding most commonly used methods.

Collections and Streams-

A collection is an in-memory data structure to hold values and before we start using collection, all the values should have been populated. Whereas a Stream is a data structure that is computed on-demand.

Stream doesn't store data, it operates on the source data structure (collection and array) and produce pipelined data that we can use and perform specific operations. Such as we can create a stream from the list and filter it based on a condition.

Stream operations use functional interfaces, that makes it a very good fit for functional programming using lambda expressions. As you can see in the above example that using lambda expressions make our code readable and short.

Stream internal iteration principle helps in achieving lazy-seeking in some of the stream operations. For example filtering, mapping, or duplicate removal can be implemented lazily, allowing higher performance and scope for optimization.

Streams are consumable, so there is no way to create a reference to stream for future usage. Since the data is on-demand, it's not possible to reuse the same stream multiple times.

Stream support sequential as well as parallel processing, parallel processing can be very helpful in achieving high performance for large collections.

All the Stream API interfaces and classes are in the java.util.stream package. Since we can use primitive data types such as int, long in the collections using auto-boxing and these operations could take a lot of time, there are specific classes for these – IntStream, LongStream and DoubleStream.

Commonly used Functional Interfaces in Stream-

Some of the commonly used functional interfaces in the Stream API methods are:

1. Function and BiFunction:

Function represents a function that takes one type of argument and returns another type of argument. Function is the generic form where T is the type of the input to the function and R is the type of the result of the function. For handling primitive types, there are specific Function interfaces-

ToIntFunction, ToLongFunction, ToDoubleFunction, ToIntBiFunction, ToLongBiFunction,ToDoubleBiFunction, LongToIntFunction, LongToDoubleFunction, IntToLongFunction, IntToDoubleFunctionetc.

Some of the Stream methods where Function or it's primitive specialization is used are:

❖ <R> Stream<R> map(Function<? super T, ? extends R> mapper)

❖ IntStream mapToInt(ToIntFunction<? super T> mapper) – similarly for long and double returning primitive specific stream.

❖ IntStream flatMapToInt(Function<? super T, ? extends IntStream> mapper) – similarly for long and double

❖ <A> A[] toArray(IntFunction<A[]> generator)

❖ <U> U reduce(U identity, BiFunction<U, ? super T, U> accumulator, BinaryOperator<U> combiner)

2. Predicate and BiPredicate:

It represents a predicate against which elements of the stream are tested. This is used to filter elements from the stream. Just like Function, there are primitive specific interfaces for int, long and double.

Some of the Stream methods- where Predicate or BiPredicate specializations are used are:

✦ Stream<T> filter(Predicate<? super T> predicate)

✦ boolean anyMatch(Predicate<? super T> predicate)

✦ boolean allMatch(Predicate<? super T> predicate)

✦ boolean noneMatch(Predicate<? super T> predicate)

3. Consumer and BiConsumer:

It represents an operation that accepts a single input argument and returns no result. It can be used to perform some action on all the elements of the stream.Some of the Stream methods where Consumer, BiConsumer or it's primitive specialization interfaces are used are:

✦ Stream<T> peek(Consumer<? super T> action)

✦ void forEach(Consumer<? super T> action)

✦ void forEachOrdered(Consumer<? super T> action)

4. Supplier: Supplier represent an operation through which we can generate new values in the stream. Some of the methods in Stream that takes Supplier argument are:

- ❖ public static<T> Stream<T> generate(Supplier<T> s)

- ❖ <R> R collect(Supplier<R> supplier,BiConsumer<R, ? super T> accumulator,BiConsumer<R, R> combiner)

java.util.Optional -

Optional is a container object which may or may not contain a non-null value. If a value is present,isPresent() will return true and get() will return the value. Stream terminal operations return Optional object. Some of these methods are:

- ↓ Optional<T> reduce(BinaryOperator<T> accumulator)
- ↓ Optional<T> min(Comparator<? super T> comparator)
- ↓ Optional<T> max(Comparator<? super T> comparator)
- ↓ Optional<T> findFirst()
- ↓ Optional<T> findAny()

java.util.Spliterator-

For supporting parallel execution in Stream API, Spliterator interface is used. Spliterator trySplit method returns a new Spliterator that manages a subset of the elements of the original Spliterator.

Intermediate and Terminal Operations-

Stream API operations that returns a new Stream are called intermediate operations. Most of the times, these operations are lazy in nature, so they start producing new stream elements and send it to the next operation. Intermediate operations are never the final result producing operations.

Commonly used intermediate operations are filter and map.Stream API operations that returns a result or produce a side effect. Once the terminal method is called on a stream, it consumes the stream and after that we can't use stream. Terminal operations are eager in nature i.e they process all the elements in the stream before returning the result.

Commonly used terminal methods are forEach, toArray, min, max, findFirst, anyMatch, allMatch etc. You can identify terminal methods from the return type, they will never return a Stream.

Short Circuiting Operations-

An intermediate operation is called short circuiting, if it may produce finite stream for an infinite stream. For example limit() and skip() are two short circuiting intermediate operations.

A terminal operation is called short circuiting, if it may terminate in finite time for infinite stream. For example anyMatch, allMatch, noneMatch, findFirst and findAny are short circuiting terminal operations.

Java Stream Examples-

I have covered almost all the important parts of the Java Stream API. It's exciting to use this new API features and let's see it in action with some examples.

Creating Streams-

There are several ways through which we can create a stream from array and collections. Let's look into these with simple examples.

1. We can use Stream.of() to create a stream from similar type of data. For example, we can create Stream of integers from a group of int or Integer objects.

```
1   Stream<Integer> stream = Stream.of(1,2,3,4);
```

2. We can use Stream.of() with an array of Objects to return the stream. Note that it doesn't support autoboxing, so we can't pass primitive type array.

```
1   Stream<Integer> stream = Stream.of(new Integer[]{1,2,3,4});
2   //works fine
3
4   Stream<Integer> stream1 = Stream.of(new int[]{1,2,3,4});
5   //Compile time error, Type mismatch: cannot convert from Stream<int[]>
    to Stream<Integer>
```

3. We can use Collection stream() to create sequential stream and parallelStream() to create parallel stream.

```
1   List<Integer> myList = new ArrayList<>();
2   for(int i=0; i<100; i++) myList.add(i);
3   //sequential stream
4   Stream<Integer> sequentialStream = myList.stream();
5   //parallel stream
6   Stream<Integer> parallelStream = myList.parallelStream();
```

4. We can use Stream.generate() and Stream.iterate() methods to create Stream.

```
1   Stream<String> stream1 = Stream.generate(() -> {return "abc";});
2   Stream<String> stream2 = Stream.iterate("abc", (i) -> i);
```

5. Using Arrays.stream() and String.chars() methods.

```
1   LongStream is = Arrays.stream(new long[]{1,2,3,4});
2   IntStream is2 = "abc".chars();
```

Converting Stream to Collection or Array-

There are several ways through which we can get a Collection or Array from a Stream.

1. We can use Stream collect() method to get List, Map or Set from stream.

```
1   Stream<Integer> intStream = Stream.of(1,2,3,4);
2   List<Integer> intList = intStream.collect(Collectors.toList());
3   System.out.println(intList); //prints [1, 2, 3, 4]
4   intStream = Stream.of(1,2,3,4); //stream is closed, so we need to create it again
5   Map<Integer,Integer> intMap = intStream.collect(Collectors.toMap(i -> i, i -> i+10));
6   System.out.println(intMap); //prints {1=11, 2=12, 3=13, 4=14}
```

2. We can use stream toArray() method to create an array from the stream.

```
1   Stream<Integer> intStream = Stream.of(1,2,3,4);
2   Integer[] intArray = intStream.toArray(Integer[]::new);
3   System.out.println(Arrays.toString(intArray)); //prints [1, 2, 3, 4]
```

Stream Intermediate Operations- Let's look into commonly used Stream intermediate operations example.

1. Stream filter() example: We can use filter() method to test stream elements for a condition and generate filtered list.

```
1   List<Integer> myList = new ArrayList<>();
2   for(int i=0; i<100; i++) myList.add(i);
3   Stream<Integer> sequentialStream = myList.stream();
4   Stream<Integer> highNums = sequentialStream.filter(p -> p > 90); //filter
    numbers greater than 90
5   System.out.print("High Nums greater than 90=");
6   highNums.forEach(p -> System.out.print(p+" "));
7   //prints "High Nums greater than 90=91 92 93 94 95 96 97 98 99 "
```

2. Stream map() example: We can use map() to apply functions to an stream. Let's see how we can use it to apply upper case function to a list of Strings.

```
1   Stream<String> names = Stream.of("aBc", "d", "ef");
2   System.out.println(names.map(s -> {
3       return s.toUpperCase();
4     }).collect(Collectors.toList()));
5   //prints [ABC, D, EF]
```

3. Stream sorted() example: We can use sorted() to sort the stream elements by passing Comparator argument.

```
1  Stream<String> names2 = Stream.of("aBc", "d", "ef", "123456");
2  List<String> reverseSorted =
3  names2.sorted(Comparator.reverseOrder()).collect(Collectors.toList());
4  System.out.println(reverseSorted); // [ef, d, aBc, 123456]
5  Stream<String> names3 = Stream.of("aBc", "d", "ef", "123456");
6  List<String> naturalSorted = names3.sorted().collect(Collectors.toList());
7  System.out.println(naturalSorted); //[123456, aBc, d, ef]
```

4. Stream flatMap() example: We can use flatMap() to create a stream from the stream of list. Let's see a simple example to clear this doubt.

```
1  Stream<List<String>> namesOriginalList = Stream.of(
2      Arrays.asList("Pankaj"),
3      Arrays.asList("David", "Lisa"),
4      Arrays.asList("Amit"));
5  //flat the stream from List<String> to String stream
6  Stream<String> flatStream = namesOriginalList
7      .flatMap(strList -> strList.stream());
8  flatStream.forEach(System.out::println);
```

Stream Terminal Operations-

Let's look at some of the terminal operations example.

1. Stream reduce() example: We can use reduce() to perform a reduction on the elements of the stream, using an associative accumulation function, and return an Optional. Let's see how we can use it multiply the integers in a stream.

```
1  Stream<Integer> numbers = Stream.of(1,2,3,4,5);
2  Optional<Integer> intOptional = numbers.reduce((i,j) -> {return i*j;});
3  if(intOptional.isPresent()) System.out.println("Multiplication = "+intOptional.get()); //120
```

2. Stream count() example: We can use this terminal operation to count the number of items in the stream.

```
1   Stream<Integer> numbers1 = Stream.of(1,2,3,4,5);
2   System.out.println("Number of elements in stream="+numbers1.count()); //5
```

3. Stream forEach() example: This can be used for iterating over the stream. We can use this in place of iterator. Let's see how to use it for printing all the elements of the stream.

```
1   Stream<Integer> numbers2 = Stream.of(1,2,3,4,5);
2   numbers2.forEach(i -> System.out.print(i+",")); //1,2,3,4,5,
```

4. Stream match() examples: Let's see some of the examples for matching methods in Stream API.

```
1   Stream<Integer> numbers3 = Stream.of(1,2,3,4,5);
2   System.out.println("Stream contains 4? "+numbers3.anyMatch(i -> i==4));
3   //Stream contains 4? true
4   Stream<Integer> numbers4 = Stream.of(1,2,3,4,5);
5   System.out.println("Stream contains all elements less than 10?
6   "+numbers4.allMatch(i -> i<10));
    //Stream contains all elements less than 10? true
7
    Stream<Integer> numbers5 = Stream.of(1,2,3,4,5);
8
    System.out.println("Stream doesn't contain 10? "+numbers5.noneMatch(i ->
9   i==10));
10  //Stream doesn't contain 10? true
```

5. Stream findFirst() example: This is a short circuiting terminal operation, let's see how we can use it to find the first string from a stream starting with D.

```
Stream<String> names4 = Stream.of("Pankaj","Amit","David", "Lisa");
Optional<String> firstNameWithD = names4.filter(i ->
i.startsWith("D")).findFirst();
if(firstNameWithD.isPresent()){
   System.out.println("First Name starting with D="+firstNameWithD.get());
   //David
}
```

Java Stream API Limitations -

Stream API brings a lot of new stuffs to work with list and arrays, but it has some limitations too.

1. Stateless lambda expressions: If you are using parallel stream and lambda expressions are stateful, it can result in random responses. Let's see it with a simple program.

StatefulParallelStream.java

```
1   package com.journaldev.java8.stream;
2   import java.util.ArrayList;
3   import java.util.Arrays;
4   import java.util.List;
5   import java.util.stream.Stream;
6   public class StatefulParallelStream {
7     public static void main(String[] args) {
8       List<Integer> ss = Arrays.asList(1,2,3,4,5,6,7,8,9,10,11,12,13,14,15);
9       List<Integer> result = new ArrayList<Integer>();
10      Stream<Integer> stream = ss.parallelStream();
11      stream.map(s -> {
12         synchronized (result) {
13           if (result.size() < 10) {
14             result.add(s);
15           }
16         }
17         return s;
18      }).forEach( e -> {});
19      System.out.println(result);
20   } }
```

If we run above program, you will get different results because it depends on the way stream is getting iterated and we don't have any order defined for parallel processing. If we use sequential stream, then this problem will not arise.

2. Once a Stream is consumed, it can't be used later on. As you can see in above examples that every time I am creating a stream.

3. There are a lot of methods in Stream API and the most confusing part is the overloaded methods. It makes the learning curve time taking.

That's all for Stream API in Java. I am looking forward to use this feature and make the code readable with better performance through parallel processing.

5. Java Time API -

It has always been hard to work with Date, Time and Time Zones in java. There was no standard approach or API in java for date and time in Java. One of the nice addition in Java 8 is the java.time package that will streamline the process of working with time in java.

Just by looking at Java Time API packages, I can sense that it will be very easy to use. It has some sub-packages java.time.format that provides classes to print and parse dates and times and java.time.zoneprovides support for time-zones and their rules.

The new Time API prefers enums over integer constants for months and days of the week. One of the useful class is DateTimeFormatter for converting datetime objects to strings.

6. Collection API improvements -

We have already seen forEach() method and Stream API for collections. Some new methods added in Collection API are:

- ❖ Iterator default method for- EachRemaining(Consumer action) to perform the given action for each remaining element until all elements have been processed or the action throws an exception.

- ❖ Collection default method- removeIf(Predicate filter) to remove all of the elements of this collection that satisfy the given predicate.

- ❖ Collection spliterator() method- returning Spliterator instance that can be used to traverse elements sequentially or parallel.

- ❖ Map replaceAll(), compute(), merge() methods.

7. Concurrency API improvements -

Some important concurrent API enhancements are:

a) ConcurrentHashMap compute(), forEach(), forEachEntry(), forEachKey(), forEachValue(), merge(), reduce() and search() methods.

b) CompletableFuture that may be explicitly completed (setting its value and status).

c) Executors newWorkStealingPool() method to create a work-stealing thread pool using all available processors as its target parallelism level.

8. Java IO improvements -

Some IO improvements known to me are:

d) Files.list(Path dir) that returns a lazily populated Stream, the elements of which are the entries in the directory.

e) Files.lines(Path path) that reads all lines from a file as a Stream.

f) Files.find() that returns a Stream that is lazily populated with Path by searching for files in a file tree rooted at a given starting file.

g) BufferedReader.lines() that return a Stream, the elements of which are lines read from this BufferedReader.

9. Miscellaneous Core API improvements -

Some misc API improvements that might come handy are:

h) **ThreadLocal** static method withInitial(Supplier supplier) to create instance easily.

i) **Comparator** interface has been extended with a lot of default and static methods for natural ordering, reverse order etc.

j) min(), max() and sum() methods in Integer, Long and Double wrapper classes.

k) logicalAnd(), logicalOr() and logicalXor() methods in Boolean class.

l) **ZipFile**.stream() method to get an ordered Stream over the ZIP file entries. Entries appear in the Stream in the order they appear in the central directory of the ZIP file.

m) Several utility methods in Math class.

That's all for major improvements in Java 8.

Core Java InterviewBrain Wash Questions and Answers

Whether you are a fresher or highly experienced professional, **core java** plays a vital role in any Java/JEE interview. Core Java is the favorite area in most of the interviews and plays a crucial role in deciding the outcome of your interview. I have already written a lot about **java interview questions** for specific topics such as String, Collections and Multithreading.

1.   **Java String Interview Questions**

2.   **Java Thread Interview Questions**

3.   **Java Collections Interview Questions**

4.   **Java Exception Interview Questions**

Here I am providing some of the important core java interview questions with answers that you should know.

1.   *What are the important features of Java 8 release?*

2.   *What do you mean by platform independence of Java?*

3.   *What is JVM and is it platform independent?*

4.   *What is the difference between JDK and JVM?*

5.   *What is the difference between JVM and JRE?*

6.   *Which class is the superclass of all classes?*

7.   *Why Java doesn't support multiple inheritance?*

8.   *Why Java is not pure Object Oriented language?*

9.   *What is difference between path and classpath variables?*

10.   *What is the importance of main method in Java?*

11.   *What is overloading and overriding in java?*

12.   *Can we overload main method?*

13.   *Can we have multiple public classes in a java source file?*

14.   *What is Java Package and which package is imported by default?*

15.   *What are access modifiers?*

16.   *What is final keyword?*

17.   *What is static keyword?*

18.   *What is finally and finalize in java?*

19.   *Can we declare a class as static?*

20.   *What is static import?*

21.   *What is try-with-resources in java?*

22.   *What is multi-catch block in java?*

23.   *What is static block?*

24.   *What is an interface?*

25.   *What is an abstract class?*

26.   *What is the difference between abstract class and interface?*

27.   *Can an interface implement or extend another interface?*

1. *What are the important features of Java 8 release?*

Java 8 has been released in March 2014, so it's one of the hot topic in java interview questions. If you answer this question clearly, it will show that you like to keep yourself up-to-date with the latest technologies. Java 8 has been one of the biggest release after Java 5 annotations and generics. Some of the important features of Java 8 are:

- ✓ **Interface changes with default and static methods.**
- ✓ **Functional interfaces and Lambda Expressions.**
- ✓ **Java Stream API for collection classes.**
- ✓ **Java Date Time API.**

2. *What do you mean by platform independence of Java?*

Platform independence means that you can run the same Java Program in any Operating System. For example, you can write java program in Windows and run it in Mac OS.

3. *What is JVM and is it platform independent?*

Java Virtual Machine (JVM) is the heart of java programming language. JVM is responsible for converting byte code into machine readable code. JVM is not platform independent, thats why you have different JVM for different operating systems. We can customize JVM with Java Options, such as allocating minimum and maximum memory to JVM. It's called virtual because it provides an interface that doesn't depend on the underlying OS.

4. *What is the difference between JDK and JVM?*

Java Development Kit (JDK) is for development purpose and JVM is a part of it to execute the java programs.

JDK provides all the tools, executables and binaries required to compile, debug and execute a Java Program. The execution part is handled by JVM to provide machine independence.

5. *What is the difference between JVM and JRE?*

Java Runtime Environment (JRE) is the implementation of JVM. JRE consists of JVM and java binaries and other classes to execute any program successfully. JRE doesn't contain any development tools like java compiler, debugger etc. If you want to execute any java program, you should have JRE installed.

6. *Which class is the superclass of all classes?*

java.lang.Object is the root class for all the java classes and we don't need to extend it.

7. *Why Java doesn't support multiple inheritance?*

Java doesn't support multiple inheritance in classes because of "Diamond Problem". To know more about diamond problem with example, read **Multiple Inheritance in Java**. However multiple inheritance is supported in interfaces. An interface can extend multiple interfaces because they just declare the methods and implementation will be present in the implementing class. So there is no issue of diamond problem with interfaces.

8. *Why Java is not pure Object Oriented language?*

Java is not said to be pure object oriented because it support primitive types such as int, byte, short, long etc. I believe it brings simplicity to the language while writing our code. Obviously java could have wrapper objects for the primitive types but just for the representation, they would not have provided any benefit.

As we know, for all the primitive types we have wrapper classes such as Integer, Long etc that provides some additional methods.

9. *What is difference between path and classpath variables?*

PATH is an environment variable used by operating system to locate the executables. That's why when we install Java or want any executable to be found by OS, we need to add the directory location in the PATH variable. If you work on Windows OS, Classpath is specific to java and used by java executables to locate class files. We can provide the classpath location while running java application and it can be a directory, ZIP files, JAR files etc.

10. *What is the importance of main method in Java?*

main() method is the entry point of any standalone java application. The syntax of main method ispublic static void main(String args[]). main method is public and static so that java can access it without initializing the class. The input parameter is an array of String through which we can pass runtime arguments to the java program.

11. *What is overloading and overriding in java?*

When we have more than one method with same name in a single class but the arguments are different, then it is called as method overloading. Overriding concept comes in picture with inheritance when we have two methods with same signature, one in parent class and another in child class. We can use @Override annotation in the child class overridden method to make sure if parent class method is changed, so as child class.

12. *Can we overload main method?*

Yes, we can have multiple methods with name "main" in a single class. However if we run the class, java runtime environment will look for main method with syntax as public static void main(String args[]).

13. *Can we have multiple public classes in a java source file?*

We can't have more than one public class in a single java source file. A single source file can have multiple classes that are not public.

14. *What is Java Package and which package is imported by default?*

Java package is the mechanism to organize the java classes by grouping them. The grouping logic can be based on functionality or modules based. A java class fully classified name contains package and class name. For example, java.lang.Object is the fully classified name of Object class that is part ofjava.lang package. java.lang package is imported by default and we don't need to import any class from this package explicitly.

14. *What are access modifiers?*

Java provides access control through public, private and protected access modifier keywords. When none of these are used, it's called default access modifier. A java class can only have public or default access modifier.

What is final keyword?

final keyword is used with Class to make sure no other class can extend it, for example String class is final and we can't extend it. We can use final keyword with methods to make sure child classes can't override it.

final keyword can be used with variables to make sure that it can be assigned only once. However the state of the variable can be changed, for example we can assign a final variable to an object only once but the object variables can change later on. Java interface variables are by default final and static.

15. *What is static keyword?*

static keyword can be used with class level variables to make it global i.e all the objects will share the same variable. static keyword can be used with methods also. A static method can access only static variables of class and invoke only static methods of the class.

16. *What is finally and finalize in java?*

finally block is used with try-catch to put the code that you want to get executed always, even if any exception is thrown by the try-catch block.

finally block is mostly used to release resources created in the try block.finalize() is a special method in Object class that we can override in our classes.

This method get's called by garbage collector when the object is getting garbage collected. This method is usually overridden to release system resources when object is garbage collected.

17. *Can we declare a class as static?*

We can't declare a top-level class as static however an inner class can be declared as static. If inner class is declared as static, it's called static nested class. Static nested class is same as any other top-level class and is nested for only packaging convenience.

18. *What is static import?*

If we have to use any static variable or method from other class, usually we import the class and then use the method/variable with class name.

```
1   import java.lang.Math;
2   //inside class
3   double test = Math.PI * 5;
```

We can do the same thing by importing the static method or variable only and then use it in the class as if it belongs to it.

```
1   import static java.lang.Math.PI;
2
3   //no need to refer class now
4   double test = PI * 5;
```

Use of static import can cause confusion, so it's better to avoid it. Overuse of static import can make your program unreadable and unmaintainable.

19.   What is try-with-resources in java?

One of the Java 7 features is try-with-resources statement for automatic resource management. Before Java 7, there was no auto resource management and we should explicitly close the resource. Usually, it was done in the finally block of a try-catch statement.

This approach used to cause memory leaks when we forgot to close the resource. From Java 7, we can create resources inside try block and use it. Java takes care of closing it as soon as try-catch block gets finished.

20.   What is multi-catch block in java?

Java 7 one of the improvement was multi-catch block where we can catch multiple exceptions in a single catch block. This makes are code shorter and cleaner when every catch block has similar code. If a catch block handles multiple exception, you can separate them using a pipe (|) and in this case exception parameter (ex) is final, so you can't change it.

21.   What is static block?

Java static block is the group of statements that gets executed when the class is loaded into memory by Java ClassLoader. It is used to initialize static variables of the class. Mostly it's used to create static resources when class is loaded.

22.   What is an interface?

Interfaces are core part of java programming language and used a lot not only in JDK but also java design patterns, most of the frameworks and tools. Interfaces provide a way to achieve abstraction in java and used to define the contract for the subclasses to implement. Interfaces are good for starting point to define Type and create top level hierarchy in our code. Since a java class can implements multiple interfaces, it's better to use interfaces as super class in most of the cases.

23.   What is an abstract class?

Abstract classes are used in java to create a class with some default method implementation for subclasses. An abstract class can have abstract method without body and it can have methods with implementation also. abstract keyword is used to create a abstract class.

Abstract classes can't be instantiated and mostly used to provide base for sub-classes to extend and implement the abstract methods and override or use the implemented methods in abstract class.

24. What is the difference between abstract class and interface?

abstract keyword is used to create abstract class whereas interface is the keyword for interfaces. Abstract classes can have method implementations whereas interfaces can't. A class can extend only one abstract class but it can implement multiple interfaces. We can run abstract class if it has main() method whereas we can't run an interface. Some more differences in detail are at Difference between Abstract Class and Interface.

25. Can an interface implement or extend another interface?

Interfaces don't implement another interface, they extend it. Since interfaces can't have method implementations, there is no issue of diamond problem. That's why we have multiple inheritance in interfaces i.e an interface can extend multiple interfaces.

26. What is Marker interface?

A marker interface is an empty interface without any method but used to force some functionality in implementing classes by Java. Some of the well known marker interfaces are Serializable and Cloneable.

27. What are Wrapper classes?

Java wrapper classes are the Object representation of eight primitive types in java. All the wrapper classes in java are immutable and final. Java 5 autoboxing and unboxing allows easy conversion between primitive types and their corresponding wrapper classes.

28. What is Enum in Java?

Enum was introduced in Java 1.5 as a new type whose fields consists of fixed set of constants. For example, in Java we can create Direction as enum with fixed fields as EAST, WEST, NORTH, SOUTH. enum is the keyword to create an enum type and similar to class. Enum constants are implicitly static and final.

29. What is Java Annotations?

Java Annotations provide information about the code and they have no direct effect on the code they annotate. Annotations are introduced in Java 5. Annotation is metadata about the program embedded in the program itself. It can be parsed by the annotation parsing tool or by compiler. We can also specify annotation availability to either compile time only or till runtime also. Java Built-in annotations are @Override, @Deprecated and @SuppressWarnings.

30. What is Java Reflection API? Why it's so important to have?

Java Reflection API provides ability to inspect and modify the runtime behavior of java application. We can inspect a java class, interface, enum and get their methods and field details. Reflection API is an advanced topic and we should avoid it in normal programming. Reflection API usage can break the design pattern such as Singleton pattern by invoking the private constructor i.e violating the rules of access modifiers.

Even though we don't use Reflection API in normal programming, it's very important to have. We can't have any frameworks such as Spring, Hibernate or servers such as Tomcat, JBoss without Reflection API. They invoke the appropriate methods and instantiate classes through reflection API and use it a lot for other processing.

31. What is composition in java?

Composition is the design technique to implement has-a relationship in classes. We can use Object composition for code reuse. Java composition is achieved by using instance variables that refers to other objects. Benefit of using composition is that we can control the visibility of other object to client classes and reuse only what we need.

32. What is the benefit of Composition over Inheritance?

One of the best practices of java programming is to "favor composition over inheritance". Some of the possible reasons are:

- ✓ Any change in the superclass might affect subclass even though we might not be using the superclass methods. For example, if we have a method test() in subclass and suddenly somebody introduces a method test() in superclass, we will get compilation errors in subclass. Composition will never face this issue because we are using only what methods we need.

- ✓ Inheritance exposes all the super class methods and variables to client and if we have no control in designing superclass, it can lead to security holes. Composition allows us to provide restricted access to the methods and hence more secure.

- ✓ We can get runtime binding in composition where inheritance binds the classes at compile time. So composition provides flexibility in invocation of methods.

33. How to sort a collection of custom Objects in Java?

We need to implement Comparable interface to support sorting of custom objects in a collection. Comparable interface has compareTo(T obj) method which is used by sorting methods and by providing this method implementation, we can provide default way to sort custom objects collection.

However, if you want to sort based on different criteria, such as sorting an Employees collection based on salary or age, then we can create Comparator instances and pass it as sorting methodology.

34. What is inner class in java?

We can define a class inside a class and they are called nested classes. Any non-static nested class is known as inner class. Inner classes are associated with the object of the class and they can access all the variables and methods of the outer class.

Since inner classes are associated with instance, we can't have any static variables in them. We can have local inner class or anonymous inner class inside a class.

35. What is anonymous inner class?

A local inner class without name is known as anonymous inner class. An anonymous class is defined and instantiated in a single statement. Anonymous inner class always extend a class or implement an interface.

Since an anonymous class has no name, it is not possible to define a constructor for an anonymous class. Anonymous inner classes are accessible only at the point where it is defined.

36. What is Classloader in Java?

Java Classloader is the program that loads byte code program into memory when we want to access any class. We can create our own classloader by extending ClassLoader class and overriding loadClass(String name) method.

37. What are different types of classloaders?

There are three types of built-in Class Loaders in Java:

❖ Bootstrap Class Loader – It loads JDK internal classes, typically loads rt.jar and other core classes.

❖ Extensions Class Loader – It loads classes from the JDK extensions directory, usually $JAVA_HOME/lib/ext directory.

❖ System Class Loader – It loads classes from the current classpath that can be set while invoking a program using -cp or -classpath command line options.

38. What is ternary operator in java?

Java ternary operator is the only conditional operator that takes three operands. It's a one liner replacement for if-then-else statement and used a lot in java programming. We can use ternary operator if-else conditions or even switch conditions using nested ternary operators.

39. What does super keyword do?

super keyword can be used to access super class method when you have overridden the method in the child class.

We can use super keyword to invoke super class constructor in child class constructor but in this case it should be the first statement in the constructor method.

SuperClass.java

```
1   package com.journaldev.access;
2   public class SuperClass {
3     public SuperClass(){
4     }
5     public SuperClass(int i){}
6     public void test(){
7     System.out.println("super class test method");
8     }}
```

Use of super keyword can be seen in below child class implementation.

ChildClass.java

```
1   package com.journaldev.access;
2   public class ChildClass extends SuperClass {
3       public ChildClass(String str){
4           //access super class constructor with super keyword
5           super();
6           //access child class method
7           test();
8           //use super to access super class method
9           super.test();
10      }
11      @Override
12      public void test(){
13          System.out.println("child class test method");
14      }
15  }
16
```

40. What is break and continue statement?

We can use break statement to terminate for, while, or do-while loop. We can use break statement in switch statement to exit the switch case. You can see the example of break statement at **java break**.

We can use break with label to terminate the nested loops. The continue statement skips the current iteration of a for, while or do-while loop. We can use continue statement with label to skip the current iteration of outermost loop.

41. What is this keyword?

this keyword provides reference to the current object and it's mostly used to make sure that object variables are used, not the local variables having same name.

```
1  //constructor
2  public Point(int x, int y) {
3    this.x = x;
4    this.y = y;
5  }
```

We can also use this keyword to invoke other constructors from a constructor.

```
1   public Rectangle() {
2     this(0, 0, 0, 0);
3   }
4   public Rectangle(int width, int height) {
5     this(0, 0, width, height);
6   }
7   public Rectangle(int x, int y, int width, int height) {
8     this.x = x;
9     this.y = y;
10    this.width = width;
11    this.height = height;
12  }
```

42. Can we have try without catch block?

Yes, we can have try-finally statement and hence avoiding catch block.

43. What is Garbage Collection?

Garbage Collection is the process of looking at heap memory, identifying which objects are in use and which are not, and deleting the unused objects. In Java, process of deallocating memory is handled automatically by the garbage collector.

We can run the garbage collector with code Runtime.getRuntime().gc() or use utility methodSystem.gc().

44. What is Serialization and Deserialization?

We can convert a Java object to an Stream that is called Serialization. Once an object is converted to Stream, it can be saved to file or send over the network or used in socket connections.

The object should implement Serializable interface and we can use java.io.ObjectOutputStream to write object to file or to any OutputStream object. Read more at **Java Serialization**. The process of converting stream data created through serialization to Object is called deserialization.

45. How to run a JAR file through command prompt?

We can run a jar file using java command but it requires Main-Class entry in jar manifest file. Main-Class is the entry point of the jar and used by java command to execute the class.

46. What is the use of System class?

Java System Class is one of the core classes. One of the easiest way to log information for debugging is System.out.print() method.

System class is final so that we can't subclass and override it's behavior through inheritance. System class doesn't provide any public constructors, so we can't instantiate this class and that's why all of it's methods are static. Some of the utility methods of System class are for array copy, get current time, reading environment variables.

47. What is instanceof keyword?

We can use instanceof keyword to check if an object belongs to a class or not. We should avoid it's usage as much as possible. Sample usage is:

```
1    public static void main(String args[]){
2        Object str = new String("abc");
3        if(str instanceof String){
4            System.out.println("String value:"+str);
5        }
6        if(str instanceof Integer){
7            System.out.println("Integer value:"+str);
8        }
9    }
```

Since str is of type String at runtime, first if statement evaluates to true and second one to false.

48. Can we use String with switch case?

One of the Java 7 feature was improvement of switch case of allow Strings. So if you are using Java 7 or higher version, you can use String in switch-case statements.

49. What will be the output of following programs?

A.   static method in class -

```
1   package com.journaldev.util;
2   public class Test {
3     public static String toString(){
4       System.out.println("Test toString called");
5       return "";
6     }
7     public static void main(String args[]){
8       System.out.println(toString());
9     }
10  }
```

B. Answer: The code won't compile because we can't have an Object class method with static keyword. You will get compile time error as "This static method cannot hide the instance method from Object". The reason is that static method belongs to class and since every class base is Object, we can't have same method in instance as well as in class.

C.   static method invocation -

```
1   package com.journaldev.util;
2   public class Test {
3     public static String foo(){
4       System.out.println("Test foo called");
5       return "";
6     }
7     public static void main(String args[]){
8       Test obj = null;
9       System.out.println(obj.foo());
10    }
11  }
```

D. Answer: Well this is a strange situation. We all have seen NullPointerException when we invoke a method on object that is NULL. The compiler will give warning as "The static method foo() from the type Test should be accessed in a static way" but when executing it will work and prints "Test foo called".

E. Ideally Java API should have given error when a static method is called from an object rather than giving warning, but I think it's too late now to impose this. And most strange of all is that even though obj is null here, when invoking static method it works fine. I think it's working fine because Java runtime figures out that foo() is a static method and calls it on the class loaded into the memory and doesn't use the object at all, so no NullPointerException.

***Remember* :** I must admit that it's a very tricky question and if you are interviewing someone, this will blow his mind off.

50. What is default constructor?

No argument constructor of a class is known as default constructor. When we don't define any constructor for the class, java compiler automatically creates the default no-args constructor for the class. If there are other constructors defined, then compiler won't create default constructor for us.

Java String
Interview Questions and Answers

String is one of the most widely used Java Class. Here I am listing some important **Java String Interview Questions and Answers**. This will be very helpful to get complete knowledge of String and tackle any questions asked related to String in interview.

1. *What is String in Java? String is a data type?*

2. *What are different ways to create String Object?*

3. *Write a method to check if input String is Palindrome?*

4. *Write a method that will remove given character from the String?*

5. *How can we make String upper case or lower case?*

6. *What is String subSequence method?*

7. *How to compare two Strings in java program?*

8. *How to convert String to char and vice versa?*

9. *How to convert String to byte array and vice versa?*

10. *Can we use String in switch case?*

11. *Write a program to print all permutations of String?*

12. *Write a function to find out longest palindrome in a given string?*

13.   *Difference between String, StringBuffer and StringBuilder?*

14.   *Why String is immutable or final in Java*

15.   *How to Split String in java?*

16.   *Why Char array is preferred over String for storing password?*

17.   *How do you check if two Strings are equal in Java?*

18.   *What is String Pool?*

19.   *What does String intern() method do?*

20.   *Does String is thread-safe in Java?*

21.   *Why String is popular HashMap key in Java?*

What is String in Java? String is a data type?

String is a Class in java and defined in java.lang package. It's not a primitive data type like int and long. String class represents character Strings. String is used in almost all the Java applications and there are some interesting facts we should know about String. String in immutable and final in Java and JVM uses String Pool to store all the String objects. Some other interesting things about String is the way we can instantiate a String object using double quotes and overloading of "+" operator for concatenation.

What are different ways to create String Object?

We can create String object using new operator like any normal java class or we can use double quotes to create a String object. There are several constructors available in String class to get String from char array, byte array, StringBuffer and StringBuilder.

1   String str = new String("abc");

2   String str1 = "abc";

When we create a String using double quotes, JVM looks in the String pool to find if any other String is stored with same value. If found, it just returns the reference to that String object else it creates a new String object with given value and stores it in the String pool.

When we use new operator, JVM creates the String object but don't store it into the String Pool. We can useintern() method to store the String object into String pool or return the reference if there is already a String with equal value present in the pool.

Write a method to check if input String is Palindrome?

A String is said to be Palindrome if it's value is same when reversed. For example "aba" is a Palindrome String. String class doesn't provide any method to reverse the String but StringBuffer and StringBuilder class has reverse method that we can use to check if String is palindrome or not.

```
1   private static boolean isPalindrome(String str) {
2      if (str == null)
3         return false;
4      StringBuilder strBuilder = new StringBuilder(str);
5      strBuilder.reverse();
6      return strBuilder.toString().equals(str);
7   }
```

Sometimes interviewer asks not to use any other class to check this, in that case we can compare characters in the String from both ends to find out if it's palindrome or not.

```
1   private static boolean isPalindromeString(String str) {
2      if (str == null)
3         return false;
4      int length = str.length();
5      System.out.println(length / 2);
6      for (int i = 0; i < length / 2; i++) {
7
8         if (str.charAt(i) != str.charAt(length - i - 1))
9            return false;
10     }
11     return true;
12  }
```

Write a method that will remove given character from the String?

We can use replaceAll method to replace all the occurance of a String with another String. The important point to note is that it accepts String as argument, so we will use Character class to create String and use it to replace all the characters with empty String.

```
1   private static String removeChar(String str, char c) {
2       if (str == null)
3           return null;
4       return str.replaceAll(Character.toString(c), "");
5   }
```

How can we make String upper case or lower case?

We can use String class toUpperCase and toLowerCase methods to get the String in all upper case or lower case. These methods have a variant that accepts Locale argument and use that locale rules to convert String to upper or lower case.

What is String subSequence method?

Java 1.4 introduced CharSequence interface and String implements this interface, this is the only reason for the implementation of subSequence method in String class. Internally it invokes the String substring method.

How to compare two Strings in java program?

Java String implements Comparable interface and it has two variants of compareTo() methods. compareTo(String anotherString) method compares the String object with the String argument passed lexicographically. If String object precedes the argument passed, it returns negative integer and if String object follows the argument String passed, it returns positive integer.

It returns zero when both the String have same value, in this case equals(String str) method will also return true. compareToIgnoreCase(String str): This method is similar to the first one, except that it ignores the case. It uses String CASE_INSENSITIVE_ORDER Comparator for case insensitive comparison. If the value is zero thenequalsIgnoreCase(String str) will also return true.

How to convert String to char and vice versa?

This is a tricky question because String is a sequence of characters, so we can't convert it to a single character. We can use use charAt method to get the character at given index or we can use toCharArray()method to convert String to character array.

How to convert String to byte array and vice versa?

We can use String getBytes() method to convert String to byte array and we can use String constructor new String(byte[] arr) to convert byte array to String.

Can we use String in switch case?

This is a tricky question used to check your knowledge of current Java developments. Java 7 extended the capability of switch case to use Strings also, earlier java versions doesn't support this. If you are implementing conditional flow for Strings, you can use if-else conditions and you can use switch case if you are using Java 7 or higher versions.

Write a program to print all permutations of String?

This is a tricky question and we need to use recursion to find all the permutations of a String, for example "AAB" permutations will be "AAB", "ABA" and "BAA". We also need to use Set to make sure there are no duplicate values.

Write a function to find out longest palindrome in a given string?

A String can contain palindrome strings in it and to find longest palindrome in given String is a programming question.

Difference between String, StringBuffer and StringBuilder?

String is immutable and final in java, so whenever we do String manipulation, it creates a new String. String manipulations are resource consuming, so java provides two utility classes for String manipulations – StringBuffer and StringBuilder. StringBuffer and StringBuilder are mutable classes. StringBuffer operations are thread-safe and synchronized where StringBuilder operations are not thread-safe. So when multiple threads are working on same String, we should use StringBuffer but in single threaded environment we should use StringBuilder. StringBuilder performance is fast than StringBuffer because of no overhead of synchronization.

Why String is immutable or final in Java

There are several benefits of String because it's immutable and final.

- String Pool is possible because String is immutable in java.

- It increases security because any hacker can't change its value and it's used for storing sensitive information such as database username, password etc.

- Since String is immutable, it's safe to use in multi-threading and we don't need any synchronization.

- Strings are used in java classloader and immutability provides security that correct class is getting loaded by Classloader.

How to Split String in java?

We can use split(String regex) to split the String into String array based on the provided regular expression.

Why Char array is preferred over String for storing password?

String is immutable in java and stored in String pool. Once it's created it stays in the pool until unless garbage collected, so even though we are done with password it's available in memory for longer duration and there is no way to avoid it. It's a security risk because anyone having access to memory dump can find the password as clear text. If we use char array to store password, we can set it to blank once we are done with it. So we can control for how long it's available in memory that avoids the security threat with String.

How do you check if two Strings are equal in Java?

There are two ways to check if two Strings are equal or not – using "==" operator or using equals method. When we use "==" operator, it checks for value of String as well as reference but in our programming, most of the time we are checking equality of String for value only. So we should use equals method to check if two Strings are equal or not. There is another function equalsIgnoreCase that we can use to ignore case.

```
1   String s1 = "abc";
2   String s2 = "abc";
3   String s3= new String("abc");
4   System.out.println("s1 == s2 ? "+(s1==s2)); //true
5   System.out.println("s1 == s3 ? "+(s1==s3)); //false
6   System.out.println("s1 equals s3 ? "+(s1.equals(s3))); //true
```

What is String Pool?

As the name suggests, String Pool is a pool of Strings stored in Java heap memory. We know that String is special class in java and we can create String object using new operator as well as providing values in double quotes.

What does String intern() method do?

When the intern method is invoked, if the pool already contains a string equal to this String object as determined by the equals(Object) method, then the string from the pool is returned. Otherwise, this String object is added to the pool and a reference to this String object is returned. This method always return a String that has the same contents as this string, but is guaranteed to be from a pool of unique strings.

Does String is thread-safe in Java?

Strings are immutable, so we can't change it's value in program. Hence it's thread-safe and can be safely used in multi-threaded environment.

Why String is popular HashMap key in Java?

Since String is immutable, its hashcode is cached at the time of creation and it doesn't need to be calculated again. This makes it a great candidate for key in a Map and it's processing is fast than other HashMap key objects. This is why String is mostly used Object as HashMap keys.

Last Deal- Now Kick on Java
And Say Good Bye Java.. ☺

Introduction :

I have already covered every single question from Java world. While Java-related questions are found throughout this book, this chapter deals with questions about the language and syntax.

Such questions are more unusual at bigger companies, which believe more in testing a candidate's aptitude than a candidate's knowledge (and which have the time and resources to train a candidate in a particular language). However, at other companies, these pesky questions can be quite common.

How to Approach -

As these questions focus so much on knowledge, it may seem silly to talk about an approach to these problems. After all, isn't it just about knowing the right answer?

Yes and no. Of course, the best thing you can do to master these questions is to learn Java inside and out. But, if you do get stumped, you can try to tackle it with the following approach:

+ Create an example of the scenario, and ask yourself how things should play out.

+ Askyourself how other languages would handle this scenario.

+ Consider how you would design this situation if you were the language designer.

What would the implications of each choice be?

Your interviewer may be equally or more impressed if you can derive the answer than if you automatically knew it. Don't try to bluff though. Tell the interviewer, "I'm not sure I can recall the answer, but let me see if I can figure it out. Suppose we have this code..."

final keyword -

I have already explained about it several time. The final keyword in Java has a different meaning depending on whether it is appliedmto a variable, class or method.

+ Variable:The value cannot be changed once initialized.

+ Method:The method cannot be overridden by a subclass.

+ C/oss.-The class cannot be subclassed.

finally keyword -

The finally keyword is used in association with a try/catch block and guarantees that a section of code will be executed, even if an exception is thrown. The finally block will be executed after the try and catch blocks, but before control transfers back to its origin.

Watch how this plays out in the example below.

```
1       public static String lem() {
2       System.out.println("lem")J
3       return "return from lem";
4       }
5
6       public static String foo() {
7       int x = 0;
8        int y = 5;
9        try {
19      System.out.println("start try");
11       int b = y / x;
12      System.out.println("end try");
13       return "returned from try";
14      } catch (Exception ex) {
15      System.out.println("catch");
```

```
16        return lem() + " | returned from catch";
17        } finally {
18        System.out.println("finally");
19        }
20        }
21
22         public static void bar() {
23          System.out.println("start bar");
24        String v = foo();
25        System.out.println(v);
26        System.out.println("end bar");
27         }
28
29         public static void main(String[] args) {
30        bar();
31 }
```

The output for this code is the following:

1 start bar

2 start try

3 catch

4 lem

5 finally

6 return from lem | returned from catch

7 end bar

Look carefully at lines 3 to 5 in the output. The catch block is fully executed (including the function call in the return statement), then the finally block, and then the function actually returns.

---

finalize method -

The automatic garbage collector calls the finalize() method just before actually destroying the object. A class can therefore override the f inalize() method from the Object class in order to define custom behavior during garbage collection.

```
1 protected void finalizeQ throws Throwable {
2 /* Close open files, release resources, etc */
3 }
```

Overloading vs. Overriding -

Overloading is a term used to describe when two methods have the same name but differ in the type or number of arguments.

```
1 public double computeArea(Circle c) { ... }
2 public double computeArea(Square s) { ... }
```

Overriding, however, occurs when a method shares the same name and function signature as another method in its super class.

```
1       public abstract class Shape {
2       public void printMe() {
3       System.out.println("I am a shape.");
4       }
5       public abstract double computeAreaQ;
6       }
7
8       public class Circle extends Shape {
9       private double rad = 5;
10      public void printMeQ {
11      System.out.println("I am a circle.");
12      }
13
14      public double computeAreaQ {
15      return rad * rad * 3.15;
16      }
17      }
```

```
18
19      public class Ambiguous extends Shape {
20      private double area = 10;
21      public double computeAreaQ {
22      return area;
23      }
24      }
25
26      public class IntroductionOverriding {
27      public static void main(String[] args) {
28      Shapef] shapes = new Shape[2];
29      Circle circle = new CircleQ;
30      Ambiguous ambiguous = new Ambiguous();
31
32      shapes[0] = circle;
33      shapes[l] = ambiguous;
34
35       for (Shape s : shapes) {
36      s.printMeQ;
37      System.out.println(s.computeArea());
38      }
39      }
40      }
```

The above code will print:

1 I am a circle.

2 78.75

3 I am a shape.

4 10.0

Observe that Circle overrode printMe(), whereas Ambiguous just left this method as-is.

Collection Framework -

Java's collection framework is incredibly useful, and you will see it used throughout this book. Here are some of the most useful items:

ArrayList: -

An ArrayList is a dynamically resizing array, which grows as you insert elements.

```
1 ArrayList<String> myArr = new ArrayList<String>();
2 myArr.add("one");
3 myArr.add("two");
4 System.out.println(myArr.get(0)); /* prints <one> */
```

Vector: -

A vector is very similar to an ArrayList, except that it is synchronized. Its syntax is almost identical as well.

```
1 Vector<String> myVect = new Vector<String>();
2 myVect.add("one");
3 myVect.add("two");
4 System.out.println(myVect.get(0));
```

LinkedList: -

LinkedList is, of course, Java's built-in LinkedList class. Though it rarely comes up in an interview, it's useful to study because it demonstrates some of the syntax for an iterator.

```
1       LinkedList<String> myLinkedList = new LinkedList<String>();
2       myLinkedList.add("two");
3       myLinkedList.addFirst("one");
4       Iterator<String> iter = myLinkedList.iteratorQ;
5       while (iter.hasNextQ) {
6         System.out.println(iter.next());
7       }
```

HashMap :-

The HashMap collection is widely used, both in interviews and in the real world. We've provided a snippet of the syntax below.

```
1 HashMap<String, String> map = new HashMap<String, String>();

2 map.put("one", "uno");

3 map.put("two", "dos");

4 System.out.println(map.get("one"));
```

Before your interview, make sure you're very comfortable with the above syntax. You'll need it.

Interview Questions

Please note that because virtually all the solutions in this book are implemented with Java, we have selected only a small number of questions for this chapter. Moreover, most of these questions deal with the "trivia" of the languages, since the rest of the book is filled with Java programming questions.

Que: 1 In terms of inheritance, what is the effect of keeping a constructor private?

Ans : Declaring the constructor private will ensure that no one outside of the class can directly instantiate the class. In this case, the only way to create an instance of the class is to provide a static public method, as is done when using the Factory Method Pattern. Additionally, because the constructor is private, the class also cannot be inherited.

Que: 2 In Java, does the finally block get executed if we insert a return statement inside the try block of a try-catch-finally?

Ans: Yes, it will get executed. The finally block gets executed when the try block exits. Even when we attempt to exit within the try block (via a return statement, a continue statement, a break statement or any exception), the finally block will still be executed.

Note that there are some cases in which the finally block will not get executed, such as the following:

+ If the virtual machine exits during try/catch block execution.

+ If the thread which is executing the try/catch block gets killed.

Que: 3 What is the difference between final, finally, and finalize?

Ans: Despite their similar sounding names, final, finally and finalize have very different purposes. To speak in very general terms, final is used to control whether a variable, method, or class is "changeable." The finally keyword is used in a try/ catch block to ensure that a segment of code is always executed. The finalizeQ method is called by the garbage collector once it determines that no more references exist. Further detail on these keywords and methods is provided below.

final -

The final statement has a different meaning depending on its context.

- When applied to a variable (primitive): The value of the variable cannot change.
- When applied to a variable (reference): The reference variable cannot point to any other object on the heap.
- When applied to a method: The method cannot be overridden.
- When applied to a class: The class cannot be subclassed.

finally -

There is an optional finally block after the try block or after the catch block. Statements in the finally block will always be executed (except if Java Virtual Machine exits from the try block).The finally block is used to write the clean-up code.

finalized -

The finalize() method is called by the garbage collector when it determines that no more references exist. It is typically used to clean up resources, such as closing a file.

Que: 4 Explain the difference between templates in C++ and generics in Java.

Ans : Many programmers consider the concepts of templates and generics to be equivalent simply because both allow you to do something along the lines of List<St ringx But, how each language does this, and why, varies significantly.

The implementation of Java generics is rooted in an idea of "type erasure."This technique eliminates the parameterized types when source code is translated to the Java Virtual Machine (JVM) byte code.

For example, suppose you have the Java code below:

1 Vector<string> vector = pew Vector<String>();

2 vector.add(new String("hello"));

3 String str = vector.get(0);

During compilation, this code is re-written into:

1 Vector vector = new Vector()j

2 vector.add(new String("hello"));

3 String str = (String) vector.get(0)j

The use of Java generics didn't real'y change much about our capabilities; it just made things a bit prettier. For this reason, Java generics are sometimes called "syntactic sugar."

This is quite different from C++. In C++, templates are essentially a glorified macro set, with the compiler creating a new copy of the template code for each type. Proof of this is in the fact that an instance of MyClass<Foo> will not share a static variable with MyClass<Bar>.Two instances of MyClass<Foo>, however, will share a static variable.

To illustrate this, consider the code below:

```
1       /*** MyClass.h ***/
2       template<class T> class MyClass {
3       public:
4       static int valj
5       MyClass(int v) { val = v; }
6       };
7
8       /*** MyClass.cpp ***/
9       template<typename T>
10      int MyClass<T>::barj
11
12       template class MyClass<Foo>;
13       template class MyClass<Bar>;
14
15       /*** main.cpp ***/
16      MyClass<Foo> * fool = new MyClass<Foo>(10);
17      MyClass<Foo> * foo2 = new MyClass<Foo>(15);
18      MyClass<Bar> * barl = new MyClass<Bar>(20);
19      MyClass<Bar> * bar2 = new MyClass<Bar>(35);
20
21       int fl = fool->val; // will equal 15
22      int f2 = foo2->val; // will equal 15
23      int bl = barl->val; // will equal 35
24 int b2 = bar2->val; // will equal 35
```

In Java, static variables would be shared across instances of MyClass, regardless of the different type parameters. Because of their architectural differences, Java generics and C++ templates have a number of other differences.These include:

> ➤ C++ templates can use primitive types, like int. Java cannot and must instead use Integer.

> ➤ In Java, you can restrict the template's type parameters to be of a certain type. For instance, you might use generics to implement a CardDeck and specify that the type parameter must extend from CardGame.

> ➤ In C++, the type parameter can be instantiated, whereas Java does not support this.

> ➤ In Java, the type parameter (i.e., the Foo in MyClass< Foo>) cannot be used for static methods and variables, since these would be shared between MyClass<Foo> and MyClass<Bar>. In C++, these classes are different, so the type parameter can be used for static methods and variables.

> ➤ In Java, all instances of MyClass, regardless of their type parameters, are the same type. The type parameters are erased at runtime. In C++, instances with different type parameters are different types.

Remember that although Java generics and C++ templates look the same in many ways, they are very different.

Que: 5 Explain what object reflection is in Java and why it is useful.

Ans : Object Reflection is a feature in Java which provides a way to get reflective information about Java classes and objects, and perform operations such as:

> ➤ Getting information about the methods and fields present inside the class at runtime.

> ➤ Creating a new instance of a class.

> ➤ Getting and setting the object fields directly by getting field reference, regardless of what the access modifier is.

The code below offers an example of object reflection.

```
1    /* Parameters */
2    Object[] doubleArgs = new Object[] { A.2, 3.9 };
3
4    /* Get class */
5    Class rectangleDefinition = Class.forName("MyProj.Rectangle");
6
7    /* Equivalent: Rectangle rectangle = new Rectangle(4.2, 3.9); */
8    Class[ ] doubleArgsClass = new Classf ] {double.class, double.class};
9    Constructor doubleArgsConstructor =
10   rectangleDefinition.getConstructor(doubleArgsClass);
11   Rectangle rectangle =
12   (Rectangle) doubleArgsConstructor.newInstance(doubleArgs);
13
14   /* Equivalent: Double area = rectangle.areaQ; */
15   Method m = rectangleDefinition.getDeclaredMethod("area");
16   Double area = (Double) m.invoke(rectangle);
```

This code does the equivalent of:

```
1    Rectangle rectangle = new Rectangle(4.2, 3.9);
2    Double area = rectangle.areaQ;
```

Why Is Object Reflection Useful?

Of course, it doesn't seem very useful in the above example, but reflection can be very useful in particular cases. Object reflection is useful for three main reasons:

1. It helps in observing or manipulating the runtime behavior of applications.

2. It can help in debugging or testing programs, as we have direct access to methods, constructors, and fields.

3. We can call methods by name when we don't know the method in advance. For example, we may let the user pass in a class name, parameters for the constructor, and a method name. We can then use this information to create an object and call a method. Doing these operations without reflection would require a complex series of if-statements, if it's possible at all.

Que: 6 Implement a CircularArray class that supports an array-like data structure which can be efficiently rotated. The class should use a generic type, and should support iteration via the standard for (Obj o : CircularArray) notation.

Ans : This problem really has two parts to it. First, we need to implement the CircularArray class. Second, we need to support iteration. We will address these parts separately.

Implementing the CircularArray class -

One way to implement the CircularArray class is to actually shift the elements each time we call rotate (int shift Right). Doing this is, of course, not very efficient.

Instead, we can just create a member variable head which points to what should be conceptually viewed as the start of the circular array. Rather than shifting around the elements in the array, we just increment head by shiftRight.

The code below implements this approach.

```
1       public class CircularArray<T> {
2       private T[] items;
3       private int head = 0;
4
5       public CircularArray(int size) {
6       items = (T[]> new Object[size];
7       }
8
9       private int convert(int index) {
10      if (index < 0) {
11      index += items.length;
12      }
13      return (head + index) % items.length;
14      }
15
16      public void rotate(int shiftRight) {
17      head = convert(shiftRight);
18      }
20      public T get(int i) {
21      if (i < 0 || i >= items.length) {
22      throw new java.lang.IndexOutOfBoundsException("...");
23      }
```

```
24        return items[convert(i)];
25      }
26      public void set(int i, T item) {
27        items[convert(i)] = item;
28      }
39    }
```

There are a number of things here which are easy to make mistakes on, such as:

> We cannot create an array of the generic type. Instead, we must either cast the array or define items to be of type List<T>. For simplicity, we have done the former.

> The % operator will return a negative value when we do negValue % posVal. For example, -8 % 3 is -2. This is different from how mathematicians would define the modulus function. We must add items. length to a negative index to get the correct positive result.

> We need to be sure to consistently convert the raw index to the rotated index. For this reason, we have implemented a convert function that is used by other methods. Even the rotate function uses convert. This is a good example of code reuse.

Now that we have the basic code for CircularArray out of the way, we can focus on implementing an iterator.

Implementing the Iterator Interface -

The second part of this question asks us to implement the CircularArray class such that we can do the following:

1 CircularArray<String> array = ...

2 for (String s : array) { ... }

Implementing this requires implementing the Iterator interface. To implement the Iterator interface, we need to do the following:

+ Modify the CircularArray<T> definition to add implements Iterable<T>.This will also require us to add an iterator () method to CircularArray<T>.

+ Create a CircularArrayIterator<T> which implements Iterator<T>. This will also require us to implement, in the CircularArrayIterator, the methods hasNextQ, next(),and remove().

Once we've done the above items, the for loop will "magically" work.

In the code below, we have removed the aspects of CircularArray which were identical to the earlier implementation.

```
I        public class CircularArray<T> implements Iterable<T> {
```

```
2
3        public Iterator<T> iteratorQ {
4        return new CircularArrayIterator<T>(this);
5        }
6
7        private class CircularArrayIterator<TI> implements Iterator<TI>{
8        /* current reflects the offset from the rotated head, not
9        * from the actual start of the raw array. */
10       private int _current = -1;
II        private TI[] _items;
12
13       public CircularArrayIterator(CircularArray<TI> array){
14       _items = array.items;
15       }
16
17       ^Override
18       public boolean hasNextQ {
19       return _current < items.length - 1;
20       }
22       @0verride
23       public TI next( ) {
24       _current++;
25       TI item = (TI) _items[convert(_current)];
26       return item;
27       }
29       ^Override
38       public void removeQ {
31       throw new UnsupportedOperationException("...");
32       }
33       }
34       }
```

In the above code, note that the first iteration of the for loop will call hasNext() and then next (). Be very sure that your implementation will return the correct values here.

When you get a problem like this one in an interview, there's a good chance you don't remember exactly what the various methods and interfaces are called. In this case, work through the problem as well as you can. If you can reason out what sorts of methods one might need, that alone will show a good degree of competency.

BOOK PART – XXX

(Advance Coding Standards for Java)
(Do-Don't & Database issues)

∞ **(Java Coding Standards.)** ∞

(Java.lang — The Math Class, Strings, and Wrappers.)

Introduction-

Use Sun Java Coding Standards:

This and upcoming chapters will help you to understand proper code guidelines. These chapers are very important and will help you to crack Java Developers Interview followed by Worlds top 10 software companies and learning Java coding standards. There are a lot of complex design issues to consider, and a host of advanced Java technologies to understand and implement correctly.

The practice assessors work under very strict guidelines. You can create the **most brilliant application** ever to grace a JVM, but if you don't cross your t's and dot your i's the assessors have no choice but to deduct crucial (and sometimes substantial) points from your project. This chapter will help you cross your t's and dot your i's.

Following coding standards is not hard; it just requires diligence. If you are careful it's no-brainer stuff, and it would be a shame to lose points because of a curly brace in the wrong place.

The Developer interview stresses things that must be done to avoid automatic failure. The interview uses the word must frequently. When we use the word must, we use it in the spirit of the interview, if you must you must, so just get on with it. Let's dive into the fascinating world of Java Coding Standards.

Spacing Standards-

This bonus section covers the standards for indenting, line-length limits, line breaking, and white space. Indenting We said this was going to be fascinating didn't we? Each level of indentation must be four spaces, exactly four spaces, always four spaces.

Tabs must be set to eight spaces. If you are in several levels of indentation you can use a combination of tabs and (sets of four) spaces to accomplish the correct indentation.

So if you are in a method and you need to indent 12 spaces, you can either press SPACEBAR 12 times, or press TAB once and then press SPACEBAR four times. (Slow down coach.) We recommend not using the TAB key, and sticking to the SPACEBAR—it's just a bit safer.

When to Indent if you indent like this, you'll make your assessor proud:

- ❖ Beginning comments, package declarations, import statements, interface declarations, and class declarations should not be indented.

- ❖ Static variables, instance variables, constructors, methods, and their respective comments* should be indented one level.

- ❖ within constructors and methods, local variables, statements, and their comments should be indented another level.

- ❖ Statements (and their comments) within block statements should be indentedanother level for each level of nesting involved. (Don't worry; we'll give you an example.)

The following listing shows proper indenting:

```
public class Indent {

    static int staticVar = 7;

    public Indent() { }

    public static void main(String [] args) {

        int x = 0;

        for(int z=0; z<7; z++) {
            x = x + z;
            if (x < 4) {
                x++;
            }
        }
    }
}
```

Line Lengths and Line Wrapping-

The general rule is that a line shouldn't be longer than 80 characters. We recommend 65 characters just to make sure that a wide variety of editors will handle your code gracefully. When a line of code is longer than will fit on a line there are some lines wrapping guidelines to follow. We can't say for sure that these are a must, but if you follow these guidelines you can be sure that you're on safe ground:

- ✦ Break after a comma.
- ✦ Break before an operator.
- ✦ Align the new line a tab (or eight spaces) beyond the beginning of the line being broken.
- ✦ Try not to break inside an inner parenthesized expression. (Hang on, the example is coming.)

The following snippet demonstrates acceptable line wrapping:

```
/* example of a line wrap */
System.out.println(((x * 42) + (z - 343) + (x % z ))
        + numberOfParsecs);

/* example of a line wrap for a method */
x = doStuffWithLotsOfArgs(coolStaticVar, instanceVar,
        numberOfParsecs, reallyLongShortName, x, z);
```

White Space-

Can you believe we have to go to this level of detail? It turns out that if you don't parcel out your blank spaces as the standards say you should, you can lose points. With that happy thought in mind, let's discuss the proper use of blank lines and blank statements.

The Proper Use of Blank Lines-

Blank lines are used to help readers of your code (which might be you, months after you wrote it) to easily spot the logical blocks within your source file. If you follow these recommendations in your source files, your blank line worries will be over. Use a blank line,

- Between methods and constructors.
- After your last instance variable.
- Inside a method between the local variables and the first statement.
- Inside a method to separate logical segments of code.
- Before single line or block comments.

Use two blank lines between the major sections of the source file: the package, the import statement(s), the class, and the interface.

The Proper Use of Blank Spaces -

Blank spaces are used to make statements_more readable, and less squished together. Use a blank space,

- Between binary operators.
- After commas in an argument list.
- After the expressions in a for statement.
- Between a keyword and a parenthesis.
- After casts.

The following code sample demonstrates proper form to use when indenting, skipping lines, wrapping lines, and using spaces. We haven't covered all of the rules associated with the proper use of comments; therefore, this sample does not demonstrate standard comments:

```
/*
 * This listing demonstrates only proper spacing standards
 *
 * The Javadoc comments will be discussed in a later chapter
 */


package com.wickedlysmart.utilities;


import java.util.*;


/**
 * CoolClass description
 *
 * @version .97 10 Oct 2002
 * @author   Joe Beets
 */
public class CoolClass {

    /** Javadoc static var comment */
    public static int coolStaticVar;

    /** Javadoc public i-var comment */

    public long instanceVar;

    /* private i-var comment */
    private short reallyLongShortName;

    /** Javadoc constructor comment */
    public CoolClass() {
      // do stuff
    }

    /** Javadoc comment about method */
    void coolMethod() {
        int x = 0;
        long numberOfParsecs = 0;

        /* comment about for loop */
        for(z = 0; z < 7; z++) {
            x = x + z;
```

```
    /* comment about if test */
    if (x < 4) {
        x++;
    }

    /* example of a line wrap */
    System.out.println(((x * 42) + (z - 343) + (x % z ))
            + numberOfParsecs);

    /* example of a line wrap for a method */
    x = doStuffWithLotsOfArgs(coolStaticVar, instanceVar,
            numberOfParsecs, reallyLongShortName, x, z);
    }
}

/** Javadoc comment about method */
int doStuffWithLotsOfArgs(int a, long b, long c, short d, int e,
        int f) {
    return e * f;
}
}
```

Declarations Are Fun-

Declarations are a huge part of Java. They are also complex, loaded with rules, and if used sloppily can lead to bugs and poor maintainability. The following set of guidelines is intended to make your code more readable, more debuggable, and more maintainable.

Sequencing Your Declarations-

The elements in your Java source files should be arranged in a standard sequence.

In some cases the compiler demands it, and for the rest of the cases consistency will help you win friends and influence people. Here goes:

- class comments.
- package declaration.
- import statements.
- class declaration.
- static variables.
- instance variables.
- constructors.

Location and Initialization-

The following guidelines should be considered when making Java declarations: Within methods:

- Declare and initialize local variables before other statements (whenever possible).
- Declare and initialize block variables before other block statements (when possible).
- Declare only one member per line.
- Avoid shadowing variables. This occurs when an instance variable hasthe same name as a local or block variable. While the compiler will allowit, shadowing is considered very unfriendly towards the next co-worker (remember: potentially psychopathic) who has to maintain your code.

Capitalization-

Three guesses. You better use capitalization correctly when you declare and use your package, class, interface, method, variable, and constant names. The rules are pretty simple:

- Package names The safest bet is to use lowercase when possible: com.wickedlysmart.utilities
- Class and Interface names Typically they should be nouns; capitalize the first letter and any other first letters in secondary words within the name: Customer or CustomTable
- Method names Typically they should be verbs; the first word should be lowercase, and if there are secondary words, the first letter of each should be capitalized:

initialize( ); or getTelescopicOrientation( );

- Variable names They should follow the same capitalization rules as methods; you should start them with a letter (even though you can use _ or $, don't), and only temporary variables like looping variables should use single character names:

currentIndex; or name; or x;

- Constant names To be labeled a constant, a variable must be declared static and final. Their names should be all uppercase and underscores must be used to separate words: **MAX_HEIGHT; or USED;**

(Clarity and Maintainability.)

(Java Code Clarity & Maintainablility)

Introduction of -
Clarity and Maintainability-

Always Write Clear and Maintainable Codes Now that you've made your code readable, does your easy-to-read code actually make sense? Can it be easily maintained?

These are huge issues for the interview, worth a very significant chunk of your assessment score. We'll look at everything from class design to error handling. Remember that you're a Team Player. Some key areas of code clarity are covered in more detail in the Documentation chapter, so we won't discuss them here.

Those areas include the importance of meaningful comments and self-documenting identifiers. The issues raised in this chapter are

- General programming style considerations.
- Following OO design principles.
- Reinventing the wheel.
- Error-handling.

General Programming Considerations-

The coding conventions covered in the previous chapter are a great starting point. But the interview is also looking for consistency and appropriateness in your programming style.

The following section lists some key points you should keep in mind when writing your perfectly-formatted code. Some of these will be explained in subsequent sections; several of these points are related to OO design, for example, and we cover them in more detail in that section.

Once again, this is no time to debate the actual merits of these principles. Again, imagine you've come into a project team and need to prove yourself as a, what? Yes! Team Player *Man* !.

The first thing the team is looking for is whether you can follow the conventions and standards so that everyone can work together without wanting to throw one another out the seventh floor window and onto the cement fountain below. (Unless you're a dot-com company and your office now looks over an abandoned gas station.)

These points are in no particular order, so don't infer that the first ones are more important than the last. You can infer, however, that your interview assessor will probably be asking if you've done these things appropriately.

Keep Variable Scope as Small as Possible-

Don't use an instance variable when a local variable will work! Not only does this impact memory use, but it reduces the risk that an object "slips out" to some place it shouldn't be used, either accidentally or on purpose.

Wait to declare a variable until just before it's used. And you should always initialize a local variable at the time it is declared (which is just before use), with the exception of try/catch blocks. In that case, if the variable is declared and assigned in the try/catch block, the compiler won't let you use it beyond that block, so if you need the variable after a try or catch block, then you'll have to declare

It first outside the try/catch. Another way to reduce scope is to use a for loop rather than while.

Avoid Designing a Class That Has No Methods-

Objects are meant to have both state and behavior; they're not simply glorified structs. If you need a data structure, use a Collection. There are exceptions to this,

However, that might apply to your interview assignment. Sometimes you do need an object whose sole purpose is to carry data from one location to another—usually as a result of a database request.

A row in a table, for example, should be represented as an object in your Java program, and it might not always need methods if its sole job is to be, say, displayed in a GUI table. This is known as the ValueObject pattern. Which brings us to the next issue.

Use Design Patterns-

When you use familiar patterns, then you've got a kind of shorthand for discussing your design with other programmers (even if that discussion is between your code/ comments and the other person.

If you've done it right, you won't personally be there to talk about it, as is the case with the Developer interview). If you need a Singleton, make a Singleton—don't simply document that there is to be only one of these things.

On the other hand, don't go forcing your design into a pattern just for the sake of using a pattern. Simplicity should be your first concern, but if it's a toss-up between your approach and an equally complex, well-known design pattern, go for the pattern.

Reduce the Visibility of Things As Much As Possible-

In general, the more public stuff you expose to the world, the less free you are to make changes later without breaking someone else's code. The less you expose, the more flexibility you have for implementation changes later.

And you know there are always changes. So, making variables, methods, and classes as restricted as you can while limiting what you expose to your "public interface,"

you'll be in good shape down the road. Obviously there are other subtle issues about inheritance (as in, what does a subclass get access to?), so there's more to consider here, but in general, be thinking about reducing your exposure (think of it as reducing your liability down the road). This is closely related to reducing the scope of variables.

Use Overloading Rather Than Logic-

If you've got a method that needs to behave differently depending on the kind of thing it was actually handed, consider overloading it.

Any time you see if or switch blocks testing the type of an argument, you should probably start thinking about overloading the method. And while you're at it...

Avoid Long Argument Lists-

If you have a ton of arguments coming into a method, perhaps you need to encapsulate the stuff you need in that method into a class of its own type.

Don't Invoke Potentially Overridable-

Methods from a Constructor You already know that you can't access any nonstatic things prior to your superconstructor running, but keep in mind that even after an object's superconstructor has completed, the object is still in an incomplete state until after its constructor has finished. Polymorphism still works in a constructor.

So if B extends A, and A calls a method in its constructor that B has overridden, well, guess what happens when somebody makes an instance of B. You got it. The B constructor invokes its superconstructor (A's constructor). But inside the A constructor it invokes one of its own methods, but B has overridden that method. B's method runs!

In other words, an object can have one of its methods invoked even before its constructor has completed! So while B isn't even a fully formed object, it can still be running code and even accessing its own instance variables.

This is a problem because its instance variables have not yet been initialized to anything other than default values, even if they're given explicit values when they're declared. *Yikes!* So don't do it. If it's a final or private instance method, then you're safe since you know it'll never be overridden.

Code to Interfaces-

Polymorphism, polymorphism, polymorphism. Use polymorphic arguments, return types, and variables whenever possible (in other words, declare a variable, return type, or argument as an interface type rather than a specific class type).

Using an interface as the type lets you expose only the definition of what your code can do, and leaves the implementation flexible and extensible. And maintainable. And all the other good OO things-that-end-with-ble. But if you can't...

Use Abstract Classes When You Need Functionality to Be Inherited-

If you really must have implementation code and/or instance variables, then use an abstract class and use that class as the declared polymorphic variable, argument, and return type.

Make Objects You're Finished-

With Eligible for Garbage Collection You already know how to do this. Either explicitly set the reference variable to null when you have no more use of the object, or reassign a different object to that reference variable (thus abandoning the object originally referenced by it). At the same time...

Don't Make More Objects Than You Need To-

Just because there's a garbage collector doesn't mean you won't have "memory issues." If you keep too many objects around on the heap, ineligible for garbage collection (but you won't, having read the preceding point), then you can still run out of memory.

More likely, though, is just the problem that your performance might be slightly degraded by the overhead of both making all those objects and then having the garbage collector reclaim them.

Don't do anything to alter your design just to shave a few objects, but pay attention in your implementation code. In some cases, you might be able to simply reuse an existing object by resetting its state.

Avoid Deeply Nested and Complex Logic-

Less is more when it comes to branching. In fact, your assessor may be applying the Cyclomatic Complexity measure to your code, which considers code to be complex not based on lines of code, but rather on how many branch points there are. (It's actually much more complex than that.

Ironically, the test for code complexity is itself a rather complex formula.) The bottom line is, whenever you see a nested if or anything other than very simple logic flow in a method, you should seriously consider redesigning that method or splitting functionality into separate methods.

Use Getters and Setters That Follow-

The JavaBean Naming Convention That means you should use set<yourPropertyName> for methods that can modify a property (normally a property maps directly to an instance variable, but not necessarily) and get<yourPropertyName> for methods that can read a property. For example, a String variable name would have the following getter/setter methods:

setName(String name)

String getName()

If the property is a boolean, then you have a choice (yes, you actually have a choice) of whether to call the read method get<property> or is<property>. For example, a boolean instance variable motorOn can have the following getter/setter methods:

setMotorOn(boolean state)

boolean getMotorOn()

boolean isMotorOn()

The beauty of adhering to the JavaBeans naming convention is that, hey, you have to name it something and if you stick with the convention, then most Java-related tools (and some technologies) can read your code and automatically detect that you have editable properties, for example. It's cool; you should do it.

Don't Be a Procedural Programmer in an OO World-

The two dead giveaways that you haven't really made the transition to a complete object "being," are when you use the following:

+ Really Big Classes that have methods for everything.

+ Lots of static methods. In fact, all methods should be nonstatic unless you have a truly good reason to make them static. This is OO. We don't have global variables and functions.

+ There's no "start here and then keep executing linearly except when you branch, of course...". This is OO, and that means objects all the way down.

Make Variables and Methods As Self-Explanatory As Possible-

Don't use variable names like x and y. What the heck does this mean: int x = 27; 27 what? Unless you really think you can lock up job security by making sure nobody can understand your code (and assuming the homicidal maniac who tries won't find you), then you should make your identifiers as meaningful as possible.

They don't have to be paragraphs. In fact, if it takes a paragraph to explain what a variable represents, perhaps you need to think about your design again. Or at the least, use a comment. But don't make them terse! Take a lesson from the core APIs. They could have called ArInBException, but instead they called it

ArrayIndexOutOfBoundsException. Is there any question about what that exception represents? Of course, the big Sun faux pas was the infamous NullPointerException. But despite the use of the forbidden word pointer, everybody knows what it means when they get it. But there could be some confusion if it were called NPTException or even NullException.

Use the Core APIs!

Do not reinvent the wheel, and do not—or you'll automatically fail for certain use any libraries other than code you developed and the core Java APIs. Resist any temptation to think that you can build something faster, cleaner, more efficient, etc.

Even if that's true, it isn't worth giving up the benefit of using standard classes that others are familiar with, and that have been extremely, heavily tested in the field.

Make Your Own Exception Classes If You Can't Find One That Suits Your Needs-

If there isn't a perfect checked Exception class for you in java.lang, then create your own. And make it specific enough to be meaningful to the catcher. In other words, don't make a BadThingHappenedException and throw it for every possible business error that occurs in your program.

Do Not Return Error Codes!

This is Java. This is OO. If you really need to indicate an exceptional condition, use an Exception! If you really want to annoy an assessor, use error codes as return values from some of your methods. Even one method might do the trick.

Make Your Exceptions with a String Constructor Argument-

Doing so gives you a chance to say more about what happened to cause the exception. When you instantiate an Exception, call the constructor that takes a String (or the one that takes another lower-level exception if you're doing exception chaining). When you create your own Exception class, be sure to put in a constructor that takes a String.

Follow Basic OO Design Principles-

In the preceding section, some of the key points touched on areas we'll dig a bit deeper into here. You don't have to be the World's Best OO Designer, but you do need to follow the basic principles on which the benefits of OO depend.

Obviously we can't make this a "How to Be a Good OO Designer in 10 Easy Pages." You need a lot more study and practice, which we assume you've already done.

This should be old news by now, but you can bet that your assessor will be looking at these issues, so a refresher won't hurt. We're hitting the highlights of areas where you might get points deducted from your assignment.

Hide Implementation Details-

This applies in so many places, but coding with interfaces and using encapsulation is the best way to do it. If you think of your code as little self-contained, pluggable components, then you don't want anyone who uses one of your components to have to think about how it does what it does. It all comes down to inputs and outputs.

A public interface describes what a method needs from you, and what it will return back to you. It says nothing about how that's accomplished. You get to change your implementation (even the class doing the implementing) without affecting calling code.

Implementation details can also be propagated through exceptions, so be careful that you don't use an interface but then put implementation-specific exceptions in the throws clause! If a client does a "search," they shouldn't have to catch an SQLException,

For example. If your implementation code happens to be doing database work that can generate SQLExceptions (like JDBC code would), the client should not have to know that. It's your job to catch that implementation-specific exception and throw something more meaningful a business-specific exception back to client code.

Use Appropriate Class Granularity-

A class should be of the right, you know, granularity. It shouldn't be too big or too tiny. Rarely is the problem a class that's too small; however, most not-quite-OO programmers make classes that are too big.

A class is supposed to represent a thing that has state and behaviors. Keep asking yourself, as you write each method, if that behavior might not be better suited for some other thing.

For example, suppose younhave a Kitchen class that does all sorts of Kitchen things. Like Oven things and Refrigerator things, etc. So now you've got Kitchen things (Kitchen being a room) and Refrigerator things and Oven things all in the same class.

That's three different things. Classes (and thus the objects instantiated from them) really should be specialists. They should do the kinds of behaviors that a thing of that type should do, and no more. So rather than having the Kitchen class include all the code for Refrigerator and Oven behaviors, have the Kitchen class use a Refrigerator and Oven in a HAS-A relationship.

This keeps all three classes simple, and reusable. And that solves your naming problem, so that you don't have to name your do-everything Kitchen class KitchenFridgeOven.

Another possible cause of a Big Class is that you've got too many inner classes defined. Too many meaning some of the inner classes should have been either top-level classes (for reuse) or simply methods of the enclosing class. Make sure your inner or nested classes really need to be included.

Limit Subclassing-

If you need to make a new subclass to add important functionality, perhaps that functionality should really be in the parent class (thus eliminating the need for the subclass—you just need to fix the superclass).

When you feel the need to extend a class, always look at whether the parent class should change, or whether you need composition (which means using HAS-A rather than IS-A relationships).

Look in the core Java API for a clue about subclassing versus composition: the core API inheritance hierarchy is really wide but very shallow. With a few exceptions (like GUI components), most class hierarchies are no more than two to three levels deep.

Use Appropriate Method Granularity-

Just as classes should be specialists, so too should methods. You'll almost certainly be docked points for your assignment if your methods are long (although in some cases, especially in your Swing GUI code, long methods aren't necessarily a reflection of bad design).

In most cases, though, the longer the method the more complex, because often a long method is a reflection of a method doing too much.

You're all programmers so we don't have to hammer the point about smaller modular functionality much easier to debug, modify, reuse, etc. Always see if it makes sense to break a longer method up into smaller ones. But while in a deadline crunch you might get away with long methods in the real world (feeling guilty of course), it won't fly for your Developer assignment.

Use Encapsulation-

Your assignment will be scrutinized for this most fundamental OO principle. Expect the assessor to look at the way in which you've controlled access to the state of your object.

In other words, the way you've protected your instance variables with setters and getters. No need to discuss it here, just do it. Allow access to your data (except for constants, of course) only through more accessible methods. Be careful about your access modifiers.

Having a nice set of accessor methods doesn't matter if you've left your variables wide-open for direct access. Again, make things as private and scope-limited as you can.

Isolate Code That Might Change from Code That Won't Have To-

When you design your classes, be sure to separate out the functionality that might change into separate classes. That way, you restrict the places where you'll have to track down and make modifications as the program evolves.

Use Core APIs -

Always always always check the core APIs, and know that occasionally you might find the class you're looking for in a package other than where you'd expect it.

So be sure to really search through the APIs, even digging into packages and classes you might think are a little off the path. Sometimes a solution can be where you least expect it, so stay open to approaches that aren't necessarily the ones you would normally take.

Flipping through a reference API book can help. A method might catch your eye and even if it turns out not to be your solution, it might spark an idea about a different solution.

In some cases, you might not find exactly what you're looking for, but you might find a class you can extend, thus inheriting a bunch of functionality that you now won't have to write and test (subject to the warnings about subclassing we mentioned previously).

Using core API's (besides being essential for the exam) lets you take advantage of a ton of expertise and testing, plus you're using code that hundreds of thousands of other Java developers are familiar with.

Use Standard Design Patterns-

We can't tell you which ones you'll actually need for your assignment; that depends on both your assignment and your particular approach. But there are plenty of standard design patterns that let you take advantage of the collective experience of all those who've struggled with your issue before you (although usually at a fairly abstract level—that's usually where most patterns do their work).

So while the core APIs let you take advantage of someone else's implementation code, design patterns let you take advantage of someone else's approach to a problem. If you put a gun to our heads, though, we'd probably have to say that Singleton should be way up on your list of things to consider when developing your assignment.

But you might also take a look at MVC (for your client GUI), Façade, Decorator, Observer, Command, Adapter, Proxy, and Callback, for starters. Pick up a book on design patterns (the classic reference is known as the "Gang of Four" (GOF) book,

Design Patterns: Elements of Reusable Object-Oriented Software, by Erich Gamma, Richard Helm, Ralph Johnson, and John Vlissides) and take time to step back and look at where your program might be trying to do something well-solved by a design pattern.

The patterns don't tell you how to construct your algorithms and implement your code line by line, but they can guide you into a sound and maintainable design.

Perhaps most importantly, as design patterns are becoming more and more well-known, developers have a common vocabulary to discuss design trade-offs and decisions.

We believe that the use of design patterns has recently become more important in the exam assessment than it has been in the past, due in large part to their growth in popularity.

Handle Errors Appropriately-

You'll be evaluated for appropriate and clear error-handling throughout your project. You might do really well with it in your GUI and then fall down in your server, but it matters everywhere in your program.

Don't Return Error Codes-

This is Java. Using error codes as return values, rather than using exceptions, is a Really Bad Idea. We're pretty sure your exam assessor knows that.

Don't Send Out Excessive Command-Line Messages-

Don't be too verbose with your command-line messages, and be sure not to leave debugging messages in! Your command-line messages should include only what's necessary to verify the startup of your programs and a very minimal amount of status messages that might be crucial if the program fails.

But in general, if something goes wrong that you know could go wrong, you should be handling it with exceptions. Whatever you do, don't use command-line messages to send alert messages to the user! Use a proper dialog box if appropriate.

Use Dialog Boxes Where Appropriate-

On the other hand, don't use dialog boxes for every possible message the user might need to know about. If you need to display information to the user that isn't of an urgent nature (urgent being things like a record-locking problem or if you need to offer a "Are you sure you want to Quit?" option). In many cases, a dialog box is what you'll use to alert the user when something in your program has caught an exception, and you need user input to deal with it appropriately.

Throw Checked Exceptions Appropriately-

There's a correct time and place for throwing checked exceptions, and being reluctant to throw them can be just as bad as throwing them carelessly.

- Use runtime exceptions for programming errors.

- Use checked exceptions for things that your code might recover from (possibly with help from the user).

- Checked exceptions are only for truly exceptional conditions.

- Do not use exceptions for flow control! Well, not if you hope to do well both on the exam and in real life.

Remember, checked exceptions sure don't come for free at runtime; they've got overhead. Use them when, but only when, you need them.

Create and Throw Your Own Exceptions When Appropriate-

Make use of standard exceptions when they make sense, but never hesitate to create your own if appropriate. If there's a reasonable chance that an exceptional condition can be recovered from, then use a checked exception and try to handle it.

Normally, the exceptions that you create can be thought of as Business Exceptions—in other words, things like "RecordLockedException" or "InsufficientSearchCriteriaException".

The more specific your exception, the more easily your code can handle it, and you get the benefit of providing specific catch blocks, thus keeping the granularity of your catch blocks useful. The opposite of that strategy would be to simply have everything in one big try block that catches Exception (or worse, Throwable!).

Catch Low-Level Implementation Exceptions-

And Throw a Higher-Level Business Exception Say you catch an SQLException (not likely on the Developer exam).

Do you throw this back to a client? Of course not. For a client, it falls into the category of "too much information." The client should not know—or care—that the database server happens to be using SQL. Instead, throw back to the client a more meaningful custom business exception that he or she can deal with.

That more meaningful business exception is defined in your public interface, so the client is expecting it as a possibility. But simply passing a low-level exception all the way to a client reflects a poor design, since it couples the client with implementation details of the server that's never a good idea in an OO design.

Never, Ever, Ever Eat an Exception-

By eat we mean the following horrible practice:

```
try {
    doRiskyThing();
}
    catch(Exception e) { }
```

See what's missing? By catching the exception and then not handling it in any way, it goes completely unnoticed, as if it never occurred. You should at the least print the stack trace. Putting something like this in your exam project might be the death blow.

(Java Database Issues)
(Understanding Core Java Database Issues)

Introduction-

This is very important area according to me , This is the area where your solution to the problem is going to have the greatest impact on your score. You're going to be asked to build a database.

From scratch. And since there will be concurrent clients (or at least the possibility of concurrent clients), you'll have to be certain dead certain that you correctly manage record locking.

How you implement your searching, updating, and locking mechanism is entirely up to you. Again, there is definitely no One Right Answer for your solutions to these issues. But however you choose to do it, be certain that the logic is sound. For example, even if you never experience deadlock during testing,

if there's even the slightest possibility (no matter how remote the chance) that it could happen, you could easily fail the interview exam even if nearly everything else in your application is perfect.

The two biggest issues are locking and searching, but locking is where the Big Money really is. We'll start with a brief overview of the key concepts, followed by yet another inspiring list of thought provoking questions.

Building a java Database-

If you remember from Chapter 10, you're the one who has to build the database; the client's too cheap or neurotic to invest in a commercial database, even a free one. So what is a database?

That depends on your assignment, but for the purposes of the exam, software-that lets-you-access-a-set-of-records will do. You have some data, in some file format somewhere, with a known schema, and your job is to write an application that allows that data to be searched and modified.

You might also need to add and delete records. So the concept is simple: the client makes a request, based on some search criteria, and your database returns a result.

Sometimes the client might want to, say, book a Horse Cruise, in which case one or more records will have to be updated. And you might need to insert a new cruise or delete a cancelled cruise. Regardless of the actual scenario, the Really Big Issue is-

How do I protect the data from concurrent access?

In other words, how do I lock the records?

NOTE:

Your locking design and implementation decisions (and execution) are the most important parts of your Developer assignment. Spend the greatest percentage of your time making sure you have a sound solution. Be sure you've met any requirements in your assignment document that pertain to locking and unlocking.

If part of your assignment specification is vague or ambiguous, you need to make an interpretation (your best guess about what to do) and then document your assumption and strategy.

And remember, the clients could be either local or remote (in other words, on the same machine as the database or on a machine somewhere else on the network), so you'll have to think of issues related to both of those scenarios.

Locking is crucial, but fortunately the Developer exam isn't asking you to implement a complete distributed transaction system using the two-phase commit protocol.

In fact, this is much simpler than transactions, but it will require you to understand the fundamental issues surrounding concurrent access to data. The one where the husband and wife both shared the same account?

If you're not absolutely clear about how to handle synchronization, then reread that chapter. In order to correctly implement your locking strategy, you're going to need a solid grasp on synchronization, wait(), notify(), and notifyAll(). So, ready for some questions? Once again, these are in no particular order.

Questions to Ask Yourself-

We've split these into two categories, searching and locking. But there's a lot about searching that also falls into the category of GUI issues (Chapter 13). Specifically, you'll need to be certain that your end-users know how to build a search query.

Searching-

How easy is it for clients to perform a search? Assuming the GUI itself is user-friendly (and we have a lot to say about that in Chapter 13), what about the criteria?

- How are the search criteria items represented? A String? A CriteriaObject?

- How does a client know exactly what they can base a search on?

- Does your search support boolean matches? Does it need to?

- The database won't necessarily be indexed, so have you thought about other ways to make the search as efficient as possible?

NOTE:

Don't sacrifice clarity and simplicity for a small performance gain. If the performance gain is big, then redesign so that you can have a reasonably efficient algorithm that is also clear and maintainable.

Have you documented your search algorithm?

- If you find yourself writing a lot of documentation to explain your search algorithm, there's probably something wrong with the design.

- Is the documentation of your search algorithm easy to read and understand?

- When the client submits a search query, is a specific piece of the search criteria explicitly matched to a particular field? Or do you search all fields for each search?

- If you're using 1.4, have you investigated whether regular expressions would help?

- What happens if nothing matches the client's search criteria?

- Will it need to be an exact match?

- Could there be a scenario in which too many records match the search criteria?

- Have you considered bandwidth issues when designing and implementing the format of the search criteria requests and server results? Are you shipping things over the wire that are bigger than they need to be?

- Is your search capability flexible for the end-user?

- Is your search capability flexible for future changes to the program?

- How much code, if any, would have to change if the database schema changes? Have you isolated the places where changes can occur to avoid maintenance problems?

- Are you absolutely certain that you've met the searching requirements defined in your assignment specification? Go back and reread them. Slooooooooowly.

Locking

- Are you absolutely certain that your locking scheme works in all possible scenarios?

- Does your exam assignment specify a particular kind of locking with respect to reads and writes?

- What happens when a client attempts to get a record and the record is already locked? What does the client experience?

NOTE: This is crucial. Think long and hard about what you want to happen.

- How will you keep track of which records are locked?

- How will you keep track of who locked each record? Do you need to know that?

- How will you uniquely identify clients in such a way that you can know which client locked which record? Is it the server's responsibility or the client's?

- Have you considered whether the ID of a thread is appropriate to uniquely identify a client?

- Have you considered whether a Math.random() number is appropriate to uniquely identify a client?

- If a client makes a request on a locked record, how will you verify that it's the same client who holds the lock?

- What happens if a client attempts to use a locked record when that client is not the client holding the lock?

- Is it possible to have a record locked for too long a time? How much time is too long?

- Is there anything you can or should do about the duration of a lock?

- What happens if a client goes down without releasing a lock?

- Does the server need a way to know a client went down? (As opposed to simply taking their sweet time or if they're on a painfully slow connection.)

- Is there any possibility of a deadlock? Where two or more clients are waiting for each other's locks?

NOTE:

- Check for this more than you check for anything else.

- Are you correctly using wait(), notify(), and notifyAll()?

- Are you clear about the implications of notify() versus notifyAll()?

Interview Dress/Body Appropriately.
(Guidelines)

Interview Attire Chart: Ladies

Hair: Short hair can be left neatly parted, longer hair should be picked up and removed from the face but can be used to frame the face.

Blouse: Blouses should hug your torso but allow you to breathe.

Skirt: Skirts should never fall above the knee, choose a neutral color.

Pants: Pants should be loose enough to not impair your walking and should also be chosen in a neutral color.

Shoes: Shoes should compliment the color of your pants or skirt. The heel should not exceed 2 inches.

How to Dress for a Job Interview

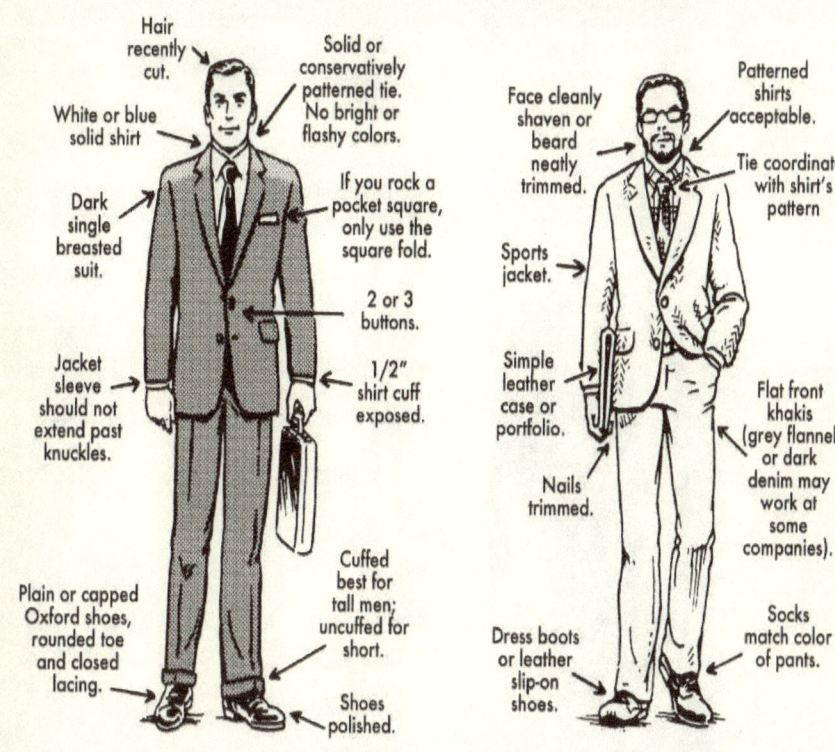

Formal Business Interview Attire

- Hair recently cut.
- Solid or conservatively patterned tie. No bright or flashy colors.
- White or blue solid shirt
- If you rock a pocket square, only use the square fold.
- Dark single breasted suit.
- 2 or 3 buttons.
- 1/2" shirt cuff exposed.
- Jacket sleeve should not extend past knuckles.
- Plain or capped Oxford shoes, rounded toe and closed lacing.
- Cuffed best for tall men; uncuffed for short.
- Shoes polished.

Casual Job Interview Attire

- Patterned shirts acceptable.
- Face cleanly shaven or beard neatly trimmed.
- Tie coordinates with shirt's pattern
- Sports jacket.
- Simple leather case or portfolio.
- Nails trimmed.
- Flat front khakis (grey flannel or dark denim may work at some companies).
- Dress boots or leather slip-on shoes.
- Socks match color of pants.

The Art of MANLINESS EST. 2008

JAVA United Hills.

Effective Core Java

The Complete Core Reference.

TENTH EDITION 2014.

ORACLE Java Harry· H.Chaudhary.

Wear conservative, minimal make-up

Jewelry should be minimal and conservative – no facial or body piercings

Perfume should be minimal

Wear a light-colored button-up blouse

Suit should be a dark-colored pantsuit or skirt suit

Carry a briefcase or portfolio

If wearing a skirt suit, the skirt should not be above the knee

Fingernails should be well-manicured

Pantyhose should have no runs or tears and should be clear or tan

Shoes should be closed-toe – no platforms or high heels (shorter heels are acceptable)

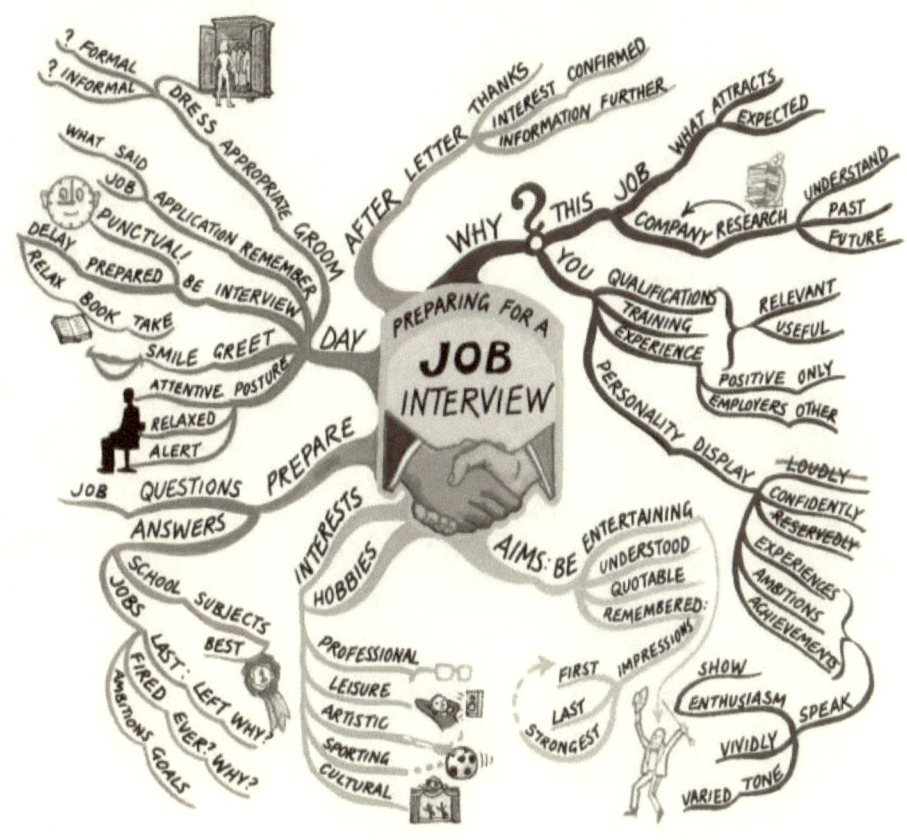

Both Physical Paperback and Digital Editions Are Available on
LuLu.com *& Amazon.com || Google Books & Google Play Book Stores ,*
Order today and Get a Discounted Copy.

According to the Last year and this year Data that we have collected from different sources, More than 5,67,000 students and IT professionals gone through this book and Successfully Cracked their jobs in IT industry and Other industries as well. Don't Forget to write a customer review or comment about this book. For Data structure and Algorithms & C-C++ Interview questions, Read Harry's Upcoming Book- "Cracking the C & C++ Interview" and Cracking the "Algorithms Interview" Tell your friends about this ultimate Java Book.

END.

www.ingramcontent.com/pod-product-compliance
Lightning Source LLC
Chambersburg PA
CBHW031813170526
45157CB00001B/43